D1606388

JUSTIFIED LIVES

■ ■ ■

MORALITY & NARRATIVE
IN THE FILMS OF
SAM PECKINPAH

Michael Bliss

Southern Illinois University Press ● *Carbondale and Edwardsville*

Library of Congress Cataloging-in-Publication Data

Bliss, Michael
    Justified lives: morality and narrative in the films of Sam
Peckinpah / Michael Bliss.
        p.   cm.
    Includes bibliographical references and index.
    1. Peckinpah, Sam, 1925–1984.—Criticism and interpretation.
2. Motion pictures—Moral and ethical aspects. I. Title.
PN1998.3.P43B57   1993
791.43′0233′092—dc20   92-37684
ISBN 0-8093-1823-7   CIP

For *Milton Bliss*

CONTENTS

PLATES

ACKNOWLEDGMENTS

I am indebted to Norman Horrocks and Albert Daub for a special favor and to Mr. Horrocks for a slang emendation incorporated into the chapter on *Straw Dogs*. Susan Field of New World Video generously provided me with an advance copy of *The Deadly Companions*. Terry Geesken at the Museum of Modern Art Film Stills Library made exceptions to the rules so that, on short notice, I could gather additional stills for the book.

My editor at Southern Illinois University Press, Jim Simmons, helped me rewrite the Introduction and proved throughout to be a supportive and compassionate friend. Paul Seydor, whom I consider to be the dean of Peckinpah scholarship, was kind enough to let me share my enthusiasm for Peckinpah with him. Garner Simmons and Stephen Prince offered extremely useful criticism. Dan Gunter, who copyedited the manuscript, not only vastly improved the book's style but also suggested interpretive shadings for which I am extremely grateful. Finally, this book would, quite literally, not have been possible without the loving support of my wife, Christina Banks.

JUSTIFIED LIVES

INTRODUCTION

Sam Peckinpah directed fourteen feature films, from Westerns to war films to popular song adaptations to contemporary spy dramas. Yet despite the diversity of his filmmaking and the commercial success of a number of his works (most notably *Straw Dogs* and *The Getaway*), Peckinpah has never received the critical attention that some of his peers have enjoyed. Although the two other major directors of Westerns, John Ford and Howard Hawks, have had their works repeatedly examined as a whole, the same cannot be said of Peckinpah. Even Paul Seydor's remarkably incisive *Peckinpah: The Western Films* treats only a few of Peckinpah's films. By contrast, the other book-length critical studies on Peckinpah—Doug McKinney's *Sam Peckinpah* and Terence Butler's *Crucified Heroes*—do not achieve the kind of attention to detail that Seydor convincingly demonstrates is so necessary when dealing with Peckinpah's work. This book gives all of Peckinpah's films the kind of close analyses that they deserve.

At the very beginning of his career, Peckinpah found the genre of the Western fully formed, but he would nonetheless adapt it to his own idiosyncratic purposes, even going so far as to use its assumptions and attributes in his non-Western films. I will show where Peckinpah's films coincide with some of the Western's traditional tendencies and sketch in some of the finer points of the films to be discussed before presenting a film-by-film analysis of Peckinpah's narrative technique, an area in which I believe Peckinpah excels.

The first critical work to observe that the West was a source of and influence on primal meanings in the American national consciousness was Frederick Jackson Turner's essay "The Significance of the Frontier in American History," which Turner delivered at a historical society meeting in 1893. Turner's central thesis is of primary importance for the student of Western films. He identified the prototypical characteristics of the West, attributes that for directors such as Ford, Hawks, and Peckinpah would become the challenging definitions and parameters to be examined, appropriated, and then adapted.

For Turner, the frontier was not only a geographical location but also a focal point in the American consciousness for a panoply of ideas concerning ambition, desire, and renewal.

> We have . . . a recurrence of the process of evolution in each western area reached in the process of expansion. Thus American development has exhibited not merely advance along a single line, but a return to primitive conditions on a continually advancing frontier line, and a new development for that area. American social development has been continually beginning over and over again on the frontier. This perennial rebirth, this fluidity of American life, this expansion westward with its new opportunities, its continuous touch with the simplicity of primitive society, furnish the forces dominating American character.[1]

Turner believed that the frontier's primary significance is twofold: as a physical border where primitivism and civilization clash, thus reminding the settlers of both their past and future, and as a conceptual locus where actuality (the old limits) and possibility (the potential for new boundaries) conflict. Each significant Western film, in the process of representing and inquiring into the nature and the ethical and symbolic import of the West, re-creates the process of discovery and inquiry that Turner elucidated.

Although Turner never uses the term in his essay, he is discussing the creation and function of a national myth. As Northrop Frye points out in *The Secular Scripture*, "Every human society, we may assume, has some form of verbal culture, in which fictions, or stories, have a prominent place. Some of these stories may seem more important than others: they illustrate what primarily concerns their society. . . . The more important group of stories in the middle of a society's verbal culture I shall call myths."[2]

Frye comments that "America has a genuine social mythology in which beliefs in personal liberty, democracy, and equality before law have a central place. Every major American writer will be found to have struck his roots deeply into this serious social mythology."[3] Frye's notion of "personal liberty" roughly equates with Turner's notion of the frontier's expansionist possibilities, just as the phrase

"American writer" can be expanded to include American filmmakers. Turner's essay focuses on the attraction of the frontier for Americans, an attraction that would become the basis for various filmmakers' obsession with the West some decades later.

In light of Turner's essay, we can view the West as a concept through which Americans confront the issues raised by the difficult birth and growth of their nation and through which, in fictive fashion, they attempt either to change or resolve these ideas. Among these issues are not only the conflict between the ideal and the real but also the clash between the values of the country's early settlers and the values belonging to those less itinerant individuals who might be characterized as the civilizers. In Peckinpah's films these persons appear in conflict as the cowboys versus the bankers, the country folk versus the city dwellers.

In conventional Western films the opposition often takes the forms of the virtuous man in white versus the villain dressed in black and the antipathy between the "good" white settlers on the one hand and the "bad" Indians on the other. Not surprisingly, this conflict was traditionally resolved in favor of the whites, who, after all, were the "authors" of this American myth and who justified their social authority through it.[4]

As Frye points out, romantic myths are perennially prone to the kind of exaggeration that divides existence into rigid categories. "Romance avoids the ambiguities of ordinary life, where everything is a mixture of good and bad, and where it is difficult to take sides or believe that people are consistent patterns of virtue or vice. The popularity of romance, it is obvious, has much to do with its simplifying of moral facts."[5]

Polarized character types abound in the West's early literature, such as the Leatherstocking books and the dime magazines that celebrated the exploits of individuals like Deadwood Dick and presented the "true to life" deeds of Calamity Jane and her ilk.[6] Turner specifies an essential conflict embodied in the dramatized actions of these individuals when he observes that "the frontier is the outer edge of the wave—the meeting point between savagery and civilization."[7] Turner goes on to note that the major representative of this savagery is the Indian (he never speculates that whites might exhibit an equal savagery), stating that "the Indian was a common danger, demanding united action";[8] this insight was not unknown to the readers of Western novels and romances. Turner's assertion thus paves the way for the consciously symbolic use of the Indian in films and presages observations that would be refined, with additional emphasis placed on the sexual element, in landmark works such as Leslie Fiedler's *Love and Death in the American Novel*. A brief glance at the character of Yellowleg in Peckinpah's *The Deadly Companions* shows how fragile Peckinpah regarded the boundary in the dramatized West between savagery and so-called civilization. Very little conceptual distance separates the behavior of a relatively traditional Western character like Yellowleg from that of a character like Turkey, who serves as what Fiedler would describe as the character's dark brother (to underscore Turkey's "dark" nature, when Turkey temporarily disappears, he is replaced by an actual Indian).

Turner's essay also identifies Indians as scapegoats who are used to compensate not only for fear of barbarism but also for an entire host of vague anxieties, a function that they serve most explicitly in Peckinpah's *Major Dundee*. *Dundee*'s title character, excessively disturbed because he has been bested by the Indian chief Sierra Charriba, persists in his pursuit of the Indians even after he has recovered the white Rostes children (who had been abducted by Indians); he thereby exemplifies the unreasoning hatred of the dark "other" that many Westerns, and much American literature, dramatizes so effectively.

From a book titled *New Guide to the West*, Turner extricates what he calls a "suggestive passage" that cites three classes of settlers, each of which represents an evolutionary stage in the maturation of the nation. (However, all three classes may have existed simultaneously.) First among these groups is the pioneer, characterized by hunting and the use of "rude" agricultural techniques. To the pioneer, who lives in a log cabin, it is "quite immaterial whether he ever becomes the owner of the soil."[9] According to the *New Guide*, the pioneer stays where he is only until he feels like leaving, since the land represents to him nothing more than a stopping-off point before his next adventure.[10] The intermediate group comprises the more sophisticated farmers, who "purchase the lands" (by contrast, the pioneers just claim it), "add field to field, clear out the roads, throw rough bridges over the streams, put up hewn log houses with glass windows and brick or stone chimneys [notice the distinction, obviously intended, with the pioneer's cabin], occasionally plant orchards, build mills, school houses, courthouses, etc, and exhibit the picture and forms of plain, frugal, civilized life."[11]

The third group is represented by "the men of capital and enterprise."[12] This group arrives, the *New Guide* notes, when "the settler is ready to sell out and take advantage of the rise in property, push further into the interior and become, himself, a man of capital and enterprise in turn. The small village rises to a spacious town or city; substantial edifices of brick, extensive fields, orchards, gardens, colleges, and churches are seen."[13] As the value-laden rhetoric makes plain, the *New Guide* is characterizing these stages in such a way as to designate an approved form of progress. Turner also approves of this supposedly laudable progression from pioneers to businesspersons, since the citation to the *New Guide*—which Turner presents without critical or analytical remarks—is the longest, most extensive quote from an outside source in his entire essay. In this respect, Turner reveals himself as a historically limited and conventional commentator, failing to see, as do practitioners of the Western like Ford and Peckinpah, that this third, capitalist stage would come into symbolic conflict with the very values and ideals that had presumably built the nation in the first place.

It is no coincidence that in Ford's *Stagecoach* and Peckinpah's *Ride the High Country* the bankers represent stultification and miserliness, an effect achieved not only by making these characters act in a niggardly way but also by having them portrayed by actors (Burton Chamberlain in *Stagecoach*, Percy Helton in *Ride*) whose elitist manners and stiff demeanors would displease the audience. Ford and Peckinpah draw on Turner's intellectual legacy but turn it on its head, reversing Turner's approbation of the move toward capitalism. In this respect, films like many of Peckinpah's return us to the idea of an uncharted wilderness that Turner claimed was the basic attraction of the frontier. It is a notable attribute of Western filmmaking that, beginning most prominently with Ford's *Stagecoach*, films began to inquire subtly into just how high a price we as a nation may have paid in achieving our manifest destiny, an inquiry that in our literature reaches as far back as Poe, Hawthorne, and Melville.

It was Turner's essay, though, that provided a kind of legitimate intellectual basis on which ambitious Western films might build. Ford, Hawks (most notably in *Red River*), and Peckinpah realized that the cinematic horse opera—which had its humble beginnings in films such as Edwin Porter's *The Great Train Robbery* and D. W. Griffith's *The Battle at Elderbush Gulch*—could be used for greater purposes. Taking a cue from non-Western works like *The Birth of a Nation*, itself an inquiry into a national myth (albeit from a rather distasteful viewpoint), Ford and other directors recognized the opportunity that this popular and populist art form offered.

As is evident from the use of the word *significance* in his essay's title, Turner is probing for the meaning of the West. Yet we must be wary of treating Turner's assertions as absolutes. What makes the Turner essay so fascinating is that, by drawing attention to abstractions, Turner inadvertently paves the way for further abstractions from the West's realities in the works of Western authors and directors, among them Zane Grey and the directors I have mentioned.

The importance of the frontier myth is that it represents a longing for an idyllic past that never existed. The Western myth reinvokes the idea of a green, fertile world, a notion that many civilizations find eminently attractive. Indeed, the myth of a new, unspoiled land crosses all territorial boundaries. If we are to appreciate the almost pre-intellectual manner in which films like those of Sam Peckinpah appeal to us, we must, if only briefly, acknowledge this background as well.

In *Virgin Land: The American West As Symbol and Myth*, Henry Nash Smith makes us aware of the cultural and intellectual ideas behind Turner's essay, although, like Turner, he stops short of identifying their mythical basis. "[Turner's] contention that the frontier and the West had dominated American development could hardly have attained such universal acceptance if it had not found an echo in ideas and attitudes already current."[14] Like the creation myth in Genesis, the Western myth is "the cultural possession of a specific society, . . . the verbal nucleus of a shared tradition."[15] By explaining our individual and national origins, the myth of the Western does more than create a national mythology; it also taps into a vast storehouse of unconscious urges and symbols, offering verbal expression of dreams and archetypes drawn from the Jungian "unconscious realm [which is] composed of elements which are the same in all men."[16] The Western myth merely expressed these desires—which intertwined with the attraction of the frontier and the desire for one's own, new territory—for Americans.

Many of these attitudes, which had to do with the West as a new Eden, a land full of opportunity for growth, were reflected in the exploits of the heroes of Western novels that set the standards for the Western film hero. According to Smith, the heroes of the Beadle romances were characteristically "benevolent hunter[s] without a fixed place of abode, advanced in age, celibate, and of unequalled prowess in trailing, marksmanship, and Indian fighting."[17] We can easily recognize these characteristics, sans the uniform insistence on age (an understandable change given the need for movies to have appealing protagonists), in the central characters of many Peckinpah films, both Westerns and non-Westerns. The description, albeit with a bit of modification mandated by its updating to a contemporary milieu, fits *Cross of Iron*'s Steiner, *Osterman Weekend*'s John Tanner and Bernie Osterman, and, in a perverse incarnation, *Straw Dogs*' David Sumner. Peckinpah even goes so far as to play against these attributes, making *Deadly Companions*' Yellowleg a capable tracker but a poor shot; demonstrating how *Ride the High Country*'s Steve and Gil have laudable ideals but diminished capabilities; showing how Amos Dundee, the title character of *Major Dundee*, is an inspired (albeit crazed) leader who yet needs help in pursuing his quarry; and dramatizing the physical and psychological failings of the protagonists of films such as *The Wild Bunch, Junior Bonner*, and *The Getaway*. When Smith comments on the prevalence of the scenario of the hero rescuing a white maiden from the Indians,[18] we see echoes of the plots of *The Deadly Companions* (in which Turkey functions as the ultimate savage, and in which Kit Tilden saves herself from an Indian), *Ride the High Country* (in which the Hammonds take the parts of the Indians), and *Major Dundee* (in which the Rostes children stand in for the maidenly abductees). *The Osterman Weekend* even goes the plot one better by having John Tanner's wife aid in rescuing him from peril.

As Smith points out, it was only after the late 1880s, when the fascination with Buffalo Bill–type heroes reached its peak, that the figure of the cowboy first began to appear in popular literature in the form of "a semibarbarous laborer who lived a dull, monotonous life of hard fare and poor shelter."[19] By this time, though, the Western story was largely divorced from the facts; indeed, as Smith observes, the Western at this time became a travesty. "The static ideas of virtue and happiness and peace drawn from the bosom of the virgin wilderness ... proved quite irrelevant for a society committed to the ideals of civilization and progress, and the industrial revolution. Devoid alike of ethical and social meaning, the Western story could develop in no direction save that of a straining and exaggeration of its formulas."[20]

Yet the prototypical Western's tale of a virtuous wanderer doing deeds of daring strikingly reemerged after the flirtation with technocracy ended in the 1930s, when the country realized that its social and ethical salvation was not to be found in industrialization. Recoiling from the rape of the wilderness by industrial progress and the unsatisfactory by-products of urbanization and industrialization, Americans turned back to their Edenic national myth, the Western, seeking a spiritual rejuvenation that they had been unable to find in the twentieth-century religion of technology. The traditional Western promised the simple pleasure derived from the romantic playing out of the conflict between good and evil, with good predominating, thereby satisfying a national need for spiritual self-justification to compensate for the loss of the wilderness. In the course of their careers, Western film directors like Ford and Peckinpah would also go through a spiritual progression paralleling that of the nation as a whole, describing the arc from idealism (e.g., *Stagecoach* and *Ride the High Country*) to disillusionment (e.g., *Cheyenne Autumn* and *Pat Garrett and Billy the Kid*).

Despite the move toward cynicism, our national need for heroes never diminished. At the same time that grim, revisionist Westerns such as *High Noon* and *Bad Day at Black Rock* were enjoying popularity, Western television shows such as *Gunsmoke* and *Have Gun, Will Travel* were celebrating the ascendancy of men who embodied the traditional values of integrity and justice. Although Peckinpah's later films make it clear that for a time he rejected the West's idealism, he could not repudiate his need for it. Peckinpah indulged his disappointment for a while in pessimistic films such as *The Killer Elite*, only to bring back traditional Western values, along with a suitably enlightened hero, in his final film, *The Osterman Weekend*. Tracking Peckinpah's intellectual odyssey, then, we track our own progression from idealism to disillusionment, with the hoped-for return to idealism held out as a desirable end.

The revulsion from industrialization, a prototypical attribute of the Western, was dramatized in Western books and films through the traditional Western hero's rejection of cities. In Peckinpah's work, this rejection is strongest in *The Ballad of Cable Hogue*, whose protagonist states, "Only thing I like about cities [is] city beds." Although Cable meets his love interest, Hildy, in town, and mechanizes certain aspects of his water station, he also rejects the city's cold-heartedness and, for a time, embraces passion as a form of escape from urban compromise. Additionally, Cable is an avatar of what Smith refers to as "the heroic figure of the idealized frontier farmer armed with that supreme agrarian weapon, the sacred plow."[21] Despite his character flaws, Cable's building his empire in the desert and making the wilderness fertile are actions that represent the best of the fruitful pioneer figure who became emblematic in

Western literature and who clearly was borrowed from the Garden of Eden story. *Cable Hogue* is a supreme example of the Western version of the Edenic myth, encompassing as it does elements of sex versus love, condemnation, death, deliverance, and a fall from grace that, in this characteristically twentieth-century version, is redeemed not by God but by a quasi-divine woman who brings the gift of love.

Yet the notion of the freedom inherent in the garden myth, which is an integral part of the Western mythos, involves a notable paradox. In *Civilization and its Discontents*, Freud, appropriating Rousseau's concept of the noble savage (a concept whose opposition between civilization and the supposedly pristine wilderness appeared in classic Western literature as well),[22] points out that "the liberty of the individual is no gift of civilization. It was greatest before there was any civilization, though then, it is true, it had for the most part no value, since the individual was scarcely in a position to defend it."[23] Applied to Westerns, Freud's observation makes it clear that a return to the "pristine" West would also return us to a time of lawlessness.

When Freud asserts that civilization is built on the renunciation of instinctual behaviors, the majority of which appear to be sexual in nature,[24] we can see how persuasively Peckinpah has constructed a number of his films. *Cable Hogue* shows us through the sexual relationship of Cable and Hildy how sexuality can be beneficial when allowed to develop outside the bounds of conventional civilization, which in this case is represented by the town and its mercantilist attitudes. Sexuality seems to infuse virtually every Peckinpah film. And though Peckinpah makes it quite clear through the behavior of many of his films' characters how inviting an open and honest expression of tenderness and desire can be, it is also plain that the director recognizes the potential for violence that sexuality also entails. The classic work in this respect is *Straw Dogs*, the only Peckinpah film that places sexuality at the center of its action. Through the person of David Sumner, Peckinpah shows us how modern man, repressed sexually and insufficiently developed emotionally, can become violent, most tellingly through the use of misdirected sexuality as a tool for power and control. It is a further, satisfying irony of *Straw Dogs* that David, the most destructive character in the film, conceives of himself as the force of civilization opposed to the supposedly anarchic tendencies of the village workmen, whom he ultimately slaughters.

In Freud's view, there is no escape from the dilemma that faces modern man, who can neither directly express his sexuality nor productively repress it. Peckinpah posits a possible resolution of this conflict through a humanism that is tied to the traditional Western's belief in the human potential for good. This resolution is given its most effective and satisfying expression in *The Wild Bunch*, in which hedonism and self-interest, which are often expressed through sexuality, are rejected in favor of a higher value—in this case, self-sacrifice in order to redeem Angel. Indeed, the Bunch's gesture of returning for Angel in order to demonstrate their faith in group solidarity borders on a religious bonding. Although *The Wild Bunch* clearly stops short of positing a transcendental answer to the problem of expressing concern for other people, it is certainly a sermon on the need for commitment.

Perhaps the most vital contribution that Freud's book makes to intellectual analysis is to treat societies as entities with individual psychologies. Thus, when critic Jim Kitses states in *Horizons West* that "*The Wild Bunch* is America,"[25] the assertion makes sense in that the Bunch seems to represent all that is best and worst in our national consciousness. Peckinpah stated at one point that "the Western is a universal frame within which it is possible to comment on today."[26] I think this assertion may distort the nature of Peckinpah's films, though, since it suggests that such commentary is one of the primary emphases in the films. Rather, I believe that what Peckinpah means is not that his films are critiques of contemporary events but that they comment on the kinds of value systems that are always the concern of the moral artist. Peckinpah's remark undercuts the effect that placing some of his Western films in the past has on the audience. The ability of the films to comment successfully on current issues derives to a degree from their being situated at a distance from us in time. Even Peckinpah's non-Western, contemporary films (which, I will argue, also operate as Westerns) succeed in this respect only to the extent that their concern is with timeless problems associated with loyalty, trust, love, death, and betrayal. And when this formula fails, as it does in *Convoy*, it does so precisely because we are not convinced of the veracity of the issues being dramatized. In all of his successful films, though, Peckinpah achieves a universality that transcends genre and time.

That the Western story often serves as a parable for our adventures as a nation may be a mixed blessing. Philip French points out that Westerns are so easily accepted and understood that it is often sufficient for a film to be characterized as a Western for a whole panoply of assumptions to come along with it.[27] The genre's prepackaged assumptions can be a curse, since they may lead the audience into drawing conclusions that can sabotage a film's intended effect. In Peckinpah's work, the film that most strongly risks being misread in this respect is *Straw Dogs*, the most "Western" of all of Peckinpah's films not set in the Old West in that it features a violent, Western-style "shoot-out" at its end. (The fact that the film takes place in the west of England only reinforces its unique status.) In *Straw Dogs*, Peckinpah must be at pains to ensure that the audience does not approve of David's successful dispatching of all of the rowdies, viewing it as some form of traditional defense of hearth and home. Certainly a casual reading of the film might make such a view possible were it not that Peckinpah is careful to demonstrate throughout that David is an obvious distortion of the idealized Western hero. Yet the power of *Straw Dogs'* sexual imagery is so strong, and our conventional reactions to an assault against the home are so ingrained,[28] that only a considered response to the film will prevent us from seeing these sequences as anything other than intentional perversions of these traditional situations.

In the hands of an inventive filmmaker, the assumptions that the audience brings to Western films can be carefully investigated and challenged by building up a productive tension between the initial assumptions of the audience and the way that the film's plot evolves. Ford's *The Man Who Shot Liberty Valance* first depicts a traditional Western myth (the innocent man who slays the evil gunman), then deflates it, and then affirms how necessary the supporting of this kind of myth is to the survival of our national heritage. As *Liberty Valance*'s newspaper editor says, "When the legend becomes fact, print the legend." The film is thus a fiction telling us that what we treat as real is a fiction that we nonetheless prefer to treat as real. *Liberty Valance* asserts that as a nation, we live by certain fictions because we believe that the truth about ourselves is unacceptable. In Peckinpah's work, the most successful example of this attitude is *The Wild Bunch*, which first embraces the common assumptions about men sticking together, then explodes these assumptions through the Bunch's abandonment of three of its members, and then miraculously, yet most convincingly, reinvokes them at the film's end.

Another important element of Western films is achieved through their location. John Cawelti notes in *The Six-Gun Mystique* that the geographic setting of many Westerns adds credibility to the genre's drama; this aspect, deriving from many Westerns' being situated in the Great Plains, involves "openness, . . . aridity and general inhospitality to human life, . . . great extremes of light and climate, and paradoxically . . . grandeur and beauty,"[29] characteristics that undoubtedly speak to a rustic yearning in many viewers. Cawelti's observation points to the recurrent geographic opposition between the town and the prairie or desert in Peckinpah's films, a distinction that complements the films' psychological situations and harks back to the frontier dividing line that Turner identified.

In his fine short introduction to the work of Peckinpah, Anthony Mann, and Budd Boetticher, Kitses sets up a chart of oppositions between the wilderness and civilization—with characteristics such as "freedom," "nature," and "the West" under the heading of "wilderness," and "restriction," "culture," and "the East" under the heading of "civilization"—that should be quite familiar to anyone conversant with classic American or British literature.[30] Kitses observes that what holds all of the generic elements of history, themes, archetypes, and icons together is "narrative and dramatic structure."[31] Yet what distinguishes the work of Sam Peckinpah from that of other practitioners of the Western—for example, Fred Zinneman and George Stevens—is precisely the manner in which Peckinpah embeds his films' meanings, making them subservient to the narrative and dramatic structure so that they emerge from these elements rather than seem grafted onto them. A comparison of *High Noon*, *Shane*, and *The Wild Bunch*, for example, reveals how in the first two films we are conscious of the manner in which the audience's reactions are being manipulated; we know we are repeatedly being given messages. By contrast, *The Wild Bunch*, despite its inclusion of sequences that amount to debates about morals, works on us implicitly through the action. The intended effect is identical, but the subtle manner in which Peckinpah achieves it is noteworthy.

I mentioned earlier that Peckinpah, like John Ford, seemed to move from optimism to pessimism in his career. This concept can be further refined by noting that Peckinpah's feature films, all of which are concerned with the presence or absence of the possibility for redemption and renewal, divide into three groups. The films from the first third, from *The Deadly Companions* to *Cable Hogue*, inquire into and support the romantic ideals of adventure and camaraderie. These are films that affirm the potential for goodness in

America. Thus, despite Steve Judd's death at the end of *Ride the High Country*, we feel uplifted, knowing that Steve's justice-oriented behavior, and all that it signifies with regard to our capability for acting in the most moral way, is an always achievable reality, a condition confirmed in Gil Westrum's return to Steve's point of view. In the second group of films, which begins with *Straw Dogs* and ends with *Bring Me the Head of Alfredo Garcia*, we see the director taking a less romantic approach to confronting the roles that Western-type heroes might take. The characters in some of these films may triumph over circumstances, but they are also more bitter than their counterparts in the films from the first period. Though it is true that, like the characters in the earlier films, these films' protagonists are delivered from corruption, they often achieve deliverance through either comically stylized violence (*Alfredo Garcia*) or near miracles, such as the kind that occurs toward the end of *The Getaway*, in which the antagonists escape into Mexico, that special Peckinpah land of release and exaggeration. With the exception of *Junior Bonner*, the endings of other films from this period plunge us into despair. *Straw Dogs* and *Pat Garrett* are the only two Peckinpah films that are devoid of hope. *Straw Dogs* inexorably leads us to its awful conclusion. *Pat Garrett*, which reflects Garrett's sensibility, is bleak from beginning to end.

In the last third of Peckinpah's work, the director achieves varying degrees of success in his attempt to ground the values of the Western in the contemporary world. *The Killer Elite* is interesting, but it exhibits a great deal of pessimism about the possibility of being delivered from corruption, this not only in spite of, but to a fair extent because of, its unrealistic ending. *Cross of Iron* suggests that escape from despair is impossible. *Convoy* presents Western ideas of moral behavior and loyalty with relatively little sophistication. Yet at the end of his career, Peckinpah gives us *The Osterman Weekend*, which not only harks back to the Old West through its return to the use of basic weaponry but also shows its protagonists using, and then triumphing over, modern technology. With the restrained but nonetheless real optimism of *Osterman*, Peckinpah seems to have been subtly renewed; his career closes the circle in a most satisfying way.

What makes Peckinpah unique among contemporary directors is that throughout his fourteen films he remained faithful to the Western format: of course, not all of the films were situated in the Old West, but they do investigate and dramatize its values, which are of far greater importance than setting. Overwhelmingly, Peckinpah's concern in his films is with issues involving morality, spirituality, and change, with attendant investigations into what progress represents, thereby bringing up the notion of the conflict between the material and spiritual realms. Since no Peckinpah film, regardless of where and when its action takes place, is devoid of these qualities, it may justifiably be asserted that all of Peckinpah's films are Westerns in the most basic sense—namely, that they are morality plays, grounded in and inquiring into the culture and values of the West.

In an ethical sense, every one of Peckinpah's films tells roughly the same story: that of a central character who must come to grips with a moral dilemma, the outcome of which will determine the course that the rest of his life will take. Invariably, we see this central character allied with another character who represents an aspect of the protagonist's psychology with which he must be reconciled if he is to productively continue his existence. Often, too, we find that these films contain virtually satanic "other selves" who tempt the protagonist with compromise, thus assuming the role of a perversion of the protagonist, a malignant projection of his own worst aspects. In *The Deadly Companions*, Yellowleg has Turkey and Billy; in *The Wild Bunch*, Pike and Thornton have Mapache and the railroad agent Harrigan; and so on. A confrontation with this "other" is represented as a prerequisite to the special kinds of redemption (some of them extremely objectionable, as in *Straw Dogs*) that invariably occur at the ends of Peckinpah's films, redemptions that involve the protagonist's ability to reconcile his values with the demands of living in the material world.

Occasionally, Peckinpah will even go so far as to insert into his films special figures who act as redeemers for the protagonists. Certainly, *The Getaway*'s Cowboy, who rescues Doc and Carol from the miasma of murder and deceit in which they have become involved, qualifies in this respect, to a certain extent, as does Hildy for Cable in *The Ballad of Cable Hogue*.

As Frye pointed out, this dual approach to characterization is endemic to the romantic story. There is a biblical precedent for this type of characterization as well. Seydor notes that the basic conflict between Steve and Gil in *Ride the High Country* seems to be based on a passage from Isaiah: "What shall it profit a man to gain the world if he lose his soul."[32] Certainly this most biblical of all Peckinpah films contains an inordinate number of references to Scripture. Yet the same kind of opposition between the material and spiritual realms contained in the citation from Isaiah is also present, at least implicitly, in all of Peckinpah's other films, either in the form of action or character conflicts or as a moral backdrop, against which the films' actions take place.

I have already noted how Turner accepts without question the notion of material progress; this attitude is understandable given the value that Turner apparently placed on America's achieving its destiny, which was traditionally linked with the country's assumption of its role as an industrial nation. Nonetheless, the Western film eventually came to reject this attitude. Peckinpah links mechanical progress with moral decline in order to bring into relief the anachronistic nature of the various films' central righteous characters, who insist on a rectitude that is wildly out of place in a universe that has accepted compromise and corruption as the inevitable price to be paid for the comforts of modernity. As a revivalist preacher says in *Cable Hogue*, "The devil seeks to destroy you with—machines." We are meant to take this statement perfectly seriously, since in Peckinpah's films, Hell is a world in which moral duplicity and loss of innocence are the consequences of progress. To take the preacher's words figuratively, the devil's machines may very well be the machinations of the machinelike people in any era whose ethically compromised actions must appear satanic to the eyes of the moralist.

Additionally, we see the director's ethical attitude reflected in his characterization of children. What Peckinpah usually shows us through children, though, is not their moral innocence so much as their indifference to the horrors perpetrated by their corrupt elders. In this respect the children at the beginning of *The Wild Bunch* are emblematic; think of them playfully romping through Starbuck's street, which is littered with bodies, and you see exemplified their outrageous moral indifference. And when, earlier in the same film, Peckinpah shows us other children idly torturing ants and scorpions, we are looking at more than just images of our own blithe attitude to cruelty; we see as well the face of an indifferent deity, which plays with mortals as though they are toys. Indeed, in Peckinpah's films only the corruption-tempered adults, having passed through their rituals of fire, can be as children. For Peckinpah, one needs to have a fully informed knowledge of evil in order to be truly innocent, since innocence is conceived of as a conscious repudiation of evil, something of which children are incapable. Peckinpah here gives evidence of a biblical moral attitude, in which a fall from grace (in the form of a compromise, near-compromise, or temptation) is a prerequisite to redemption. In many of his films Peckinpah shows us a character with a *felix culpa*, a happy fault that vouchsafes grace to the tempted protagonist. However, characters in Peckinpah films achieve redemption only by dying or through the deaths of others. (The striking exception to this formula is *Junior Bonner*, the gentlest of all Peckinpah films.) The suggestion here is that one cannot be truly reconciled to the world's compromises without somehow rising above them, either through apotheosis or excessive actions. In Peckinpah's work, the classic example of this paradigm appears in *The Wild Bunch*, in which the Bunch achieve their greatest unity after they die.

All of Peckinpah's central characters (even the misguided David Sumner) are, in the words of Steve Judd, attempting to live in such a way so as to "enter [their] house[s] justified." Appealing as they do to what I consider to be the innate human need for ethics, to our desire for something greater than the material world, and to our essentially religious yearning for some realm in which spirituality and an attendant divinity of purpose coalesce, Peckinpah's films manage to satisfy our hunger for a candid yet ethical art in eminently notable ways.

Although I touch on those bearers of cinematic significance that support the meanings in Peckinpah's films—aspects such as framing, sound and image juxtapositions, and acting—my central concern is with how Peckinpah tells his stories through the accretion of fine details. For me, Peckinpah's genius emerges most clearly in his mastery of narrative, an aspect that I have tried to elucidate in as objective a manner as possible.[33] In this respect, I am reminded of a piece of dialogue spoken by Clive Langham, the fictional author who appears in Alain Resnais's film *Providence*: "Of course, it's been said about my work that the search for style has often resulted in a want of feeling. I'd put it another way. I'd say that style *is* feeling—in its most elegant and economic expression."

If in approaching Peckinpah's films I at times seem to accentuate formal aspects at the expense of feeling, I do so in order to demonstrate just how much feeling there is in the man's work. Whether it be the ineffable loveliness of *Cable Hogue* or the awesome horrors of *The Wild Bunch*, Peckinpah never fails to evoke the most powerful emotional reactions in the most economical way, evidencing a mastery of technique that it is the purpose of this book to illuminate.

CHAPTER ONE

Couples

Peckinpah's deprecating remarks to the contrary,[1] *The Deadly Companions*, his first feature film, is a creditable work. Although some parts of the film detract from its overall success, there is also a great deal to admire in it.

Peckinpah's concern with isolated visual elements that communicate meanings—a concern that quite possibly derives from his work in television, whose limited resolving power mandates a reliance on close-ups and medium shots rather than grandiose vistas—is present from the film's opening, which is shot from ground level. We see a man photographed from the knees down enter a bar and walk across the room. Yellowleg (Brian Keith), so called because he still wears the yellow-striped pants from his Union Army days, is then shown in a full-length shot. He orders tequila. We next see that someone has been hung from the bar's ceiling. To make us aware of this man, Peckinpah has the camera, now representing Yellowleg's point of view, concentrate on another isolated visual element that is initially divorced from its context—in this case, the man's feet, which are barely scraping the top of a barrel. Already, then, the camerawork alone, which initially revealed each man by showing us his feet, has established an affinity between these characters.

Seizing on the image of the hanging man's feet scraping the barrel, Yellowleg asks wryly, and somewhat cruelly, "Having a dance?" The bartender's reply is just as ironic: "Five-ace card player." Indeed, the damning five aces have been pinned to the man's chest, branding him in a manner comparable to the way that, as we shall see, Yellowleg himself is branded. Then, vision once again becomes fixated. Yellowleg focuses on the scars on the hanging man's hand, a brand that identifies this man, Turkey (Chill Wills), as the individual who tried to scalp Yellowleg during the Civil War. Yellowleg tries to rescue Turkey only because he doesn't want anyone other than himself killing Turkey; however, just as Yellowleg is about to cut Turkey down, Turkey's sidekick, Billy (Steve Cochran), enters the room and severs the rope with a shot from his gun.

Plate 1. Yellowleg, Turkey, and Billy in *The Deadly Companions*. Yellowleg is holding the knife with which he had been scalped.

The three characters emerge into the street. Yellowleg once again proposes to circumvent justice, in this case suggesting that because Gila City has "a new bank and an old marshal," they travel there to rob the bank. At this point, the viewer might well imagine that Yellowleg is serious about this undertaking. Only later do we realize that this suggestion, like Yellowleg's attempt to release Turkey, is merely a device to get the apparently inseparable Turkey and Billy out of town. Indeed, it requires at least two viewings of the film to realize how much germinal information Peckinpah gives us in the first ten minutes. We know that Yellowleg is interested in Turkey, but we don't know why; we know that he suggests robbing a bank, but we don't know if he is serious or not. We also know that the boy whom we see playing a harmonica in Gila City (and who also takes care of the horses for Yellowleg) is given an inordinate amount of attention in the film: Peckinpah shows him standing on a building's roof and then pans down to include Yellowleg, Turkey, and Billy in the shot, the visual connection implying a thematic connection. Thus, we know that he will play some important role, but we don't know what. We also know that Kit will figure prominently in the lives of these men, but precisely how is unclear. All of this information becomes related as *Deadly* continues.

Plate 2. An unholy alliance, watched over by Death, in the form of Kit's son.

We have already met prejudice in the film (one of the card players refers to Yellowleg as "Yank"); now we see a female character assessed on comparably flimsy evidence. Kit Tilden (Maureen O'Hara) is maligned before the beginning of a prayer meeting that takes place in the Gila City bar.[2] Two of the women sitting behind Kit criticize her for presuming to be respectable, at which point Kit's son, whom the women think is illegitimate, tells his mother, "If they're going to heaven, let's you and me not go."[3]

The opening and Gila City bar scenes do more than introduce the film's four major characters; they also show these characters involved in actions that are emblematic of their personalities and that prefigure later events in the film. Turkey has been caught cheating at cards. Similarly, the republic that Turkey wants to set up involves a cheat as well: as Turkey tells Billy, "[We'll] start making up a lot of laws, only not one of 'em would apply to us." Moreover, Turkey's precarious balance atop the barrel, a situation in which he finds himself as a result of his compulsion to cheat at cards, parallels his psychological imbalance, the most blatant example of which is his obsession with his fantasized republic.

Yellowleg unsuccessfully attempts to cut Turkey's rope with a knife, the same knife that he pulls out at the film's end and shows to Turkey, saying, "Remember that?" It is the knife that Turkey used when he tried to scalp Yellowleg. In trying to cut Turkey down with the man's own knife, Yellowleg is merely freeing Turkey so that later he can use the knife against him. However, Yellowleg's use of the knife is interrupted (as was Turkey's).

Turkey's main characterizing device is his fantasy; Yellowleg's is his knife scar; Billy's is his gun.[4] Billy interrupts Yellowleg's cutting of the rope by severing it with a bullet, just as Kit later stops Yellowleg from scalping Turkey. The identity of action (although not intent) prefigures the link between Billy and Kit that will soon emerge; this link is further emphasized by Billy's entrance from the bar's back room with a couple of women, who, like Kit, are obviously barroom whores.

When we first see Kit, she is also involved in an extremely representative activity. Kit and her son, both dressed quite "properly," are attending the Gila City barroom church service, partly in order to appear respectable to the town's more conventional citizens. This desire for public and religious acceptance for herself and her son anticipates the motives behind Kit's trip to Siringo. Only after Yellowleg has detoured to the Gila City doctor's office to try and have a gun ball removed from his shoulder do we learn that Turkey is the man who nearly scalped Yellowleg.[5] When Yellowleg tells the doctor that he left his teethmarks in the man's hand, we realize that the camera's zooming in on Turkey's scars represented Yellowleg's visual obsession with them: when he saw the scars, everything else became unimportant to him.

In a similar manner, the camera, which often operates in the film as the audience's eyes, has fixations of its own, zeroing in on Yellowleg's pants, on the Tilden boy's dropped harmonica, and on the gun Yellowleg drops at one point. The representation of the four main characters' obsessions, combined with the "objective" camera's concentration on various objects, creates an inescapable pathology. All of these visual fixations are extensions of extremely narrowed thought (internal vision), suggesting a universe in which compulsion is the motivating principle behind all actions. As will become standard in Peckinpah's films, liberation occurs only at the film's end, after violent acts deliver certain characters from obsession.

In a further example of the film's striking unity, we find that all of the major characters are attempting either to legitimize past actions or to change the manner in which past actions have been viewed. Yellowleg intends to give meaning to his previous five years of searching by scalping Turkey; Kit wants to have her son buried in Siringo next to her deceased husband so that the boy will be viewed as legitimate, a justification that she feels will also serve to change the opinions about her held by many of Gila City's residents. Turkey aims to set up his own republic and buy a group of "slave Indians" to drill, all the while wearing the stolen general's cap that he carries around with him; the realization of these dreams will compensate him for his anxiety about having deserted from the Confederate Army. As for Billy, getting the best of Yellowleg will dispel the gnawing feeling that he has finally met someone who, despite his poor shooting ability, represents an extremely troubling problem: a man who speaks and behaves like his superior but who refrains from actively challenging him.

While fleeing the scene after the bank robbery, Yellowleg accidentally kills Kit's son, a result of his shoulder injury's causing him to shoot inaccurately. (This is another example of the crippling effect of the past on the present.) Kit then resolves to take the boy's body to Siringo. We know then that a powerful affinity, predicated on death, is going to be asserted between Kit and Yellowleg. Yellowleg and Turkey are already joined by the near-death of Yellowleg's scalping, just as Billy and Turkey are joined through the murders they've undoubtedly committed. One more death-based linking therefore seems quite apt. The idea of Turkey's death keeps Yellowleg on his journey; Yellowleg's death fascinates Turkey, who keeps urging Billy to shoot Yellowleg in the back. The possibility of death resulting from a quick-draw contest animates Billy. As for Kit, she travels to Siringo in order to ensure that her son's death will have some meaning.

This last consideration brings up another interesting aspect of the film: each of these characters undertakes the journey for selfish reasons. Yellowleg goes along with Kit to ease his conscience over killing her son. Despite her protests to the contrary, Kit is using Yellowleg to shield her from her surroundings and from Billy. Billy

Plate 3. The high-tension trio has their anxiety level raised with the addition of a woman, Kit.

journeys with them because of his attraction to Kit, and Turkey goes with Billy because he needs him for his republic. (As Turkey says to Billy at one point, "You the kind of trigger-happy young fella I can use.")

Although they all travel together, each character is also isolated, lost within his or her own musings: Yellowleg about Turkey, Kit about her son and husband, Turkey about his phantom republic, and Billy about Kit. Simultaneous with these tendencies toward alienation are the constant affinities that Peckinpah establishes in the film. One of the most subtle of these is the connection between the doctor's statement that he realizes Yellowleg is from Missouri and the Gila City storekeeper's giving Kit an umbrella from St. Louis. The implication is that Yellowleg will serve as some form of protection for Kit, which he does in defending her from Billy.

This affinity between Yellowleg and Kit is later reaffirmed using another prop as a connecting symbol. Carrying the body of her dead son, Kit walks past the boy's harmonica, which is lying in the street. The camera's attention is fixated on the ground, so that all we see when Kit passes the camera are her legs. Later we see Yellowleg, also photographed from the knees down, approach the instrument and pick it up. The boy's harmonica—which as a prop disappears after this point, but which recurs in the film in the form of music played either on a harmonica or on an accordion, which sounds similar to it—reminds us of the death linkage between Kit and Yellowleg, as does the title theme, which the boy had been playing when Yellowleg, Turkey, and Billy entered Gila City and which recurs throughout the production.

Repeatedly, we see Yellowleg, Kit, Turkey, and Billy involved in scenes in which hostile statements are followed by exaggerated reactions or powerful revelations (sometimes both), as though it requires violence, usually verbal, to prompt candor among these characters. This abuse/insight paradigm initially surfaces in an exchange between Kit and Yellowleg after they leave Gila City. Yellowleg first implicitly brings up the subject of Kit's son's death by saying, "Lady, I'm just trying to help." Although Kit is pained by Yellowleg's statement, since it reminds her of the boy's death, she responds quickly. Moreover, as is clear from the way that she smiles when speaking the following lines, hurting Yellowleg gives her pleasure. "Help who?" Kit asks. "Riding shotgun on this wagon isn't gonna buy you a clean conscience." In response, Yellowleg attempts to hurt Kit.

YELLOWLEG: I'm beginning to wonder if you figured on going to Siringo at all.
KIT: What are you trying to say?
YELLOWLEG: I mean right here is as good as Siringo for the boy. You don't have to prove anything to me.

Regardless of the hostility behind both characters' statements, there is a large amount of truth in them as well. Guilt, not charity, is the prime motivating factor in Yellowleg's accompanying Kit. Similarly, although Kit may use the ideal of establishing her son's legitimacy as the reason for her journey, there is, as Yellowleg realizes, a certain degree of self-interest involved in her actions. Despite her repudiation of the biased residents of Gila City, Kit is concerned about what people think and is just as interested in changing people's opinions about her marriage as she is about changing her son's status.

When Kit tires of Yellowleg's calling her "lady," she says, "My name is Kit," to which Yellowleg responds, "I don't know you well enough to call you Kit." In Yellowleg's view, using Kit's name would imply an intimacy that at this point he would prefer to avoid.

However, this attitude changes after Yellowleg steals the Indian's horse and returns to camp to find Kit bathing nude in a stream. Kit's physical exposure leaves her extremely vulnerable, thereby making the situation greater than others involving revelations and exposures of a verbal kind. It is therefore appropriate that with this intimacy between them (Yellowleg watches Kit bathe, and Kit sees him watching her), Yellowleg should respond by using Kit's name for the first time, shouting, "Kit—pack up. We're moving out'" Yet even by the film's end, Kit is never given the chance to use Yellowleg's real name (which we don't know either). "Is Yellowleg a name?" she asks at one point, to which Yellowleg replies, "It'll do."

Throughout the film, Yellowleg prefers to remain an enigma, successfully hiding his name (a passageway into his identity) and trying to hide his scar (a passageway into his psyche). Turkey and Billy never ask Yellowleg what his real name is (Yellowleg never asks for Turkey's real name, either); if they did, he would doubtless field the question as effortlessly as he does with Kit. But Turkey and Billy do bring up the issue of Yellowleg's scar, causing him to reveal how extremely sensitive about it he is.

Yellowleg's defensiveness doesn't stop him from constantly challenging Turkey and Billy concerning their vulnerable points. Yellowleg taunts Turkey about deserting and looks over at him after the two of them discover a scalped man as though he expects Turkey to admit to the connection between the dead man and what happened between Yellowleg and himself. Yellowleg also seems compelled to assault Billy verbally (and thereby challenge him physically), ordering him about, goading him into reacting. The following conversation among Yellowleg, Billy, and Turkey is not only characteristic but is also identical to the kind of verbal abuse that goes on between Yellowleg and Kit; it also looks forward to the nonverbal abuse that the Indian will visit on Kit and Yellowleg. Turkey begins by making an insightful observation.

> TURKEY: I think Yellowleg's kind of taken a shine to that woman; all the time we thought he was feeling sorry for that boy.
> YELLOWLEG: Shut up.
> TURKEY: Touchy, too.
> BILLY: Yeah, like he is about that hat he keeps wearing.

Billy then teases Yellowleg about his vulnerable point. "Take your hat off or I'll shoot it off," he says. Yellowleg responds by audaciously challenging Billy's gunmanship. "You do and I'll kill you," he says, to which the usually good-natured Billy replies, "You know Yellowleg, there's something about you I just gotta like"—undoubtedly the man's outright bravado.

Yellowleg's hostility and reticence are prescribed by the rules of the cat-and-mouse game he is playing with Turkey and Billy. Yellowleg's reluctance to be revealed to Kit derives from his embarrassment concerning his partial scalping, which he seems to regard as a judgment against his male prowess. (He was, after all, bested by a rebel, and one who, as the Gila City doctor recalls the story, was drunk at the time as well.) Yet Kit easily overrides Yellowleg's hesitation when she says, "I've seen you without your hat." However, even after this point, which seems to represent the ultimate example of understanding and intimacy between them, Yellowleg will still slip back into his old behavior, in this case by leaving Kit in order to try to scalp Turkey. But since the scalping attempt occurs after Yellowleg has been reconciled to his disfigurement, the action seems implausible. If anything, it would have made more sense for Yellowleg to have scalped Turkey in the desert, soon after Billy left the group. One can assume only that the attempted scalping occurs late in the film in order to serve the scriptwriter's purpose of deferring Yellowleg's redemption, which supposedly takes place after Kit stops him from scalping Turkey by crying out, "Don't do it!" In any case, Turkey's final descent into madness satisfies Yellowleg (and the audience) far more than a scalping would have and further allows Turkey to be brought to conventional justice.

Kit cannot accept the truth in Yellowleg's observation about her motive for the journey any more than Yellowleg could accept the truth in Kit's previous statement about his. In response to Yellowleg's verbal lashing, Kit lashes out at Yellowleg with her whip. Billy and Turkey recognize this behavior as the beginning of intimacy. Turkey remarks to Billy, "Look at 'em fighting," which he says immediately after observing that in riding next to Kit, Yellowleg has already "done got his claim staked out." (This comparison of women and mining for precious metal looks forward to the identical equation in *Ride the High Country*.)[6]

When Yellowleg returns to the side of Kit's wagon, he says, "You don't know me well enough to hate me that much."[7] This assertion carries within itself an inherent contradiction, since after knowing someone fully, one might very well not hate him, which is exactly what happens between Kit and Yellowleg. Later in the film, Kit remarks to a sleeping Yellowleg, "Strange, I feel as though I know you better than any man I've ever known, yet I hardly know you at all";[8] Kit then tries to remove Yellowleg's hat, occasioning a bitter physical and verbal response on his part. Despite the disclaimer appended to Kit's speech, the statement achieves full significance in its implication that it is possible to feel close to someone with whom you are not familiar. Taking Yellowleg and Kit's last two statements in tandem would suggest that in *The Deadly Companions*' view, human nature, despite episodes of hostility and violence, generally tends toward understanding. Yet there is a striking contradiction in the film's attitude. On the one hand, *The Deadly Companions* chronicles alienation; on the other, it tries to preach affinity. Given the compelling nature of the former and the awkward and unconvincing quality of the latter, we must conclude that the film really believes only in alienation and that the "tender" aspects of its plot have been included in order to satisfy the need for a conventional love interest.

After the whip-lashing incident between Kit and Yellowleg, Yellowleg narrates a story about animosity.

> Hating's a subject I know a little something about. You gotta be careful it don't bite you back. I know somebody spent five years looking for a man he hated. Hating and wanting revenge was all that kept him alive. He spent all them years tracking that other man down and when he caught up with him it was the worst day in his life. He'd get his revenge, all right, then he'd lost the one thing he had to live for.

The speech is interesting not only for the way that Yellowleg talks in the third person about what is obviously himself and Turkey—a rhetorical distancing meant to mask the men's identities—but also because it suggests that Yellowleg's guilt about killing Kit's son temporarily displaces his need for aggression against Turkey. (When Kit's husband's grave is found in Siringo, thereby resolving the problem about the boy's legitimacy, Yellowleg's desire for revenge returns.)[9] After Turkey deserts their camp during the night, thereby denying Yellowleg his revenge, Kit asks Yellowleg, "You can't forgive me for asking you to give up those five years, can you?" We realize then that Kit knew that Yellowleg was referring to himself and Turkey in his story about hating someone; Yellowleg does not respond to Kit's statement, indicating that he is not surprised by her insight. Though Yellowleg and Kit do not acknowledge it until

Deadly's end, the two characters repeatedly achieve sporadic insights into each other during the film.

Peckinpah never abandons the film's revenge theme. Yellowleg banishes Billy from their camp; Turkey then steals away to follow Billy, after which Yellowleg rides off in pursuit of Turkey. While Yellowleg is gone, Kit startles and then loses her horse. After apparently accepting the unconscious prompting that Kit and her son mean more to him than Turkey does (one of the rare instances in which Yellowleg seems to understand how destructive his obsession with revenge really is), Yellowleg returns. He then decides that they will need another horse, which he steals from one of the Indians whom he and Kit had seen staging a mock re-creation of their attack on a stagecoach. Thus, no sooner does the film eliminate the revenge-based character pairing of Yellowleg and Turkey (whose dress and behavior, furred clothes and scalping, are quite like those of an Indian) than it replaces it with another: Yellowleg and the Indian from whom the horse is stolen.

Seeing how quickly and successfully this Indian fits into the film's plot throws into relief the motivations behind Kit and Yellowleg's behavior. The Indian has had an important possession stolen from him, as have Kit (her marriage's legitimacy and her son) and Yellowleg (his sense of well-being, destroyed by the near-scalping he underwent). For the Indian, who has been bested by a white man, regaining his horse is a matter of pride and honor. Kit and Yellowleg are also involved in regaining honor: for Kit, the honor accruing from a socially accepted marriage; for Yellowleg, the honor of not being degraded in battle. Unfortunately, *The Deadly Companions* doesn't use Indians simply for comparison; it also renders them as catchall symbols for evil. Thus, it is the "bad" Apaches who killed Kit's husband, the "bad" Indians who rob the stagecoach (and undoubtedly also killed its passengers), the "bad" Indian who taunts Kit and Yellowleg, prolonging their anxiety.

In intentional near-misses, the Indian repeatedly looses two arrows against Kit and Yellowleg (one for each of them), taunting the couple in a reflection of the way that they taunt each other. The anxiety that the Indian causes also duplicates other situations: the uncomfortable way that Kit is made to feel in Siringo, the uneasy way that Yellowleg feels about his scar. Robbed at night, pursuing them in the shadows, always appearing either in the evening or late day, standing silhouetted against a dark sky, finally seen peering out of the darkness in the cave where, just before being shot, he is illuminated by a bolt of lightning (whose flash is followed by the judgmental burst of light from Kit's gun), the Indian functions most successfully as a creature from Kit and Yellowleg's dark, tormented side.

Plate 4. Yellowleg and Kit nervously scanning the horizon.

Yellowleg seems to recognize that the Indian is treating him and Kit the same way that he himself treats Turkey. Near the apex of her anxiety, Kit cries out, "What is he waiting for; why doesn't he kill us?" Using words that could apply to his situation with Turkey, Yellowleg replies, "Well, he's got a little score to settle with me first." Finally, Kit shoots the Indian with a shotgun filled with buckshot (the buckshot is apparently meant to explain how Kit is able to kill the Indian without aiming).[10] Without meaning to, Kit kills the Indian just as, also without meaning to, Yellowleg had shot her son. The similarity doesn't end there, though. Both the Indian and Kit's son represented a problem for at least one member of the couple. The Indian is a threat to Kit and Yellowleg's safety; the boy attracted attention to the fact that Kit didn't seem to have a husband. The film does little to encourage a sympathetic attitude toward either the Indian or the boy, using each as a disposable means of throwing

Kit and Yellowleg together. Indeed, it would seem that Peckinpah's criticism of the film's "gimmicks—the scarred head, the dead boy being carried across the desert"[11]—could be applied to the character of the Indian as well.

Just as the separate anxieties that Turkey and Billy represent for Yellowleg and Kit are replaced by the anxiety that the Indian creates for both characters (this despite Yellowleg's brave response), the killing of the Indian, who seems to be the last barrier to the successful completion of Kit and Yellowleg's trip, is soon followed by Turkey and Billy's reappearance. The Indian's essentially elementary threat (another denigration of the character's role) is replaced by the threats represented by Turkey and Billy, who once again pose problems for Kit and Yellowleg involving their sexual identities. Turkey reminds Yellowleg of a time when he was unable to take care of himself; Billy's leering and assaults remind Kit of her past as a prostitute.

The Deadly Companions tries to use the love between Kit and Yellowleg as an answer to these problems, but this resolution merely sidesteps the issues. It seems unlikely that the hate Yellowleg has been building up for five years can be dispelled by his affection for Kit, which has developed in a suspiciously short amount of time, perhaps to compensate for his guilt over having killed her son. As for Kit, her anxiety about her self-image cannot be easily resolved by her merely going off with another "true love."

It has been noted by other critics that Peckinpah intended both that Billy shoot Turkey (an event that occurs in the present version) and that Yellowleg kill Billy.[12] Despite the director's plans, the film as received has a resolution that seems just as functional. With Billy having shot at him, it seems only natural that the temperamentally mercurial Turkey would want to immediately avenge himself on his former partner. It also seems unlikely that Yellowleg, who is a very bad shot, could actually kill Billy. (In Siringo, Yellowleg is unable to hit Turkey, even after firing three times, which prompts Billy to remark, "All this shooting and he ain't even touched him yet.") If Yellowleg had killed Billy, it is difficult to envision how the film's end, which has Yellowleg and Kit united and riding off into the sunset, could have been made even marginally plausible. Yellowleg would have been morally unacceptable to Kit, who had said, "I could never love a man who was a cold-blooded killer."[13]

Turkey's fantasy about starting his own republic provides occasions for rewarding comic moments. Toward the film's end, when

Turkey is backing away from Yellowleg, he delivers a speech that is wonderfully complemented by Chill Wills's exaggerated vocal delivery. "Listen to reason; why can't a Yankee join up with a Rebel? . . . I'll make a general out of you. General Yellowleg. Think of how you'd look in one of these caps. . . . Oh, you'd look good in a gold braid."

Later, when the posse is leading him away, Turkey is still ranting about his subject, addressing his captors as though they are his new recruits. One of the men puts Turkey on his horse, to which Turkey responds, "Thank you, orderly. Gentlemen, you gonna make great officers in my army. I'll soon have your uniforms for you and gold braids, and then we'll start training. Now, captain, if you'll say 'forward yo' and dress these ranks, we'll go."

Much of the film's camerawork is quite remarkable. We are given panoramic vistas and impressive color renditions of early evenings and sunsets. Peckinpah also employs a tracking technique during the final "showdown" between Yellowleg and Billy that not only draws out the sequence's drama but also anticipates the more refined use of the same technique at the end of *Ride the High Country*. The shots photographed from Yellowleg's perspective (Yellowleg is moving toward Billy) work successfully until the point at which the camera reaches Billy and then passes him, something that occurs not once but twice. Since the advancing camera is here functioning as Yellowleg's point of view, such duplication should not be occurring. Moreover, the first subjective track-in on Billy shows him being passed by, even though a cutaway at this point to an objective shot of Yellowleg indicates that he has not yet reached Billy. I can only assume that this is merely another example of the sloppy work of producer Charles FitzSimons, who re-edited the film after Peckinpah had finished his first cut, and that the duplication results from FitzSimons's forgetting to remove one of the track-in shots.

Peckinpah employs an interesting cutaway in the scene in which, for a brief moment, real tenderness is demonstrated between Kit and Yellowleg. After Kit's statement about knowing Yellowleg better than any other man, Kit attempts to remove Yellowleg's hat in order to make his sleeping easier. Yellowleg abruptly wakes up and reacts violently; Kit explains her motive. At this point Yellowleg's horse moves. Peckinpah then gives us Kit's point-of-view shot of the horse, which, as the horse moves to the left, shifts over to include a view of Kit's son's coffin. When Yellowleg attempts to explain his reaction by saying "There's something about me you don't understand," Kit replies, "You killed the only person I ever loved in this whole world; that's all I need to know about you." Having said this, she angrily moves away. The horse obviously reminds Kit of Yellowleg; the coffin reminds her that it was Yellowleg who shot her son. Far more effectively than through dialogue, Kit's emotional reasoning has been communicated through a succession of images.

As one might have expected given the conflicts during production between Peckinpah and the film's producer,[14] certain elements in *The Deadly Companions* are quite awkward.[15] In particular, much of Maureen O'Hara's dialogue strains credulity.[16] For example, scriptwriter A. S. Fleischman provides her with the following cliché-ridden speech.

> Bury him here? You think I haven't heard all the whispering? You [the men in Gila City] and your gossiping little wives with their pinched little faces and their noses in the air. "That dance hall woman with her freckle-faced wood colt, no telling who the father might be." They smell brimstone every time I walk by. They hated us both, me and the boy. Well, he's dead now and you can tell your wives that there was no sinning and there'll be no funeral. I'm taking him to Siringo.

Nonetheless, *The Deadly Companions* is a noteworthy effort. The film is satisfying in so many ways, and is so strongly a precursor of the great films to come, that it deserves our careful attention. Although not a major work by any means, *The Deadly Companions* always repays repeat viewings. That is no small achievement.

Riding High on Morality

There is a significant improvement in technique, symbology, and theme between *The Deadly Companions* and *Ride the High Country*, a distinction that is apparent from the very beginning of the latter film. We are immediately treated to smooth arcing pans from Lucien Ballard's camera, whose point of view moves gracefully up and then down through wooded vistas, the images effortlessly dissolving among a number of settings so that we are virtually unaware of the transitions. This smoothness would seem at odds with the apparent differences among the film's various locations were it not that the film will reveal a skillful thematic overlapping of these settings.

Peckinpah introduces the film's major theme, age versus youth (with attendant polarities of wisdom versus ignorance and integrity versus corruption), in the first post-title shot. An older cowboy, Steve Judd (Joel McCrea), enters a western town where some sort of contest is going on. The cheering crowd, seen at times from Steve's point of view, is not exulting over Steve but something else; that much is quite clear to us, but not to Steve, who acknowledges the crowd's stares (which to us appear either amused or indifferent) as though they were applauding him. He responds to this presumed acclamation by touching his hand to the brim of his hat. Such a split in perceptions, between what we know and what Steve seems to know, might lead us to believe that Steve is something of a fool and that we are superior to him. This is merely the first of the illusions with which *Ride* will tempt us.

A traffic cop yells at Steve, "Get out of the way, old man, can't you hear, can't you see you're in the way?" This statement suggests not only that there is something seriously wrong with Steve's senses, possibly resulting from a debility of age, but also that Steve is unimportant in the normal course of events that take place in this microcosmic town: that Steve has, in essence, lost touch with the world. However, given the way that the film approves of Steve's morality and criticizes that of civilization, it seems more likely that it is the world that has lost touch with Steve. To the policeman, though, Steve is nothing more than an old man, an individual whose anachronistic status is brought into relief by the automobile that nearly runs him down.[1]

As we see, what the crowd is gathered for is an example of bread and circuses: a race between a camel and a horse. Again we encounter the clash between ignorance and knowledge, although in this case knowledge is being used for a rather deplorable purpose. The camel, owned by Heck Longtree (Ron Starr), bests his opponent's horse, which, as Steve later remarks, it will do every time. (It doesn't take long at all for our initial view of Steve as naive to be deflated.) Thus, although both Steve and Heck know that a camel is faster than a horse, each man uses such information differently: Steve merely comments on the race; Heck uses his knowledge for deception. As *Ride the High Country* will repeatedly demonstrate, knowledge is morally neutral; it acquires a moral force only as a result of the way that it is used—as do the forces of arms, money, and religion in the film. The implication is that people attain a moral realm appropriate to their freely chosen actions. The universe in which *Ride* takes place allows for either salvation or damnation, depending on how one lives. Moreover, as the young boys queued up in front of the belly dancer (and the people whom we will later meet in Kate's Coarse Gold saloon) demonstrate, people are also at times creatures of appetite (a quality that will be jestingly referred to by Gil at the Knudsen dinner table).[2]

There are other snares in wait as well, such as the tendency toward self-deception. Deception, already presented in an innocent guise (Steve's wide-eyed, ignorant reaction to the crowd), now assumes another incarnation as we are shown the sideshow booth in which Gil Westrum (Randolph Scott) is occupied in cadging money from the local populace. Gil poses as the Oregon Kid, billed as "The frontier lawman who tamed Dodge City and Wichita and who singlehanded sent the notorious Omaha Gang to their graves." Like this claim, Gil's make-up is similarly exaggerated: he sports a wig and false beard and affects a mode of dress that makes him the picture of a storybook gunslinger.

Steve, though, is not fooled. Recognizing Gil, he walks up to the booth and attempts to deceive the deceiver, who apparently, like Steve (as we learn later), has poor eyesight. Turning the booth's patrons' ignorance of his chicanery to his advantage, Gil uses buckshot to hit the targets, a reflection not only on his aim but also on his ability to see the targets. Steve here turns the notion of deceived vision to his own account by approaching the booth with his head down, his hat obscuring his face from Gil's sight. Implicitly, Gil is being challenged to look beyond visual appearances (and sound as well, since Steve has disguised his voice) and somehow recognize Steve. After Gil completely recognizes Steve, he says, "Well, I'll be damned"—a judgment that, given Gil's proclivity toward petty theft and deception would, but for Steve's intervention in Gil's life from this point on, have come to pass.

At the outset of *Ride*, the notion of religious judgment, like the other themes in the film, has first been offered in a predominantly humorous way. Later, as the film's action becomes more complex and the presentation of the moral issues becomes more sophisticated, the ideas being dramatized assume greater seriousness, with occasional comic relief to allow for necessary changes in tone.

At this point in *Ride*, we take great pleasure in watching McCrea and Scott have fun with the roles of two men casually jousting with one another. Yet though Gil offers many of his remarks humorously ("It takes all the free drinks I can get to put me to sleep at night"), we already know that there is a serious example of self-diminishment at work here. Gil's transparent sideshow con appears to be the last refuge of a man without resources. Steve seems to have fallen on hard times, too: after the joking about the betting at the booth is over, Steve is careful to remove the dime he had put down to bet with. Steve's ironic comment "Quite a *little* enterprise you've got" (emphasis added) and Gil's reply that he is the "hero of the small time" not only suggest diminishment but also work in league with what we already know about Steve to make us regard these men's present conditions as truly moving and pathetic. Yet from the outset, even before Steve enters the bank to discuss his job, he seems to have far too much integrity to abase himself in the way that Gil has. Steve's dated and worn clothes may very well occasion as much ridicule as do Gil's, but because Steve does not make a show of himself, we view him as having more self-respect than his friend does.

As we will see, Gil is prone to the greatest deception of all: believing that material goods can relieve him of the universal responsibility to reflect on the morality of his actions. The moneyed characters in the film—the bankers, Knudsen, the inhabitants of Coarse Gold—seem to have acquired a moral dullness through their lust for lucre. As a result of their attempt to find salvation in riches, Heck and Gil have been corrupted by lust for money, whereas Steve and Elsa, who do not feel the need for riches, appear much better off because of their wealth of morality.

For now, though, we return to the theme of material diminishment, as Steve makes his way to the bank. Before speaking to banker Luther Samson's son Abner, Steve pulls a loose piece of material from his clothes, whose threadbare state will be recognized by Abner. The theme of the past versus the present—already hinted at through the opposition of Steve's horse versus the automobile, Steve's rather dated clothes versus those of the modern-dressed townspeople, Gil's claim to a fanciful past (as the Oregon Kid) versus his actual present status—surfaces again when the banker's son says to Steve, "We're more than familiar with your reputation . . . but that was made many years ago and we're dealing with the present, not the past." This assertion about chronology is echoed in his father's statement: "The days of the '49ers are past and the days of the steady businessman have arrived." Again, we see another character falling prey to illusion. The bankers judge Steve solely by his current appearance. From Steve's apparent age and ragged clothing, they assume that his capacities are diminished and that he is incapable of handling the job that they have for him. (Indeed, the job itself is diminished: only twenty thousand dollars is to be transported, not the quarter-million that the bankers' letter mentioned.)

It would certainly be unwise for *Ride the High Country* to fall prey itself to illusion by attempting to characterize Steve as being at the height of his powers. I fact, *Ride* shows Steve making a number of poor judgments: initially trusting Gil and Heck, forgetting to reload the rifles before the party leaves Coarse Gold, assuming Joshua Knudsen to be alive when returning to Knudsen's farm, and leaving the rifle on the horse when the party moves in on the farm. Nevertheless, Steve's essential ideas and attitudes are consistently shown to be worthwhile, and by its action, *Ride* shows us that Steve is indeed of great value, in the moral sense of the word.

The film repeatedly equates eyesight with insight. Steve, who is physically far-sighted, takes the figuratively far-sighted view of things, judging events against the context in which they occur. For example, given the self-determining nature of the Coarse Gold miners' justice, Steve feels that it would be unwise to challenge them on the validity of Elsa's marriage. But Steve is often rather weak on reacting to particular, fine details. Thus, Steve initially ignores the obvious fact that Gil's numerous references to their past aren't mere nostalgia but serve to distract Steve from his concern with morality. In a figurative sense, because Steve is too close to Gil to see his shortcomings, he overlooks them. Steve gains some perceptual distance after he sees Gil attempting to steal the bank's money, and only then does he acknowledge Gil's faults. At that point, with his moral vision cleared, Steve reconsiders Gil's references to the past, now realizing conclusively where all of them were leading.

Having already attempted a mild form of deception on the bankers (trying to conceal his worn cuffs), Steve perpetrates a further deception by speaking in a voice far bolder than his usual one in order to encourage the bankers to accept him as their courier.

> STEVE: My usual fee is twenty dollars a day; I'll have to charge you forty.
> THE BANKERS (in tandem): Forty dollars a day?
> STEVE: For two extra men. I don't intend to go four days without sleeping.
> LUTHER SAMSON: The question is . . .
> STEVE: The question is, can I do it. I can't answer that by talking about it, only by doing it. If you two want to talk about it, go ahead. I'll read the contract.
> LUTHER SAMSON: Well, I guess that'll be all right.
> STEVE: In private, if you please.

Steve retires to the bathroom for privacy; the unaccustomed audacity has obviously been difficult for him, since the first thing he does on entering the room is to wipe the sweat off his forehead. He then produces a pair of reading glasses, which he apparently needs to correct his far-sightedness. Despite the glasses, Steve still has to hold the contract far away from him in order to read it, thereby indicating not only that the prescription is out of date (another anachronism) but also that he apparently cannot afford to purchase new glasses.

Returning to the main part of the bank, Steve walks up to the Samsons and says, "Well, the contract's all right, any doubts about me? If not, I'll sign it." Luther Samson reluctantly replies, "Well, I guess it's all right."

After the contract signing, the scene dissolves to a Chinese restaurant where Steve is eating. Gil and Heck look in from the outside. Heck refers to Steve by saying, "That old man is Steve Judd? He don't look like much to me." This is another mistake in perception, since Heck is here equating age with the inability to pose a threat. Gil, as yet not totally convinced of Steve's weakness, isn't quite as confident. "I hope you're right, boy; I surely hope you're right," he says. Both Heck and Gil here underestimate Steve, to their mutual disadvantage; however, youth does best age, in that Heck reforms before Gil does. Heck's reformation, though, is prompted by his love for Elsa. Gil loves Steve, but he doesn't admit that love until later.

Gil and Heck enter the cafe, where Heck begins to flirt with a waitress until he is pulled away by Gil; this is the first indication in the film that Heck's attraction to a woman may pose a threat to his and Gil's compact of deception. Gil tells the waitress that Heck, despite his willingness, won't be meeting her later. When Heck asks why not, Gil replies, "Because if I can't you won't." This ambiguous statement means literally that for the sake of their plot, he and Heck must soon go off with Steve, but it also suggests that Gil is incapable of such assignations; perhaps because of his age or his lack of self-respect, he has been rendered both sleepless and impotent.

Overhearing their interplay, Steve good-naturedly remarks, "Showing your age, aren't you—interfering in a young man's love life?" The statement's reinvocation of the theme of youth versus age reminds us of the serious moral undercurrent always at work in the film. Indeed, two significant elders later intrude into the love lives of younger characters: Joshua Knudsen (R. G. Armstrong) interferes with his daughter's assignations in a way suggesting incestuous desire, and Gil interferes when Billy Hammond (James Drury) doesn't want Elsa to leave him (although Gil does so for an ulterior motive). In each of these cases, we see that Steve's comical comment about interference assumes a serious and grim form later, another example of the movement from lightheartedness to solemnity that is characteristic of the film.

Gil tells Steve that he may decide to help him with his assignment, invoking the past but with an application to the present by stating that he's "hankering for a little old-time activity." Gil refers to Heck as his "partner," although given the fact that their partnership is based on deception and theft, it cannot really (in *Ride*'s moralistic universe) be considered a true partnership. Similarly, there can be no truly sincere feelings behind Gil's calling Steve his "partner" until he repents of his intentions to steal the bank's money, something he does only after Steve is shot at the Knudsen farm.

Gil says that Heck has been dying to meet Steve, an obvious lie, as is evident from Heck's still looking at the waitress while absently greeting Steve. Heck's attraction to this woman is interesting in light of his later meeting with Elsa. First drawn physically to Elsa, as he obviously is to the waitress, Heck finds Elsa denying him her sexuality. Elsa thereby implicitly indicates that her love must be earned. This attitude eventually reforms Heck. Accustomed to easy love (thus the slap on the backside that he gives the waitress, whose only rebuke is to tell him not to do that in the restaurant), Heck must examine his motives when he finds that Elsa, who doesn't seem to be teasing, is interested in him but cannot reciprocate his attentions until he demonstrates that he is serious. Heck accomplishes this by repudiating Gil and showing his respect to a man worthy of it: Steve (thus Heck's transfer of "sir" from Gil to Steve). *Ride* demonstrates that one person can be the catalyst for another's salvation, a mechanism that operated in the film's past (via Paul Stanaford, who rescued Steve from a life of self-indulgent destructiveness) and reappears in its present in Elsa's reformation of Heck and in Steve's eventual reformation of Gil.

Attempting to meet Steve's objection that Heck seems to lack experience, Gil replies, "Steve, this boy's a good deal less than green; he's been dogging after me for better than three years." The reference is hardly complimentary to Heck: he has cast off idealism for expedient cynicism, while the phrase "dogging after" places him in the role of a dependent puppy. Steve silently counters this assertion about Heck's supposed maturity by covertly slipping Heck's revolver out of its holster and revealing the youth's lack of self-respect through the way that he cares for one of his most important possessions. "Pretty," Steve remarks of the gun. "Too bad he can't keep it clean." This statement links up with Steve's later remark about Heck's littering: "These mountains don't need your trash."[3] In both cases, literal dirtiness is equated with spiritual soiling—the corrupt morals that are often used to justify theft. The trash reference also seems to anticipate the appearance of the Hammonds, who are literally and, to a certain extent, morally dirty men whom one might very well refer to as trash.[4] Yet since he is hopeful not only of his own regeneration but that of others, Steve credits Heck's efforts in the cafe fist fight, granting Heck the benefit of the doubt. "He'll do; he'll do just fine," Steve says, with only a hint at the compromise involved in accepting a somewhat less than perfect assistant.

The trio finally arrives at the Knudsen farm. Joshua Knudsen, dressed in black in an obvious attempt to look like a preacher, greets them. Once more appearance pales beside reality, for Knudsen is far from pious; rather, he represents the perversion of true religious values, which are embodied in Steve. Knudsen is extremely dogmatic and lacking in compassion, qualities that combine with hubris and cold-hearted mercantilism. When Steve asks about buying some eggs for food, Knudsen says that the group can have the first egg for free—"because the Lord's bounty is not for sale"—but that each subsequent egg will cost one dollar, implying that everything after the first egg is his bounty, a horribly covetous attitude.

The tendency to joust with people, using the Bible as a tool, emerges when Knudsen replies to Heck's sarcastic comment about the high-priced eggs by saying, "Levity in the young is like unto a dry gourd with the seeds rattling round." At this point Peckinpah first inserts a shot of Heck and then one of Knudsen's daughter, Elsa (Mariette Hartley), thereby establishing a linkage among sterility (the dry gourds), Heck, and Elsa.[5] The association suggested here by the editing is borne out by the film's action until Heck begins to treat Elsa not as an object but as another human being. For now, though, Heck is attracted to Elsa only because of his greed, just as he is greedily attracted to the money that Gil promises. This attitude toward Elsa, which compares her with riches and which will be developed in the Coarse Gold sequences, is reaffirmed by further dialogue. When Heck comments, "Think of all that [Elsa] going to waste up here," Gil replies, "Like the fella said, gold is where you find it"; by contrast, Steve responds, "If it's not yours, don't covet it." Like his later parody of Knudsen's rhetoric (Steve's humorously offered biblical citation about "The mouth of a strange woman [being like] an open pit"), Steve's assertion actually contains a falsehood, since Steve doesn't really believe one should "covet" anything (indeed, it is impossible to covet something that is yours); the word is used only because Heck treats people and (unbeknownst to Steve at this point) money in a covetous way. ("Covet" may also tie in with the incestuous atmosphere at Knudsen's farm.)

During dinner at Knudsen's, the characters are appropriately seated at the table: the moral pair (Steve and Elsa) are on one side; the deceivers (Heck and Gil) are on the other, with Knudsen at the head of the table. For the dinner benediction, Knudsen says, "Teach thy children to be grateful for thy goodness, to walk in thy path." Peckinpah cuts to Elsa on the phrase "grateful for thy goodness" and to Heck on the phrase "walk in thy path." Knudsen then adds, "That they may not suffer thy wrath and thy vengeance." On the last two words, Peckinpah cuts away from Heck and back to Elsa. From the editing, it is clear that the self-righteous Knudsen, who conceives of God in his own unyielding image, is really speaking about his own "wrath and vengeance" and his own "goodness," for which he feels Elsa should be grateful. (This view is confirmed later when he tries to convince Elsa that he struck her for her own benefit.) The shot of Heck on the word "path," though, has a dual meaning: first, it affirms Heck's status as a moral novitiate still on the "path" to enlightenment (thus linking him with Steve, who will become a positive moral instructor for him); second, since it follows our view of Elsa (who lifts her eyes to Heck, who then does the same), it tells us that Elsa, as much as Steve, will have a beneficial influence on Heck. However, Knudsen not only fails to see the role he has assumed but cannot even connect his plea to God to forgive the assembled company "the mercenary desires that brought them here" with his own mercenary side, a failure that points up his pitiful ignorance.

What follows is the fascinating catechistic duel between Knudsen and Steve, which both underscores the film's religious subtext and brings into relief Knudsen and Steve's different attitudes toward religion. Knudsen begins by stating that "gold is a stumbling block to them that sacrifice to it, and every fool shall be taken therewith." This assertion is founded on the unproven assumption that Steve, to whom Knudsen addresses the citation, intends to sacrifice to gold. Nevertheless, Knudsen's statement is somewhat correct, in that there are two fools quite taken with gold: Gil and Heck, to whom he looks (briefly averting his eyes from Steve) on the word "fool."

Moving the level of the discussion from the abstractly moral to a more humane level, Steve says, " 'A good name is rather to be chosen than great riches, loving favor rather than silver or gold'—Proverbs, chapter 22." To Steve, what is most important is how he is regarded—primarily, it would seem, how he is regarded by himself, since if he meets his own high ideals of behavior, such a state would be recognized by others as well. Moreover, the film suggests that the only being outside of Steve whose evaluation of him really matters is God, who would confer on him the blessing of a redeemed life.

Knudsen counters, " 'Into the land of trouble and anguish come the old lions, and they shall carry their riches on the shoulders of young asses to a people that shall not profit them'—Isaiah, chapter 30, verse 6.' " From the severity of the quote's delivery, we can see that Knudsen—unlike Steve, who regards their exchange as good-natured banter—intends to do rhetorical battle. The quote is both harsh and insulting, since Knudsen means it to refer to Steve and Gil as old (and therefore impotent) lions and to the more physically powerful among them (Heck) as a young ass who is bearing a great deal of the journey's chores. Of course, greed ("profit") doesn't motivate Steve (although it obviously applies to Gil and Heck); the only reward that Steve wants is self-respect.

Knudsen's citation is also interesting for what it modifies and deletes. The original passage in Isaiah refers to "the young and [the] old lion," a pairing that would seem to apply to Steve and Heck, or Gil and Heck, only. Knudsen also excises the verse's reference to the "viper and fiery flying serpent" that accompany the lions; these are animals of prey (the viper) and judgment (the serpent, which also suggests Edenic connotations) that one would have expected the judgmental Knudsen to have included.[6] Moreover, the verse's phrase about "treasures" being carried "upon the bunches of camels" was eliminated by the film's scriptwriter, even though it would have nicely recalled Heck's use of a camel for profit.

We can appreciate the distinctions between Knudsen and Steve by tracing their quotations back to their sources. Steve's source, Proverbs, derives from a time in Israel's history when wisdom and compassion were being offered as alternatives to violence. Knudsen, though, quotes from Isaiah, a late prophet renowned for delivering violent warnings to a people who had drifted away from God's morality by transgressing. There is a bitterness in Isaiah not found in many Old Testament books. However, what is most fascinating about Steve and Knudsen's "books" is that both Proverbs and Isaiah are also characterized by qualities that relate to each man's "opponent." Thus, Steve's book, although filled with practical maxims, also repeatedly asserts that wisdom derives from fear of the Lord, a characteristic that would appeal more to Knudsen. Alternatively, although Isaiah is quite judgmental, its latter half holds forth hope for the exiled Jews, thereby suggesting a compassion we would expect from Steve, not Knudsen.[7]

To accentuate the scene's significance, Peckinpah cuts away from Knudsen twice during his last citation, first on the word "riches," when he shows us Elsa, and again on the word "asses," when he shows us Heck. Knudsen means to shame Heck through the reference, although he could not possibly know that Heck will also be the animal who initially bears the yoke of Gil's disgrace; however, Heck nonetheless accepts this yoke as his first step toward moral and spiritual regeneration.

At this point Gil speaks up, not only to divert attention from the "mercenary desires" being identified but also to relieve the scene's tension with a bit of humor. "You cook a lovely hamhock, Miss Knudsen, just lovely," Gil says. When the company looks at him, he parodies the war of citations by stating, "Appetite, chapter one." Yet the mock textual reference also identifies Gil as a creature whose desire to satisfy baser hungers is that of a man fallen on hard times, a man who intends to purchase fulfillment with stolen money. Gil's statement, then, reveals more than he intends it to.

Steve's citation (Prov. 22:1) does more than reproduce the Bible accurately. When one looks a bit more in Proverbs, one finds that the entire chapter to which Steve alludes is concerned with issues relating to self-knowledge as it conflicts with the desire for wealth; with righteousness as opposed to blasphemy; and with teaching and discipleship, themes clearly applicable to the interactions among Steve, Gil, and Heck. The chapter's mention of "cast[ing] out the scorner" (22:10) anticipates Steve's throwing Gil out of camp after he discovers Gil's perfidy. Heck fits the part of the chapter's child, who should be "train[ed] up . . . in the way he should go . . . and when he is old, he will not depart from it"; this reference to moral instruction applies not only to Steve's instruction of Heck but also to Paul Stanaford's instruction of Steve.

Proverbs 22 seems to be a special favorite of Steve's. Later he kids Heck about the disappointing meeting with Elsa by saying, "The mouth of a strange woman is a deep pit; him that is abhorred of the Lord shall fall therein."[8] In the context of the film, this reference suggests an affinity between a woman's mouth and the mouth of a mine. This is one of many references to Elsa as a piece of wealth. The linkage between women (albeit corrupt ones) and money is made again in Coarse Gold when Kate, the town madam, stops by Steve's tent to have her gold weighed.

GIL: Looks like you got a pretty good claim.
KATE: Aw, it's a gold mine, honey. Why don't you come on over and take a look?

Certainly the whorehouse (where Elsa's marriage takes place) is a gold mine in the sense that it produces a significant amount of profit from the gold that miners redeem there for whisky and lodging. (It is no coincidence that a sign outside the building's entrance reads, "Men taken in," a punning reference to the place's taking advantage of its clientele.) But the establishment's primary source of income is prostitution. We can thus see how the vagina yields forth gold for Kate, just another example of an "open pit" strewing forth riches.

Knudsen's farm comprises all of the worst aspects of the film's universe. The lack of respect for elders is present, yet at the farm it is justified, since the self-righteous Knudsen does not warrant respect. Like the city, the farm is a place of plenty, but it is also a place of unrequited desires (in the form of Elsa's need for affection and attention). There is a self-sufficiency to Knudsen's place that rivals that of the town and Coarse Gold, but it is a self-sufficiency born of an attempt to withdraw from the world. The farm seems to be a mutated version of the town that feasts on gold and the mining encampment that produces it. In town, money is the governing principle, although it is expressed in terms of progress ("The days of the steady businessman have arrived"). In Coarse Cold no such hypocrisy prevails: unadulterated passions and lusts (for gold, whiskey, and women) are ascendant. Knudsen embraces both of these attitudes. He subsumes greed under the rubric of some abstract principle (the "bounty" supposedly dictated by the Bible), but at the same time he allows unbridled passion to hold sway by permitting a "mercenary desire" (to use his own words) to rule in the form of the exorbitant price for all of the eggs after the first one. And though he probably doesn't drink, Knudsen certainly seems to suffer from lust. One has only to point to Knudsen's inveighing against all of Elsa's suitors, which makes it clear that he suffers from incestuous jealousy. As Elsa remarks, "According to you [Knudsen], every single man is the wrong kind of man, except you."

Following the meal, the film's two couples—Steve and Gil, Heck and Elsa—retire to reflect on romantic notions, the former in conversation that touches on the past, the latter in conversation as part of a courtship ritual in the present. While Elsa is doing the dishes, Heck arranges for an assignation with her. The couple's complementarity is evident in Elsa's pumping the water while Heck offers to dry. Later, spotting Heck waiting at the haystack, Steve says to

Gil, "That boy you trained personally shows a substantial lack of judgment." This is another pronouncement that means more than the speaker intends, since at this point Steve couldn't possibly know that Heck has also shown poor judgment by agreeing to steal the bank's money.

Steve and Gil undress down to their long underwear: Steve's is white, reflecting the purity of his intentions; Gil's has a touch of red, hinting at the satanic urgings that are prompting him to betray his friend. (Gil had said earlier, "The Lord's bounty may not be for sale, but the Devil's is . . . if you can pay the price.") The two men begin to talk about a former lover of Steve's, Sara Truesdale; Gil remarks that Elsa reminds him of Sara. Though Steve denies the resemblance, the connection is nonetheless significant given the way that the film attempts to establish Heck as a successor to Steve's morality.

The next morning, the trio departs. Knudsen is seen kneeling at his wife's grave (we learn on the group's return to the farm that this is his daily custom). Knudsen looms large in the foreground of the shot, initially dominating our attention in a corollary of the way that he tries to achieve the same effect verbally; nevertheless, the framing of the shot draws our attention to the three small figures moving off in the background. In a comparable manner, *Ride* directs our attention to Gil by virtue of his more dynamic personality, his use of humor, and his loquaciousness, characteristics that may result in some viewers being more interested in watching him than in noting Steve's words and actions. Indeed, the manner in which the shot at the farm foregrounds the morally inferior character and relegates the essentially religious party (the righteous Steve and his flawed but redeemable associates) to the background challenges us to reject the more obvious allurements in favor of concepts such as Steve's idealism, which may be more difficult to grasp but which are nonetheless worth the effort. This shot underscores the theme of vision to tell us that, here as well, we must set our sights on the far view, that we must concentrate on the morally high country, in order to perceive what is really important.

The visit to the Knudsen farm proves to be fateful in a number of ways. As we shall see, Joshua Knudsen's description of Coarse Gold is quite apt. But it is the attributes of the two women at Knudsen farm's that prove to be most significant. Although we never meet Knudsen's wife, his attitude toward her is characterized by the words that Knudsen has had inscribed on her tombstone: "Wherefore, O Harlot, hear the word of the Lord. I will judge thee as women that break wedlock and shed blood are judged. I will give thee blood in fury and in jealousy." The inscription's words smack of sanctimonious judgment against Mrs. Knudsen and prophesy of events to come. Ironically, not only does the prophecy come to pass, but the first part of the inscription, which initially seems to be unjustifiably harsh, seems to be correct as well—that is, if we are to judge by the actions of Elsa, the inheritor of Mrs. Knudsen's role as woman of the family.

As the focal point from which much of the film's emotional energy derives—in particular that regarding lust (be it for women or for gold, which in the film amount to the same thing)—Elsa is responsible for setting in motion all of the film's subsequent deadly machinery. It is Elsa's presence that occasions harsh words between Mr. Knudsen and Heck at the haypile, her presence that causes blows to be exchanged between Steve and Heck and estrangement to occur between Gil and Heck. In Coarse Gold, it is while delivering Elsa to the Hammonds that Heck first runs afoul of the family (although at this point all that the Hammonds do is taunt him and then stone him out of the camp). Elsa occasions the fights in the brothel and the drunken assault against her. She "break[s] the wedlock" with Billy and catalyzes the abrupt departure from town of Steve, Gil, and Heck, which leads to the shoot-out in the mountains and the final decisive gun battle at the Knudsen farm (where her father, himself reaping a harvest of "blood in fury," kneels dead at his wife's grave). It is Elsa, through her sexuality, who rules over the majority of the film's conflicts, a fact that makes the salutary effect she has on Heck pale by comparison.

Despite what we might expect given the town's rough reputation, no deadly encounters occur in Coarse Gold itself. True, there may be a fistfight or two and a threatened rape, but the violence played out in town simply does not compare to the deaths and terrors that occur either in the mountains or at the Knudsen farm. Coarse Gold, that demiparadise of base desires, is witness to relatively benign incidents. Instead, corruption seeps down from the high country and takes root at the Knudsen farm in the form of the essentially jaded Hammond family.

The gold ore itself, which almost always leads to disaffection, functions in the film along with Elsa as a precious commodity that causes enmity among men. It is for lust of money that Gil and Heck bilk the townspeople; it is to shield the ore from gold lust that Steve becomes its protector. (He also uses this job as a means of redeeming himself from base occupations.) It is lust for wealth that suggests the plan for theft to Gil; and it is through lust for the possession of Elsa's body that the Hammonds, first in their camp and later at the saloon and whorehouse, argue among themselves. Later, after Elsa's flight from town, they are undone by their lust for vengeance against the men who take her away. And although we may object to their resolve to carry out a deadly vendetta against Steve, Gil, and Heck, we cannot justifiably condemn the Hammonds for feeling wildly offended by what amounts to Elsa's being illegally separated from her husband. Only by invoking a higher law than the one of marriage (for compassion's sake, Elsa should not be compelled to stay married to a man whom she doesn't love) can Elsa's determination to leave Billy be justified. However, we are here dealing with a moral anachronism, since this compassionate attitude, although it is obviously present in Steve, is far from characteristic of the ideas concerning wedlock that were contemporary to the period in which *Ride* takes place.

From virtually her first appearance Elsa is referred to in words that suggest that she is the gold being retrieved from the high country and brought back to the safety of the town; thus, we can in one respect understand the Hammonds' communal attitude toward her as a form of wealth that should be shared. (We would expect that as equal partners in their gold claim, they would democratically share in whatever they discovered.) Nor is the mercantile attitude toward Elsa confined to the Hammonds alone, as we have seen from the comments about Elsa that Heck and Gil (in all seriousness) and Steve (partly in jest) offer on first seeing her.

By the time Kate refers to her business as "a gold mine," the equivalence of Elsa and a precious metal is virtually complete. (To juxtapose moral and mineralogical terms, Elsa's supposed refinement is opposed to the moral dross of the whores in Coarse Gold's saloon.)[9] After the marriage ceremony, Kate enjoins Elsa to "have a good time"—presumably meaning that Elsa, like the other women in the scene, should relax, drink up, and carouse with any man who wants to have her—indicating that she views Elsa as no different from the whorehouse's other residents: she is the rightful property of anyone who can possess and retain her. One might expect such an attitude in a town named Coarse Gold: the coarser one's behavior, the more gold you're likely to have.

Yet the film's real gold, the important ore that Steve is mining, is the golden ideal of justice and righteousness. Applying this righteous attitude to Elsa reveals that what is being referred to when Elsa is compared to gold is her virginity, which is, significantly, unviolated throughout the film. Although Elsa is assaulted three times—first by Heck, then by Billy, and then by Billy's two brothers—Elsa in each instance emerges intact. Indeed, in the first and third situations she is dramatically rescued by the film's moral paragon, Steve Judd.

The trip into the high sierras is first a journey upward, into God's country; the region is beautiful and pristine. The journey's religious aspect is made clear by Peckinpah's following the shot of Knudsen praying at his wife's grave with a scene in which, after the ascension into the mountains, Steve performs a pleasurable self-baptism by washing his aching feet. Heck ridicules Steve, indicating that at this point Heck is still too intolerant and lacking in empathy (short-sighted) to realize that he too will grow old, which is just what Steve tells him. "In about thirty years you'll like the feel of it, too," Steve says. Gil then comes on the scene. Putting on his boot, Steve remarks about the hole in its bottom that Gil has noted (Gil is once more trying to make Steve regret his poverty). Steve humorously comments on the hole, stating that he had "a hell of a time getting [the bootmaker Juan Fernandez] to put [it] in there" and referring to Fernandez's inability to understand the "principle of ventilation." (A vision reference surfaces again here, as Steve refers to Juan's being "short-sighted.") The worn boot, like Steve's frayed cuffs, is merely another indication of the hard times onto which he has fallen, although it's notable that Steve responds to all of these adverse conditions with extraordinarily good humor. Admittedly, Gil does the same, but the distinction between the two men is worth keeping in mind. Steve accepts personal responsibility for his present state, whereas Gil blames the world for his poverty. In this sense, the difference between Gil and Steve is very much like that between Pat Garrett and Billy the Kid in Peckinpah's later film. Garrett uses a rationale to justify his compromises: the supposed fact that, in the character's words, "Times have changed." No one disputes this; it's the manner in which a man responds to this change that is of significance. The Kid says, "Times maybe, not me," a response that would be worthy of Steve.[10]

Gil then begins to mention the past again, attempting to turn Steve's obvious weakness for nostalgia to his own account. However, Gil has seriously misjudged his friend: Steve may be sentimental, but he is not naive. Gil relates the story about Doc Franklin's funeral—which was attended only by himself, the mortician, and the gravedigger—in order to imply that he was at the funeral solely out of loyalty, a quality that Gil is nonetheless now willing to suppress for material gain. Gil's various attempts to have Steve admit to Gil's (and, by extension, Steve's) present impoverished condition and the way that money would alleviate this state fail, though. Steve knows himself too well, and is too determined to act honorably, to be swayed by the comparatively weak ministrations of morally inferior characters (whether it be the bankers, who try to shame him; Knudsen, who tries to best him; or Gil, who tries to take advantage of him). "The only gratitude I expect," says Steve, "is my paycheck." "And that satisfies you?" asks Gil, to which Steve replies, "That's all I can hope for." (However, Seve is referring only to the job's material aspect here.) When Gil baits him by saying, "Is it?" Steve answers, "According to my contract it is." The reply makes plain that the pay is important only as an acknowledgment of Steve's worth and, further, that whether or not an actual written contract existed between Steve and the bank, Steve would honor his commitment, since his word is his bond.

Elsa then appears, saying that she's left home and is traveling to Coarse Gold to marry Billy Hammond. "Our business is transporting gold, not girls," says Steve. The statement once again asserts

Plate 5. Elsa, Heck, Steve, and Gil in *Ride the High Country*.

the equivalence between women and precious ore and looks forward to Gil's later assertion (when Steve suggests that they take Elsa, who has just been married to Billy Hammond, back to her father), "We're packing gold, not petticoats"; the similarities between these two statements demonstrate the strong affinity between Steve and Gil. But Heck, whom they need for support, threatens to leave with Elsa if she isn't accepted, so the older men reluctantly allow her to accompany them.

It is no criticism of Steve's capabilities that he needs both Gil and Heck's assistance to transport the gold, since reinforcements would be needed by anyone carrying large amounts of money. Steve later says that he has served as "bartender, stick man, bouncer, what have you" and that his current job represents part of an attempt to regain his self-esteem, which he "intend[s] to keep . . . with the help of you and that boy back there." This acknowledgment of his need for assistance does not indicate that Steve cannot achieve redemption on his own. All we are meant to understand is that on the present job, which is only one of the many conceivable ways in which Steve could have acted honorably, two (or, better yet, three) couriers are needed. However, Gil is not as self-assured as Steve. Later, when Heck once again threatens to stay behind with Elsa (this time in Coarse Gold), Gil talks him out of it by appealing to their "deal," an invalid tactic, since no agreement between unprincipled parties can truly be binding. As Dutch says in *The Wild Bunch*, "What counts [is] who you give [your word] to."[11]

It's a measure of Gil's sorry state that he doesn't consider himself Steve's equal (which he had been in the past, as when Steve was a deputy to Gil, just as Gil was later to Steve). When Steve discovers Gil attempting to steal the money, he challenges him to draw, saying, "You always fancied yourself faster than me"; perhaps Gil was faster, but he now relents. Yet Gil could have employed something other than gun skills to get the better of Steve, possibly by striking Steve when he was asleep. Instead, what really puts Gil at a disadvantage is that he doesn't respect himself and his capabilities. As a consequence, he is significantly weaker than Steve and could overcome him only with the force of greater numbers. When Gil tries to act alone, though, he fails.

Later on in the journey (but before Gil's robbery attempt), the two couples again split up. As before, the older two talk of the past (a discussion about old man Kiefert), and the younger pair deal with the present (an exchange about Elsa's hair). Heck distracts

Elsa, then kisses her and finally starts pushing her down on the ground. At this point, using the "isolation of elements" technique also used in *The Deadly Companions*, Peckinpah shows us Steve, at first shot from the ankles down, moving into the frame. He pulls Heck away; Heck strikes him, and Steve knocks Heck down. Gil picks Heck up and asks if he's learned a lesson; the youth then modifies his earlier opinion of Steve ("He don't look like much") by saying, "That old man is about half rough." Gil asks Heck, "Got room for another [lesson]?" Heck replies yes, and Gil knocks him down. Gil's chastisement doesn't have a moral purpose, though; he merely wants Heck to attend solely to their business: "We're not here for romance; understand me, son?" The word *son* implies a closer relationship between Gil and Heck than really exists; and though Heck uses the respectful *sir*, he has not considered whether Gil deserves his respect or not. As we will see when he rejects Gil, one of Heck's major lessons in the film is perceiving the threat to his own soul of committing a crime, a realization that occurs in response to Steve's object lessons in morality. Later, when Heck replies to Steve with "sir," we can conclude that the feeling of respect behind it is genuine and well-founded; Heck has obviously had to carefully consider rejecting Gil, especially since at that point he is under the threat of imprisonment, something that might befall him should he remain allied with Gil against Steve.

The first views we have of Coarse Gold confirm Joshua Knudsen's description of the place as a "sinkhole of depravity," a reference that harks backs to Steve's "open pit" quote, thereby accentuating the town's aura of female sexuality. As the quartet's horses move through the street, a woman throws a pail of slops in front of Steve's horse. In all, it's an appropriate welcome to this depraved town in which people live and die by money. Gil wishes Elsa "all the happiness in the world," at which point we hear a woman's raucous laughter, which has the effect of deriding Gil's statement. Peckinpah then intercuts a shot of the place of Elsa's greatest sorrow: Kate's whorehouse and saloon, with Kate, holding a bottle of whiskey, seated in front of it. "This seems to be the place to find it [happiness]," says Gil, a statement that is not only ultimately cruel (in light of Elsa's near-rape at the saloon) but is also an indication that Gil might very well regard Kate's carnal emporium as a source of pleasure.

Heck leaves to accompany Elsa to the Hammond camp, where we get a bit of the male roughhouse humor that Peckinpah seems

Plate 6. The delivery of Elsa to Coarse Gold.

to favor. Elsa is initially identified by Elder Hammond (John Anderson) as "the girl [Billy's] been going down the mountain to see." Elder goes on to say, "She's sure *worth* the trip" (emphasis added), another example of the film's coordinating women and valuables. Elder then says, "She can have the pick of the litter; no rush about making up your mind," giving us the first example of the Hammonds' communal attitude toward women. (There is also an unintentional and apposite pun in Elder's use of "litter" to refer to members of the clan; the word recalls Steve's comment about Heck's littering in the mountains and anticipates Steve's reference to the Hammonds as "trash" just before the Knudsen farm shoot-out.) The Hammonds' communal attitude is made more obvious later, not only in the attempted gang rape of Elsa by Henry (Warren Oates) and Sylvus (L. Q. Jones) but also in Henry's earlier statement that at their cousin's wedding the bride didn't seem to mind being accosted en masse, to which Billy replies, "Now there'll be none of that"—this despite the fact that Billy himself, right after the ceremony, brutally kisses one of Kate's women. Similarly low principles come into play in the taunting of Heck, whom the Hammonds deride for acting "the perfect gentleman" with Elsa while on the trail and, later, in Sylvus's intention to spend the night of Billy and Elsa's wedding in the tent with them.

Elsa's wedding procession into town is accompanied by the Hammonds singing (with some new lyrics) "When the Roll Is Called up Yonder," thus linking the wedding with death; this association is soon confirmed, since the wedding eventually leads to the deaths of Steve and all of the Hammonds. This fatalistic linkage is affirmed as well in the verse "The knot that binds them till they die"; the knot is in fact undone only at the end of the shoot-out at Knudsen's farm.

The wedding occurs at Kate's Place, a proper setting for the prostitution of Elsa's purity. It is a wedding conceived in Hell, presided over by a dipsomaniac judge and attended by the leering, drunken patrons of the saloon, who are presented to us in carefully staged shots that show their dirty clothes and uneven faces; some of the shots are photographed with a short focal-length lens, which accentuates the scene's grotesquerie. The visuals are complemented by the characters' slurred speech, and the entire ceremony is orchestrated by the overweight town madam, with a trio of sorry-looking prostitutes serving as Elsa's bridesmaids.

Despite being totally drunk, Judge Tolliver (Edgar Buchanan) acquits himself of a fine speech about marriage that has a truly touching naivete about it. The latter part of the speech is worth quoting in full.

> [Marriage is] not to be entered into unadvisedly, but reverently and soberly. A good marriage has a kind of a simple glory about it. A good marriage is like a rare animal—it's hard to find, almost impossible to keep. You see, people change. That's important for you to know at the beginning; people change. The glory of a good marriage don't come at the beginning; it comes later on, and it's hard work.

It's a curiously moving sermon, not the least significant aspect of which is Tolliver's comparison of a good marriage to a rare animal whose qualities ("hard to find, almost impossible to keep") invite comparison with gold (also "hard to find" and "almost impossible to keep"), thereby once again affirming for us the analogies between women and gold that are drawn throughout the film.

After the ceremony, Peckinpah cuts to a shot of Steve and Heck outside. Heck is standing next to a sign for the Coarse Gold market, implying a connection between the marriage and the marketing of goods; this shot not only links up with Elsa's being effectively sold to the Hammonds but also correlates with Kate's Place, where men and women are paired for money. Finally, after Billy tries to force himself sexually on Elsa, followed by Henry and Sylvus breaking into the "bridal chamber" with similar intent, Steve enters the saloon. With gun drawn, Steve saves Elsa in a classic Western manner comparable to the way that, later, Gil comes riding back to the scene of the final shoot-out, his horse at a gallop, his gun drawn and firing.

Steve proposes to take Elsa back to her father; Gil protests, believing that this action might complicate his designs on the money. This time, however, Gil finds that Heck will not support his protest, so he convinces Tolliver to lie about the marriage's legality, thereby assuring Elsa's release.

Heck's refusal to back Gil obviously derives both from his emotional attraction to Elsa and his respect for Steve's saving her. Heck must also realize that Gil's objection to taking Elsa, and Gil's subsequently ensuring that she can leave town, are done only so that Gil can later use Heck against Steve. Heck's alienation from Gil is virtually complete, signaled by the youth's assignment of unqualified respect for Steve. Whereas earlier Heck had withheld total admiration for Steve, he now indicates his changed attitude. "I started out thinking he was an old mossback but I changed my mind," Heck says. For the rest of the film, Heck will remain loyal to this view.

What follows is Steve's statement about his earning back his self-respect. Still trying to sway Steve's allegiances, Gil once again attempts to shift a discussion from a moral level to one concerned solely with material matters. "What's on the back of a poor man when he dies? The clothes of pride; and they're not any warmer to him than when he was alive. Is that all you want, Steve?"

But Steve immediately guides the conversation back to a moral level, expressing his desire in spiritual terms. In the film's most succinct and affecting expression of its theme of salvation and redemption, he says, "All I want is to enter my house justified."

When Steve apprehends Gil in the act of stealing the money, Peckinpah again uses isolated elements to tell a story. The director shows us Gil's tiptoeing feet and the hooves of his horse, which are cloth-bound to prevent noise. By the time the Hammonds encounter the party, Gil's hands are bound, and Steve must turn to Heck for assistance, which is freely given. Steve asks for Heck's word that he will return his gun after the shoot-out, and Heck gives it; because Heck respects what Steve stands for, Steve is now willing to repay this trust with some of his own. Heck's insight here reminds us of an important dialogue between Steve and Gil concerning the manner in which one recognizes values.

The morality by which Steve lives is an outgrowth of his previously mentioned encounter with Paul Stanaford, who had physically corrected Steve when he was acting wild. The exchange on this subject is of major importance.

> STEVE: Would it surprise you to know that I was once a law-breaker?
> GIL: Well, bless my stars.
> STEVE: 'Bout the age of that boy back there, skinny as a snake and just about as mean, ran around with the Hole-in-the-Wall bunch, gun-happy, looking for trouble or a pretty ankle. Had the world by the tail, so to speak. Then one night Paul Stanaford picked me up. He was sheriff of Madeira County then. There'd been a fight and I was drunk, sicker than a fat dog. Well sir, he dried me out in jail and then we went out back and he proceeded to kick the bitter hell right out of me.
> GIL: That took some doing.
> STEVE: Not much; see, he was right and I was wrong. That makes the difference.
> GIL: Who says so?
> STEVE: Nobody. That's something you just know.

Here we can see the clearest identification of the source of Steve's values: intuitive knowledge of morality. Such intuition is significant partly because it yields empirically productive attitudes (witness Steve's admirable example). It is also significant, though, because such values are not imposed by either an external authority figure (e.g., Knudsen) or a deity but are instead spiritually apprehended from within and then integrated into a mode of behavior. Moreover, unlike Knudsen's rule-bound approach to morality, Steve's morality is compassionate and places faith in the ability of the individual (with a little help from others who have already been enlightened) to realize his or her own ideals. Moreover, the interchange between Steve and Gil affirms Steve's view that good must always triumph over evil: Stanaford wins the fight because "he was right" and Steve "was wrong." The fact that Steve characterizes the result of the fight in colloquially transcendent terms ("kicked the bitter hell right out of me") once again reveals his divine aspirations and shows us that in Steve's simple piety, to be right (moral) is to be close to heaven; to be wrong (immoral) is to consign oneself to Hell.[12]

The shoot-out in the hills between Steve's party and the Hammonds results in the killing of Sylvus and Jimmy Hammond (John Davis Chandler). When Billy notes that Heck is now carrying the loaded rifle he took from the dying Sylvus Hammond (Steve had neglected to load the party's rifles before they left Coarse Gold, an inexcusable oversight), Billy says he wants to clear out, although Elder wants to stay. (Their morality later reverses, with Elder playing the coward at the farm shoot-out and Billy encouraging a moral response.)

ELDER: We'll catch them when they raise up.
BILLY: Ain't you got no sense of family honor?"

Elder, Billy, and Henry do eventually leave, though, after Heck shoots at and narrowly misses Elder.

Finally, Steve's trio (Gil has stolen away during the night) once again approach the Knudsen farm. Having gone ahead, Steve comes back to report, "I saw your father; everything's all right." Heck and Elsa apparently assume from Steve's colloquial use of the word "saw" that Steve has had personal contact with Knudsen. This one time, though, Steve's far-sightedness has not been put to good use. Steve saw Knudsen, but because of the angle from which he was watching him, he did not note that Knudsen was dead. Unlike earlier, it is not Steve's literal (eye) sight that has caused him trouble but his inner sight, his reasoning, which he uses to draw conclusions from his sense perceptions. Regardless of the farm's tranquility (itself an illusion: Steve didn't notice Henry Hammond's black crow, a harbinger of death, causing havoc among Knudsen's chickens), Steve should have been prepared for trouble. After all, three of the vengeful Hammonds are still at large.

It is only when Elsa remarks that her father is visiting the grave at the wrong time of day that Steve deduces that something is wrong; the trio must abase themselves by "going to the ditch" in order to survive. Gil then returns in a blaze of glory, deceiving the Hammonds by feigning injury after his horse is shot out from under him ("That got him," says Henry).

Pinned down, there isn't much that the party can do. Heck is taken out of action when he is shot—a dramatic ploy to ensure that the shoot-out involves only the two elder gunfighters, who once again are friends (thus Gil's compassionate use of "partner" for Steve at this point). Steve gets a rise out of the Hammonds by calling them "redneck peckerwoods" and "dry-gulching Southern trash."

(The Hammonds have already insulted Gil by referring to him as "old man.") Steve has the Hammonds agree to meet them in the deception-free manner in which he likes to operate: "Head on, halfway, just like always," to which Gil assents. "My sentiments exactly," Gil says.

Plate 7. The maligned Hammonds, just before the final shoot-out.

The shoot-out occurs amid a dizzying number of explosions, and though all three remaining Hammonds are killed, Steve is mortally wounded. He falls in a symbolic half-light region between life and death: near the edge of a group of mottled shadows, his position viewed from a god's-eye vantage point. What follows is the film's most moving exchange. "Don't worry about anything," Gil says. "I'll take care of it just like you would have," thereby indicating that he will indeed carry on his friend's essentially religious quest. Steve is gracious to the end. "Hell, I know that," he says. "You just forgot it for a while, that's all." He thus implies that all along Gil had intuitively understood what was morally correct (a repetition of Steve's earlier contention that morality, like an article of faith, is "something you just know"). "So long, partner," Steve says, thus affirming that he has totally accepted Gil as his equal. Gil replies, "I'll see you later," suggesting how close he, too, is to death.

Peckinpah ends the film with a masterful low-angle shot of Steve, who looks one last time at the high country of morality (to which he had raised his eyes when making the assertion "All I want is to enter my house justified") before slowly lowering himself to the ground. The music swells and the film ends. It's a great close to a simple yet powerfully affecting film.

What Peckinpah gives us in *Ride the High Country* is his first fully developed meditation on progress. By making the film's moral heroes anachronistic old men and contrasting their attitudes with "progressive" beliefs, Peckinpah shows us that mechanical and social progress is purchased at the price of morality.[13] Although the film's script attempts through the characters of Heck and Elsa to establish a continuity of morality, its thematic intent is compromised by the undynamic actors playing these roles; their weak performances make us wonder if after Gil's death there will be anyone left to carry on Steve's tradition. Nevertheless, the overwhelming emotion of *Ride the High Country* is classically tragic; after all, Steve's death is the death of a very great man. Yet we are also uplifted by the purity of the film's dramatic conception and therefore hope that, somehow, Steve's quest will be continued. It's quite rare in any medium to be so powerfully affected by both longing for the past and hope for the future, a divine admixture that Peckinpah will repeatedly create in his subsequent films.

CHAPTER THREE

Dandy Tyrant

Perhaps because of the significant amount of postproduction editing—none of it approved by Peckinpah—to which *Major Dundee* was subjected, most commentators on the film have failed to note that even in its surviving, truncated form, *Dundee* evidences a great deal of structural and symbolic unity.[1] Much of this unity derives from two characteristics of the film's plot: the well-defined conflict between Dundee (Charlton Heston) and Tyreen (Richard Harris) and the monomaniacal nature of Dundee's quest.

However, investigating the nature of *Major Dundee* is not the straightforward task it may at first seem. Uniformly overlooked in discussions of the film is the fact that the plot is supposedly not communicated by the usual omniscient narrator but is instead rendered by the bugler Timothy Ryan (Michael Anderson, Jr.), whose diary notes (according to the film's opening) are the only factual source for the information about the events that *Major Dundee* will depict. Initially, then, we need to determine how reliable a chronicler Ryan is, since his reliability will determine how much validity we assign to the events that he relates.

Excluding the male Rostes children (who have no part in telling the film's story), Ryan is the sole survivor of the Indian raid led by Sierra Charriba, the end of which is depicted at the film's opening. We would expect that as a result of such a traumatic experience, Ryan has no small fear of, and grudge against, Indians. Indeed, Ryan's reference to Sam Potts's Indian scout Riago ("I still don't trust him") is a clear indication of Ryan's racism, which is not limited to Indians, as witnessed by Ryan's use of the word "Confederate" in the malediction "Damn it to bloody Confederate Hell!"

We also must note that, somewhat improbably given Ryan's naivete and Charriba's usual cautiousness, Ryan is revealed at *Dundee*'s end as Charriba's executioner. This visitation of justice on the Indian leader by the film's major "wronged party" seems to settle the score against Charriba rather too neatly, suggesting that Ryan the storyteller has altered the facts and cast himself in the role of successful avenger simply because it pleased him to do so.

There are other indications in the film of Ryan's unreliability, such as his characterization of the fight between Sam Potts (James Coburn) and his scout as a "friendly conflict," although the fight could easily be interpreted in precisely the opposite fashion. Likewise, his assertion on Christmas Eve that "there is a deep and reverent sense of peace and tranquility in the camp tonight" is contradicted not only by the aforementioned fight but also by the obvious uneasiness among the men. Later, we are again reminded of Ryan's callowness in his comment about Teresa Santiago (Senta Berger) that she is "somewhat old."

Ryan's attitude is extremely important because it draws attention to *Major Dundee*'s racial theme, something we would expect to find in any film set during the Civil War. We can see many of Ryan's attitudes in a more developed form in Dundee. Thus, Ryan's fixation on Charriba invites comparison with Dundee's similar obsession. It is clear that Dundee's pursuit of the Apache is meant less to effect the rescue of the Rostes children than it is to satisfy the major's racism, which is highlighted in an exchange between the major and Sam Potts. The major asks Potts about his Indian scout, saying, "That's Riago rode in with you, isn't it?" Potts replies, "They all look alike to you, Amos?" Here Potts both bests Dundee verbally and accurately identifies the major's prejudice. (Later, after Dundee refers to Riago as a "camp dog," Potts totally loses patience with Dundee and insults the major by putting their friendship on a purely mercantile basis. Dundee: "Sam, you take this camp dog and go find me Charriba." Potts: "That's what you pay us for, Amos.")

A subsequent scene demonstrates that prejudice encompasses virtually everyone in the command. When Jimmy Lee Benteen (John Davis Chandler) calls out "Boy!" the first reaction shot Peckinpah gives us is of Ryan, as though the word were being applied to him and his immaturity. A subsequent shot reveals that the intentionally demeaning term is directed at a black soldier, Aesop (Brock Peters). When Mario Adorf's Gomez (who at one point calls members of the troop "gringos") tries to put down the altercation that Benteen's epithet threatens, he wrongheadedly does so by using an epithet of his own, telling the Confederates, "You Southern trash, sit down." The Confederate sergeant Chillum (Ben Johnson) responds by insultingly referring to the Union soldiers as "blue bellies." Given the moment's potential for violence, it is laudable how Tyreen defuses the entire situation by directly praising Aesop (whom he refers to as "Mr. Aesop") and the other black soldiers under Aesop's command, first speaking on his own behalf and then speaking for, and thereby apologizing on behalf of, all of the Confederates: "I . . . we would like to compliment you and your men on the way you handled the river crossing this afternoon."

Indeed, factionalism (which will take another form in the animosity between the French and American soldiers) enters quite early in the film, even before we realize Dundee's prejudice. In the fort's courtyard, Dundee asks for volunteers. After Tyreen defies Dundee, the Southern soldiers start whistling "Dixie"; they also rattle their chains as applause for Tyreen's speech. At the same time, their prime rivals in the film, the black soldiers, menacingly advance on them. This implied racial antagonism is only somewhat tempered later by Tyreen's compliment to Aesop and the good-natured exchange between Aesop and O. W. Hadley (Warren Oates). Aesop tells Hadley that the blacks will easily best their counterparts in the French battalion since the latter are "soft." When Hadley asks Aesop what he means, Aesop replies, "They've never been south," a statement that prompts Hadley (who, unlike Tyreen, calls Aesop simply by his last name) to smile in an extremely friendly way.

Much like Ethan Edwards of *The Searchers* and Owen Thursday of *Fort Apache*, Dundee uses an Indian assault against a group of which he is not a member as the pretext for a campaign of violence that is prompted far more by his obsessive personality than it is by the need to avenge any particular act. Edwards, Thursday, and Dundee carry out inherently racist vendettas. Although Dundee is accused by both Tyreen and his temporary successor to command of the fort of pursuing nothing more than a promotion (in a manner similar to his unspecified, exaggerated actions at Gettysburg), it is quite clear that the type of aggrandizement that Dundee seeks is not higher military rank. Instead, Dundee is searching to satisfy the anxieties resulting from his own bigotry, which derives in turn from his insecurity, specifically, his poor understanding of precisely who he is. This lack of self-knowledge highlights further similarities between Dundee and Ryan. It is apparent that Ryan develops in the film, advancing to a measured maturity. (Unfortunately, Peckinpah chooses to represent this maturity in awkward, clichéd terms, as in the embarrassing sequence after Ryan's sexual initiation during which he shaves for the first time.)[2] However, Dundee remains a man who "hath ever but slenderly known himself." It is to the credit of Ryan, who must see many aspects of himself in the major, that such an unflattering characterization of Dundee is allowed to emerge through the bugler's reportage.

Fortunately, as is evident from the sophistication of *Dundee*'s characterizations and symbols, the film soon violates the dictates of the limited point of view that a strict derivation from the diary of a young recruit would mandate. In fact, in representing to us a number of situations whose details Ryan could never have perceived (e.g., Dundee and Teresa's assignation by the water or the specifics of the events in Durango), it is clear that significant portions of the film are rendered by an omniscient observer, not by a single narrator.

Even when it occasionally returns to the limitations of Ryan's point of view, *Major Dundee* nonetheless reveals important facts about the major and his campaign. Although Ryan writes after Hadley's execution that Dundee "bears the burden of command and I do not feel fit to judge him," the manner in which Dundee is repeatedly represented in a negative fashion (as in the execution sequence or at the points at which he gives vent to his raging racism) virtually compels a viewer's judgment against him. Ryan may at another time assert that "the major's present war is not with the South but with the Apache," yet the corporal unwittingly betrays a contradiction in one of his later diary entries, which asks, "How can we catch the wind or destroy an enemy we never see?" The impalpability of the noun *wind* in the sentence's first half carries over into its second part, suggesting that the unseen enemy is not the Indians so much as it is some opponent whose elusive and symbolic status inheres potentially in everyone. In fact, despite the external conflicts and rivalries that the film depicts, one of its predominant concerns is with psychological rather than material action, with wars between various states of the self rather than between North and South, Indians and whites.

The film's central conflict is the rivalry between Dundee and Tyreen, whose antagonism derives not only from their having fought on opposite sides in the Civil War but also from Dundee's having served on the court-martial jury that convicted Tyreen of murder in what was apparently a duel of honor, a conflict that would fall within the purview of law only in a Northern state.

Tyreen isn't the only outlaw whose aid Dundee solicits. Dundee is compelled to enlist the help of all sorts of outsiders, not only town rowdies, horse thieves, drunkards, and black soldiers but prisoners as well. In sum, the troops are an alienated and disaffected bunch, appropriate for the pursuit of a group of comparably alienated renegade Indians. Dundee's band of men wage war against a nationalist group, the Indians, who will eventually replace Southerners as the most aggrieved and persecuted sector of the population and against whom racist, murderous campaigns will somehow be justified.

Yet such justifications are clearly without basis. As the old Apache who enters Dundee's camp one night observes, all of the land is the Indians'; and certainly in terms of primacy of territorial rights, he is quite correct. The film's major example of racism derives from the unnatural fear and loathing of the Indians by the whites, who have usurped the Indians' land and are now engaged in using the Indians' perfectly understandable reprisals against these offenses to justify killing them off. The fact that this racism against a common enemy unites the disparate members of Dundee's troop indicates on an individual level what presumably positive cohesion may derive from war; on a national level, this cohesion suggests that as a country, we are never so firmly united as when we join together in unreasoning hatred of another nation. In many ways, then, *Major Dundee* is not only a commentary on its obsessed central character but also a gloss on our deficiencies as a country.

The relationship between Dundee and Tyreen is multifaceted. In one sense, Dundee and Tyreen assume the roles of God and Satan, with Dundee the rule-obsessed lawgiver (who nevertheless isn't above using stolen horses and guns and journeying into Mexico, where he has no jurisdiction) upbraided by his rebellious former compatriot, who states, in appropriately Miltonic terms, "I damn your flag and I damn you and I would rather hang than serve"—a wonderful expression of the stance of *Non serviam*. Nonetheless, despite being cast in the role of the traditionalist here, Dundee is as much of an alienated outsider as Tyreen. Dundee's nebulously described rebellion at Gettysburg confirms this view, as does the major's comment that he has offended so many people in his career that "my executioners will have to stand in line." Moreover, despite Dundee's emphasis on rules, it is clear that his campaign against Charriba is illegitimate—he is pursuing the Indian into Mexico, where he has no jurisdiction—and involves a repudiation of the law in the major's use of stolen guns and horses. Dundee thus seeks advancement in the service of a country whose laws he breaks, a clear indication of his egotism.

Yet as one of Dundee's later statements reveals, both his and Tyreen's intransigent natures have less to do with rebellion in political or nationalistic terms than with the alienation of an inherently individualistic man from his contemporaries. As Dundee accurately tells Tyreen, "You were a rebel before you ever saw the South." Given Dundee's Southern background and his stormy career as a Northern officer (a dual status mirrored in Tyreen's present enlistment in Dundee's cause, which transforms him into a troubled Southerner serving the North), we may infer corresponding conflicts (although in inchoate form given the major's lack of self-knowledge) in Dundee as well. In fact, considering the significant amount of screen time that the film devotes to the highly personal, idiosyncratic actions of Dundee and Tyreen, it would appear that the overwhelming determinant of their rebellion is their constant struggle, both within themselves and between each other, for either the discovery (in Dundee's case) or maintenance (in Tyreen's case) of each man's identity.

Early in the film, we realize that despite his status as an outsider and a rebel, Tyreen knows precisely who he is. This is evident from his sense of grace, which contrasts so harshly with Dundee's stiff, awkward bearing. Thus, on first meeting Teresa (Senta Berger), Dundee is cold and clinical, asking questions that have to do with official matters only: "Are you speaking for these people?" "You're not Mexican, are you?" Alternatively, Tyreen immediately speaks to the human level, complimenting Teresa on her attractiveness. "With beauty such as yours, this village is rich beyond comparison," he says.[3] Even when Dundee calls to Tyreen in an attempt to draw Tyreen away from Teresa, and throws Tyreen's sword to him as though to remind the lieutenant of his military, nonamorous obligations, Dundee can do little to stifle Tyreen's essentially compassionate and humanistic nature. Tyreen catches the sword, makes a lovely bow, and retires in style.

Throughout virtually the entire film, Dundee seems inhuman; by contrast, Tyreen is graceful and relaxed. Tyreen is impressively

Plate 8. Dundee and Tyreen during the village interlude in *Major Dundee*.
Note the lieutenant's stylish mustache, tie, and ruffled shirt.

courteous to Teresa at the village feast; and whereas Dundee talks
only about Teresa's charm, Tyreen does something about being
attracted to her, jumping up to greet her and asking her to waltz
with him before the major can even get to his feet. Teresa later tells
Dundee, "I liked the way he [Tyreen] asked me to dance, as though
we were in a ballroom in Vienna"; Dundee replies, "The lieutenant
has style." (Even before this point, Dundee reveals that he is aware
of Tyreen's flamboyant nature by drawing attention to Tyreen's
most obvious symbol of fancy: in Dundee's words, the lieutenant's
"plumed hat.") Teresa goes on to observe, "He must be a fanciful
man." Dundee then aborts the entire train of thought by focusing the
discussion on moral rather than personal attributes: "He [Tyreen] is
corrupt, but I will save him," Dundee says, implicitly equating gracious appearance and behavior with moral laxity, as though fancifulness, style, and corruption were inherently linked.

However, Dundee later unconsciously realizes how poorly he
compares with Tyreen. When the major receives no emotional response from Teresa after kissing her, he resolves (probably for purely
self-aggrandizing and therefore insincere reasons) to emulate his
alter ego. "Next time I'll be more fanciful," he states, an obvious
impossibility, since fancy is a characteristic that cannot be con-

sciously acquired. Soon after this exchange, the split in personality traits between Dundee and Tyreen is reaffirmed. In taking leave of Teresa, Dundee stiffly salutes good-bye, whereas Tyreen first nods, then smiles, and then casually salutes. Appropriately, Dundee receives only a straight-faced look from Teresa, whereas Tyreen merits a smile.

Dundee does eventually acquire a modicum of style (and with it an attendant degree of corruption, his drunkenness, thereby seeming to prove the major's point about corruption in his comment on Tyreen), but only after figuratively dying, entering Hell, and being reborn, actions prepared for by a series of symbolic events.

Major Dundee repeatedly shows us characters moving toward bodies of water, which operate in the film as sources of both life (replenishment) and, more commonly, death (destruction). Thus the command, which heals and takes rest by bodies of water, also suffers its first grave defeat, at the hands of the Indians, by the water. While his brother and his compatriots pleasurably frolic in the water, Hadley (much like the character Henry Hammond in *Ride the High Country*, who was also played by Warren Oates) does not bathe, claiming that he's already had his bath. This refusal looks ominous in light of the film's symbolic terms and is, in fact, followed by Hadley's desertion and execution.[4]

After Hadley's execution, Dundee and Teresa meet by a waterfall—in Teresa's words, in order "to feel alive, for both of us to feel alive" after experiencing so much death. Alternatively, there is the repudiation of the possibility for renewal in Tyreen's shredding of his hat's feather by the water, where he goes in order to come to terms with Hadley's death. Tyreen's action, however, seems well conceived, whereas Dundee's is characteristically strained and ineffective. Indeed, despite the scene's sexual content, Dundee and Teresa's water-linked assignation, which the director represents in clichéd, almost parodic terms (e.g., the rising and falling passions represented by the camera's panning up and then down; the conjugal swim awkwardly standing in for postcoital relaxation), is filled with awkward moments. Yet this awkwardness is nonetheless quite appropriate, since at this point in the film Dundee, stripped of his uniform's camouflage, is patently unable to act the part of a lover precisely because he is not sufficiently humanized. (In fact, he will never be so, even during his brief low point in Durango.) Despite Teresa's intentions, the assignation she engineers connotes death. While still in the embrace of postcoital warmth, Dundee is shot

Plate 9. The waterside tryst between Dundee and Teresa.

with an arrow in the right leg (the same leg in which Gomez had shot Hadley and a rather shocking duplication of one of the returned Rostes children's shooting an arrow into a gourd in an earlier scene).

For Dundee, the initially baptismal swim signals an eventual, albeit qualified, rebirth, but only after many deadly setbacks. We have already seen Dundee bested by three men in his command. Tyreen's ascendancy over him has previously been noted. At the village feast, the supposedly callow Ryan inappropriately but nonetheless correctly lectures Dundee on the disadvantages of solitude: "Sitting alone is bad for the soul," he says. Likewise, the bumpkinish Graham (Jim Hutton), displaying one of the few positive effects ascribed in the film to liquor and drunkenness, successfully cuts in on the waltzing Dundee and Teresa. (Dundee had earlier cut in on Tyreen and Teresa, but by contrast with the situation involving Graham, Tyreen had graciously allowed the cutting in.) Graham then bests the major a second time by outperforming him in a rendition of a lively Mexican dance that makes the waltz seem lifeless and overly formal.

Dundee's wounding follows these humiliating scenes and should be seen as merely a further, more pronounced, humiliation, mandating his removal to Durango. (Dundee's eventual fall is presaged before the arrow wounding when, during the midstream attack by the Apaches, he is shot from his horse.) The major's wrongheaded tryst ends with Dundee being excoriated by Tyreen: "You were trapped by the river, cornered like a shavetail. You caused the boy's death and you split your own command. And how do you explain being outside your own picket lines? What are you doing, major, easing your conscience in the arms of a woman?"

Dundee's banishment to Durango signals the beginning of his death, descent, and rebirth, after which the major, in an appropriately equivocal fashion, starts to change subtly. In a somewhat fanciful but largely unconscious way, the normally clean-cut Dundee (who strikingly contrasts with the mustachioed Tyreen) begins to sport a beard and takes to excessive drinking.

The emphasis on liquor at this point causes us to focus on its symbolic uses in the film. Whereas water in the film signals either life/rebirth or death/immersion, whiskey connotes self-indulgent weakness, as in Tyreen's use of liquor to dull the pain of a shoulder wound; Dundee's request for "medicinal brandy," which he obviously intends to use to assuage his shame over the Indians' defeating his troop; the drunkenness in Teresa Santiago's village, which is used to effect the nonetheless awkward revelry; and Dundee's use of whiskey in Durango to obliterate his self-awareness.

The reply to Dundee's request for brandy after the initial Indian ambush hints at what we may later expect of the major with regard to liquor. Ryan says, "There is no more brandy . . . except at the bottom of the river." Truly, it is only when Dundee has hit absolute moral bottom and is figuratively drowned in Durango (through a submersion of identity) that he finds what appears to be an endless supply of liquor, from which he turns away only after repudiating his immersion in self-pity.

Interestingly, *Major Dundee* also uses water imagery in tandem with action to presage Dundee's hellish interlude in Durango. While the troops frolic by the water (with Ryan commenting that "We were healing, becoming a command again"), Dundee is shown walking away from the revelry and into the infernal desert, a milieu where shortly after his being wounded, he will be consigned in the water-dry (but liquor-wet) streets, cantinas, and rooms of Durango. Indeed, the Durango doctor's humorous comment that the drunken Dundee's blood "is mostly alcohol" has truth in light of Dundee's subsequent self-pitying behavior, during which the major's usually

Plates 10–11. Martinet turned souse: Dundee before (*top*) and after (*bottom*) losing to the Indians.

hot-blooded spirit is on the wane, replaced by the emotions and lowly actions of a man whose only internal spirit comes from the spirits that he imbibes.

Exiled in the Mexican city, Dundee's status sinks. He begins as an incapacitated man in a doctor's office, bragging that he will somehow miraculously recover. (The doctor tells Dundee that he will be able to walk in seven days and ride in twelve, but the major asserts that he will "walk in two and ride in one more.") He sinks from there to being a dissipated roué lounging in the bedroom of a Mexican woman and ends a drunkard suffering the discomforts of a bed in the gutter. Given his dissolution, and his pursuit by a French spy whose actions presage nothing but trouble for him, Dundee is clearly in Hell. Ironically, it is Tyreen, the man who had earlier been cast in the role of satanic rebel, who angelically delivers the major from this inferno.

Although the literal meaning of Tyreen's statement that "I've come to rescue you . . . so I can kill you myself" is apparent, a figurative reading of the assertion is also possible—namely, that the murder involves the death of the major's former personality, a reading that ties in with Dundee's assertion that his drinking stems from doubts about his identity. (As Dundee says to Tyreen, "Why don't you drink . . . or don't you ever have any doubts about who you are?") Ironically, the threat to Dundee's self-confident self began earlier: before Hadley's execution, when Tyreen had told Dundee, "If you kill that boy it's not the end, it's the beginning." In light of subsequent action, the statement implies that what transpires from Hadley's execution onward is Dundee's fall and subsequent rise to his former status, a death-to-life progression concurrent with Tyreen's earlier realization that the execution of Hadley (who secedes from the command just as the South had seceded from the Union) signals the death of the Southern spirit in the film. Actually, Tyreen twice mentions killing Dundee: once before Hadley's death, and later when he rescues him in Durango.

Unfortunately, despite Tyreen's laudable efforts, it is evident from Dundee's subsequent actions that the major's former intractable self does not die in Durango; in fact, it survives intact. Only Dundee's outward show of fancy, in the form of the beard that he decides to retain, reminds us of his period of suffering.

Dundee is a poseur, more a figure of a man than a man. It would appear that it was precisely to highlight Dundee's habit of posturing that Peckinpah tailored the characterization of Dundee to suit Charl-

ton Heston's bigger-than-life cinematic presence. Moreover, although Peckinpah reportedly found it impossible toward the production's beginning to have Richard Harris subdue his British accent,[5]
it's quite obvious how Harris's fanciful traits, especially his florid
gestures and speech patterns, are well-suited to Tyreen's character.

The yoking of Heston and Harris in the film works marvelously,
with each actor setting off the other. To ensure that the viewer of
Major Dundee doesn't miss the significance of the differences between Dundee and Tyreen, Peckinpah gives each man a symbol
of adornment. Dundee's beard is an essentially empty symbol, as
appropriately meaningless as his other grandstanding gestures
throughout the film. However, Tyreen's adornment, the feather in
his cap, has great symbolic resonance, as is consonant with the
depth of his character.

Early in the film, Tyreen walks under a tree branch that grazes
the top of his hat. He takes off his hat and inspects it to make sure
that the feather, which is obviously important to him, is undamaged.
At this point, the feather functions as little more than a symbol of
the character's somewhat dandyish aspect. However, after he is
compelled to shoot Hadley, Tyreen retires to the water's edge and
plucks out and shreds the feather. (Characteristically, the shredding
of the feather is a private, unobserved gesture with great meaning;
by contrast, Dundee's drunkenness is a public display that is all
show and no substance.) The literal feather in Tyreen's cap is a
figurative expression of Tyreen's love for the South, which has been
ritually sacrificed through the shooting of his fellow countryman.
Hadley's death signals the killing off of Tyreen's birdlike, carefree
air, which he is not to regain for the remainder of the film. From
this point on, Tyreen's actions begin to seem more and more premeditated. As a result of Hadley's death and Tyreen's vow to kill Dundee,
the formerly lighthearted Tyreen begins to be weighed down by a
sullenness that previously had been only Dundee's.[6] The desire for
vengeance oppresses Tyreen from this point onward. Ironically, the
only way that Tyreen can deliver himself from his hatred for Dundee,
and the compromised position in which the major has placed him,
is to adopt the Union position, as a pretext and prelude to self-
destruction. After the gloriously improbable act of saving the flag
in which he does not believe, a flag that in the film comes to represent
narrow-mindedness and bigotry, Tyreen is left with no other alternative but to commit suicide on the swords of the French lancers.

With a fascinating consistency, *Major Dundee* casts Dundee and Tyreen in roles that are antithetical to their natures. Thus, Dundee, who fancies himself a military man, is seen at the film's beginning as a mere jailer. (At one point, he protests, "I am a professional soldier, not a prison keeper.") He regards himself as a lover but is at first spurned by Teresa Santiago; and though he apparently thinks of himself as something of a fighter, Dundee is nonetheless initially bested, and rather easily at that, by Charriba and his men. Tyreen sees himself as an independent spirit, yet he enters into an agreement with Dundee whose terms dictate servility. His emotional and political allegiance is with the South, yet he must agonizingly repudiate this allegiance in his execution of Hadley.

In consonance with these rather perverse variations on the characters' desires are the names that each man bears. The characters' names are inappropriate to the bearer's status; in fact, each man's name is more applicable to his counterpart. "Dundee" suggests the dandyish quality to which the major unsuccessfully aspires; "Tyreen" connotes the tyrannical behavior that only Dundee exhibits.

Although all of Peckinpah's films involve contentious relationships among characters, nowhere does this opposition assume such blatantly cinematic form as it does in *Major Dundee*. Toward the film's beginning, when Tyreen is in chains, Peckinpah photographs the character so that the shadows from the prison bars bracket him, effectively enclosing him in a cell whose bonds are as intangible and restrictive as the constraints placed on his action not only by his word (which Dundee highly prizes) but also by some of his men's racism and his own rebelliousness. When Tyreen, still in chains, stretches out both of his arms and assumes the posture of the Crucifixion, we see a hint of the sacrificial status that the character will, unfortunately, be compelled to assume.

Subsequent scenes make concrete through symbolic positioning and framing the antagonism between Dundee and Tyreen. This overt framing occurs in the film's two most emotionally intense and psychologically exaggerated episodes. The first involves the execution of Hadley, during which Dundee is in the ascendant while Tyreen is at an emotional nadir, constrained to kill his countryman because he has given Dundee his word to serve. (Hadley asks, "You gonna let them shoot me, Captain?" and Tyreen forlornly replies, "I'm obliged to, son; you should have remembered you belong to the major and not to me.") The second sequence, which follows shortly thereafter, depicts Dundee's ultimate low point: his wounding by an Indian and his subsequent relegation to Durango.

During Hadley's execution, Dundee is at screen left and stands on level ground, so that his figure in the frame seems well-grounded and secure. By contrast, Tyreen is at screen right and stands on a slant, with his shoulders tilting down to screen left. The character's slant compels us to perceive Tyreen as somewhat off-balance, understandable given the extremely upsetting situation. Additionally, the tilt of the character's shoulders throws the majority of Tyreen's weight in Dundee's direction, suggesting that Tyreen may carry out the shooting, but the weight of responsibility for Hadley's death is on Dundee.

Later, after Dundee is shot with an Indian's arrow and Tyreen enters the scene, we find that the two characters have changed screen positions and postures, reflecting the reversal of their roles. Tyreen is now standing on level ground while he passes harsh judgment on Dundee (thus Tyreen's earlier excoriation and his assertion, "You're getting leave, major," which not only has Tyreen giving Dundee an order but further has the effect of relieving Dundee of his command and banishing him).[7] Dundee has to look up at Tyreen; then, after trying to attack Tyreen, Dundee trips and falls and again must look up at him, but this time from a lower vantage point. This sequence is an obvious replay of the scene in which Hadley, pushed off his horse by Gomez and injured in his right leg (as Dundee will later be), has to look up at Dundee and then drag himself along the ground. Additionally, before tripping and falling, Dundee holds himself so that he tilts to screen right. Unlike Tyreen earlier, Dundee slants away from his counterpart in an obvious attempt to avoid confronting Tyreen and thereby be compelled to suffer judgment at his hands. Very soon now, with Dundee in Durango and Tyreen coming to rescue him, jailer and jailed will have switched roles, with the notable difference that whereas earlier, in the fort's prison, Tyreen was triumphant although literally in chains, Dundee in Durango is in defeat and is constrained by his own personal weaknesses.

In the Durango scenes, symbolic framing and positioning are reprised, with the upright character at screen left represented as superior to the relatively powerless individual at screen right. Tyreen and Gomez confront the drunken Dundee in Durango. At first Dundee, attempting to affect power, puts up a good front from his position at screen left. Gomez, still predominantly Dundee's man, is at the major's side while Tyreen stands motionless at the right. Dundee then opposes himself both to Gomez and his avowed rival by refusing to leave Durango with them; as a result, Tyreen and Dundee fight. The screen-left (and thereby, in terms of symbolic placement, assertive) Dundee initiates the battle by throwing a punch at Tyreen. However, Dundee misses and is knocked down to far screen right by Tyreen, who now occupies the superior, upright position at screen left while Dundee lies prostrate and powerless at screen right. After goading Dundee, Tyreen manages to have the major reassert himself.[8] Dundee mounts his horse, regaining a position of power; appropriately, he is now once more at screen left while Tyreen, also mounted but now again only a single man in the major's service, is at screen right.

There is a significant amount of divisiveness in the film, with friend turning against friend, French against Americans, Southerners against Northerners, youth against elders, Mexicans against Americans, Americans against Indians, even Indians (Riago, who helps Dundee) against Indians (Charriba). Jim Kitses asserts that the nature of Dundee's amalgamated force suggests the anomalies and divisions of early America.[9] Paul Seydor disagrees, stating that the tendency to see "Dundee's divided command as a microcosm of a nation desperately in search of a unifying identity . . . is a tenuous reading at best." Seydor believes that "the composition of the command . . . although diverse, is not diverse enough to encompass the whole country" since "the middle class and mercantile interests" are missing.[10]

Despite Seydor's assertions, the film can still stand as a paradigm for national divisiveness. The class representations do not have to seem all-inclusive for viewers to feel that they are watching a representation of the country as a whole. This approach to the film, supported by Ryan's statement that "we are a command divided against itself," suggests that we also regard the troop's predominantly racist mission as an attempt through war to produce a modicum of peace. The film's last series of resolved conflicts, which shows us the troop finally united, is nothing less than a depiction of the salutary effects of war, leading us to the melancholy conclusion that *Dundee* is a prowar film, a view in keeping with the contentious personality of its lead character, for whom war is essential. When Dundee remarks, "The war won't last forever," Teresa Santiago replies, "It will for you, major."[11]

Since *Major Dundee* is redolent with contention, the viewer should not be surprised by the film's emphasis on symbolic, horizontal oppositions, as when characters clash while facing each other (e.g., the scene in the fort in which Dundee, Tyreen, the Southerners and the blacks confront each other). Yet equally significant is the symbolism expressed through vertical oppositions. This symbolism first appears during the scene depicting Tyreen's imprisonment at Dundee's fort. Enchained and awaiting execution in the prison's lower depths, Tyreen is in a kind of Hell, an underworld where he writhes on a lake of uncertainty regarding his fate: will Dundee execute him or not? Later, we are given the shot of the unobserved Sierra Charriba, on a mountain, looking down at Dundee's ragtag troop passing by. Just as the earlier shot of the degraded Tyreen was at odds with our high estimation of him, so in the present instance, although Charriba is clearly in a literally ascendant position, the Indian's high physical location is at odds with our low moral regard for him, which derives from the merciless slaughter at the Rostes ranch.

The number of role reversals in the film (prisoners become free, drunks are sobered up, youths turn mature) virtually dictates that the initially buried and bound Tyreen ascend and be free, a state that he achieves only at the film's end through his death; by contrast, Charriba is "laid low" by Ryan, the troop's least accomplished and imposing member, and is last seen being kicked by Dundee, who propels Charriba's corpse down the side of a dusty hill, where it winds up facedown in the dirt. (This scene recalls the sequence in Durango, when the humbled Dundee was kicked by Tyreen.)

As men highly conscious of symbols, Dundee and Tyreen are powerfully sensitive to figurative placements and gestures. When Hadley is returned to the troop after deserting, Dundee insists that he be brought down from his high horseback perch, saying, "I don't want to look up at him." Dundee also seems to appreciate figurative language involving heights and depths when, commenting on the troop's loss of spirit after being bested by the Apaches, he states, "We lost a lot at the bottom of the river."

The inordinate importance that both Dundee (with his constant posing) and Tyreen (with his ultrarefined gestures) seem to attach to figurative actions makes it quite fitting that for their most symbolic acts in the film the two men should choose equivalently suggestive modes of behavior. Thus, Tyreen's solitary charge against the French is certainly an awe-inspiring move (the entire troop watches with astonishment), but it is also utterly illogical, although it does show us Tyreen, having jettisoned his fancifulness, redeeming himself in a way that Dundee would approve. Tyreen moves against the French single-handedly, just as the egocentric Dundee conceives of his pursuit of Charriba as a one-man crusade that achieves mythical significance; as Sam Potts remarks, "I guess he [Charriba] figures to leave stories about you to be told by the campfires of his people for a thousand years." Dundee similarly allows the self-aggrandizing reference to himself as "El Tigre" when he is by the water with Teresa.[12] Comparable to the illogicality of Tyreen's last act is Dundee's grandstanding bid for sympathy in the role of the unshaven, unwashed, self-pitying hulk who wallows facedown in the filth of a Durango street while he is licked by a dog.

The animal symbolism in that last image has an ironic aptness. Throughout the film, Dundee treats the Indians as little more than beasts; we should recall that he refers to the Apache scout Riago, whom he obviously thinks is no different than any other Indian, as a "camp dog." Dogs are further associated with the Indians through the dog meat that apparently served as the primary food for the Rostes children while they were in Indian captivity. It would not be taking things too far to see that Dundee, at his lowest ebb as a result of his having been "licked" by the Indian/dog Charriba, should again be licked by a dog, this time literally, so that the viewer is reminded through the imagery of Dundee's most humiliating defeat.

Sometimes the viewer has to extrapolate from the film's images to infer figurative connections among them. At one point in the Durango sequence, we find Dundee and Tyreen once more symbolically linked. The major's wounded leg causes him to limp, inviting a comparison between this debilitation and Tyreen's impairment while he was shackled in the prison. Again, though, as is characteristic throughout the film, the distinction between the two men's situations is instructive despite the similarity of personal attributes. Whereas Tyreen's chains were real, limiting him physically but leaving his indomitable spirit free, Dundee is for the majority of the film a physically free man bound by the psychological chains of his self-ignorance and racism.

Even the times of the year when the film's major events take place assume significance. The massacre of the original troop from Fort Benyon occurs on Halloween, an appropriate night for what must have seemed the frightening show (involving painted devils and spooks) that the Indians visit on the whites. Christmas Eve brings the return of the Rostes children, but as Tyreen divines,

Charriba "gave us what we wanted only because he intends to take it back again." In this case, the gift is rescinded when Charriba presents the troop with his Christmas Day present: a daytime ambush of Dundee's command that by Graham's reckoning results in "fourteen killed, thirteen wounded—four critically" and the loss of 70 percent of the batallion stores, 20 percent of the ammunition, and 60 percent of their livestock.

Down and almost out despite the brief respite at Teresa Santiago's village and the successful raid on the French batallion, Dundee will again be bested by Charriba on the day when the major is shot. Yet scarcely a week after Easter (April 16, to be exact), the resurrected Dundee and his troop rally and, having killed Charriba, are all effectively reborn when they return to the United States.

Admittedly, *Major Dundee* is something of a botch. The film contains glaring elisions, doubtless the result of heavy editing of either the script or the film's rough footage. Missing events include the escape from the fort by Tyreen and his associates and their wounding of the Fort Benyon guard, who subsequently dies.[13] Moreover, the meaning of some scenes seems to have been excised, presumably because footage was eliminated (e.g., the encounter with the Confederate patrol, from which no action follows). Some scenes are notoriously lax in continuity. For example, given the scene's dialogue and visual information, one would assume that the ambush against Charriba takes place at night (the footage looks like it was shot "day for night," and there is the unnatural, nightlike quiet in Dundee's camp and Gomez's feigning of sleep). Yet immediately afterward we have the encounter with the French, which obviously occurs during the day. This same sequence contains a horrible mistake in continuity. Dundee's troop, still in Mexico, attack the French, who advance from the American side of the Rio Grande. After the battle, Ryan states that the troop "re-enter[s] the United States"; however, the men not only never cross the river but are actually shown doubling back into what must represent Mexican territory.

Other elements work against the film as well. At the beginning, Charriba asks, "Who will you send against me now?" The answer is overdramatically provided with the title *Major Dundee* blasting onto the screen. Equally embarrassing is the repeated musical sting that signals the presence of an Indian, a device that undermines suspense. As for the lyrics to the "Major Dundee March," they are too awful to quote.

However, the majority of *Major Dundee* has sufficient symbolic and dramatic sophistication to convey the impression of, if not wholeness, at least integrity. In sum, the film is like a magnificently formed vessel that has been damaged. Figuratively cracked, *Dundee* at times fails to hold logical water, springing a few leaks here and there; nor can we do more than merely guess at how grand a film it might have been had we received it in the form that Peckinpah intended. Taken as it is, though, *Major Dundee* not only entertains and at times even impresses us strongly but further manages to consistently engage our attention with its great, ruined beauty.

CHAPTER FOUR

Like It Used to Be

The Wild Bunch is Peckinpah's masterpiece, the purest, most satisfying expression of the director's main concerns. Once again we have a central pair of characters, with one pursuing the other. Each of the two men has a past in which the other plays an extremely significant role; as a consequence, each is intrinsically involved with the other's fate, especially as this fate embraces the quest for redemption and liberation. As we might expect, it requires the death of one of this duo to make possible the survivor's complete deliverance. Indeed, if we consider *The Wild Bunch* as a whole, we must conclude that deliverance may be achieved only through death.

With the film's expansive breadth and scope providing a suitable backdrop, *The Wild Bunch* qualifies as Peckinpah's only truly epic film, the only one in which he makes comprehensive statements about essential matters—life, death, love, and sex. Primarily, though, *The Wild Bunch* is about responsibility, about the need for individuals to remain faithful to themselves and their fellows. In this respect, the film invites comparison with Polonius's speech to his son in *Hamlet*, during which Polonius makes statements that at the time seem to border on cliché before concluding, "This above all, to thine own self be true, and it must follow, as the night the day, thou canst not then be false to any man" (2.2.78–80). I do not offer this comparison lightly, for *The Wild Bunch* not only stands as Peckinpah's great tragic film but also, in its pronouncements about life, successfully negotiates between profundity and triteness. If taken out of context, some statements—for instance, Pike's assertion that "we're gonna stick together, just like it used to be. When you side with a man you stay with him, and if you can't do that you're like some animal"—border on the homiletic. Yet assertions like these are so integral to the film's action and its characters' personalities that they tend to communicate their meanings virtually subliminally. We are so distracted and enthralled by the film's events and characters that these observations pass directly into our consciousness, almost as though we hear them whispered to us in a dream. When we consider that despite all of the talk about loyalty and faithfulness, the Bunch gains our respect only when they finally act on their assertions, we see that Peckinpah very carefully constructs the film so that we withhold approbation from men's words but not from their actions, thus making *The Wild Bunch* a mixture of the ideal and the material—more specifically, the ideal manifested through the material.

In true epic fashion, *The Wild Bunch* repeatedly alternates between actions on a grand scale (e.g., the train heist) and scenes that have the most delicate intimacy (e.g., when Angel [Jaime Sanchez] plays guitar in the adobe after the Starbuck debacle),[1] between sequences of frenzied activity (the assault on the supply train; the beginning and ending slaughters, which surround the film like a fateful circle) and sequences that are doubly reduced in scale by virtue of their smaller number of participants and their inclusion of the most concentrated of details (e.g., the sequence with some Starbuck children in which the camera fixates on the ants and scorpions; the sequence with Tector and Lyle Gorch [Ben Johnson and Warren Oates] and the Mexican prostitute in which the camera moves in and lingers on the image of the small, panting baby bird). Here we can see Peckinpah's insistence on including in the film the polarized realms of perception, macro and microcosmic vision, an insistence that, like the divergence between the large scale of the film's various verbal pronouncements and the intensely personal nature of their application, ensures that *The Wild Bunch* encompasses as much of the spectrum of existence as is possible.

The precision with which *The Wild Bunch* is constructed and its emphasis on an exhaustive representation of reality are manifest in its employing more highly visible linkages than any other Peckinpah work does. People, things, and events aggregate in twos and threes, thus creating a sense of fullness and completion, with many of the groupings pointing up structural and conceptual connections. These doublings and triplings (only some of which I'll draw attention to) not only make the film seem more sumptuous but also create a special kind of awareness for us. Because *The Wild Bunch* is to a great extent about memory, the memory of past deeds and the uneasy knowledge that regrettable deeds cannot be changed, it is appropriate that an emphasis on memory be created for the audience as well. Consequently, when the film recalls its most significant events, we take note of these repetitions and realize that the mechanism through which we make these discoveries is memory. I believe that when we achieve this awareness, we tend to think about Thornton (Robert Ryan) and, especially, Pike (William Holden), whose curse is to ruminate over past events and how he would have acted differently if only he had been wiser or more thoughtful. What all of this reflection points us to is that moral realm with which *The Wild Bunch* is so powerfully concerned.

The film gives us two sets of Mexicans (Mapache's people, who are corrupt, and Angel's people, who are fighting them); two rival male figures, Pike and Thornton, leading two morally opposed collections of ragtag associates, each of which contains a comic pair (the Gorch brothers on one side and T. C. [L. Q. Jones] and Coffer [Strother Martin] on the other); two heists pulled by the Bunch (the one in Starbuck and the one against the train).

We are also presented with two elders, one American (Sykes [Edmond O'Brien]), one Mexican (Don José [Chano Urueta]). The film also presents two notable oppressors (Mapache [Emilio Fernandez] and Harrigan [Albert Dekker]), who inadvertently induce the film's two major protagonists, Pike and Thornton, to move toward redemptive actions: Pike redeems himself by carrying out Angel's wish that he and his people will, in Dutch's words, "Kick [Mapache] and the rest of that scum like him right into their graves"; Thornton redeems himself by joining Sykes and Don José's army and thus continuing the fight against oppressive men like Mapache and Harrigan. There are two visual recognition shots between Pike and Thornton, each juxtaposed with literally explosive action and each reinforcing the two men's complementarity. The first occurs during the shoot-out in Starbuck, in which Pike, surrounded by chaos, looks up and sees Thornton; the second comes after the Bunch's train job, when Thornton, about to be engulfed in the chaos created by the bridge explosion, looks across the water and sees Pike.

The film also contains two realization dialogues, each concerning Deke Thornton's pursuit of the Bunch, in which Pike and Sykes trade roles. In the first instance, Pike knows of Thornton's pursuit and Sykes is unaware.

Plates 12–13. The two groups in *The Wild Bunch*, a study in contrasting styles of dress, behavior, and, ultimately, morals: Pike's Bunch (*top*) and Thornton's group (*bottom*).

SYKES (somewhat sarcastically): They, who the hell is they?
PIKE: Railroad men, bounty hunters, Deke Thornton.
SYKES: Deke Thornton—he was one of them?

Later, it is Sykes who is knowing and Pike, as a result of unconscious denial, who seems ignorant.

DUTCH: At least we won't have to worry about Deke Thornton.
PIKE: Hell no, not after riding half a case of dynamite into the
   river.
SYKES: Well, don't expect him to stay there. He'll be along and
   you know it.

Indeed, this complementarity between Pike and Thornton extends to each man's prescience regarding the other. (In this respect, though, Thornton is obviously more thoughtful than Pike.) Thus, Thornton foresees that Pike will raid Starbuck and rob the train; Pike knows that Thornton, as the representative of the opposition, will follow the Bunch after the train heist.

Additionally, there are two significant leg wounds: Pike's (in the left leg) and Sykes's (in the right leg), the complementarity suggesting that Pike and Sykes are counterparts of the same individual, with Pike as the man still young enough to be engaged in vigorous action, and Sykes as the elder who speaks with the voice of moral reason (yet it is Sykes who assumes Pike's leadership role after Pike's death).

The Wild Bunch also features two approaches to the Texas/ Mexico border: one by the Bunch and one by Thornton's group. Each involves at least one comic character's inability to properly perceive what another character is saying.

ANGEL: Mexico lindo!
LYLE: I don't see nothing so lindo about it.
TECTOR: Just looks like more of Texas far as I'm concerned.
ANGEL: Ah, you have no eyes.

Later, Thornton's group reaches the same spot.

COFFER: From here on it's Mexico, Mr. Thornton.
THORNTON: What's the closest town of any size?
COFFER: Agua Verde.
THORNTON: What's in Agua Verde?
COFFER: Mexicans, what else?

The film's dualities are exemplified in the Bunch itself, with the men forming important pairs that evidence their various kinds of bonding until their decisive coming together at the film's end. Pike and Dutch (Ernest Borgnine) are the two prominent leaders. Pike is usually characterized by emotional reticence; Dutch speaks up for considerations involving compassion. We recognize the high regard that each man has for the other in many ways. For instance, Dutch, obviously seconding Pike's sentiments, makes the point about what folly it would be (considering that they're being followed) for the Bunch to stay behind and bury Abe, after which Dutch and Pike look at each other in silent appreciation of Dutch's appropriate use of irony. Likewise, Dutch repeats Pike's statement "I wouldn't have it any other way."

The Bunch's second obvious pair are the Gorch brothers, who seem to go everywhere together (e.g., to Hondo, into Agua Verde to collect their share of the money from Mapache) and who are linked not only in action but even in speech ("Me and Tector figured . . ."). The two Bunch members most closely associated with the Mexican gentry, Angel (with his important link to the mountain Indians) and Sykes (e.g., Sykes's playing with the Mexican child at the film's beginning and his alliance with Don José and the mountain Indians at the end), are the last pair.

However, the pairings are not always made up of the same two characters. Thus, before Pike and Dutch were linked, Pike and Thornton were a close duo. Angel and Dutch also link up in that Dutch is the only non-Mexican Bunch member who speaks Spanish in the film (although they all seem to understand the language). Dutch and Angel are linked in that it was Dutch who suggested giving Angel the rifles, Dutch whom Angel saved during the train heist, Dutch who rode into Agua Verde with Angel to claim their share of the gold, and Dutch who seems to be the most despondent about Angel's abandonment. Dutch and Sykes match up in their concern for Angel. As Dutch states at one point, "Sykes says we oughta go after him," a statement whose open expression of a need for redressing a wrong to one's "family" echoes Angel's insistence on knowing who killed his father. Moreover, in their recognition of the political elements of the struggle in Mexico between the oppressive President Huerta and the revolutionary Pancho Villa[2]— Dutch through his later statement about the difference between the Bunch and Mapache, Sykes through his eventual affiliation with the mountain Indians—Dutch and Sykes evidence a political awareness shared by only one other Bunch member, Angel. This awareness paves the way for the uniting of Thornton (whose recognition of

Harrigan's injustices radically politicizes him), Sykes, and the mountain Indians at the film's end. Finally, there is the link established between Pike and Sykes, the two senior Bunch members, each (ultimately) a leader of his own bunch, with Sykes the successor to the original Bunch's tradition.

Plate 14. One of *The Wild Bunch*'s frozen moments, after Angel has shot Teresa.

The film contains three successive uses of the technique of a moment of extreme violence followed by an anxious pause or frozen moment, which is then followed by a discharge of tension. In one scene, Angel shoots Teresa, and after a pause there is laughter when Dutch reveals Angel's supposed motive.[3] After one of Herrera's men shoots at the Bunch's machine gun, Lyle and Tector ready the gun for retaliation; Herrera shouts "Quien fue?" (Who was it?), and after a pause the offending soldier is shot. Pike shoots Mapache and then, after a pause, shoots Mohr (at which point we know that a massive discharge of tensions, through some kind of blowout, is in the offing).

Many of *The Wild Bunch*'s linked statements and actions reflect oppositions between cohesion and dissent, idealism and materialism, altruism and selfishness. The total significance of this opposition, which underlies many of the film's antagonisms, emerges only toward the film's latter half. Nevertheless, from the earliest moments these examples dramatize the clash of elemental attitudes that will eventually assume the form of full-fledged debates in two sequences to be examined in detail later.

The materialistic realm, which involves an emphasis on money and selfishness (with an attendant destruction of group unity), is characterized most aptly after the Starbuck massacre when an argument about apportioning the "silver" occurs. The Gorches don't want Sykes or Angel to have shares equal to everyone else's, which leads to guns being drawn on all sides. The dissension is most aptly characterized by Pike when he says, "Go on, go for it, fall apart." Opposed to this strain is the idealistic realm, in which, despite petty antagonisms, the men stay together because of their feelings of loyalty to one another, a state also successfully characterized by Pike after Tector threatens to "get rid of" Sykes. Pike then delivers the speech mentioned above: "When you side with a man you stay with him, and if you can't do that you're like some animal, you're finished, we're finished, all of us." The use of the plural pronoun signals precisely the kind of unity about which Pike is talking.

The two elements are vital to *The Wild Bunch* because, if nothing else, the film is about the difficulty of making choices. It's significant that in the majority of the cases in which we find moral linkages, the example signifying dissent, materialism, or selfishness occurs before the one signifying cohesion, idealism, or altruism. The implication is unavoidable: what we witness in *The Wild Bunch* is the triumph of the ideal over the material realm.

Thus, we get two massacres: the one in Starbuck committed for the selfish reason of stealing silver, and the one in Agua Verde committed for the altruistic reason of avenging Angel, who for the Bunch represents the golden ideal of fidelity.[4] The film also presents two childlike duos within each bunch: the always selfish T. C. and Coffer, and the Gorches, whose apotheosis after T. C. and Coffer's deaths affirms the Gorch brothers' discovery of true fidelity and idealism. There are two militarily precise marches by the Bunch, each accompanied by snare drums: one enacted for selfish reasons (in Starbuck), and one (in Agua Verde) in the service of an ideal, when the Bunch marches into town to reclaim Angel. Dutch laughs twice in joyous assent: in Starbuck when he accedes to Pike's suggestion that the Bunch callously use the temperance union marchers as a diversionary human shield, and outside the Agua Verde adobe,

Plate 15. The regimented march toward the railroad company office; the temperance union parade is not far behind.

when he looks up and realizes that the Bunch will expose themselves to danger to help Angel. There are two screams by Lyle: once while self-indulgently shooting the wine vats in Agua Verde, and, again in Agua Verde, while at the helm of the machine gun, which he is using to avenge Angel's murder. There are two different attitudes toward leaving behind wounded Bunch members: that displayed toward Thornton (in a flashback), Abe, and Sykes, about all of whom Pike attempts to reject any sentimentality, and the attitude toward Angel, who so strongly plays on the Bunch's emotions that they simply cannot abandon him. Twice Thornton half-dozes with his back to a wall, each instance occurring at one of the film's moral poles: at the film's opening (the beginning of Thornton's travails), before the Bunch rides into Starbuck, and at the film's end, when Thornton leans against Agua Verde's wall, before Sykes and Don José's men ride up and take Thornton with them (which represents the beginning of Thornton's redemption). There are two different moral implications of the phrase "Let's go" as used by Pike: either as a call to escape in order to save oneself or one's booty (before and after Starbuck, and after the train heist), or, as in Agua Verde toward the film's end, as a call to save someone else (Angel) at the expense of one's own well-being. There are two significant uses of the term "Why not?": first in a negative mode, in an expression of resigned disgust, when Pike decides to let the Bunch avail themselves of the distractions in Agua Verde and thereby, at least for a while, forget about rescuing Angel; and later in a positive sense, when Lyle, speaking for himself and Tector, readily accedes to Pike's invitation—"Let's go"—to go back for Angel. The film also offers a morally balanced entrance into and exit from Angel's village: the entrance in a scoffing mood, when the Gorches taunt Angel (who rather reluctantly brings the Bunch to his village, since he is ashamed of his outlaw status) about wanting to meet his sister, mother, and grandmother);[5] the exit in an extremely emotional and touchingly reverent mood. The film features two Mexican characters who know a deadly secret and use it differently: Teresa's mother, who out of selfish pique betrays Angel, and Angel, who knows of the Bunch's complicity in the diversion of guns and remains silent. There are two uses of the machine gun, one by the oppressors (Mapache and his men), one by the unwitting liberators (the Bunch). The Bunch takes two very important rides: at the film's beginning, as they head into a place of confinement (Starbuck) where they intend to satisfy their selfish desire to steal gold, and at the film's end as, angel-like, their images—hovering over the riders in the new Bunch, which is led by Sykes and Thornton—pass from Agua Verde's confines along with Sykes, Thornton, Don José, and the mountain Indians, all of whom are embarking on their idealistic, revolutionary campaign. At two points the Bunch is serenaded to the tune of "La Golondrina": when leaving Angel's village and heading toward Agua Verde, where the deal with the oppressor Mapache and the abandonment of Angel take place, and at the film's end, when the music acts as the accompaniment to the Bunch's grand apotheosis.

Two ritualistic activities, drinking and laughter, demonstrate how *The Wild Bunch* will repeatedly alternate between actions involving either bonding or alienation, fidelity or abandonment, notions that correspond to the moral categories of the ideal versus the material, the altruistic versus the self-centered. Liquor serves as a communal drug that is employed for its chastening and bonding effects—for example, after the antagonisms about dividing the Starbuck "gold" have passed, during the fiesta in Don José's village, in the steam-bath and wine-vat sequences, and after the train heist. Drinking also occurs when a character tries, without success, to reduce his sorrow, alienation, or anxiety and thereby regain a sense of unity and purpose. However, the opposite effect is often achieved, as when Pike self-indulgently talks about how he "ain't getting around any better" while he is drinking in the adobe after the Starbuck debacle. (This statement is a virtual repetition of the remark Sykes had made after the Bunch discovered the washers: "You boys ain't getting any younger.") Likewise, Angel, while drinking, ruminates over an obsessive concern, in this case the question of who killed his father; Angel's ruminations are halted by Pike's threatening to expel him from the Bunch, but this threat does not prevent Angel from crying out later in the scene, "Where is Mapache?"

Liquor's greatest failure as a diversion occurs after Angel has for the second time been "captured" by Mapache. When we see Pike in the room with the Mexican woman and her child, the disgusted look on his face after he drinks the last of the tequila indicates that drinking cannot alleviate his guilt over Angel's abandonment; if anything, it exaggerates that guilt. At this point, only a new form of intoxication, the giddy drunkenness that will be released during the mass slaughter in Agua Verde, can create for the Bunch the kind of Dionysian unity that they all desire.[6]

As might be expected, the temporary unity deriving from consumption is also present among Thornton's gang as well, but in a reduced form, which is consistent with the group's status as a poor reflection of the Bunch. In one scene, Peckinpah cuts from the Bunch drinking to a shot of Thornton's men indulging in a comparable, albeit less intense, communal activity: eating. These and other parallel scenes constitute additional linkages in the film.

The film's drinking sequences have a tremendous power. Mapache's drinking scenes, which twice show us the "general" in a state of advanced alcoholic stupor, are characterized by a degree of overindulgence that establishes a striking contrast with the famine in Angel's village, which has been sacked by the Federales.[7] As Lyle comments when the Bunch is approaching the village, "Hey Angel, why in the hell don't you tell your folks to feed them dogs?" Apparently, the people in Angel's village don't even have enough food for themselves.[8]

Nevertheless, liquor can also increase one's pleasure, an effect most notable during the fiesta in Angel's village. Sometimes, though, the desired effect is not achieved, a situation evident when Mohr asks the Bunch to drink with him and Mapache, a gesture intended to establish an amiability among the Bunch and Mapache's men that never materializes.

Laughter also has two effects.[9] Like liquor, it may produce bonding, as when the Bunch (while drinking) laugh about the botched job in Starbuck. A great deal of laughter occurs during the fiesta in Angel's village, during which the yearnings for diversion and pleasurable bonding are allowed to be satisfied. We can see an idealized, childlike purity in the Gorches' laughter when they are playing cat's cradle with a young Mexican woman. (However, the game is not as innocent as it might first appear. The brothers' interest in the young woman—the two are, as usual, jointly interested in one female—is not without seductive overtones. Their game involves drawing a string back and forth through an opening in another part of the string, an act suggesting intercourse. Later the woman's mother, most likely in a protective act, calls her away.)

Watching the Gorches at play, Don José remarks, "We all wish to be a child again, even the worst of us." But there's more to this statement than what Don José intends. Although Don José's comment is in response to the Gorches' childlike game-playing and the Bunch's outlaw status (Peckinpah cuts to a shot of Pike for the phrase "even the worst of us"), Peckinpah interposes a meaning of his own through the editing. Just before Don José ends his assertion by saying, "perhaps the worst most of all," Peckinpah cuts to a shot of Angel, who is drunkenly walking away from the festivities. Although the director obviously means for us to draw a connection between the visuals and the words, it is clear that no simple relationship between these two realms is being asserted here. Don José is apparently reacting to Angel's idealism, which, even if it is at this point disappointed, represents the Bunch at their best. Through the editing, Peckinpah suggests that one of the worst parts of our existence is the part that experiences this disappointment.

Don José is commenting on the tragedy of Angel's loss of innocence, not only with regard to his finding out about the death of his father at Mapache's hands but more painfully about Teresa's having gone off with Mapache. The agony of disappointment in romantic love, then, takes precedence over the loss of familial love. Mapache has thus killed two people in Angel's life, one literally (his father), and one figuratively: Teresa, whose image for Angel as someone pure is destroyed by Mapache. What has died in Angel is a dream of innocence relating both to family and loved one. As we see beginning with the upcoming steam-bath sequence, Angel attempts to revive this dream by embracing the cause of his countrymen, who represent his extended family (thus Angel's later "my village, my people, Mexico" speech).

The fact of Angel's bruised idealism is made more specific with Don José's statement about Teresa: "To him Teresa was like a goddess, to be worshipped from afar. Mapache knew she was a mango, ripe and waiting." This statement strongly suggests that Angel never had sexual relations with his girlfriend. (Given Mapache's relations with Teresa, the sexual reticence must have been Angel's, not hers.) When Pike responds to Don José's comment by saying, "Angel dreams of love and Mapache eats the mango," the statement's form and meaning remind us of earlier assertions made about Pike that, as with Angel, contrasted his idealism with a simultaneous sexual, material reality. Pike's "dreaming of washers" (to use Dutch's phrase) occurred at the same time as the Gorches' sexual cavorting. As Lyle puts it, "While you [Pike] was doing all that planning, me and Tector was getting our bell rope pulled by two, mind you, two Hondo whores." The linkage is merely one of a series of connections established between Pike and Angel, including a striking parallelism between Angel's later statement about "my people, my village, Mexico" and Pike's assertion about the significance of disaffection among the Bunch, which he characterizes as meaning that "you're finished, we're finished, all of us." This statement, like Angel's, progresses toward increasingly greater inclusivity. These connections make more poignant and understandable the extremely sensitive reaction that Pike has to Angel's final capture by Mapache. What Pike attempts to hide throughout the film—as when he speaks sternly to Angel in Don José's village and threatens to abandon him, or when, during the steam-bath sequence, he calls Angel "a pain in the ass"—and what he demonstrates most conclusively at the film's end is his fatherly love for Angel. Indeed, for all of the Bunch's braggadocio, taunts, kidding, and drinking, the one quality that is more genuine and profound than their desire for money is their affection for and devotion to one another, characteristics that seem all the more poignant for the Bunch's attempts at masking them throughout the film.

Much of the time, laughter in the film is generated at the expense of some character's sense of well-being; in these instances, it causes a dual reaction, bringing together the majority of a scene's characters but simultaneously alienating one of them. We see laughter arising out of discomfort in the Bunch's amusement over denying Lyle whiskey and in what they apparently consider the ludicrousness of his "engagement." Some of the laughter occurs in extremely nasty incarnations, as when characters take sadistic pleasure in another's pain; examples of such cruel laughter include Coffer's cackling about the fake gun play with Thornton and the laughter of Mapache and his townspeople, which is caused by Angel's capture and torture.

All of these examples ultimately take us back to those scenes at the film's beginning when the children take pleasure in torturing the ants and scorpions and playing in the corpse-littered street of Starbuck. The latter scene is noteworthy because of the sound technique that Peckinpah uses in it. The children's delighted voices from a previous scene are first carried over onto the sight of the massacred Starbuck citizens, a view accompanied by the cries of the wounded and their relatives and the blended-in children's squeals.[10] These sounds conceptually segue into the actions and sounds of T. C. and Coffer, who are childishly haggling over the spoils and over which one of them killed a certain man. (Later they will virtually repeat this behavior when each tries to blame the other for shooting one of the soldiers who had been following Thornton's gang.) Then, the children's "pretend shooting" shouts of "bang bang" from the Starbuck scene (which link up with Coffer's later pretend shooting of Thornton, thus establishing a further link between Coffer and children) are superimposed on the shot of Abe falling off his horse. The juxtaposition of sounds and images makes it seem that, in the first case, the children are pleased by the massacre and, in the second case, that they cause Abe's fall and death; both assertions are, in a sense, correct. The massacre not only mirrors the torturing of the ants and scorpions but is also perpetrated by two childishly reckless individuals, Harrigan and Pike. Because Abe's wounding occurs during the massacre, the causality seems complete. In Starbuck (whose residents suffer) and on the trail (where Abe succumbs), the children's voices seem to float over the visuals, interacting with the images without revealing the source of the sounds; these voices thus have an offstage, *deus ex machina* quality that nicely complements the children's capricious, godlike aspects, which are at other times asserted in *The Wild Bunch*.

The laughter we remember most, though, is the kind that occurs when the members of the Bunch are in good spirits and are emotionally closest to one another. The best example of this kind of humor occurs after the tension created by the Gorches' demand for equal shares of the Starbuck heist.[11] When the "gold" is discovered to be washers, disgust (with a bit of amusement when Tector refers to the washers as "silver rings") is followed by Sykes's derisive laughter, which gives rise to anger and the threat of a shoot-out between Angel and the Gorches. At this point the Bunch is very close to self-destructing, as Sykes, Dutch, and Angel, all of whom have their guns out, bracket the Gorches. But then hostility, lessened by the threat of guns, is transmuted to good humor; the tensions subside as the Bunch laughs about the Gorches cavorting with whores while Pike was planning the Starbuck job. Indeed, it is this very sequence of laughter that Peckinpah reprises for the Bunch's apotheosis at the film's end, by which time they are in their most perfect cohesion: that of mutual death.[12] This last view of the Bunch causes a dual reaction, one of both happiness and sorrow, reminding us of the Bunch's better selves, their ability to laugh about their shortcomings and to be joined in joyous union. These final images also create an unavoidable sense of nostalgia, a feeling that Peckinpah complements by following these shots with a reprised view of the Bunch leaving Don José's village. These images encourage us to miss these men not only for their boisterous good humor but also for their admirable sentimentality, which takes complete hold of them during the fiesta; in that scene, only Pike maintains a degree of distance as, acting as the Bunch's wise man, he reflects along with Don José on the creation of tender feelings.

Despite focusing on images of the Bunch, the end of *The Wild Bunch* nonetheless makes us recall the film as a whole, and thus every other character in it as well, not just the endearing ones but the despicable ones too—and not only the comically despicable (T. C. and Coffer) but even completely unsympathetic characters such as Harrigan and Mapache's German advisers. It is a measure of its greatness that by the time it is over, *The Wild Bunch* can cause us to say about all of its characters what was well expressed by Holden Caulfield in *The Catcher in the Rye*, when he commented on the people whom he had met, including, perhaps most especially, the sadistic hotel elevator operator, Maurice. "About all I know is, I sort of *miss* everybody I told about, even old Stradlater and Ackley, for instance. I think I even miss that goddam Maurice. It's funny, don't ever tell anybody anything. If you do, you start missing everybody."[13]

As one might expect, the significances of *The Wild Bunch* are present from the film's very beginning. We see the Bunch riding into the town of Starbuck and are then given shots of them in black-and-white still frames, each of which communicates a meaning concerning the character being depicted.[14] The shots of Pike and Dutch freeze as these men look at the children torturing the scorpions and the ants. It's not just that Pike and Dutch, the Bunch's two most prominent members, demonstrate a greater yearning for a childlike simplicity of ideals and actions than do the other members. The shots additionally demonstrate that, although the Bunch might prefer a world without opportunism and pain, they also know that such a world is not to be found through so-called childlike innocence. Indeed, the children's behavior here makes it quite clear that childhood can be a time of awful cruelty and discomfort.

The ants and scorpions image suggests another meaning as well. The sight of the relatively powerful scorpions being rendered helpless by the ants, who connote industriousness, makes it clear that a group of weak individuals, if united in a common purpose, can vanquish a greater one, precisely the situation during the Bunch's slaughter of virtually all of Mapache's men. (Of course, there is a contrast being drawn here as well, since the ants act from instinct, whereas by the film's end the Bunch does know the purpose of their final action: in the most basic sense, to redeem their friend.)

Finally, the image's meaning becomes more complex. Toward the title sequence's end, the children cover the insects with twigs and set them afire, the burning wood eventually settling down on the ants and scorpions and killing them. It's clear that the children's act suggests a deity visiting a fiery fate on men as recompense for their deeds. When we consider that the figures for the deity here are children, it seems that we are meant to recall the speech toward the end of *King Lear* concerning insects, fate, children, morality, the deity, and death: "As flies to wanton boys are we to th' gods, / They kill us for their sport" (4.1.36–37). Indeed, Peckinpah gives us evidence that this is one suggested meaning here, especially when we consider that at four different junctures the Bunch, like the ants and scorpions, are surrounded in a cagelike area and threatened with assault from above by morally regressive, childlike individuals: in Starbuck when Thornton's group fires on them from a rooftop; when they first enter Agua Verde and young children pelt them with stones that they toss through bars that resemble the straw barriers enclosing the ants and scorpions; when they show the stolen munitions to Herrera in a canyon on whose cliffs Mapachistas with rifles are situated; and once again in Agua Verde, when they are surrounded by Mapache's men, many of whom are perched on high parapets.[15]

Given these examples, one might be tempted to cast the depressing pall of the Shakespeare quote on the film, which after all is bracketed by two fiery judgments against a group of people who are insectlike: the townspeople at the film's beginning, whom Peckinpah, by not characterizing, makes seem little more than props (a function they certainly serve in the shoot-out),[16] and the immoral, insectlike members of Mapache's town at the film's end. However, both the film and the play that it here seems to cite speak against such a reading. In the manner in which it shows us that the ends to which all of its major characters come are just—from the deserved deaths of T. C., Coffer, and the rest of Thornton's gang, to those of Mapache and his men, even to those of the Bunch themselves (all of the Bunch members who die in Agua Verde do so in the name of a higher morality)—*The Wild Bunch* demonstrates that, in the words of Edgar, the character in *Lear* who rejects a fatalistic reading of comparably excessive events, "The gods are just, and of our pleasant vices / Make instruments to plague us" (5.3.172–73). *The Wild Bunch*'s universe is indeed a moral one; only men who are morally blind would blame the gods, rather than themselves, for what happens to them, failing to realize that just as we are penalized for our vices, we are also rewarded for our virtues.

Meanings arise from the rest of the title sequence as well. Robert Ryan's name appears over a shot of railroad tracks, an appropriate image not only because of Deke Thornton's association with a literal railroad (his being blackmailed by the railroad man Harrigan and his involvement in the pursuit of the Bunch after they rob a train) but also because his fate is as determined as the destination of a train. The same image over which Ryan's name appears also shows the Bunch riding away from us; thus, we see the Bunch from the perspective of someone pursuing them, exactly the situation in which Thornton finds himself for most of the film.

The names of Edmond O'Brien, Warren Oates, and Ben Johnson, who play the Bunch's most childlike members, are superimposed over a still of an innocent-looking girl. (Jaime Sanchez's name appears here too, but Angel's morality embraces mature political values, a state achieved by neither of the Gorches—played by Oates and Johnson—and demonstrated by O'Brien's Sykes only at the film's end.) Clearly, though, these characters are no more innocent than the children we've been watching: Sykes has a long history of robbery and killing, and the Gorches are wanted for rape and murder. The names of actors Strother Martin, L. Q. Jones, Emilio Fernandez, and Albert Dekker are superimposed over a shot of the ants and scorpions, keying us in to the rapacious, insectlike characteristics of the men whom these actors portray. Among the players listed next, the most prominent are Dub Taylor (Mayor Wainscoat) and Bo Hopkins (Crazy Lee), whose names are superimposed over a shot of the temperance congregation, a suitable juxtaposition given Taylor's role as the speaker at the temperance union rally and Hopkins's role in leading his prisoners in a rendition of "Shall We Gather at the River," the marching song for the temperance union.

Finally, Peckinpah's directorial credit appears. It occurs superimposed over an image of Pike after Pike says to his men about the railroad employees, "If they move, kill 'em." The statement's first half leads us to believe that Pike will not use the word "kill" but "shoot," a usage that suggests not only the discharge of a weapon but the photographing of a scene or character. As the orchestrator and instigator of most of the film's action, Pike certainly serves as a corollary for a film director; what and who get shot in the film are often the result of Pike's decisions.

Just to be playful, we might surmise that there is significance in the fact that the name of producer Phil Feldman, whom Peckinpah and others accused of sabotaging the film by allowing it to be trimmed unmercifully after its initial release, appears after the railroad office manager says, "I don't care what you meant to do; it's what you did I don't like."[17] A disputatious producer might very well have made such a statement concerning a director's intentions versus the final version of a film that the director delivered to him.

Mention of Feldman brings up the issue of the film's cutting. Among the cuts were a number of flashbacks and footage that situates and integrates them; these cuts include Pike's explanation of his previous encounters with Harrigan, information that explains Harrigan's otherwise curious obsession with Pike's capture. In addition, the producer cut a present-tense sequence involving the assault by Villa's forces on Mapache's train, during which the "general" is shown to be a brave and audacious man. Certainly all of these scenes should have remained in *The Wild Bunch*. Although the concepts dramatized in the cut flashbacks—the sense of regret over past mistakes and the connections that exist between Pike and Thornton—are to a degree successfully communicated in the film's shortened version, the profound sense of loss and poignancy created by the excised footage is unavailable to the viewer of the truncated film.[18]

The film's short version retains the flashback concerning Thornton's whipping while imprisoned; the scene, which occurs after Harrigan threatens to send Thornton back to jail, represents Thornton's internal vision. The short version also includes the repetition of Crazy Lee's vow to hold the Starbuck hostages (which represents an internalized vision of Pike's). However, the full-length version contains the flashback explaining Thornton's capture as a consequence of Pike's stupidly not reckoning that, after a robbery, he and Thornton might be followed. The long version also includes Pike's insistence that he knows they are safe because "being sure is my business,"[19] a statement that is followed by a knock at the door of their room. Pike says that the person at the door is merely someone delivering champagne that he ordered. When opened, though, the door reveals an armed man who raises his pistol and fires at Thornton, at which point Pike flees. Intercut with the flashback are present-tense shots of Pike and Thornton. In the first of these shots, Thornton is rolling a cigarette; Pike, seen in the adobe after the Starbuck massacre, is rolling a half-smoked cigar between his fingers. Seydor states that the insertion of the present-tense shots establishes "a structural arc that binds these two men . . . by way of a common memory,"[20] but more is being asserted here than that.

The way that Peckinpah cuts back and forth from Pike to Thornton and shows each man in a comparable attitude of repose, when considered along with the total conjunction of the memory that Pike and Thornton share (each man ruminates over the selfsame details at the exact same time), leads us to conclude that Pike and Thornton are not only similar but are virtually the same person. For Thornton and Pike, their past "sticking together" has taken the form of almost complete emotional and psychological unity. We are thus reminded of Thornton's ability to intuit Pike's moves, his amazingly accurate knowledge of where the Bunch is at nearly every moment, and his virtually overwhelming need to be with the Bunch, a desire for a unity that he finally achieves at the film's end when he assumes Pike's role, thereby ensuring that the Bunch's existence will continue unbroken.

The other excised flashback explains how Pike got his leg wound. He was visiting a married woman who told him that her husband was not due back immediately. However, the husband (who is first seen reflected in a wardrobe mirror) returns precipitously, kills his

Plate 16. Thornton during the dual flashbacks scene.

wife, and wounds Pike.[21] As in the earlier flashback with Thornton, Pike again displays his arrogant ignorance. With the gift of hindsight, Pike says, "He [the husband] wasn't around and I got careless," but it's obvious that Pike hasn't learned much from his past actions, even if he does swear (before the train assault sequence) that "this time we do it right."

Pike is the film's most prominent example of a man whose words and deeds are often at variance, as demonstrated by his memory of Thornton's capture and his own escape. Seydor views this kind of disparity as evidencing another one of Pike's failings, and his point is well taken. Seydor states, "The point here is not so much that Pike is a hypocrite as that he fails to live up to his own standards from time to time."[22] In fact, as we'll see, Pike repeatedly says one thing and does another; he continues to disappoint himself and his ideals. Pike's realization of his shortcomings, which are presented to him as he thinks over his past errors (e.g., those involving the Starbuck job and the losses of Abe and Crazy Lee), cause him to take Thornton's side concerning his friend's pact with the railroad. In this matter, Pike defends Thornton in response to his need to

Plates 17–18. Pike's two modes: woefully ignorant, with Aurora (*top*), and impressively self-assured, during the train heist (*bottom*).

believe in a man's word, a need that arises from Pike's realization that his own word has always seemed worthless. And though Pike's defense of Thornton's deal with Harrigan is misinformed, we should not understand it merely as a function of Pike's feeling that it was his fault that Thornton was captured (as Seydor suggests that we do);[23] Pike's statement is also an example of his simple admiration of Thornton's ability to remain true to something even if to do so is painful, an ability that Pike achieves only at the film's end when he at last hazards his own life for the sake of someone else—something that, with his constant running away, he has never done before.

At the end of this flashback sequence, we are returned to the adobe in which the Bunch is resting. Dutch asks, "How about us, Pike: you reckon we learned, being wrong today?" (Dutch seems to be attempting to remind Pike that one must learn from one's mistakes.) When Pike answers, "I sure hope to God we did,"[24] it is only a hope that is being expressed (although Pike does learn how to harness the power of the machine gun). Two more men, Angel and Sykes, are to be abandoned before Pike finally asserts his true leadership by changing the Bunch from unfeeling men into heroes. Until that point, though, Pike will insistently dwell on his mistakes and is thus that worst of all moral beings: the man acutely aware of his shortcomings but unable, or unwilling, to do anything about the situation. (Indeed, Pike's obsession with his constantly updated list of errors seems to serve as self-flagellation.)

The contradiction between what Pike says and does emerges most tellingly immediately following the "stick together" speech. After the speech, for which Pike is complimented by Sykes, Sykes asks how Crazy Lee performed in Starbuck. Once assured that Crazy Lee did not disgrace himself, Sykes is satisfied. Yet surely the viewer—like Pike—recalls at this point that despite all of the preceding talk about unity, Pike (and the rest of the Bunch) abandoned Crazy Lee, just as Pike abandoned Abe and will abandon Angel and Sykes himself. What we witness in these conflicts between words and deeds is Pike's having to balance considerations regarding the individual against those of the group. Crazy Lee would obviously have been a liability on the trail; Abe could no longer ride; Angel was being held by a formidable number of men; and Sykes, after being shot, seemed very badly wounded. Yet opposed to these practical considerations is Pike's basic desire—doubtless in response to his guilt over having abandoned Thornton—to remain loyal to the men in the Bunch. This quality emerges most notably in Pike's early attitude toward Sykes. Pike defends Sykes when Sykes loses control of the horses on the sand dune, despite the fact that, as Lyle makes clear, such a loss of control signals rank incompetence. This quality is again in evidence when Sykes hands Pike and Dutch cups of coffee that are not only far too hot to handle (although Sykes does warn them, saying, "Them's hot") but also contain a concoction that Dutch likens to poison. Yet in answer to Dutch's complaint ("Where did you find him?"), Pike invokes Sykes's past usefulness as a rationale for retaining him in the present. Clearly, Pike's personality is far more complex than it would initially appear to be.

Plate 19. Crazy Lee during the Starbuck assault: "I'll hold 'em 'til Hell freezes over or you say different."

Despite Pike's prominence of place, *The Wild Bunch* holds out the most important redemption of all for Deke Thornton. Thornton is the film's most sympathetic character in that he is the only man who is not only branded by his past but is also, for most of the film, unable to do anything about making up for past mistakes. Thornton is trapped by that most abominable of forces in Peckinpah's universe: morally retrograde moneyed interests. Moreover, Thornton's deliverance exceeds that of the Bunch in that he survives to translate his higher morality into action. In the manner in which Thornton reminds Pike of one of his major shortcomings (abandoning his associates) and in the way that Thornton emerges as a viable moral force at the film's end, it's clear that by virtue of his greater sensitivity to and awareness of oppression, he represents the conscience not only of Pike but of humankind in general. Whereas the Bunch is characterized by blind impulse, Thornton combines instinct (e.g., his ability to sense the Bunch's presence when he and his group are being watched by men they cannot see) with reflection and compassion. He thereby embodies Peckinpah's optimism for some future time when meaningful social and political change will be possible.

By blending Sykes and Thornton's laughter at the film's end with that of the Bunch, Peckinpah makes it plain that Sykes and Thornton epitomize the Bunch at its most idealistic. Moreover, through our simultaneous realization that Thornton succeeds the Bunch, we recognize that Thornton, finally liberated from oppression himself, will consciously carry on the work of liberation that the Bunch only began, doing so by liberating others as well. In the film's final sequence, laughter heals the wounds of misjudgment and regret over past mistakes and is itself a liberation, in this case from compromise and pettiness, allowing a passage into a world in which disunity (discontinuity between what one intends—planned actions—and what one actually does) yields to the unity arising from being reconciled to the imperfection inherent in human activities.

During the fiesta in Angel's village, Pike tells Angel that he must "learn to live with" Mapache's killing his father or they will leave him there. It's a curious statement, since Pike recommends that Angel forget about his family yet threatens him with the loss of the Bunch, his other "family." Pike's later actions, though, make it clear that he cannot learn to live with the loss of a family member—in this case, Angel. As noted, though, Pike has exhibited such contradictory behavior before.

Don José does not suffer from Pike's division of feelings. In the midst of the celebration, Don José counsels Angel not to take his father's death so personally. Angel asks for "the name of the soldier who killed my father." Don José replies, "Why do you wish to know?" Although he does eventually give Mapache's name to Angel, we may intuit in Don José's remarks the notion that what is essential in the national struggle are groups, not individuals (an attitude that might resolve many of Pike's dilemmas if he were only able to jettison his guilt and achieve it). However, Angel seems to understand what Don José means, as evidenced by his later saying that what is important to him are "my people, my village, Mexico": he has realized that all three realms are united and that the individual achieves significance only as part of a greater whole. This stance corroborates the implication in Pike's "stick together" speech that there is a quality to group cohesiveness that exceeds individual loyalties. No such group loyalty exists among Thornton's gang. When one of their members, who has been tracking the wounded Sykes, fails to return to Agua Verde on time, T. C. asks if they should wait for him; Coffer impatiently replies, "No, no, no, we'll pick him up on the way." To these men, the idea of group honor simply doesn't exist.

T. C. and Coffer's counterparts, the Gorches, also have trouble accepting the concept of group honor. Until the film's end, the Gorches fail to realize that honor is the key to alliance, that force is simply not necessary to compel unity (although, after the Starbuck job, the threat of force must be used to quell the Gorches' rebelliousness). After the "stick together" speech, Pike falls while mounting his horse, and Lyle says to him, "How in the hell are you going to side anybody when you can't even get onto your horse?" However, Lyle is obviously missing the point: Pike's fall does not in any sense indicate an inability to lead. Pike's leadership depends not on his physical condition but rather on his personal force. Don José may say, "If we had rifles like these [we could fight]," yet even with guns, a character or group may still be powerless: Mapache's well-armed people are morally misled and thus doomed to failure. Only when morality is allied with personal dynamism can a man be an effective leader, one who is capable of achieving meaningful change.

National honor and fidelity are verbally denied in the film. (Mohr: "Are you men associated with the American army?" Dutch: "No, no, we're not associated with anybody.") Nonetheless, these qualities are an important part of the Bunch's make-up. Thus, when Mohr points out the intended location for the train heist, Dutch says, "That's hitting pretty close to home, ain't it?" However, Peckinpah is not above humorously treating the sense of honor about country or family. (In *The Wild Bunch*, the two concepts seem to be equivalent, a notion that refers us back to Angel's equation of his people with his country.) When the Bunch approaches Angel's village, Angel says, "Any disrespect to my family or to my people, I will kill you." This remark doesn't prevent Lyle from asking Angel, "You got a sister?" Receiving an answer in the affirmative, he goes on to state, with obvious intentions, "I'd be proud to make her acquaintance, and that of your momma, too," to which Tector adds, "That goes for your Grandma too, sonny."

A number of traditional Peckinpah conceits emerge in the film. Mexico is portrayed as a land of exaggerations, of great contrasts. It is in Mexico that we find both heaven and hell. Heaven, of course, is suggested by the peaceful respite in the village of the aptly named Angel. This village, as is obvious both from its lushness—in contrast to the aridity of the film's other locations—and its description in the film's script, is part of the "green world" of moral and spiritual fruitfulness. Hell appears in the awful explosion of death in Agua Verde, which easily dwarfs the violence in Starbuck. It is in Mexico, too, that the Bunch's apotheosis takes place. Thus, *The Wild Bunch* shows Mexico producing three important effects in two realms: pleasure and pain in this life, justice in the next.

Other important themes appear in *The Wild Bunch* as well. Moneyed interests (in the persons of Harrigan and Mapache, who are corrupted by wealth and power) are in conflict with the actions of individuals who are working outside the law, either those like the Bunch, who seem to have no particular ideology, or those like Don José and the mountain Indians, who consciously fight against repression. In this respect, until the film's very end we must view the Bunch's actions as useless in working out the political dialectic. In fact, the Bunch's robberies serve to strengthen the ruling classes by giving them a very visible, apolitical antagonist that they may oppose for the supposed benefit of "the people." What the Bunch demonstrates is that opposing the system from within (which is, after all, what the Bunch does in their thefts) is pointless. Instead, the system as an entirety must be abolished. Only in their first (and final) revolutionary act does the Bunch seem to realize this, but this dim realization comes too late for them to do anything except to help establish, through wanton destruction, a new egalitarianism that not only grows out of the barrel of a machine gun but that also arises from the ashes of the old order. What the Bunch finally accomplishes is to reduce the number of tyrants with which the revolutionary forces have to deal.

The Bunch also represents another familiar Peckinpah concept, anachronism, through their outmoded methods of robbery, characterized by their tending to rely more on force than intellect. Yet force alone does serve the Bunch well at the film's end, when they appropriate an example of another traditional Peckinpah conceit, new technology. The machine gun is clearly a device that results from a kind of thinking that, to appropriate Pike's words from another context, is "beyond [their] guns." It is obviously a very special instrument, something worthy of reverence. Even the Gorches handle the gun respectfully when it is discovered. When Lyle first sees the gun he says to Pike, "Think you can handle that?" Pike answers, "What I don't know about I sure as hell am gonna learn."[25]

Unlike Mapache (who is apparently incapable of progressive thinking), the Bunch early on demonstrates that they appreciate the weapon's power by immediately (to use Mapache's words) "put[-ting] it on the tripod." Also notable is the way that, after the gun's recoil knocks Mapache down, he rises grinning with admiration for the gun's unearthly power. The camera technique that Peckinpah uses to reveal the gun (a technique repeated during our first view of another piece of relatively new technology, Mapache's car) indicates that Peckinpah wishes to emphasize the gun's extraordinary status.[26] While it is being unloaded from the supply train, the gun is twice photographed in an overhead crane shot (representing Pike's point of view) that causes us to look down on the gun, thus emphasizing its unusual nature while inviting comparison with the height from which the Starbuck children viewed the ants and scorpions that they were so dispassionately manipulating. The children functioned as the insects' godlike executioners. Pike, godlike, dispassionately observes the gun, not yet aware of what kind of execution it will occasion. The god-man imagery reappears in Agua Verde, where the Bunch, childlike in the simplicity of their motives (but superior to the film's other children in their implicitly perceived morality), brings down a fiery fate on the town's residents, who seem like moral insects. True, the Bunch pays for their appropriation of fire by eventually being destroyed, yet they are reborn like the phoenix when they are reinvoked by the words and laughter of Thornton, Sykes, and the others.

Yet before this point, the Bunch must overcome major character faults. Predominant among them is Pike's persistent lack of prescience. Thornton describes Pike as "the best, he never got caught," which is literally true; but then Pike usually escapes capture by leaving other people behind. Pike anticipates some form of opposition to the train heist. When Dutch says, "They'll be waiting for us," Pike responds, "I wouldn't have it any other way." Yet the "way" that Pike has it threatens the success of the entire operation, since he (and the rest of his men) never suspect that the train might carry significant opposition aboard it, which explains Dutch's amazed stare when he sees the horses being led out of one of the boxcars. Although Pike certainly surprises Thornton with the dynamiting of the bridge and is one step ahead of Mapache in knowing that the "general" will try to violate his agreement with them, he fails to anticipate the possibility of a trap in Starbuck. Later, along with Dutch, Pike watches Thornton and his men pursuing them. Noting that Thornton's gang are riding east, Pike asks, "Are they bluffing or did they really miss it?" Dutch replies, "I'd say they missed it." Yet Thornton knows exactly where the Bunch is hiding, which makes Pike's mistake in perception that much more striking.

> COFFER: Hell, we lost 'em.
> THORNTON: We haven't lost 'em. I could point to them right now. You think that Pike and old Sykes haven't been watching us? They know what this is all about and what do I have? Nothing but you egg-sucking, chicken-stealing gutter trash with not even sixty rounds between you. We're after men and I wish to God I was with them. The next time you make a mistake I'm gonna ride off and let you die.

Thornton's statement is quite prophetic. T. C., Coffer, and the rest do make one more mistake: they try to ride back to Starbuck with the Bunch's bodies, not realizing that they will be passing through territory controlled by Don José and the mountain Indians. By staying behind—knowing, as he must, precisely what will happen to T. C. and the other men—Thornton has in effect left them to die.

Just as Pike underestimates the ingenuity of Harrigan and Thornton, Mapache underestimates the Bunch's resourcefulness. This is clear from the way that he mistakenly assumes that the Bunch will be unprepared for any subterfuge from his emissary, Herrera. Similarly, Mohr, the German munitions adviser, remarking on Pike's ownership of an army-issue gun, says, "That pistol is restricted for the use of army personnel; it can't be purchased or even owned, legally." Pike replies, "Is that so?" Mohr then goes on to state, "It would be very useful for us if we knew of some Americans who did not share their government's naive sentiments." Apparently demonstrating disdain for the legal authority in his country, Pike replies, "Well, we share very few sentiments with our government." The German misreads this statement, failing to realize that Pike has shrewdly sidestepped politics and has instead merely commented on some series of undefined attitudes. Yet by giving rifles to Angel, the Bunch reveals that they do believe in the kinds of admirable ideals on which America was founded (e.g., justice and equality) and that they respect Angel's attempt to help his people.

Mohr intends the word "naive" to be pejorative, but the "naive" values in the film are those that *The Wild Bunch* most highly regards: friendship, camaraderie, loyalty. Of course, to the observer who is even slightly cynical, the embracing of such values might very well seem naive. Yet it should be apparent that through our final identification with the Bunch, the film virtually compels us to accept these ideals, thus making us over in its own image.

These and comparable values emerge most forcefully toward the film's latter half in three important sequences: during the "debates" in the Agua Verde steam bath, on the mountain outside Agua Verde, and during the events preceding, during, and following the film's major set piece, the Agua Verde shoot-out. These sequences demand close attention.

The steam-bath sequence features Pike, Dutch, Sykes, and Angel in a setting that is used for its dramatic symbolism. The characters, literally and figuratively stripped down, are dealing with unadorned attitudes and ideas. There are no pretensions here, as is indicated by the innocently playful attitude of Dutch, who splashes water on Pike and Sykes (and who is splashed back by Pike in a rare example of unbridled pleasure on Pike's part). What we witness in this and the mountaintop scene is a debate on materialism versus idealism. It is a testament to *The Wild Bunch*'s sophistication that the scene works on both a dramatic and ideological level. As with the discussion on the mountaintop, I will cite a line of dialogue and identify the moral realm in which it is situated.

PIKE (to Angel): I don't know why I didn't let them kill you.

The ideal is expressed in material terms. This restrained expression of affection is cautiously couched in a humorous reference to possible abandonment (a form of selfish behavior).

ANGEL: Listen, I'm not going to steal guns for that devil to rob my people again.

Idealism ("oppression is wrong") is expressed practically.

DUTCH: Noble, very noble.

Admiration for idealism is here masked by irony.

SYKES: I didn't see no tears running down your cheek when you rode in from Starbuck.

Irony again masks idealism. Sykes is not criticizing Angel for his lack of tears but is instead prodding him for an explanation of the distinction between his people and those in Starbuck.

ANGEL: They were not my people. I care about my people, my village, Mexico.

Again, idealism is tempered with practicality. One cannot help everyone; one's allegiance is initially to one's family, no matter how "family" is defined.

SYKES: Listen, boy, you ride with us, your village don't count. If it does, you just don't go along.

This statement (which is based in the realm of the ideal) is essentially a repetition of what Pike told Angel in Don José's village. Sykes's assertion is not so much a criticism of Angel's idealism as it is a simple restatement of Angel's point about the impracticality of dividing allegiances. All that Sykes means here is that Angel's first loyalty should be to the Bunch, a point that Angel later affirms by not implicating the Bunch in the diversion of the guns.

ANGEL: Then I don't go along.

In this statement from the material realm, Angel is being petulant because of his wounded idealism. He is acting as though he is morally superior to the other men and implies that his loss will seriously affect them.

DUTCH: Angel, one load of guns ain't gonna stop them raiding villages. Why, you ought to be thinking about all the money you're gonna have.

The ideal is here stated in material terms in a very interesting speech. Dutch tries to ensure that Angel will not leave the group, thereby signaling to him that he is indeed important to them. Further, Dutch seems to imply that Angel could place the material realm in the service of the ideal by using the money from the train heist to help his people battle for their rights, a meaning consistent with his revolutionary statement earlier about the need to rid the country of Mapache and men like him.

PIKE: Buy 'em a ranch; move 'em a thousand miles. Buy 'em two, three ranches.

Pike's materialistic comment suggests that he either misses Dutch's meaning or simply changes it. In essence, Pike says, "Don't fight oppression; run away from it."

DUTCH: One—a very small one.

In this "ideal" statement, Dutch plays along with Pike's meaning to avoid offending him. Yet he nonetheless contradicts Pike in two very important exchanges: the one in which Pike compares Mapache to the Bunch (an assertion to which Dutch bitterly replies, "Not so's you'd know it, Mr. Bishop. We don't hang nobody") and the one on the mountaintop about how one determines whether or not one's word is binding. For all of their camaraderie, Pike and Dutch often have serious ideological differences.

ANGEL: Don't you see, this is their land and no one is gonna drive them away.

This "ideal" statement answers Pike's suggestion. Angel is in no mood for kidding.

SYKES: I'll drink to that sentiment, and to love. But most of all, I'll drink to gold.

More playful—and material—comments to match Pike's tone. Sykes and Dutch realize that Pike does not want to respond seriously to Angel's suggestion.

DUTCH: Salud, salud!

There follows a return to the simultaneous wine-vat interlude with the Gorches, a sequence whose sensual aspect reminds us of the Bunch's self-indulgent qualities. At this point, the Gorches seem like nothing more than men in love with violence (e.g., shooting the wine vats) and ribaldry (the tasteless playing with and comparing of the women's breasts). The scene is meant to provide both a contrast to the serious steam-bath scene and a reminder of the Gorches's comparatively lighter natures, a quality unrelieved until the film's end. Having achieved these effects, Peckinpah returns us to the steam bath.

PIKE: Angel, you're a pain in the ass.

The conflict between the material and the ideal here surfaces directly. Pike indicates that Angel is reminding him of his own wounded idealism.

ANGEL: Would you give guns to someone to kill your father or
your mother or your brother?

Angel reiterates the all-important ideal of loyalty to one's family,
a term that can be taken to refer to one's close friends as well.

PIKE: Ten thousand cuts an awful lot of family ties.

This "material" statement is a lie. Pike would like to believe
this himself, but he cannot. Even though Pike offers Mapache only
half of his share of the gold for Angel, the Bunch as a whole, at
Pike's initial prodding, will eventually cash in everything for their
friend, whom they regard as a family member with whom they
cannot sever their "ties."

ANGEL: My people have no guns. But with guns, my people
could fight. If I could take guns, I would go with you.

The ideal may now be achieved through the material. Angel
makes the bargain plain: I will stay with you, but only for the sake
of my people, who come first. This is a lesson in loyalty that the
rest of the Bunch eventually learn. Later, Angel will place the Bunch
first when he keeps quiet about their making it possible for him to
give guns to the mountain Indians.

An extremely critical juncture has been reached here, a characteristic cued by the disappearance of the scene's music when Pike says
the words "ten thousand." It is left to Dutch, as the Bunch's most
vocal idealist (that is, until his role is taken over by Sykes), to make
a proposal that is physically fatal, in that it ultimately leads to the
Bunch's demise, but fatefully bountiful, in that it compels them all
to make the one truly moral decision in their lives.

DUTCH: Say, how many cases of rifles did Zamorra say was in
that shipment?
PIKE: Sixteen.

The moral realm here is indeterminate. Pike looks quite grim:
he knows what's coming and doesn't like it, although at this point
he doesn't know why.

DUTCH: Well, give him one.

Again, this statement suggests that the ideal may be achieved
through the material. The music returns at this point with an ominous sting. Dutch's offer, prompted by both practicality (the desire

to have Angel remain with the Bunch for the train job) and idealism (Dutch's hope that the mountain Indians may be able to strike a blow against oppression), sets in motion a chain of events resulting in effects that are similarly dual. The Bunch's triumph over Mapache is a victory for idealism, but it is paid for materially with the deaths of these men (which in turn makes possible their idealization through myth).

> PIKE (after a very thoughtful pause): All right. One case and one case of ammo. But you give up your share of the gold.

Idealism is here masked as materialism. Apparently embarrassed by his gesture's idealism, Pike tries to obscure this aspect by emphasizing the material trade of gold for guns.

> ANGEL: I will.
> PIKE: We know you will.

The "we" makes it plain that although Pike is speaking, this is a group decision, one with which even the usually materialistic Gorches would probably concur. Excluding the Gorches, who act altruistically only at the film's end, the other members of the Bunch show their idealism in different ways. Pike tries to mask his idealism with his supposed toughness: he keeps his pain and vulnerability, physical and moral—all of which derives from his having abandoned Thornton and others like him—to himself. In order not to appear an overt sentimentalist, Dutch usually mixes idealism with humor to lessen its impact, as does his moral counterpart, Sykes. Like Pike (who appears callous but isn't), Sykes projects a public persona strongly at variance with his real self. Sykes uses his age as a cover; his grizzled asides give the impression that he is merely a cantankerous old man. Yet it's clear by his toughness (exemplified through his surviving a serious leg wound and his vitality at the film's end) that he's far less debilitated than he pretends to be.

As is apparent from the film's conclusion, Sykes is at least as much of an idealist as Pike or Dutch. He ends the discussion with a note of humor in order to relieve the overt seriousness of the pact to which the "debate" has led. "Sure glad we got that settled," he says, to which Dutch, catching the need to restore a light mood, growls, "Why you!" and splashes water on him. Peckinpah knows that the audience also needs a bit of relief from this high-temperature discussion, so he brings in the Gorches, whose comic announcement of Lyle's engagement not only implicitly contrasts with what Angel regarded as his serious relationship with Teresa but also provides a humorous comment on commitment. Lyle has become engaged while drunk; there's a strong implication that the moral "engagement" with Angel that the other members of the Bunch have just made official is also the result of a form of drunkenness: the delirious embracing of ideals.

After Angel is detained by Mapache, who knows of his diversion of the rifles, another battle takes place between the ideal and material realms, with the ideal quickly yielding to the material in a demonstration of the Bunch's growing disappointment over Angel's capture and their apparent inability to do anything about it. The scene opens with Pike, Dutch, and the Gorches at the top of a mountain clearing. The elevated setting conflicts with the group's extremely low spirits. The men are standing apart, their placement reflecting their dejected and alienated status. Yet at the same time, they are paradoxically united by their dejection and alienation, since they are all upset by what has happened to Angel.

LYLE: Well, he had guts.

This statement is an ideal appreciation of Angel's sacrifice for the sake of the group.

PIKE: We're just lucky he didn't talk.

Pike demonstrates a materialistic concern for saving oneself, even if that self is a member of a group.

DUTCH: He played his string right ut to the end.

Dutch here offers an idealistic affirmation of Lyle's point about Angel's selfless gesture.

LYLE: Her own mama turned him in, like some kind of a Judas.

Teresa's mother, a Mexican, turned against one of her own people by identifying Angel to Mapache, thereby violating an ideal ("one should remain true to one's people"). Lyle views this act as a materialistic betrayal; in fact, Teresa's mother merely opted for one ideal over another, siding with her immediate family against her country's best interest (this in spite of the fact that her daughter consorted with Mapache, who decimated her village).

DUTCH: Sykes says we oughta go after him.

Dutch voices an idealistic need, for the sake of fraternity, to come to Angel's defense.

LYLE: How in the hell are we gonna do that? They got guns and
    two hundred men.

This statement combines both the material and the ideal, but practical considerations take precedence. However, there is a hint of idealism as well, since Lyle's first statement allows for the possibility that some way of rescuing Angel might be found.

PIKE: No way, no way at all.

Bitter resignation. Pike yields to the supposed sway of being outnumbered, yet the same overwhelming odds do not deter the Bunch later in Agua Verde.

At this point, Sykes is shot by Coffer. At first, Lyle believes that Mapache's men have shot Sykes. Pike corrects him, stating "Thornton," as though Thornton himself had done the deed. Either way, Pike is ascribing a villainous status to Thornton that is undeserved, an attitude that reveals a great deal about Pike's guilt concerning his former friend; Pike makes Thornton out to be a man as compromised as he himself is as a way of assuaging his own shame.

PIKE: They got Freddy. Looks like he's hit pretty bad.

Pike is concerned, but not deeply so; his attitude is primarily materialistic. Like Crazy Lee, Abe, and (for now) Angel, Sykes is to be abandoned.

The debate between Pike and Dutch about the effect of circumstances on the binding effect of one's word then occurs.

DUTCH: Damn that Deke Thornton to hell!
PIKE: What would you do in his place? He gave his word.
DUTCH: Gave his word to a railroad.
PIKE: It's his word.
DUTCH: That's not what counts; it's who you give it to!

The point being made here is apposite not only to Thornton's deal with Harrigan—which, unbeknownst to Pike and Dutch, is founded on an agreement into which Thornton was blackmailed (which in my view nullifies the pact)—but also to the promise that the Bunch made to Mapache to deliver the ordnance on the train. That Mapache's word to the Bunch is worthless is made obvious when he tries to double-cross them. (In fact, Pike may be partially relying on his knowledge that Mapache is corrupt to justify to himself the diversion of guns to Angel.) There's no need to be totally honest with Mapache since Mapache is not totally honest with the Bunch. This situation demonstrates quite clearly that a binding word can exist only between two honorable individuals, each of whom voluntarily gives it.[27]

The discussion then turns back to the immediate situation. One final idealistic assertion is made, after which materialism predominates. Lyle first suggests that the Bunch avenge Sykes's shooting.

> LYLE: We can stay up here and kick hell out of 'em, that's what we can do.

Lyle idealistically proposes that the group ("we") avenge the attack on one of their members (an anticipation of the attitude that impels them to return for Angel).

> PIKE: No, we're running short of water.

The group thinking is here expressed in practical terms, a realm that is rejected when the Bunch decides to rescue Angel.

> DUTCH: Make a run for the border?
> PIKE: They'd follow us every step of the way. I know Thornton. I'm tired of being hunted.

Pike's statement is predominantly materialistic, blending self-concern and group considerations. The entire group would be followed, but Pike expresses the wearying effect of being pursued in terms relating only to himself.

> PIKE: Go back to Agua Verde. Let the general take care of those boys.

This materialistic statement urges the Bunch to abandon not only Sykes but also their responsibility to avenge his wounding.

> LYLE: You're crazy. That general would just as soon kill us as break wind.

A group dilemma is being considered, but the terms in which it is being considered are still self-centered and therefore materialistic.

Pike's tone then becomes overtly callous and selfish as the bitterness over what appears to be the elimination of Angel and Sykes begins to reach its peak.

> PIKE: He's so tickled with those guns he'll be celebrating for a week and happy to do us a favor. Thornton's not gonna

> follow us in there. While they're busy picking over Freddy,
> we'll find a back trail off this mountain and head for town.

The vulture imagery ("picking over"), which recalls T. C. and
Coffer's actions after the Starbuck massacre and anticipates the real
vultures and vulturous T. C. and Coffer after the carnage in Agua
Verde, is present here. Pike's language suggests that Sykes is already
dead, thereby revealing his increasing sense of despair.

> DUTCH: What about our gold?

Despite the plural possessive, this question exemplifies the same
kind of repellent materialism that the Bunch has displayed all along.
Pike's response continues in this vein:

> PIKE: We'll take one sack to pay our way—bury the rest.

Dutch and Tector cast suspicious looks at each other, suggesting
that even now, when the Bunch should be united by external threats,
they still do not think and operate as a group: some of the men
anticipate that one of them will steal the money. Pike solves the
problem, ending his last statement by saying, "together." In concert,
the Bunch will protect their individual greed. The passage from the
realm of the ideal (which predominated in the steam-bath sequence)
to the material realm is now complete. At least for the time, materialism has triumphed. It remains for the film's ending sequences to
shift the moral emphasis back toward the ideal, a move brought to
fruition with the return for Angel.

It's important to keep in mind that the Bunch does not return
to Agua Verde for Angel; they go there to ask Mapache to deal
with Thornton and his gang. In other words, they intend to ask
Mapache to do something that they should do themselves. However,
although the Bunch wants to abdicate one responsibility, they nonetheless wind up taking on an even greater one: rescuing Angel. Yet
before that point, the group is still reluctant to oppose morally
objectionable acts. Even after witnessing the terrible treatment to
which Angel is subjected, the Bunch does nothing. Despite the fact
that they are all disturbed by what they see—with Pike and Dutch
commenting to each other on their anger—the only statements made
to Mapache are those by Pike: "I want to buy him back; I'll give
you half my share for him." The statement is interesting for a number
of reasons. There is the accent on selfish practicality (Pike offers
only half of his money), a carryover from the discussions among

Plate 20. The torture of Angel in Agua Verde: Zamorra and Herrera bracket Angel while Mapache approvingly looks on from the back of the car.

the Bunch in the previous scenes. Additionally, Pike's offer implies that Angel has already been sold, which indeed he has. By virtue of Dutch's silence about the Bunch's complicity in the diversion of the rifles and ammunition, the Bunch, to invoke the colloquial phrase, has sold Angel out.

Mapache refuses Pike's offer, expressing himself, like Pike, in mercantile terms that mask the emotional reason for his statement: "I need no gold, and I don't sell this one." Mapache will not sell Angel back to Pike because Angel betrayed him. The issue is now one of his honor, which Mapache intends to satisfy by publicly humiliating his betrayer. Moreover, even if Mapache had known of the other men's involvement in the theft of the rifles, Angel's act is probably more offensive to him since Angel is Mexican. In this sense, Mapache is undoubtedly very much like Angel. Angel cannot forget that it was Mapache who killed his father; Mapache cannot forget that it was a Mexican, one of his own people, who acted against him.

We might also surmise that since Mapache learns from Teresa's mother that Angel stole the guns (this despite Mohr's aide's description of Mapache's "superb intelligence corps"), it is also possible that Mapache learned from the same woman that the man he killed in Don José's village was Angel's father; knowledge of this fact may suggest to Mapache that this Mexican youth has both personal and political grudges against him, thereby posing a double threat that should be dealt with as quickly as possible.

Pike's practical reply to Mapache's refusal to sell Angel ("Why not? You've had your fun with him") completely discounts the issue of honor, an intentional oversight considering that the return for Angel is prompted by a desire to do the honorable thing. Pike also overlooks that fact that Angel has embarrassed Mapache politically (a realm of which Pike, like the Gorches, is only vaguely aware) and that the "general" needs to have his political pride satisfied as well.

In the steam-bath and mountaintop sequences, a profusion of words is used, in the first instance to divert the emotional conflict in the Bunch between their ideals and their selfishness to the safer realm of a verbal debate between the moral and material realms, and in the second case to try to mask the sorrow over Angel's capture by expressing it through discontent and aggression. In both instances, though, words fail to hide the fact that the topics under discussion are really the most elemental matters concerning what is right and wrong. The sight in Agua Verde of Angel being tortured dismisses all abstract considerations, ultimately making it quite plain to the Bunch that what is needed is something at which they excel: action.

Dragged like a toy at the end of a rope behind Mapache's car, a symbol of mechanistic progress (another example of which, the machine gun, will prove to be the entire village's undoing), Angel seems to be fulfilling the ambiguity implicit in Dutch's statement that "he played his string right out to the end." More important, though, the string that Angel is playing out is his keeping silent about the Bunch's involvement in the diversion of the guns, a gesture that ultimately plays on the sentimental strings of the Bunch's sensibilities, until at last they return their Mexican friend's grand gesture with an appropriately grand gesture of their own.

Before that point, though, an anxious and awkward period must be passed through. The Agua Verde adobe sequence is notable not only for its tension but also for its virtual lack of speech and simultaneous richness of communication.

The guilt over Angel's abandonment, which in these sequences seems virtually palpable, first surfaces in Pike's awkwardness with his Mexican lover. Fortunately for Pike, the squabbling over money coming from the Gorches' room next door provides him with an excuse to leave his room temporarily. Pike has already gone through a series of gestures with the Mexican woman that exemplify his shame at trying to avoid being emotional with her, a shame that the liquor he has been drinking before and during the sequence has done nothing to diminish. Repeatedly, the woman's candid and direct looks at Pike cause him to avoid eye contact with her, something he can at this point achieve only with the members of the Bunch, which makes it quite clear how emotionally immature these men are.

After strapping on his gun, Pike walks across the room and parts the curtain between his and the Gorches' room. As Pike stands in the doorway, we see that Tector is idly playing with a tiny baby bird;[28] in this image, which reinvokes the image of the children torturing the ants and scorpions, humans again manipulate animals for their amusement. What follows are a series of "statements" conveyed through eye contact that signify what Pike, Lyle, and Tector are thinking; the direct way that these men meet each other's gazes shows that Pike and the Gorches are finally confronting the emotional issue that is bothering them all: Angel's capture.

First Tector and then Lyle look up at Pike, silently questioning his presence. Pike challenges the Gorches to ask more aggressively what he wants by looking at, and thereby confronting, each of his inquisitors in the order in which they first looked at him—first Tector, then Lyle. Lyle narrows his eyes in thought, trying to understand fully what Pike wants in the same way that he tried to divine Pike's reaction to Angel's mistreatment when the Bunch first rode into Agua Verde. Tector is still looking at Pike. Pike looks again at Tector, then at Lyle. Then, still keeping Lyle's gaze, Pike simply says, "Let's go." Lyle again narrows his eyes as if to divine the statement's true significance, then looks over at Tector. Tector meets his brother's gaze, understands his confusion, and looks over at Pike for an answer. Pike looks at Tector to reiterate the implications of his statement and, having "answered" Tector, looks once again at Lyle, ending this gesture by narrowing his eyes to indicate determination. As though to confirm what he has understood by this series of communications, Lyle looks one last time at Tector, then at Pike. Then, for the first time in the film, Lyle acts as the sole spokesman for himself and Tector, no longer invoking his brother in the reply (as in the "me and Tector figured" during the argument about the division of the Starbuck "gold") but simply and resolutely speaking for both of them. "Why not," he says. Unlike earlier in the film (as when Pike reluctantly agrees to join the revelry in Agua Verde after the train heist), this statement is not an expression of despair but a direct affirmation of the fact that there is only one right thing to do.

When Pike returns to his room and pays the Mexican woman, awkwardness and averted eye gestures again occur; he simply cannot express himself forthrightly with a woman (that is, except through violence, as he does when returning the fire of the woman who shoots him in the back). Pike's treatment of the Mexican woman here is so terribly materialistic and insulting that at one point the woman must avert her eyes from Pike out of embarrassment for the way that he is betraying his essential humanity. After tossing a few gold coins at the woman, Pike walks out.

After the men leave the Gorches' room, Peckinpah zooms in on the panting baby bird, a poor plaything worn out by the kind of moral indifference that the Gorches and Pike have finally repudiated. As they emerge from the adobe, the men all look in turn at Dutch, who is dispiritedly whittling and, like Thornton at the film's beginning and end, forlornly sitting with his back to a wall. In response, Dutch directly meets Pike, Tector, and Lyle's gazes in a replay of the order of eye contact during the adobe sequence. Then Dutch looks again at Pike.

The communication between Pike and Dutch outside the adobe is nonverbal, a quality we might very well expect given the great understanding that always exists between the two men. Moreover, we are given an interchange of gestures and reactions that not only mirror those that Pike and Dutch exchanged when they were watching Angel being tortured but that will also be repeated at the film's end when Sykes and Thornton face each other. The relative physical positioning will be repeated as well, with the superior, authoritative member looking down at his second in command (or, in Thornton's case, potential second in command), who is seated on the ground with his back to a wall: here, Pike looks down on Dutch; later, Sykes will look down on Thornton. The secondary member's physical position (the low vantage point and the fact of being backed up against a wall) indicates an impasse that somehow must be overcome.

Pike and Dutch engage in a communication even more perfect than the one just achieved among Pike, Tector, and Lyle, since here no words are used. Dutch looks at Pike, "reads" him, and just barely begins to smile; Pike not only looks back but for one of the few times in the film also smiles. Dutch smiles broadly and then laughs. (This is the same triad of gestures that Thornton and Sykes will exhibit at the film's end.) Only Dutch responds to the men's unspoken common intentions with laughter, thus indicating that he realizes more clearly, a bit more consciously, the true purpose behind their return to the center of town: not just to redeem Angel but to redeem themselves as well through a final, concerted act that will surpass everything else they've done. Dutch's laughter demonstrates his ability to intuit and anticipate the joy to which such a pure act can give rise and signals the fact that the compact, begun inside the adobe, has been sealed through good humor (a reinvocation of the bonding through laughter we've previously seen). Everything is now in readiness. This time the Bunch will indeed "do it right."

The four men prepare their guns; once ready, they pause for a fraction of a second to line up, thereby asserting in physical terms the unanimity that they have already reached emotionally and psychologically. As the Bunch move into formation, they repeat the response to Pike's "fall in" from the Starbuck scene and echo the clockwork precision of the train heist, with the difference that in the present case, we see the Bunch displaying the kind of "sticking together" that Pike has always wanted them to have, a unity deriving from fidelity to a common cause that has compassion, not greed, as its basis.

The regimentation of this march befits the essentially military mission that these men are on, right down to the military-sounding snare drum accompaniment. There are further parallels with the Bunch's first march. In both scenes, a counterpoint to the Bunch's precision is provided by an essentially buffoonish collection of people: the temperance union marching band in the first scene (whose music, although it comes later than the Bunch's march, nonetheless contrasts with it) and the drunken Mexicans in the Agua Verde scene. Additionally, whereas at the film's beginning the Bunch, drunk with desire for money, had their actions contrasted with an accompaniment associated with sobriety, here music is played and sung by a literally drunken group of people whose inebriation con trasts with the sobriety of the Bunch's mission, which nonetheless turns to a kind of joyous drunkenness after the shooting begins.

Agua Verde also provides an important comparison with the departure from Don José's village. When the Bunch left Don José's village, after a life-affirming fiesta, they were a unified group being

Plate 21. The Bunch's final march, as they head back to rescue Angel.

serenaded as benefactors and heroes. In Agua Verde, after a series of situations connoting death—the abandonment of Angel, the failed attempt at diversion with prostitutes, the terrible emotional estrangement in the adobe scenes with Pike and the Gorches—the Bunch is once again alienated.

Physical separation as a sign of alienation, used with success in the mountaintop scene, reappears in the adobe sequences. Pike and the Gorches are in separate rooms. Dutch is even further removed; he is totally outside the building in which the other men are located. The manner in which the Bunch, when leaving the adobe, is reassembled piece by piece—first Pike, then the inseparable Gorches, then Dutch, all then proceeding toward Angel—signals a rebuilding of the united Bunch and suggests a return to the type of fidelity and life we felt when they left Angel's village. (Moreover, the men leave the adobe in the same order used in the eye-contact sequence in the Gorches' room—first Pike, then Tector, then Lyle—a note of directorial precision that ranks these men according to the strength of their influence. As usual, Lyle is the minor member.) Yet in opposition to the positive connotations created by this orderliness, the insistent snare drum and the drunken trivialization of the Mexican song cast an apprehensive gloom over the proceedings. What we are being prepared for is the contradictory nature of the scene of Angel's reclamation, with Angel being restored to the Bunch, then abruptly stolen away, then (figuratively) recovered again as the Bunch make all of Agua Verde pay for Mapache's brutality. Finally, Peckinpah will end the film with two more recoveries, first by resurrecting the Bunch in the flesh through their successors—Thornton and the Sykes gang—then resurrecting them through the images that hover spiritlike over Thornton, Sykes, and Don José's men as they ride away.

It's significant that at the film's end, the Bunch's newfound unity of purpose and action doesn't occur in the United States but in Mexico. In other words, we're on the other side of the mirror, in that special Peckinpah region where anything can happen. The film has been leading us here all along. We have to wait for that final moment, though. By photographing the first part of the Bunch's march through Agua Verde's heat-shimmering, dust-filled air, Peckinpah lends a dreamlike unreality to the image. Additionally, the flattening of the perspective (caused by the use of a telephoto lens) prolongs the drama of the moment, giving the sequence the quality of the kind of nightmare in which one is moving but making no progress; the telephoto lens also collapses the Mexicans in the foreground against the Bunch, so that the Mexicans seem at every moment to be threatening the Bunch with their (apparent) proximity.[29]

However, this anxious part of the scene lasts only a short time. When the Bunch rounds a corner, Peckinpah photographs them with a shorter focal-length lens, which gives a more normal perspective. Having turned the corner, Pike, Dutch, and the Gorches can now be seen by Mapache and his retinue. Once again, the Bunch pauses. The nightmare is finally over; a fantastic reality, full of a different kind of horror, one made up not of compromise and abandonments but of forthright explosions of revenge, is about to take place.

At this point, Mapache uses words whose literal meaning masks what he really feels: "You want Angel, no? All right, I am gonna give it to you." Mapache is quite careful not to state in what condition he intends to deliver him, though.

Immediately before Angel shot Teresa, Dutch, anticipating what was about to happen, cried out "No!" Here, just after Mapache starts to bring his knife near Angel's throat and before he actually cuts it, Dutch once again opens his mouth to cry out. But he cannot speak; this is one of his own being killed. Dutch can only look and stare.

After Mapache is shot (first by Pike, then by Dutch and Lyle),

Plate 22. The shooting of Mapache.

the whole village freezes. Herrera, Zamorra, Mohr—everyone is struck immobile by the act's swiftness and daring. Seeing this reaction, and knowing that despite the odds the Bunch has once again achieved an effect quite out of proportion to their strength in numbers, Dutch laughs once more, just as he laughed before the Starbuck escape when contemplating Pike's plan to use the temperance union marchers as a diversion, and just as he smiled during the train heist when, after getting the drop on some soldiers, he knew that the plan was going to succeed.

At this point, Pike makes his final decision for the Bunch. It's possible that having so outrageously stunned Agua Verde, the Bunch might conceivably be able to move beyond this exaggerated Mexican standoff and safely ride out of town. However, it's more likely that Pike reasons that there's simply nowhere for them to go from here. In Pike's words from an earlier scene, they are about to complete their "last go 'round." Pike turns and shoots Mohr, who is clearly the second most objectionable man in the village. After Mohr's death, Mapache's two seconds-in-command—Herrera and Zamorra—are shot, followed by Mohr's aide, thereby killing off everyone with any degree of military authority in the town. Having rid the village of its leaders, the Bunch now turns their full attention on the troops.

The chaos that breaks loose in Agua Verde is similar to that in Starbuck, in that the Bunch initiates it and bests their opponents. The Bunch is in full control, right up to the end, when a young boy delivers the first of three *coup de grace* shots to Pike. (Since the child shoots Pike with one of the weapons that the Bunch had stolen, his act replays the manner in which the Bunch turned Mapache's machine gun against him.)[30] Except for Dutch, who has never seemed as brutal as the rest, each man takes his turn at the machine gun, first Tector, then Lyle, then Pike. As we might expect, Pike exceeds everyone else's efforts. Dutch uses grenades; Pike does him one better by using machine-gun fire to detonate boxes of dynamite. With one last (unanswered) call to Dutch to "Come on, you lazy bastard," Pike and Dutch go out in a blaze of protesting gunfire.

After the massacre, the vultures arrive, first as animals, then in the form of their human counterparts: T. C., Coffer, and the rest of Thornton's gang, who are preceded by glimpses of mourning villagers, women in black, and grim funeral processions, images that create a sensation of depression and despair that contrasts with the feelings of transcendence and hope that Peckinpah will soon create. There follows the looting of the bodies, a replay of the aftermath of the Starbuck slaughter. Then Deke Thornton moves forward and tenderly removes Pike's gun from his holster. For Thornton, the gun has obviously assumed talismanic significance; his taking of it presages his assumption of Pike's newfound political mission. This gesture also marks the beginning of reverence and acts as an affirmation of tradition, effects that are undercut somewhat by Thornton's forlornly sitting down outside the village walls. Finally, after Thornton acknowledges the truth of Coffer's observation that he "ain't coming," the gang leaves.

T. C., Coffer, and the other members of Thornton's gang, with the dead members of the Bunch hanging over their saddles as Harrigan wanted them, ride off to their doom. When Thornton, sitting with his back to one of Agua Verde's walls, hears the shots that finish them off, he smiles. After a few moments, whose desolation is underscored by the sound of the whistling wind and the sight of blowing dust (a silent interlude that Peckinpah uses to build up our expectations for the film's finale), Sykes, Don José, and the mountain Indians come riding up.

Plate 23. Pike, during the Agua Verde massacre, about to spin around and shoot through a mirror before he is shot (in the back) by the woman.

Plate 24. Pike and Dutch toward the massacre's end.

Plate 25. Thornton, after the massacre, just before he takes Pike's gun.

SYKES: I didn't expect to find you here.
THORNTON: Why not? I sent 'em back; that's all I said I'd do.

Thornton's comment demonstrates how closely allied the film's three leaders—Pike, Thornton, and Mapache—are. Each of them makes a statement whose literal meaning is intentionally at variance with what the speaker really feels. Pike's "We share very few sentiments with our government" and Mapache's "I . . . give [Angel] to you" are both intentionally duplicitous. In the present sequence, Thornton lives up to the letter of his pledge to Harrigan when he sends his gang, with the corpses of the Bunch, back to the United States, but he retains what he obviously regards as the spirit of his deal by remaining behind.

SYKES: They didn't get very far.
THORNTON: I figured.
SYKES: What are your plans?
THORNTON: Drift around down here. Try to stay out of jail.

Thornton undoubtedly has no real plans, although I think it's safe to say that he intentionally omits his hope that he can join up with Sykes. Then, the great offer: to fight with purpose, for idealism,

125

Plate 26. The departure from Angel's village, whose lyricism is reinvoked at the end of *The Wild Bunch*.

for social change, to fight back against the oppression that we've seen throughout the film.

> SYKES: Well, me and the boys here, we got some work to do. You wanna come along? It ain't like it used to be, but it'll do.

Yet, for one last time recalling Pike's "stick together" speech, we realize that in an important sense, it *is* "like it used to be." The Bunch, in a new incarnation, is spiritually and physically together again, a fact affirmed by the next action: the repetition of bond-creating gestures that occurred between Pike and Dutch outside the Agua Verde adobe (which tells us that Sykes now equals Pike and that Thornton is now his sidekick).[31] Thornton looks up and begins to smile; Sykes laughs, and then Thornton laughs. Finally, the men, laughing, ride off together. As they do, the old Bunch comes back to life, reappearing in images, and *they* all laugh,[32] which tells us more successfully than words that because fidelity is now linked to political purpose, it's not only like it used to be, it's better, and that eventually all of them—Pike, Thornton, Angel, Dutch, the Gorches, and Sykes—will finally be united—in legend, in memory, forever.[33]

126

This Cactus Eden

The Ballad of Cable Hogue counters the common belief that Peckinpah is capable of producing only action pictures about violent men. Instead, *Cable Hogue* clearly demonstrates that when he wishes to do so, Peckinpah can create extraordinary scenes of tenderness and compassion between men and women.

That Peckinpah should have chosen to follow *The Wild Bunch* with *Cable Hogue* indicates an apparent desire to move away from films involving predominantly male ethics toward a more comprehensive view of human nature. True, *Cable Hogue* does evidence a typical Peckinpah nostalgia for a tradition-valuing past and an aversion to mechanistic progress, and the film does contain significant amounts of effective comedy. Yet for all of its good humor, *Cable* despairs of the possibility of sustaining compassion and companionship at the same time that it dramatizes the need for these attributes.

Like all of the films in the Peckinpah canon, *Cable Hogue* involves the necessary interaction of one or more pairs of central protagonists, each of whom has in some sense an important lien on the other's existence. Actually, the film provides us with three pairs of characters. The first pair consists of Cable (Jason Robards) and Taggart and Bowen; the latter two characters (played by L. Q. Jones and Strother Martin, respectively) actually function as an evil presence that has been bifurcated into two individuals, with one, Taggart, evilly conceived, and the other, Bowen, comically conceived. The other pairs are Cable and Josh (David Warner) and Cable and Hildy (Stella Stevens). As the film unfolds, we watch how, regardless of the fundamental nature of their relationships—

either deadly (Cable and Taggart and Bowen), amiable (Cable and Josh), or life-connoting (Cable and Hildy)—these pairings lead inevitably to death. Indeed, *Cable Hogue* is a tragedy, one that leaves us with a distinct sense of regret.

To appropriate the words of Cable himself, the film is the story of a desert rat who "found [water] where it wasn't." That phrase conveys two distinct, contradictory meanings. Obviously, water cannot be found where it doesn't exist but only where it simply hadn't been discovered before. The fact that in *Cable Hogue* the stage company has been searching for water in the desert for thirty-five years without finding any, and that they work for thirteen days immediately adjacent to Cable's property with similarly uneventful results, suggests that Cable's discovery of water is indicative of nearly divine good fortune, as though he has found salvation in the wilderness.

Indeed, it is quite clear that *Cable Hogue* not only follows the Edenic story but also incorporates a number of other motifs culled from Genesis: the presence of the untouched, pristine wilderness; the invocation of God; the granting of what is essentially a garden in the desert; the strong opposition between spirituality on the one hand and the tendency toward selfishness and self-aggrandizement (which appears in Genesis in the form of pride) on the other; and the conflict between carnality and transcendental qualities. *Cable Hogue* goes so far as to include serpents, not only literal snakes but snakelike figures. The most prominent of these figures are Taggart and Bowen (whom Cable torments with snakes), who are presented as despoilers of the garden. Likewise, Cable initially views Josh as a snakelike seducer of Claudia, another man's wife.

Josh also functions as a biblical corrupt priest, while Hildy most clearly recalls Mary Magdalene, the saintly whore. Yet the roles that the film's main characters essay are not exclusively realized. With admirable economy, *Cable Hogue* grants each of its three main characters a dual status. Cable not only fills the role of Adam, but also partakes of God-like characteristics, acting as both lawgiver (establishing rules and geographic boundaries for the water station) and avenger. Hildy is both a saintly figure, reviled by the so-called good people of the town (who, with their phony piety, function as the hypocritical Pharisees), and a pronounced materialist, a woman who intends to use her physical charms to attract and secure a rich man who will provide for her. Josh is, quite obviously, at once a truly religious man (he is named for a strongly religious figure—

Plate 27. A snake for two snakes: Taggart and Bowen in *The Ballad of Cable Hogue.*

Joshua) and the worst kind of zealot: one who uses his religiosity to seduce women.

The manifest irony in *Cable Hogue* is that whereas in the Bible Adam and Eve are cast out of Eden for eating the forbidden fruit, Cable is simultaneously redeemed and condemned because of his passion for Hildy. Surely it is no accident that Cable's death takes place almost immediately after Hildy returns to the desert. However, we must recognize as well that as Adam and Eve are fated to fall, so too is Cable destined to fail in his desire to leave the desert. In fact, one of the major regrets that the film creates in its viewers results from our realization that Cable is doomed to perish at the water hole precisely because he is not constituted to survive and prosper anywhere. Cable can neither leave the desert with Hildy (and thereby repudiate his loneliness and his need for revenge) nor live out his life where he is. With vengeance and materialism condemning him to his fate, the only way that Cable can be redeemed and released is through his death.

Cable Hogue also offers a parable for the growth and development of the United States. Quite simply, the film is the tale of a prospector-like character who finds riches beyond anything he expected and who fights an internal battle between his desire to be satisfied with what he has and the temptation to take full advantage of the fiscal possibilities of his domain. In this tale, we can recognize the story of the growth of America and a sketch for the kind of temptations to which the country will be subjected as it evolves into a monstrous mercantile beast. Despite its love theme, with Hildy functioning at times as the country's better, idealistic, and compassionate aspect, *Cable Hogue* does not hold out much hope for America's moral development, especially if the country continues along the opportunistic path that it has already mapped out for itself. The film makes it quite plain that materialism's greatest incarnation, capitalism, is an obsessive disease that compels the practitioner to treat virtually all things, whether goods or people, as commodities. By the way that its action is resolved, *Cable Hogue* emphasizes that unchecked materialism will inevitably destroy us through the very impulses toward progress that initially vitalized us; the land, which was once bursting with promise, must eventually fall to ruin, with no promise of regeneration. This is, after all, the Edenic warning: that disobedience to the way of faith—expressed as acting either in accordance with a divine injunction or in response to the behest of one's conscience, both of which tendencies are antithetical to materialism—must result in ruination and expulsion from happiness. In this sense, *Cable Hogue* operates not only as a historical fable but as a religious one as well.

Given water's life-giving and life-sustaining properties (qualities underscored in Cable's parched wanderings during the film's title sequence), Cable's discovery is clearly the sign of a blessing, one vouchsafed to a man who immediately before finding water has totally submitted himself to God's will. In fact, the film's religious subtext continually asserts itself, first in Cable's addresses to God while he is dying of thirst and then in the satiric form of the itinerant preacher Josh, who despite his wryness is, like Cable, a man of great faith. Religion surfaces again in the touchingly compassionate interaction between Cable and Hildy and in the obsessive grudge that Cable holds against Taggart and Bowen.

In the desert, Cable is forcibly abandoned by Taggart and Bowen because there simply isn't enough water to sustain all three of them. When Cable finds the water and restores himself with it, the restoration suggests to him a series of actions that are, without exception, mercantile. In fact, in the initial stages of the film, before redemption through love affects Cable and Hildy, each character is afflicted with a taint endemic to civilization: a selfishness that manifests itself in uniformly materialistic ways.

Despite Cable's acknowledgment of the kindness shown him by the stage drivers (which he nonetheless sullies by appending to his offer of thanks the statement, " 'Til you're better paid"), he is concerned only with money. In fact, it is from the drivers that Cable learns that the forty-mile stretch between the towns of Dead Dog and Gila City is totally arid, a fact that suggests to him the value of his discovery of water. However, what sustains Cable before he meets the stage—indeed, even before he discovers water—is his desire to wreak vengeance on Taggart and Bowen. To express the desire for revenge in appropriate terms, Cable wants to repay Taggart and Bowen for their cruelty. Thus, Cable's statement after being refreshed by the discovered water ("I licked them bastards; now all I gotta do is wait") not only asserts the revenge theme but seems to drive out any thoughts of gratitude toward God for vouchsafing him the means with which to continue living.

In fact, throughout *Cable Hogue* characters approach and then retreat from religious notions involving either love or God (in the film's terms—especially as it shows love expressed in sacred ways—these concepts are virtually equivalent), sheltering themselves in the petty values and attitudes of materialism. *Cable Hogue* repeatedly dramatizes the antagonism between the realms of the sacred (fidelity, kindness, friendship, and love) and the profane (betrayal, selfishness, and hate). The most significant action in the film takes place in the desert, whose ambiance and associated values are opposed to those of the town, thus suggesting quite strongly that the characters' actions represent a debate about how people should live. In this sense, *Cable Hogue* obviously intends to be taken as a parable with a very valuable lesson to teach.

After the interlude with the charitable stage drivers, Cable immediately begins to pervert water's life-sustaining, merciful aspect to material ends. He shoots his first customer (who tries to leave without paying) after the man attempts to shoot Cable. Earlier, we had seen Cable unable to shoot either Taggart or Bowen, whom he obviously recognized as mercenary characters. The fact that Cable can now kill in order to survive points up the distinction between the two situations: Cable's capacity for fiscal self-protectiveness is greater than his presently weak sense of self-preservation. By the film's end, though, when Cable saves Bowen from being run over, we realize that through love, Cable has completely changed, eschewing self-protectiveness in favor of a higher ideal: helping a fellow man. What Cable is looking out for at that point is neither himself nor money but the health of his soul.

However, when he first discovers the water and thereby is delivered from death by an act of mercy, Cable begins to plan on how to capitalize on his find. As soon as Josh (who seems to be a truly kind man) turns up, the preacher's statement that the discovery of water could mean "a lot of money" to someone motivates Cable to travel to town to stake his claim—in Cable's terms, to "go in among 'em."

Like Cable, Hildy, a town whore, is at first characterized as overwhelmingly self-centered. In fact, it is precisely at the moment when Cable contracts for his two acres of desert that Hildy brings in a second customer. The simultaneity of materialistic actions confirms a simultaneity of materialistic intentions. After failing to convince the stage company manager that he has discovered water (thereby affirming the man's lack of faith), Cable then enters the bank, where a predictably mercantile discussion takes place. We might be tempted to conclude that the banker lends Cable a hundred dollars solely because of Cable's plea for faith (even if Cable does express his request in fiscal terms: "I'm worth something, ain't I?"); however, the banker's generosity is tempered by our realization that he is also making a relatively small investment in hopes of a significant return on his money. If, after thirty-five years of searching, there does turn out to be water in the desert, whoever owns the rights to that water stands to make a great deal of money.

No sooner does Cable leave the bank than he spots Hildy bidding adieu to her second customer. The comic business with the animated Indian face on the money does not temper the fact that the first thing Cable does with his loan is to indulge his selfishness by carrying out a powerfully impersonal transaction: the purchase of Hildy's sexual favors. Thus, when Cable appears at Hildy's room (which is situated above another place of commerce, a saloon), she asks, "Did you want to see me?" while staring at Cable's bankroll. As soon as she sees that Cable can pay for sex, Hildy tells him, "Come on in."

Just as money and monetary references function in the film as the major examples of life's material aspects, emotional and sexual longings, when they are allied with genuine tenderness, stand in for the truly spiritual aspects of existence. This opposition between the material and spiritual is made concrete (albeit within the context of a comic episode) when, during the saloon liaison with Hildy, Cable loses his erection, his desire thwarted by his fear that Josh might be betraying him out at the water hole. As Cable puts it, "Gotta go; that pious son-of-a-bitch coulda sold me out." This consideration is prompted by the reference that the film's second preacher, the leader of a revivalist meeting, makes to the devil: "The devil seeks to destroy you with—machines!" Judging by his worried reaction, Cable is obviously reminded of Josh and apparently feels that Josh may very well be involved in truly satanic, snakelike machinations as the despoiler of Cable's economic Garden of Eden.

In the saloon scene with Hildy, we see Cable collapsing into a sole concern with his monetary prospects. The identical kind of protectiveness, a manifestation of innate human pettiness, is echoed at this point by Hildy, who, when she sees Cable preparing to leave, says, "What about me and my money?" Cable coarsely tells her that she doesn't deserve any money because no business has transpired between them. Cable explains, "I got business at the springs," and hastily departs.

The contrast between the physical and spiritual realms is also exemplified through Josh. Josh is first seen using his status as a preacher to seduce a woman, an activity in which he has apparently been involved for quite a while: thus his mention of "sisters of the spirit" when he is showing Cable photos of naked females and his reference to "baptizing them," an obvious euphemism for sex. Nevertheless, Josh is eventually undone by a true affection for Claudia, which develops in spite of his intentions.

Like Josh with Claudia, Cable at first treats his eventual love interest in the film as little more than an object. It is only later in the film, after Cable and Hildy develop true affection for one another, that Cable finally understands love. (However, there is a minor lapse when Cable, in a materialistic argument with Josh about payment for the preacher's lodgings, replies to Hildy's "You never charged me nothing" by saying, "That's because you never charged me nothing," thereby reducing their lovemaking to prostitution.)

The realization about love that Cable comes to does not differ significantly from the insights in the film concerning other important values that transcend earthly, material considerations. The film's moments of stillness and wonder don't occur just in the scenes of tenderness between Cable and Hildy (or at the times when Josh is powerfully missing Claudia); rather, they happen whenever some idealistic passion takes hold of one or more characters. At each of these points, characters experience feelings that without exception cause them to embrace values greater than those that might typically concern any one individual.

Although selfless love of another person certainly qualifies as one such ideal, so too does another kind of love: the love for one's country. Immediately after Cable signs the contract with the stage company, the stage driver, Ben (Slim Pickens), gives Cable a package. Ben says, "I reckon this is about the most important thing of all." Cable, still mindful of the material realm, replies, "Yeah, what's it gonna cost me?" Ben replies, "Nothing." Yet as soon as Cable sees that the package contains an American flag, all commercial considerations disappear. "Gonna have to buy you a flagpole," Ben says. "I'll make my own," Cable replies.

To underscore the scene's significance, Peckinpah employs two techniques that he will repeatedly use at special points throughout the film: a reverential lack of dialogue and an editing technique that magically elides time. In the present scene, we see Josh silently walking away from the camera and into the desert after Cable accepts the flag; in the next shot we see Josh walk back toward the water station and doff his hat (Cable does the same) after the flag is raised on the pole. The editing makes the time between the acceptance of the flag and the flag's raising (during which period the flagpole must have been erected) disappear into insignificance; indeed, compared to the importance of the tenderly patriotic feelings engendered by the gift of the flag and its raising, that intermediate time must have seemed quite unimportant.[1] Here, as with other special times in the film, Peckinpah shoots the flag raising at the magic hour just before sunset, which lends the scene a golden glow and emphasizes the unique aspect of this and similar portions of the film.

Cable Hogue is full of events that might very well qualify as miracles. At the film's beginning, Cable, nearly dead from thirst, realizes that he must give himself up to God: "Lord, you call it; I'm just plain done in. Amen." At that moment, he finds mud caked on his boot, indicating that there is water nearby. This capitulation to divine will comes after Cable's contentious effrontery to God (he requests water with the ironic comment, "Just thought I'd mention it") and his subsequent attempt to bargain with the deity: he says that if God would just send him a drop or two of water, he would never again commit the sin that he must have committed, "whatever in the hell it was." These statements immediately reveal Cable's ambivalent religious attitude, for while he addresses his requests to

God, he insults God at the same time, even bringing in considerations of mercantilism: the bargaining for only a drop or two of water in exchange for a repudiation of disobedience, which qualifies as a false bargain at that, since Cable obviously doesn't believe that he has sinned.

Despite these affronts, water is nonetheless granted to Cable in a gesture whose merciful aspect is lost on him. No sooner does Cable refresh himself with the water than he repudiates the God with whom he had pleaded by claiming that it was through his own efforts that he was saved. "Told you I was gonna live," Cable says, echoing what he had earlier told Taggart and Bowen. Cable goes on to claim that he alone was responsible for discovering the water, an assertion that he emphasizes by repeating his name over and over in a quasi-religious litany affirming his power and authority: "This is Cable Hogue talking, Hogue, me, Cable Hogue, Hogue, me, me, I did it, Cable Hogue, I found it, me." In the same mood, Cable goes on to alter the facts of his last meeting with Taggart and Bowen so that he emerges as a heroic figure. "I whipped 'em both; now all I gotta do is wait," he says, although, as in the discovery of the water, Cable's survival has less to do with his own efforts than it has to do with either chance or some divine plan. The choice of explanation obviously depends on the viewer's inclinations, since the film's attitude toward its events is intentionally ambiguous.

Regardless of the cause of the film's actions, it is nonetheless plain that *Cable Hogue* encourages a humanistic attitude in which morality, whether divinely or humanly derived and inspired, must take precedence over materialism. Moreover, the film makes it clear that true religion springs not from the apparently pious (like the hypocritical, Bible-quoting stage rider at the film's beginning) but from those who act with compassion and humanity.[2] Whether it be the tenderness between Cable and Hildy or the empathy between Josh and Cable, this is the film's real religiousness. Indeed, it is not by chance that virtually all of *Cable Hogue*'s truly inspiring moments (aside from the flag-raising ceremony, which involves love of a special sort) involve either sexual passion or earthly love. *Cable Hogue* means to make it quite plain that desire and piety not only are not antithetical but are intimately wedded. What is in conflict with religion, though, is materialism. *Cable Hogue* asserts that the repudiation of materialism is a necessary prerequisite to true love and salvation.

Eventually, Hildy rides out to the water station to be with Cable; apparently, she has been driven out of town for having the effrontery to do the town's materialism one better by selling not just goods but love. By this time, a true emotion, one divorced from any consideration other than the need for affection and companionship, has taken hold of both characters. Hildy must have recognized in her second meeting with Hogue that Cable was treating her as a person, not as a purchased object, as is witnessed by a later scene in which Hildy asks, "Didn't it bother you none, Hogue, what I am?" Cable's reply shears away the fiscal aspect of Hildy's trade. "Human being," he answers. Cable cleans out the shack for Hildy's stay, and the good graces of his faith in her vouchsafes him the rarity of a lovely portrait: Hildy, bathed in the golden light of the shack's oil lamp, asking Cable to come in and join her.

There is clearly something special, and virtually divine, in the image of Hildy in a white nightgown beckoning Cable into the shack. Hildy remarks, "You've seen it [this picture] before," and Cable responds, "Lady, nobody's ever seen you before." Such is the force of the scene that we can readily attest to the truth of Cable's reply.

The montage sequence that follows, orchestrated to the strains of the song "Butterfly Morning," which is sung by Hildy and Cable,

Plate 28. Hildy with Cable during her second desert visit.

is indisputably the tenderest scene that Peckinpah has ever created. Only the most hardened filmgoer will not regret the point, after Hildy's bath in the rain barrel, when the stage arrives and breaks up the couple's revelry. Yet a later interruption of a similar sequence (this time by the bickering between Cable and Josh) is overcome by having Hildy, who has thrown Cable and Josh out of the shack, emerge near dawn, extend her hand to Cable, and in a gesture of forgiveness take him back inside.

For all of the film's loveliness, though, there is a powerful suggestion of despair in the way that *Cable Hogue* assigns to its three major characters such antithetical tendencies. Of course, given the film's abundance of opposite qualities inhering in the same individuals, one could conclude that human beings are full of the potential for both growth and destruction. Yet the manner in which characters abruptly change their attitudes—from selfishness to charity, hate to love—suggests that the universe in which the film takes place may best be described as chaotic. Moreover, although we see Hildy, Josh, and Cable redeemed by love, at the film's end we also witness the characters' redemptions coming to naught. Hildy eventually returns to San Francisco and her materialistic existence; Josh undoubtedly goes back to his occasionally hypocritical behavior; and Cable is never allowed even to leave the desert and attempt to begin a life free from vengeful and selfish impulses. Even the overriding charitable gesture that Cable evidences (his forgiving Bowen and leaving him in charge of the water station) yields no positive consequences; as we see from the film's conclusion, Bowen has not remained at the station, which has fallen into ruin.

The essential element in *Cable Hogue* that, in league with materialism, triumphs over the positive aspects of love is revenge. With vengeance in the forefront, the film qualifies as a tragedy that is both typical and idiosyncratic. *Cable Hogue* begins with, and shows the growth of, Cable's enmity toward Taggart and Bowen. Cable is quite aware that the only thing keeping him in the desert and preventing him from leaving with Hildy, who represents the blossoming of his affections (thus the flower he shyly presents to her at one point), is his waiting for Taggart and Bowen's return. The death wish here seems greater than the life force, although ironically, for all of the positive associations attendant with Hildy, she nevertheless brings with her on her last visit the instrument of Cable's death— a car, symbol of deadly progress, fueled not by life-giving water

(Bowen: "I guess you need the water . . . for the steam?") but a newer, more "advanced," and explosive liquid (the chauffeur: "No, it burns gasoline").

The return of Taggart and Bowen to the desert sets in motion the machinery of revenge that Cable has been constructing all along and that eventually becomes his undoing. The opposition between love and revenge is made manifest in an exchange between Cable and Josh.

> JOSH (reclining on a mattress): My little Claudia springs to mind.
> CABLE: Burning with passion, eh preacher?
> JOSH: What about yours, brother Hogue?
> CABLE: Hell, I ain't never had a passion.
> JOSH: What do you call that vengeance that gnaws at the very walls of your soul?
> CABLE: Taggart and Bowen left me out there to die. If my feet don't turn cold and my back don't turn yellow and my legs stay under me, I aim to kill 'em for it. I don't call that a passion.
> JOSH: That's a passion that will water the dandelions over your grave.

Here, the "passion," an intentionally ambiguous word referring to both sexual and emotional desire as well as to a religious kind of suffering, signals the unfortunate obsession that presages destruction for Cable. (However, Josh's reference to watering the dandelions on Cable's grave somewhat tempers our sense of despair here by suggesting that tears of mourning will water the flowers.) One would hope that Cable's love and desire for Hildy would purge his soul of the need for vengeance, yet such a purging does not occur. Love provides only a brief respite from Cable's doomsday watch. (Indeed, even while Hildy is with Cable in the desert, the topic of revenge and its pointlessness is discussed, to no avail.)

Ironically, for all of its redemptive promise, even love itself has a painful, virtually destructive potential. Its fateful aspect is recognized by both Cable and Josh in the following exchange.

> JOSH: Funny thing—doesn't matter how much or how little you've wandered around, how many women you've been with, every once in a while one of them cuts right through, right straight into you.
> CABLE: What do you do about it?
> JOSH: I suppose maybe when you die you get over it.

Despite the melancholy conclusion to which the above dialogue leads us—that Cable is doomed either to suffer or to die—the real tragedy of *Cable Hogue* is not that Cable must remain in the desert to await Taggart and Bowen, nor that he is never given the chance to have a truly productive relationship with Hildy. The film's real tragedy is that even the best kind of love simply isn't enough to redeem Cable—and, by extension, all humans—from an obsession with death. Indeed, in the manner in which death is viewed as the only cure for love, we can see how powerfully disposed Cable is to remain trapped in this tragic paradox, with no possibility of escape.

Death crowns the film's final lovely moments. Josh's funeral peroration achieves an apotheosis of the all-too-human central character. Yet, as in the "Butterfly Morning" sequence, many of *Cable Hogue*'s most moving episodes have no dialogue. In particular, the points at which the usually verbose Josh is reduced to silence give evidence of how special the action really is. At each of these points, the film assumes a mythical status from which it very rarely departs.

Cable Hogue also has a pronounced fabulist tone; indeed, with its essentially religious text about love, money, and death, the film could justifiably be retitled *The Fable of Cable Hogue*. This fabulist aspect is most evident in the film's time elisions. At these points, *Cable Hogue*'s unique nature asserts itself, making us aware (as does the use of fast motion in the comic scenes) of how much this film differs from the director's other films.

Taggart and Bowen return to the desert toward the film's end. In self-defense, Cable justifiably kills the more evil of the two, Taggart, and spares the sniveling Bowen. Unfortunately, this compassionate act has extremely deadly consequences, since it makes way for a second act of compassion toward Bowen: saving him from being hit by Hildy's car, which results in Cable's being fatally run over by the vehicle. (The causality isn't quite as simple as it appears, since the car's emergency brake is disengaged when Cable slings his gear into the cab.)

Peckinpah splits our reactions to the film's resolution. Emotionally, we yearn for Hildy and Cable's successful departure for San Francisco. Yet intellectually we know that Cable is not a creature of the town: "Only thing I like about cities—city beds," Cable had commented. He would not spiritually prosper if trapped in a city's squalid emotions and mercantilism. Indeed, Cable seems unable to exist profitably outside of the desert, where his assertions of self

Plate 29. Cable as the victim of progress.

must be viewed as the solitary voice of one crying in the wilderness, a voice that, subsumed by those of other people, would be reduced to merely another noise within a frightfully loud din. Cable's childishness (he dances for joy after getting his loan) and bashful nature make him unsuitable for society.[3] Clearly, Cable is ruined by progress, by the movement of the United States from a predominantly rural to an urban nation, manifested in the shift from the physical expansiveness of the desert to the constricted, fiscal expensiveness of the town. Cable is unsuitable not only for the city but also for his lady, who prefers cities. The quest for money and the preference for cities emerges in Hildy's early statement to Cable: "I'm gonna marry me the richest man in San Francisco—maybe the two richest men." Judging by her fancy car and stylish appearance at the film's end, she has apparently accomplished her goal, although it is to her credit that she returns to the desert to share her good fortune with Cable.

Cable is fated to live out his life in the desert, watering the garden of his own desires, a garden that for all of its beauty must eventually yield to the desert's wasting nature: thus the skinny coyote seen rummaging around the ruined station at the film's end. Ulti-

140

Plate 30. Cable's death scene, which ironically recalls Cable's statement, "Only thing I like about cities—city beds."

mately, the positive notions associated with water yield to the deadly progress symbolized by the automobile, a device that will soon help people lay waste to the land in their headlong rush for bigger cities, greater wealth, and the types of materialistic emotions that a man like Cable Hogue, especially after he is delivered from his death-oriented yearnings for wealth and vengeance, would never be able to appreciate or understand.

CHAPTER SIX

Dogs of War

All of Peckinpah's films challenge their viewers to evaluate their reactions to what is being depicted, but no film does so with more deftness and urgency than *Straw Dogs*. The film speaks especially to the audience's male members because of its concern with prototypical male ideas and responses involving the assertion of power and dominance in heterosexual relationships. And although female attitudes are dramatized in the film as well, it would seem that *Straw Dogs* is interested primarily in its male characters.

Whether such a choice of focus is a consciously artistic one or is an unconscious reflection of the filmmakers' biased attitude may be determined from the evidence. *Straw Dogs* is far too structured and sophisticated to be anything other than a consciously created artifact rather than the result of prejudiced moviemaking. The film shows unsympathetic men abusing women and then links this activity with other forms of objectionable behavior; it should thus be clear where the director's sympathies lie. *Straw Dogs* is a dramatization of sexual bigotry, not an example of it.

Like the beginnings of *The Wild Bunch* and *Cross of Iron*, the title sequence of *Straw Dogs* keynotes the film's theme. We see children playfully circling around a gravestone, certainly a prescient image in light of the various horrible deaths that the film metes out. The director begins the shot by having it photographed out of focus, gradually sharpening it throughout the title sequence until by the sequence's end, when Peckinpah's name appears, the background image is sharp and clear. (In a comparable fashion, the film's undercurrent of sexually created and sustained violence becomes clearer the closer we come to the revelatory end.)

After the titles, Peckinpah quickly places us in the midst of the conflicts between David Sumner (Dustin Hoffman) and his wife, Amy (Susan George). The opening interplay between the two characters reveals a jockeying for dominance that only seems like good-natured kidding. David's conservatism is communicated through Hoffman's mild demeanor and awkward gestures. The character's supposedly meek, academic manner is further suggested by his tasteful, steel-rimmed spectacles. David's restrained attributes immediately conflict with the carefully framed shots of Amy's braless breasts as the voyeuristic camera seems to become fixated on them. There is an immediate doubling of this almost leering sexual concern with Amy when we see Janice Hedden (Sally Thomsett), whose short skirt and tight sweater reveal her as a younger version of David's wife. Janice is further yoked with Amy through the manner in which, having been spurned by David, she and Amy become involved with other men in encounters that finally lead to death.

The relationship between Amy and David is mirrored not only in the desire that one of the town locals (Charlie VENNER [Del Hen-

Plate 31. Amy and David, *Straw Dogs*' supremely contentious couple.

ney], who turns out to be one of Amy's former lovers) has for Amy but in the mocking form of the relationship between Janice and the town idiot, Henry Niles (David Warner). Right up to the film's end, Henry functions as an exaggerated embodiment of David's initially repressed instincts. (In the film's early stages, David seems to represent pure intellect as opposed to pure impulse, which Henry appears to represent.) Moreover, the relationship between Henry and Janice re-emphasizes the dangers inherent in the physical passions that Amy, Charlie, and Henry represent, passions strikingly at odds with David's wholly academic work.

From its very beginning, then, *Straw Dogs* splits human existence into two supposedly exclusive realms, the intellectual and the physical, thereby reducing it to its barest essentials. The apparent equivalences between Charlie Venner and Henry Niles, especially with regard to their open displays of sexual desire, further suggest how nonintellectual, and virtually preconscious, sexual reactions and passions can be. (Later, as Amy's provocations become more studied and David's reactions more exaggerated, she and David seem to trade roles, although not completely, as is evident throughout the assault/ defense sequence, during which David carefully premeditates most of his reactions.) By dividing human responses into the exclusively intellectual and the emotional, and convincingly dramatizing this division, Peckinpah encourages us to treat as real a series of actions that seem objectionably stylized. Such bifurcation can obviously result only from exaggeration, yet exaggeration is present throughout the entire film. Yet the film exhibits increasing degrees of conceptual sophistication. At first, we may believe David to be the typically repressed intellectual, despite his playfulness; in this scheme, Amy, Henry, Janice, and the local rowdies (Venner, three of his friends, and Janice's father, Tom Hedden [Peter Vaughan]) occupy the physical realm. On closer examination, though, this division seems to be only a partial reflection of the characters and action.

Virtually every action and speech in the film may be construed both as normal behavior or speech and as a sexual gesture or double entendre. Each character seems to occupy a physically symbolic space within which his or her actions can be viewed as either friendly or threatening, at the same time suggesting either sexual submission or dominance. Throughout its running time, *Straw Dogs* returns us to a bestial universe in which grunts, groans, and actions carry greater force than communication with words and "civilized" behavior. The film leaves its characters and audience almost shamefully naked.

Thus, the presumably playful fighting between Amy and David that opens the film has a quite serious side, acting out in physical terms the very real struggle for control (which David always initiates) that is present in virtually all of the couple's exchanges. This aspect emerges most notably when Amy attempts to describe David's work. "He's writing a book on the computer analysis of celestial . . . ," Amy says. David finishes the statement in a way that insults his wife and asserts his superiority to her. "Good try," he says to her. Even in the midst of the assault on the farmhouse, David is still smug and composed, treating Amy in a patronizing fashion. When she refuses to help him repel the attack, he sneeringly tells her, "Why don't you entertain Niles?" This suggestion comes shockingly true a bit later when Niles attacks her. Earlier in the film, Charlie Venner inadvertently gave voice to David's smugness. In answer to Amy's question about David when he is on the moor, Charlie had replied, "He's fine; he's enjoying *himself*" (my emphasis).

A struggle identical to the one between Amy and David emerges in the exchanges between David and the rowdies and, most notably, between David and the Reverend Mr. Hood (Colin Welland). In fact, the film suggests that for many men traditional academic education

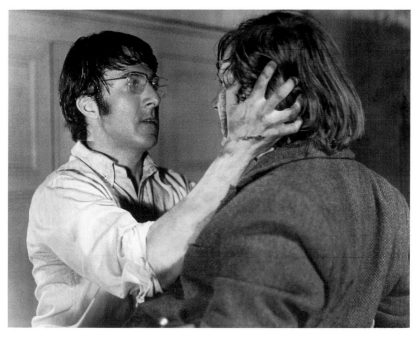

Plate 32. David and Henry Niles after Niles assaults Amy.

inevitably leads to arrogance. The reverend, an educated man like David, first engages in a bit of repartee with David into which David characteristically introduces a bit of sarcasm.

> DAVID: There's never been a kingdom so given to bloodshed as that of Christ.
> REVEREND: That's Montesquieu isn't it?
> DAVID: Oh, really?

The reverend's wife then asks, "Who's that [Montesquieu]?" and the reverend replies, patronizingly, "Somebody well worth reading."

In their only significant scene together, the reverend is being hosted by David and is thereby bound to defer to him to a degree, a power imbalance of which David takes advantage: thus the lack of amiability between the two men. However, no such rivalry emerges in the interaction between David and the film's other central "civilized" character—the local policeman, Major Scott (T. P. Mc-Kenna)—perhaps because Scott represents the law and thereby has at his command the type of power that can effectively uphold the status quo of sexual imbalance between women and men that David repeatedly exploits.

These immature power plays characterize David, as do his nightly physical exercises, which seem at best sophomoric. David's little boy body pales besides Amy's sexuality and the passions suggested by the most sexually and intellectually mature of the four rowdies, Venner. During the rape sequence, shots of Venner removing his shirt are juxtaposed with shots of David similarly disrobing; the distinction between the two men's bodies works to David's disadvantage.

Just as David is first seen as less accomplished physically than mentally, his wife is initially represented as less accomplished mentally than physically. Amy's approach to chess is that of a novice, and the glasses she wears in the scene make her look as awkward as David appears while exercising. She reads a book on chess, perhaps because she is not always able to go to David for advice. (It is interesting that just as Amy is tutored in the intellectual realm, David, through exposure to the rowdies, is educated in how to act physically.) Predictably, David downplays his wife's intelligence during their chess game. While Amy tries to decide on her next move, David distracts her by jiggling the chessboard from under the covers. David then further makes light of Amy's intellectual endeavor by turning it into a bedroom physical farce with an only mildly amusing joke. David pretends that he lost a rook under the bedcovers, thus reducing the game piece to a sexual toy. Throughout the sequence, Peckinpah nervously cuts back and forth between conventional and mirror shots of David and Amy's activities. The technique not only encourages us to gain a distance from what is going on and consider it as more than just simple interaction but also lends to the scene an unnerving quality, as though we are actually seeing an unsettling dualism at work. This feeling is underscored by Amy's statement after David closes the chessboard that the final move "puts you [David] in," an ambiguous statement in light of the lovemaking that is about to take place. Yet even this physical intimacy is not without problems. After Amy and David start kissing, David interrupts their activity three times, pausing first to take off his watch, then to remove his glasses, and then to pick up the bedside clock. When Amy protests, David denies that he has done anything wrong. "Just setting the alarm," he says, as though his behavior doesn't have annoyingly manipulative overtones.

This scene is of further interest since we also witness a reversal of the couple's roles. Usually, we see Amy making the physical advances in the relationship, with David insistent on playing out his role as the intellectual. In the bedroom chess scene, David sees his wife involved in an intellectual pursuit and encourages her to renounce this activity, since it apparently threatens his intellectual dominance of her. Clearly, David wants to play only when *he* wants to play. Moreover, for all of his supposed self-knowledge, David is not only childish and impetuous but maladjusted. Unsure of himself intellectually as well as physically, David can feel secure only by degrading others. In this respect, he is as irrational and impulsive as those other characters in the film (Amy and the rowdies) whom he implicitly accuses of suffering from these faults.

Four crucial scenes demonstrate the precise nature of David and Amy's relationship and prepare the way for the horrors to come. The next scene after the chess sequence takes place in the village pub, where the rowdies are gathered. In a distasteful display, Chris Cawsey (Jim Norton) throws a pair of Amy's panties to Norman Scutt (Ken Hutchison). Scutt dangles the panties in front of Venner, who looks at them with fascination and dismay: Venner is both attracted to what the panties represent and somewhat reluctant to claim it, whereas Cawsey and Scutt seem to evidence no such scruples. This scene also comments wordlessly on its predecessor; whereas David contrives innocuous games for sex, Cawsey, Phil

Riddaway (Donald Webster), Scutt, and Venner apparently regard sex as something brutal, characterized by taunting and derision.

In the following scene, David has retreated to his study. Trying to get David's attention, Amy moves one of the four dangling metal balls of a desktop ornament (which works on an action/reaction principle that is emblematic of the film's relationships). The balls begin to clack back and forth, distracting David.

> DAVID: Look, Amy, don't play games with me. I've got a lot on
> my mind.
> AMY: You're not being fair; I'm just trying to help. [At this
> point, we hear Cawsey's high-pitched laugh, which com-
> ments on the uselessness of Amy's suggestion.]

David rejects Amy's offer of emotional consolation and relief, telling her that all he wants is his privacy.

> DAVID: If you want to help, then get your friends to finish. Get
> the garage makers and rat catchers, get them all to fin-
> ish—and fix the toilet and clean up the kitchen. That
> would be a terrific help. I love you Amy, but I want you
> to leave me alone.
> AMY: OK; I'll leave you alone with your blackboard.

At this point, Amy draws a vertical chalk mark down the board's center as though delineating the battle lines between herself and David. David once again responds by rejecting the serious intentions behind Amy's words and deeds. "Don't play games with me," he says. When, like a rebellious student, Amy threatens to stick her chewing gum on the board, David says, "No, don't do it, Amy," which she nevertheless does. Later, when Amy is alone in the study, she commits a similar act of defiance. Immediately after David makes a rather brutal remark about the cat, Amy reacts by changing a plus sign in one of David's equations to a minus. This retaliatory gesture highlights the negative aspect of Amy and David's relationship.

Amy gives David two more chances to respond to her on human terms. In the following scene, Amy drives up to the farmhouse after shopping. As she gets out of the car, she inadvertently lifts her skirt and reveals her panties, a sight that the workmen are quick to notice. After Amy goes into the house, the subsequent exchange between her and David indicates that he disclaims responsibility for the volatile situation developing at the farm—a situation that is, to a great extent, the result of the workmen's perceiving what a weak, presumptuous, and emotionally undemonstrative person David is.

Moreover, David apparently believes that Amy provokes the men's reactions to her and would thus be culpable in her own rape.

AMY: They were practically licking my body.
DAVID: Who was practically licking your body?
AMY: Venner and Scutt.
DAVID: I congratulate them on their taste.
AMY: Damn rat catcher staring at me.
DAVID: Why don't you wear a bra?
AMY: Why should I?
DAVID: Shouldn't go around without one and not expect that
      type to stare.

Amy then challenges David's masculinity, using a work-related sexual reference (the forceful driving in of a nail, an image that Peckinpah showed us just before Amy drove up) to underscore the point that she finds David essentially impotent.

AMY: Look it, if you could hammer a nail, Venner and Scutt
      wouldn't be out there.
DAVID: Listen, Amy, fixing the toaster and getting the garage
      built is not exactly the reason I came here in the first
      place.
AMY: Are you saying you'd be happier if we hadn't left?
DAVID: We left because I got a grant to do work which I haven't
      found the time to do.

The dialogue then sketches in an aspect of David's personality first mentioned in an earlier scene. In that scene, Scutt and Cawsey (who are native to the Cornwall village where the film takes place) had asked David about political violence in the United States. David had denied any familiarity with the problem; Amy now returns to that issue:

AMY: You left because you didn't want to take a stand, commit.
DAVID: Commit to what? Huh? I was involved with my work.
      You want something out of me that it's not right to de-
      liver. That's not what I was there for.
AMY: I know why you're here.
DAVID: Why?
AMY: Could it be because there's no place else to hide?

A long silence ensues. Then, slyly using an appeal to emotion, but with the obvious intention of silencing his wife on the subject under discussion, David says, "I'm here because you once said you thought we could be happier here, remember?" Amy then smiles and says, "I'm sorry." David cannot let it go at that, though, pressing the point in order to make sure that the argument's resolution represents a decisive moral victory for him, something he achieves by humiliating his wife. "Are you sorry sorry or just sorry?" David asks, to which Amy replies, "Sorry sorry."

In David's view, this response earns for Amy some physical intimacy with him: "Then come here," he says. Amy crosses the room and lies next to David on the couch. However, a moment later, Amy says, "I'm gonna take a bath." Amy may simply desire to cleanse herself of Venner and Scutt's figurative licking of her body; however, the immediate context suggests that she instead wants to wash away the feelings engendered by her husband's treatment of her. (Indeed, we soon know that Amy is not trying to rid herself of the effect of the men's watching her, since in a few moments she will intentionally expose herself to them in defiant response to David's smugness.)

Unfeeling as always, David cannot intuit why Amy would want to bathe just then. "Why? You don't need [a bath]," he says, to which Amy replies, "I think I do." David's parting statement is, "By the way, I never claimed to be one of the involved." As far as Amy is concerned, though, the jousting match is not over. After going upstairs and removing her sweater, Amy throws it down onto David. Patronizingly protective, David says, "Don't forget to draw the curtains." Amy's response, unseen by David, is to let the workmen see her naked torso. However, the gesture is not as meaningful as we might at first believe. By restricting Amy's most significant act of defiance to the physical rather than the verbal realm—a position she is compelled to assume as a result of David's rhetorical one-upmanship—*Straw Dogs* relegates Amy to a subsidiary role in the film's moral scheme. Only David is given the opportunity to demonstrate his supposed superiority in both the intellectual and physical realms.

In the next scene, Amy tries once more to coax an affectionate and compassionate response out of David. David is writing; his being seated in a swing suggests his regressive state. Amy asks him to take time off from his work to go for a walk, which he tells her he will do later. Two of the workmen walk by, and David greets them; Amy then starts calling for the cat, the violence against which signals the beginning of the physical aggression that will eventually blossom into the assault on the farmhouse.

The viewer might object at this point in the film that *Straw Dogs'* Manichaean conception of human existence, while perhaps interesting, seems far too artificial to ring true. It would appear that the filmmakers anticipated this reaction: any possible objections to the film's violent distinction between the physical and intellectual realms are answered in *Straw Dogs'* most crucial sequence, during which Amy is first raped by Venner and then sodomized by Scutt, a sexual act anticipated verbally in Scutt's statement about the pair of Amy's panties that Cawsey has stolen. "Bugger your trophy," Scutt says. "I want what was in them." Later, he makes good on both intentions by literally "bugger[ing] . . . what was in them."[1]

The rape sequence is certainly shocking, as it should be. However, its frightening aspect does not derive from surprise; we expect some sort of exaggerated response from the workers given the dialogue concerning the expedition, the subtle teasing of David, and the repeated suggestive references to shooting.

VENNER: Mr. Sumner, would you like to shoot with us sometime?

DAVID: Oh, I've, uh, I've never hunted much.

SCUTT: Oh, but you've shot, Mr. Sumner? . . .

VENNER: At Trencher's good shooting's right outside the door.

The references to hunting not only anticipate part of the farmhouse assault, during which Major Scott and Tom Hedden are shot "right outside the door," but also emphasize the hunt's dual status as both objective journey and figurative display of sexual prowess, the latter quality predictably being acted out against David's wife. The only question that might have arisen regarding the film's first instance of violence against the Sumners is when it would have occurred, and it is easily minutes before the attack that we know it is coming, since Venner, Scutt, Cawsey, and Riddaway clearly intend to lure David away from the farm on the pretext of a hunting expedition, abandon him in the bush, and go back and do some form of mischief. Instead, the shock of the rape derives from the very special nature of our personal reactions to it.

Let's first be clear that the second sexual encounter, which obviously represents anal intercourse, is loathsome. Scutt is able to have sex with Amy only because he overpowers her. (The action is repugnant even to Venner, who watches but does nothing.) However, the sex between Venner and Amy starts out as a forcible encounter but then seems to change into consensual intercourse. This doesn't mean that we are meant to approve of what is going on. Indeed, *Straw Dogs*' consistent criticism of violence, whether physical or psychological, makes this point quite obvious.

Like the shower scene in *Psycho*, the voyeuristic element of the *Straw Dogs* rape scene directly implicates the audience in its concerns. What implicates us even further than the act of watching, though, is that what is apparently played out here is a primal scene of shocking graphic directness, one that follows a series of attempts at deplorable manipulation (David and Amy manipulating each other, Amy attempting to manipulate the rowdies, the rowdies teasing David) that break down in the face of elemental human tendencies. I am not arguing that the film's characters are in the grip of forces beyond their control, that they aren't accountable for what they do. What I am saying is that throughout *Straw Dogs*, Peckinpah is working on an extremely instinctual level, representing actions that to a significant degree defy dispassionate interpretation.

Despite its equivocally tender end, the sex between Venner and Amy leaves us with mixed feelings of both interest and abhorrence, much like the manner in which David and Amy seem at once attracted to the violence that the rowdies stand for and repelled by its intrinsically coarse, brutal nature. Despite violence's objectionability, Peckinpah probably recognizes that he is drawn to it, although no Peckinpah film depicts violence without also critiquing it. Those filmgoers who see in *Straw Dogs* (or any other Peckinpah film, for that matter) an endorsement of violence rather than a mere portrayal of it are mistaking representation for approval.

During the assault on David and Amy's house each assailant is dispatched with methods or devices that suggest sexuality, a quite appropriate conceptualization since the entire siege on the farm, in an extension of the attack on Amy, is a figurative embodiment of rape. Thus, all of David's defensive reactions to the siege involve repeated excisions (suggesting castration) or violations of the body through penetrations. First, Tom Hedden and Charlie Venner are assaulted with boiling oil, which is directed against their most susceptible uncovered orifices: their eyes.[2] Scutt is figuratively castrated by having his hands tied with wire and his head poised precariously over broken glass; he is later killed (by Venner) with a shotgun blast that rips a sexually suggestive hole through him. Tom Hedden is figuratively castrated by having part of his foot blown off. Riddaway, the least imposing and least featured of the gang, is first struck down with a tire iron and is later fatally penetrated by shotgun pellets fired by Amy. Cawsey, who wears a sexually suggestive, bulbous false nose (similar to the one worn by Alex in Stanley Kubrick's *A Clockwork Orange* during a scene that also involves an assault on a home), has his head bashed in.

Plate 33. The two rapists, Venner and Scutt, square off toward the end of the farmhouse assault sequence as David and Amy watch.

The most powerfully suggestive of the sexually figurative deaths is reserved for Venner, whose head is crushed in the man trap in an obvious trope for castration. This trap, with its sexually suggestive name, is, of course, an emblem of the *vagina dentata*, a point made graphically when Venner and Scutt first bring the trap into the farmhouse: they lay it down for a moment on a rug so that the rug's pile emerges around and protrudes through the trap like pubic hair. The trap is also a fitting weapon to cause Venner's death because of his early comment that such devices were traditionally used "for catching poachers"; in primal terms, Venner and Scutt's assault against Amy represents poaching on David's territory.

Much of the film's dialogue reinforces its representation of undercurrents of meaning in even the most casual words and deeds.[3] Commenting on Amy's hobby of buying antiques, David says, "My wife is a collector but I wind up with them." Reading the pronoun as referring to men instead of antiques yields the meaning that Amy likes to engage men's attention but David must deal with the consequences of such behavior.

When Janice Hedden asks David what he is going to catch with the man trap, David replies, "Peace and quiet"; these are, of course, the precise qualities that descend on the farm after the siege is over. We should also note that Amy buys the trap for David's birthday. For the viewer, David is truly born (as his own dangerous self) on the night that the trap is first used.

When the trap is delivered, Cawsey, who is a rat catcher, comments on it: " 'Fraid it's a bit large for my price, sir; won't do at all." As he speaks, he gestures with a mousetrap, a smaller version of the antique. (David contradicts Cawsey replying, "Don't count on it," which makes it seem that David knows that the trap may be of some future use.) The equation of the man trap and mousetrap implies that if any man is caught in the larger trap, he will be nothing more than a large rodent or rat, a nasty view of the trap's victim, Venner, with which David would nonetheless agree.

Riddaway and Cawsey then offer to bring the trap into the house, stating, "We'll get it up for you," a statement that acts as a precursor of the manner in which, by virtue of their assault on the house, the men enable David to respond in a way that involves a physical demonstration of his sexual prowess.

Inadvertently equating wild animals with himself and his friends, Cawsey says of the ducks they intend to hunt, "If you can't catch 'em, shoot 'em." During the siege, though, David has no need to resort to shooting, since he manages to "catch" all of the men without firing a shot.[4] Cawsey also says, "They [the ducks] might try to come from behind as well, sir, but don't move"; this statement seems to prefigure both Scutt's sexual assault of Amy from the rear and David's subsequent behavior, which is characterized by his doing nothing when his wife, after the rape, hints that something terrible happened to her that afternoon.

By encouraging us to draw these types of connections and make us see sexual suggestions virtually everywhere, *Straw Dogs* not only compels us to return to a time inhabited by "man the hunter" but also proposes the caveman view of woman as chattel. By contrast, David's claim toward the beginning of the farmhouse assault sequence that, like a piece of property, Henry Niles will be protected from the rowdies is obviously unfounded. David's attempt to keep Niles out of the rowdies' hands may appear humane. However, since David has never before acted humanely, the sanctuary claim impresses us as a self-imposed lie that David uses to antagonize the men. Ironically, in their insistence that Niles be brought to justice, the rowdies seem far more devoted to law than David is, whose appeals to territorial rights are little more than hypocritical justifications for violent retaliation.

It's notable that during his defense of the house, David does not protect the female element, as he might have done earlier in the film in attempting to defend Amy against the various provocations and suggestive behaviors directed against her. Though the house, with its many openings, is clearly a feminine symbol, David chooses to ignore its female sexual aspect. He justifies his indignation against the assault by referring to the rowdies' threat to a masculine object: Henry Niles, who, like the rowdies and David himself, has displayed hostility to a female. Teasing Henry in a manner comparable to the way that Amy teased the workmen, Janice Hedden is repaid with a literal death that invites comparison with the figurative murder (of identity) that Amy suffers during the rape.

In the midst of the rape sequence the basic forms of these ideas begin to take shape. During the rape, David is alone on the moor. Appropriately, quite soon after Venner and Amy's climax, David succeeds in shooting a duck, thereby reconfirming the film's linkage between sex and shooting; Peckinpah emphasizes this link by overlaying the shots of David with the sounds of Venner and Amy's passion. The scene also invokes the idea of the orgasm as death, not only in the classic sense of the "petit mort" or "little death" but also in the sense of sex leading to a literal death. With the simultaneous killing of the duck and the end of the intercourse, we see David reach over into the bush where the bird has fallen and retrieve the animal, whose head he gently caresses. (The duck's head droops from its neck like a flaccid male member.) Then, in a Pontius Pilate gesture, David figuratively denies his complicity in the assaults against Amy by washing the bird's blood off his left hand, which is photographed in such a way as to feature his wedding ring.

The equivalence between David and the rowdies is made clear not only by David's homicidal actions toward the film's end but also by the various match cuts that Peckinpah employs throughout the film as a means of creating a feeling of equivalence and fostering the sense that the film's actions are inevitable and that free will is virtually nonexistent. During Venner's rape of Amy, we are given shots of David, abandoned out on the moor, putting on his coat, followed by a complementary shot of Venner, who is poised above Amy, unbuckling his pants. David's assumption at this point of a garment to shield himself from the elements is consistent with his self-concerned actions, while Venner's disrobing not only contrasts with David's gesture but highlights Venner's curious emotional openness at the same time that he is carrying out an act of aggression against Amy. (The scene also gives us identical shots from David and Venner's vantage points of Amy's naked chest as seen from above during sex, which suggests that David, too, rapes Amy, albeit in a more insidious way than does Venner.)

Later that same day, David is seen leaning over in bed to kiss Amy, followed by a flash cut (representing Amy's internal vision) of Venner, on the couch, kissing her. During a later church social, Peckinpah even goes so far as to suggest a linkage among Venner, Scutt, and the Reverend Mr. Hood. The director accomplishes this linkage by match-cutting a shot of the reverend bowing during an intonation with shots of Venner's humping motions during the rape, thereby implicating the reverend, as a manipulative male, in the rape as well as conveying the impression of an unbridgeable gap between physicality on the one hand and repressed, sensuality-denying religion on the other. And as though to emphasize the nightmare aspect of the whole rape experience for Amy, whose interior reactions are the basis for many of the film's intercut images, Peckinpah inserts what can only be described as a subliminal ghost image of Venner's face, which he superimposes on the frame's relatively blank right side, during the scene in which Amy is walking past Venner and his friends when she enters the church on the night of the social.

Such match cuts also embrace action involving Amy and David's counterparts, Janice Hedden and Henry Niles. When Janice kisses Henry that same night, we are given a flash cut of Amy being grabbed by Venner. This linkage hints at the violence that is soon to occur between Janice and Niles when Niles lifts Janice by her head off her feet, breaking her neck. (This scene recalls Steinbeck's *Of Mice and Men*, in which Lenny inadvertently breaks the necks of his pet mice and, later, Curly's wife.) At this point, with Peckinpah providing shots of Janice's limp head, we cannot avoid comparing this image with the one of David tenderly lifting the head of the dead duck and then laying it down in a fashion similar to the way Niles slowly lowers Janice to the barn floor.

The sequence involving Janice's death is worth examining a bit more closely. Janice has left the evening entertainment organized by the reverend; Peckinpah repeatedly cuts back and forth between the entertainment and the encounter between Janice and Henry that occurs after the two leave the church. The reverend performs an amateur magic trick in which he apparently tears paper, saying at the trick's end, "It hasn't been torn at all." Peckinpah immediately cuts to shots of Janice and Amy, implying that the reverend's statement ironically refers to sexual violence, including both the rape of Amy and the literal tearing of Janice's hymen during her encounter with Henry Niles.

The equation of sex and violence is underscored when Janice asks Henry, "Would you like to kiss me?" The statement is followed by a shot at the church gathering showing Tom Hedden brutally throwing Henry's brother to the floor. The reverend then says to the assembly, "Will you all now please stand?" The standing up acts as a corollary for Henry's rising sexual excitement; the almost holy delirium that Henry presumably experiences when he touches Janice's breast is ironically compared to the feeling of being in the presence of "God, the Blessed Virgin, and all the saints," to whom the reverend now refers. Yet the holy aspect of Janice and Henry's encounter is immediately replaced by the sternness of judgment (the view apparently being the Edenic one of sex followed by damnation) when the reverend refers to "eternal fire, world without end, unless ye repent" while we see Henry and Janice kissing. When Janice says to Henry, "I have to go now," Henry (as a prelude to inadvertently breaking her neck) grabs her around the throat and says, "No, no, they might hurt you." (Henry obviously shares the view that strict judgment is the payment for sex.) At this point Peckinpah cuts to a shot of two children at the assembly toying with blowing out candles, a figurative representation of the small amount of flickering life left to Janice as Henry unwittingly chokes her to death, his actions accompanied by the grim tolling of the church bell.

Despite the slight threat to David's person when he early on allows Venner, Scutt, and the other men to talk to Niles, it is clear that the initial stages of the attack, before first blood is drawn (when Major Scott is killed),[5] are against the farmhouse itself and not the persons of David and Amy. This aspect is quite important, since it represents a playing out of one of the main elements of the typical horror film: the assault against the home.[6] As in the classic horror film, the house, with its many vulnerable orifices, is a symbol of the body.[7] It is thus interesting to note David's reaction to the gang's attack on his home. Quite soon after the initial assaults have been parried, David, replying to Amy's requests that he allow the assailants to enter and take Henry Niles, yells out to the men, "This is where I live; this is me. I will not allow violence against this house." Of course, David has already allowed violence against his house— that is, if we conceive of the house not only as a representation of the body but also as a symbol of the family. In the rape's aftermath, when Amy is clearly upset, David chooses to ignore her reactions. We shouldn't be surprised by David's attitude, though. It is quite evident that he does not conceive of the household as including Amy or, for that matter, any female. (Given his hostility toward the cat, it is clear early in the film that the animal must be female.) David is motivated to defend the home only when it is regarded as an extension of his own male self ("This is me"). Thus, David's comment to Riddaway, "You don't come in here," is as telling an antirape statement as there might be, although its figurative meaning applies only to the sanctity of David's body, not Amy's. When the issue is the safety of his wife, the film's most important woman, David, like the gang, is as much of an assailant against her as any member of the gang has been. One need only draw attention to the first instance of David's direct physical aggression against Amy to affirm this point. During the assault, Amy says that she intends to open one of the barred doors and leave; David slaps her and then in caveman style drags her across the room by her hair, acts that Venner performed just before the rape.

It is true that during the assault David is being given a lesson in the type of vulnerability to which women are often subjected.[8] Yet the outright threats against the house are much easier to deal with than the insidious insults and assaults that many women in Western society experience. Still, one wonders whether David would have been as adamant in his defense of the house and Henry Niles— his "innocent until proven guilty" ward—had the person being sought been a woman instead of a man. Given David's past responses, I doubt that he would react at all in such a situation.

It is only when David is placed in the role of a female, as someone quite likely to be violated, that he retaliates. David characterizes the humiliating deceit that the hunting party played on him that day by saying, "They stuck it to me on the moor today"; his words reveal the sexually suggestive element of penetration and stand in for the literal penetration of Amy by Venner that was simultaneously taking place. Yet when Amy, not speaking directly about the rape, hints that she was sexually assaulted at home that day, David fails either to listen or to understand. "They also serve who sit at home and wait," Amy says, suggesting through the use of the word "home" and its implicit contrast with the moor a parody of the distinction between a woman's traditionally domestic aspect and the conventional conception of man as hunter. Both Venner and David prey on women, an aspect that adds significance to David's repeatedly telling Amy to go to the kitchen (during the assault he also tells her to go to the bedroom), away from rooms like the study, which, in *Straw Dogs*, are identified with men. David cannot fathom what Amy means by her remark, though, because he is too self-centered to understand what Amy is telling him: that some cruelty infinitely greater than an insult to one's pride has occurred—namely, an insult against the body, the most vulnerable repository of the self. Unfortunately, despite the graphic way in which essentially sexual vulnerability is brought home to David during the farmhouse assault, it is clear from the film's ending that David cannot (or will not) comprehend the assault's symbolic significance.

Throughout the film, David chooses to ignore his wife's feelings and needs. With all of the assailants dead, David returns to his willful blindness to a woman's right to a security as real as that which he and his male counterparts usually enjoy. When Henry says at the film's conclusion, "I don't know my way home," and David replies, "That's OK; I don't either," we realize how powerfully equivalent the two men really are: both are sexual idiots who respond to pure impulse. Although David may comfort himself with the notion that he is intellectually superior to Henry, it's clear that he is little more than a brute. If anything, David is more dangerous than Henry, since he is conscious of many of his abuses. What we witness with Henry and David's departure in the car is the release into the world of two dangerous men. It's not too much to presume that David, when he is out and about, will remain smugly confident that his good little wife is sitting at home, busy about some domestic duty, and waiting for her great white male to return from the latest hunt, bloody in tooth and claw and ready (but only when it strikes his fancy) to have his selfish way with her.

The Taoist text from which *Straw Dogs* borrows its title provides us with further insight into David's psychology.

Heaven and Earth are not humane
They regard all things as straw dogs.
The sage is not humane.
He regards all people as straw dogs.[9]

To properly apply this text, one must first arrive at a satisfactory understanding of its terms. Translator Chan Wing-Tsit's annotations on this verse are most instructive.

> The term "not humane" is, of course, extremely provocative. It may be suggested that this is Lao Tzu's emphatic way of opposing the Confucian doctrine of humanity and righteousness. Actually, the Taoist idea here is not negative but positive for it means that Heaven and earth are impartial, have no favorites, and are not humane in a deliberate or artificial way. This is the understanding of practically all commentators and is abundantly supported by the Chuang Tzu. To translate it as "non-benevolent" is grossly to misunderstand Taoist philosophy.[10]

With this elucidation in mind, it immediately becomes obvious that David in no sense qualifies as "not humane" in the way intended by the Tao; we must therefore regard the manner in which David acts toward other people as extremely reprehensible. One could approve of David's attitude toward the film's sacrificial straw dogs only if one were psychologically constituted like him and therefore prone to pervert the observation about human nature inherent in the text. Only a cruel man could act in the self-serving way that David does.

Yet by entering into the perverted spirit of David's psychology, revealed in *Straw Dogs* and highlighted by the Taoist verse, we arrive at some startling revelations concerning the film. Reading the text from David's perspective suggests that we view him, the film's academically oriented character, as the sage who uses the rowdies in a ritual offered toward a presumably violent god who must somehow be placated. Such a reading implies that in a very subtle way—first by acting superior, then by snubbing the men, and finally taunting them by insisting that Henry is his responsibility, not theirs—David engineers the attack on the farm so that he might dispassionately sacrifice the gang in order to shore up his insecure masculinity.[11] In line with such a reading, we must also regard Amy as a disposable commodity whom David would be ready to sacrifice to further his solipsism; indeed, given his unfeeling reaction after the rape, David appears to evidence this attitude.

This reading of the film's action also dictates that we view David's being lured away from the farm onto the moor as an intentional self-deception, a withdrawal from home engineered by David to allow the rape, which he may very well regard as a justified chastening of Amy in payment for what he views as her various provocations. In this sense, Venner and Scutt inadvertently act as David's surrogates (one of the meanings suggested by the cross-cutting that occurs during the rape), assaulting Amy in characteristically direct fashion, a mode of behavior that the supposedly civilized David has presumably repressed. Such an approach to David's personality mandates that we also hold him responsible for two other deaths, those of the cat and Janice Hedden.

We have seen that in *Straw Dogs*, animals sometimes stand in for people and people often act like animals. The equation of Amy with a cat (with an apparently intentional, albeit unstated, reference to the sexual epithet "pussy") is made most clear when Amy asks Venner, "I'd like to know what you think of cats"; Charlie replies, "I do fancy cats," and then kisses her. Yet David, in his statements and deeds, makes the equation far more explicit. Early in the film, when Amy is looking for the cat, the following exchange takes place.

> AMY: I can't find the cat.
> DAVID: It doesn't answer my call.
> AMY: Do I?
> DAVID: You'd better.

I have already noted how much David dislikes Amy's interrupting him in his study. Here, David demonstrates the identical attitude toward the cat, thereby equating it with his wife. "If she's in my study, I'll kill her," he says.

When the cat is discovered hanging in their closet, David and Amy look shocked, at which point we might be tempted to agree with Amy that Scutt or Cawsey killed the animal in order, as Amy says, "To prove to you [David] they could get into your bedroom" (which is, after all, where Cawsey obtained his souvenir, Amy's panties, which stand in for her body). Yet despite David's astounded expression on seeing the cat (a reaction that could be explained as necessary to maintaining a ruse), it seems more likely that it was David, who throughout the film has been displacing his aggression against Amy, who hanged the cat in order to demonstrate his escalating impatience with his wife. (He is not physically direct until the film's end.) David's raising of the stakes, from pelting the cat with food to killing it and then making sure that the workmen get the blame for its death (an accusation that he cunningly leaves it to Amy to make), would also serve the purpose of alienating his wife further from the workmen, whose friendly relationship with Amy worries David. I recognize the fact that my hypothesis regarding the cat's death posits an extremely convoluted and pathological sensibility. Nevertheless, such maneuverings of thought and deed are consistent with the psychology of someone like David, whose personality is characterized by a maladjusted sexual relationship and an overtly analytical bent.

As for Janice's death, it should be noted that it is only because of David's petulantly ignoring her that Janice goes off with Henry Niles. Thus, like Venner and Scutt, Henry qualifies as a stand-in for David, as do all of the assailants against the home. This view of Henry suggests that David's protecting him is an example of one murderer's sheltering another, thereby making that much more appro priate the pairing off of Henry and David at the film's end. David and Henry's similarity is also suggested through Tom Hedden's awareness of Janice's attraction to David. At one point, after Janice greets David as he enters the pub, Tom gives David a look that is as worried and concerned as the one he evinces when he is talking about the potential threat to the town's children represented by Henry Niles. David's passive-aggressive behavior thus results in a total of seven deaths: Janice, Major Scott, and the five rowdies, an impressive number of homicides for a supposedly reclusive and peaceful man.

Regarding the film in this way makes possible a provocative insight into David's character, suggesting that his meek demeanor is an intentional ruse to mask his aggressions. Indeed, despite David's desire to isolate himself in academic fashion from the world and his presumed good-humored gentleness, we have seen that David repeatedly exhibits hostility. Even in the pub and farm sequences in which he and the rowdies are involved, David continually asserts his supposed superiority. In one scene, after Tom Hedden has offered to pay for David's cigarettes and then left the pub, David insists on paying for the cigarettes; when the pub owner says, "They're paid for, sir," David replies, "They are now." David's haughtiness is much like Major Scott's. David never asks the rowdies to stop calling him "Sir," a term he obviously regards as an affirmation of his social ascendancy over them. Scott is always addressed by the rowdies as "major" (and by Henry's brother as "sir"), although he introduces himself to David as "John Scott" and visits David socially at home. Like David, Scott spurns gestures from Tom Hedden (e.g., he refuses Tom's offer of a drink). On the other hand, David acts like Scott when he buys the men a drink, since he does so in a patronizing manner.

David's reaction to the assault against the home might very well be made up largely of outrage: "How dare these peasants attack the lord of the manor's dwelling?" Considering the many affronts to which the rowdies are subjected throughout the film, it is little wonder that, given the added provocation of David's harboring Henry Niles, the men cry out for some redress. Once launched, the attack allows David to demonstrate to himself, his wife, the rowdies, and the entire village that he is not afraid. "I'm not [a coward]," David insists to Amy after the rape, and the perfect situation arises for David to demonstrate that he can hunt and kill as well as anyone.

It would be logical to assume that David's dispatching of the farm's assailants might lead us away from the violence into a peaceful region where we could breathe a bit easier. Peckinpah does not intend to let us off so easily, though. David may smile at the end as he drives off with Henry, although it's clear that David is no different at that point than he always has been. Having discharged his pent-up frustrations, having finally proved himself a man, David might be expected to act a bit more humane and well-adjusted. All that the successful defense of the farmhouse has accomplished, though, is to merely affirm for David in concrete form his antifeminine, prejudicial prowess. David has passed beyond taunting the vicar, torturing the cat, or cruelly manipulating his wife. Having done murder, he is now totally the beast. When he smiles at the film's end, we can only be horrified at the idea that such a sexist, vindictive man is free to commit even more mischief. In charting David's passage from acts of verbal homicide to physical murder, Peckinpah brilliantly shows us a supposedly cultured man acting on the level of an animal. In no other film has Peckinpah given us such a chilling view of human nature.

The essential point that *Straw Dogs* makes is that David, like many men, lacks the courage to be compassionate. For all of his intelligence, he is too ignorant to realize that his insecurity, which is based on his failure to measure up to the traditional conception of the "rough and tough" male, does not derive from a fault in himself but from the rigid, conventional conception of what it means to be a man. If nothing else, *Straw Dogs* clearly demonstrates that it is men who are afraid to exhibit true tenderness and compassion, and thereby risk being called unmanly, who are the real cowards.

CHAPTER SEVEN

Memory and Desire

Junior Bonner is the best-natured of all of Peckinpah's films. It tries for neither the dramatic intensity of *The Wild Bunch* and *Straw Dogs* nor the sentimentality of *Cable Hogue*. Instead, *Junior Bonner* tells its story simply and directly, without many of the stylistic devices, such as exaggerated action sequences or dramatically excessive behavior, that we have come to expect from Peckinpah. Moreover, *Junior Bonner* is notable in that unlike any other Peckinpah film, it does not contain a single villainous character. Nevertheless, *Junior Bonner* does have strong affinities with Peckinpah's other films. The most notable similarity derives from Junior's anachronistic status as a rodeo cowboy; as a cowboy, Junior (Steve McQueen) is called on to demonstrate his mastery of skills that are associated more with the past than the present. Yet the film is less concerned with the opposition between the past and the present as historical entities than it is with the antagonism between those events, past and present, that have occurred during the lifetime of its central character. However, this characteristic in no way lessens the significance and intensity of the film's temporal conflict. If anything, the shift in focus allows a greater emphasis on the struggle between the immutable past and the promise of the present.

Despite its air of unassuming simplicity, *Junior Bonner* reveals its conceptual sophistication in that a number of its major scenes are designed to establish significant differences among the characters. The functioning of these scenes is vital to the film's dramatization of past and present. Yet the conflict between these realms is

164

Plate 34. Remembering the past, anticipating the future: Steve McQueen as the title character in *Junior Bonner*.

actually given to us right at the film's beginning, in the title sequence, which shows Junior's first ride on the bull Old Sunshine and his recollections of this event.

The sequence's opening images are extremely grainy, as though the events that they depict, already distant in memory, have somehow begun to be affected by the vagaries attendant with recollection, so that the sharpness of their reality has been dulled. (Later, Junior remembers the event in sharp, well-defined images. Here, though, almost immediately after the event being recollected, Junior is still so pained and upset by being thrown that his memory does him a kindness by softening the outlines of this embarrassing event.) We first see Junior riding the bull; after a brief dissolve, we are given an image of Junior walking out of the rodeo arena and into a corral-like building adjacent to it.[1] Junior has obviously been thrown by the bull before the qualifying eight-second mark, as is evident first from Junior's defeated expression and then from the rodeo announcer's statement, "Old Sunshine is still champ." This assertion blatantly contrasts the bull's present status with that of Junior, whom the announcer previously referred to "the former champion in the event, [who] drew for himself the current champion brahma bull."

The repetition of the word *champion* establishes both an affinity and a contrast between Junior and the bull that will be explored further as the film continues.

The title sequence uses images and images set within images; the latter are set into the former like intrusive memories, which is precisely the meaning that they are meant to suggest. After a cutaway shot of Old Sunshine, now riderless and still bucking, and a cut back to Junior walking in the corral, the first of the insets appears: a shot of stall number 4, the one from which we see Junior, mounted on the bull, eventually emerge. This inset intrudes into the shot of Junior walking away from the arena and into the corral. The juxtaposition of the two images signifies that memory has already begun to press on Junior in a most uncomfortable way, reminding him of his defeat. The memory becomes even more intrusive through the subsequent use of another of the title sequence's techniques. The inset image soon enlarges, spreading out and completely engulfing the shot of Junior in the corral and eventually occupying the entire frame, thereby graphically demonstrating how the past can dominate the present. This memory image then freezes and moves up to occupy the frame's upper half, the bottom half of which shows us Junior, seen from the knees down, walking back into the corral. At least in terms of frame space, past and present are equally forceful here, although the past occupies the superior, upper position. The emphasis then changes as the lower half of the frame moves up to take over the image.

But then memory intrudes again; the image of Junior in the present is cut in half horizontally, the bottom half of the frame yielding to an image of Old Sunshine and Junior once more coming out of the stall. The image of Old Sunshine bucking then freezes again; the lower quarter of the frame, which has been blocked off to feature one of the actors' names, dissolves to an image of Junior once again walking back into the corral; at this point we hear the rodeo announcer's comment about the impressive amount of money that has been won by Junior's rival in the rodeo, Red Terwiliger (Bill McKinney). This reminder of Junior's being bested by Red apparently prompts Junior to think about the bull besting him, too. Thus, the frame, as always here representing aspects of Junior's consciousness, reflects Junior's divided awareness by dividing vertically between Junior on the left and the bucking bull on the right. Eventually, though, the right-hand image moves left and takes over the entire frame as the bull, representing the past and defeat, once again dominates.

Alternations like these continue throughout the sequence, with sounds and sights repeatedly impressing on us the war between the past and the present that is going on inside of Junior. Finally, as an image of Junior taking off his rodeo gear is presented, we see Red stop by to help Junior hitch his horse trailer to his car. Junior says, "Maybe I oughta take up another line of work," to which Red replies, "Sheesh; see you at Prescott [the site of the next competition]." Red's comment makes it plain that for both Junior and himself, giving up the rodeo is simply not possible. Despite the pain and humiliation and essentially lonely existence to which the rodeo subjects Junior, his skills have mandated this life for him. Moreover, as we see, this is the way that Junior prefers to live, taking the rodeo's pleasures and discomforts in good-natured stride.

After the next editing cut, which occurs just before Junior is seen driving on the highway, the sound-track music changes. The title sequence's mournful guitar music is replaced by the song "Arizona Morning," the word "morning" suggesting the possibility of renewal attendant with the start of another day. The song's optimism is not unqualified, though. In consonance with the title sequence's melancholy ambiance, the song's notion of the future is balanced with reminders of the past, notable here in the verses "And in my mind I hear a gentle warning / You've been a rounder and a rambler much too long." (The reminder that Junior may now be too old to compete in the rodeo will soon reemerge in Buck Roan's (Ben Johnson) assertion about Junior's not being "the rider [he] used to be.")

This reinvocation of the antagonism between past and present, which intrudes on the only extended present-tense shot that we have so far received in the film, reinstitutes the war of images culled from the two temporal realms. The frame splits horizontally: the bottom half now shows Junior driving to his new destination, which represents open-ended possibility; the upper (and therefore symbolically dominant) half shows Junior once more entering Old Sunshine's stall, thereby reminding us of the unchangeable past. This visual alternation repeats itself in successive images and divisions, finally ending when Junior pulls up at a combination gas station and roadside fruit stand, where he buys some "fuel" for both of his modes of transportation—apples for his horse and gas for his car. The scene at the gas station suggests Junior's impoverishment: he buys only four gallons of regular gas. As we see in the next scene, Junior can't afford lodgings, so he sleeps outside.[2] When he wakes up in the Arizona morning, the sylvan scenes's beauty and serenity are undercut by the first thing that Junior does after putting on his hat: he touches his bruised side. The pain that gave rise to the gesture reminds Junior (and us) of his defeat. Even here, at the very beginning of a new day, the influence that the past has on Junior is emphasized.

Junior's arrival at the house of his father, Ace Bonner (Robert Preston), signals the beginning of a visually rich series of images. On the way to Ace's house, Junior passes images of obsolescence and transience—an abandoned car, a broken windmill, and a tumbleweed—all set within a dusty, bleak landscape. The shack itself is filled with a number of objects associated with the past, which thereby evoke a host of memories; among them are a photograph of Ace riding, an old-fashioned radio, and a wall-mounted poster, which also seems to be of Ace. Equally poignant and suggestive is the condition of all of these items. The glass over the photograph is broken, the radio looks decrepit and dusty, and the torn poster hangs from the wall. In addition, Ace's bed is threadbare and unmade; the house is obviously not being lived in. Together, these images create a depressing sense of abandonment.

In many ways, the inside of the house is also emblematic of Junior's present situation. Its poverty echoes Junior's financial circumstances; the torn photo and cracked glass hint at the ravages of time of which Junior, during the rodeo, has been made painfully aware; the still photos recall the freeze frames from the title sequence, many of which communicated the sense of Junior's defeat. The old-fashioned radio reminds us of the voices of radio announcers and, through that memory, the rodeo announcer from the film's opening, who narrated and commented on Junior's defeat. Finally, a pair of crutches leans against the house's wall, drawing our attention not only to the hazards of rodeo life in general but more specifically to the injury that Junior sustained during his ride. In all of these instances, these objects, now left behind, not only convey a sense of the past or defeat (sometimes both) but also propel us, like Junior, back in time as well, mandating that we experience and share Junior's feeling that the past is inescapable.

After Junior leaves the house, he looks across the land; in a point-of-view shot, the camera zooms in on some of the mobile homes that Junior's brother, Curly Joe (Joe Don Baker), is having constructed, homes that are destined to be successors to the house in which Ace Bonner had lived. (Indeed, Curly bought Ace's land so that he could knock down the house and build more houses on it.) The sterility of the mobile homes will shortly become clear to us; what is significant now is how out of place these structures look. By contrast, Ace's house, despite its dilapidation and quite possibly because of its rough-hewn façade, seems to be appropriately placed out here on the prairie.

The entire area around Ace's house is teeming with construction activity; as a result, there is a constant noise of machines on the soundtrack. This persistent reminder of destruction in the name of progress creates a sense of despair that links up with the feeling created when Junior realized that Ace was not at home. What follows is Junior's shouted dialogue with a man working on a machine. (The noise of the machine hinders communication, another sign of the alienating effects of progress.) Judging by the man's protective gear, the machine is obviously moving some sort of toxic substance, toxins and pollution being further indications of the kind of progress that the future portends. Junior asks the man if he has seen Ace; the man replies that he never heard of him. Junior's desire for contact with his father, even if only through recognition by someone else of his father's existence, is once again frustrated, at which point Junior drives away.

The scene that follows, which most effectively evokes the past and the present and brings them into striking conflict, is the most intricately rendered and visually suggestive in the entire film. We already know from the title sequence how essential to the film Junior's internal images will be; we also know that Junior obviously has a very rich interior existence. (By failing to dramatize the internal life of any character other than Junior, the film not only compels us to identify with Junior but also uses the emotional distance between the audience and the other characters as a corollary to the distance between the characters themselves.) After driving a short distance, Junior stops and looks back at Ace's house. A bulldozer approaches the house and, without stopping, knocks down Ace's mailbox, on which Ace's name is prominently displayed.[3] What we witness in the destruction of the mailbox with Ace's name on it is the symbolic destruction of the man himself. Just as the man at the toxic machine had never heard of Ace, neither, apparently, does the man driving this bulldozer attach any importance to Ace's name or to this act of destruction. Indeed, without a sense of either the rodeo (of which Ace is an important part) or of history and tradition, how could these destructive construction workers see any significance in their actions outside of a routine way to earn money?

After the shot of the mailbox being knocked down, we see

another bulldozer approaching. When Junior, whose car is at a standstill, sees the approaching bulldozer, he rises up slightly out of his seat. In response, the driver leans over his steering wheel and looks down at Junior. Obviously, with regard to both sheer horsepower and physical placement (the man is seated a number of feet higher than Junior), Junior is at a disadvantage here, powerless before the onslaught of progress. Moreover, the fact that in the present scene, as in the film's title sequence, Junior is confronted by a force greater than he can presently master suggests that what is also being portrayed here is a replay of Junior's ride on Old Sunshine. Until he has conquered his doubts and thrown off the weight of the past, Junior will be unable to overcome the forces that oppose him, whether they're in the form of a bulldozer or a bull. Having eliminated his doubts, he will be able to triumph in the present and, by extension, the future.

Next, another bulldozer knocks down part of Ace's house. In response to this sight, Junior makes what appears to be a derisive comment to the driver of the bulldozer facing him. However, the man doesn't react; indeed, Peckinpah next presents us with a close-up of the impassive face of this man, whose features are obscured by the sun at his back shining into the camera lens.[4] The bulldozer working near Ace's house crushes another part of the dwelling, at which point the man in the bulldozer in front of Junior shifts gears and begins to move the machine toward Junior's car, challenging him in Western showdown fashion either to stand his ground or to yield. Obviously, though, what we are seeing here is not a typical Western showdown, since in that situation, each participant's individual abilities are being tested. If two men face each other in a shoot-out, each is armed; the deciding factor is each man's skill with his gun. In the rodeo, although the bull is more powerful than the man, the man has the advantage of tactics that give him a relatively equal chance at winning. Here, though, the bulldozer's bulk and power give its driver the decided advantage. As a consequence, when the man moves the bulldozer forward, Junior has no choice but to back up his car.

After more shots of the other bulldozers, we see another view of the driver's face.[5] The driver then starts to move the bulldozer forward, an obviously threatening gesture. Rocks begin to fall out of the bulldozer's scoop as Junior backs up his car; a shot of the roof of Ace's house, which is now lying on the ground and is being lifted a bit for further demolition by one of the bulldozers, is followed

170

by the driver's lowering his scoop slightly and dumping some rocks right in front of Junior's car. After this point, the driver complements the upward, destructive movement being used on Ace's house by causing the scoop of his bulldozer to ascend; in a symbolic expression of the machine's impersonality, the scoop completely obscures the driver's face. The scoop rises until a large rock is prominently featured in the middle of the frame. Quick cut shots follow of the working bulldozers, the driver's face, and the rocks in the scoop, melding all of the sequence's destructive and impersonal elements. This part of the sequence ends as Junior backs up his car and drives away. At least for a time, destructiveness has prevailed.

When Junior begins to slow down briefly, he looks back and witnesses the final destruction of Ace's house, which is now leveled. Yet the house has not completely disappeared; the following sequence of shots, which appropriates the already dramatized notions of conflict and alternation and uses them in intriguing ways, demonstrates this point.

First we are given another shot of mechanical destructiveness and progress as Peckinpah shows us a bulldozer pouring dirt into a dumpster. Junior again looks back at the house site; the house is gone, destroyed. Peckinpah then cuts back to Junior; obviously quite upset, Junior begins to bite his lip. Junior's internal vision then renders him an image of the house being destroyed again, as we see a part of the house being knocked down, its pieces flying away from a bulldozer. Remembrance has restored the house to life, but only to show it dying once more. Thus, memory here serves as a tormentor, as it does periodically throughout the film by bringing back to Junior reminders of his failed attempt to ride Old Sunshine longer than the mandatory eight seconds. In this instance, the memory of the house becomes even more poignant and painful as the former image is followed by a memory shot of the framed picture of Ace that Junior had examined in the house. This movement from the relatively personal outside of the house to the more personal object within it does more than act as a corollary of the distinction, which is dramatized in the film, between Junior's public consciousness and his more private one. It also serves to show how greater acuity of perception (in the form of the passage from external to internal vision) intensifies the accompanying emotional response. In this sequence, the emotional response is at best melancholic, at worst depressing. Of course, Junior chooses to remain sensitive to his impressions, taking the chance that such sensitivity, although it may increase his capacity for pain, will also maximize his capacity for pleasure. In contrast to Ellie Bonner (Ida Lupino) and Curly (Junior's mother and brother), who have withdrawn emotionally, Junior remains an emotionally receptive and therefore vulnerable character, one who, like his father, earns our sympathy and respect.[6]

Another shot of the house in pieces follows. But then Junior's internal vision performs a blessing for him. We are given a shot of the house intact; memory has restored its physical integrity. This restoration is a decidedly mixed blessing, though, since it represents only an abstract, internal reality, not a concrete, external one. Certainly we know that memory can comfort us at times, helping us to remain in touch with people and things that no longer exist. But just as certainly, the person remembering also recognizes the powerful discrepancy between the internal and external realms, a distinction that can cause great pain. The corollary conflict between living for one's dreams (the internal reality) and facing up to so-called facts (the external realm) is one that all four of the film's principals seem to have resolved. Ace and Junior attempt to translate their dreams into reality: Ace by trying to reinvoke the life of an old-time prospector, Junior by attempting to live the honest life of a rodeo man. Alternatively, Ellie and Curly have chosen to live totally within the harsh realities of the everyday world. Yet *Junior Bonner* is careful to maintain important distinctions between the characters in each realm. Ace is reckless with money and acts irresponsibly; Junior is fiscally circumspect and considerate of others. (Junior—and doubtless Ace as well—owes Ellie money, but Junior doesn't try to borrow any more and he shows profound regret at being unable to repay his mother.) As for the two materialistic Bonners, Curly is rather ruthless and unfeeling, whereas Ellie, although she is doubtless as materialistic as Curly (an attitude that she has had to adopt in order to survive), does not try to manipulate other people. (A case could be made for her influencing other people through her passive manner, which invites attention and sympathy.)

What is especially sad in the film is that although all of these characters want something in the future, they are willing to sacrifice closeness to the other members of their family in order to achieve what they want. *Junior Bonner* shows us how depressing these characters' futures are. Curly and Ellie will be financially secure but emotionally isolated (this despite the two "emotional contact" scenes that the characters are later given). Ace and Junior will each have his dream, but each man will be alone: Ace by himself in

Australia, Junior by himself traveling on the rodeo circuit.[7] Indeed, by the time that *Junior Bonner* is over, we come to realize that in spite of all of its touching emotional scenes, the film is about loneliness and isolation, showing us how the contacts that people establish are fleeting and intermittent at best.

After the shot of the house intact, the ambiguous nature of internalized vision once again asserts itself as memory renders an opposing truth: the house in pieces, but breaking up at a slightly later point than the last time that we saw it being demolished. Next, we get another shot of the intact house, but seen from farther away, the greater distance in this internal view suggesting that the longed-for reality (the house before destruction) is receding into memory. As if to further dramatize the conflict between the ideal and the real, two more shots of the house intact and in pieces are alternated. Only the irresolution of the two realms offers a modicum of solace. Comfort is then withdrawn, though, as two successive images of the house breaking apart are shown. But then memory becomes kind again by offering another image that seems to derive from an impulse of grace. Junior's mind reaches even further back in time, effectively restoring the house by offering up images representing the vitality of its owner. The framed photo of Ace riding was somewhat compromised in its effect because it was static. In what is apparently a vision experienced by Junior, we now see a shot of Ace, also riding and roping in a competition, but in motion.

These shots of Ace riding are culled from the Prescott rodeo wild cow–milking contest, which occurs later in the film. Whether Peckinpah used these shots because he needed footage of Ace riding and didn't want to shoot any additional footage, or whether the image's inclusion in the earlier scene is meant to represent a prescient vision on Junior's part, cannot be determined; however, given the strong affinity between Ace and Junior, the latter interpretation seems more likely. This view would mandate our feeling that Junior sees the image of Ace riding in the event because he is looking forward to it (he has, after all, already paid for the event before he even reaches Prescott). Moreover, it is obvious that other people in the film are anticipating Junior and Ace's participation in the event as well. The man at the rodeo registration desk says to Junior, "Good to see you and your dad together again." Similarly, when Buck Roan hears about Junior and Ace being in the event together, he says, "That's a pair to draw to," to which Junior replies, "That's me and Ace all right." The comfort resulting from the image of Ace

Plate 35. Junior and Ace Bonner.

in motion is then sabotaged by our seeing the house once again breaking up, followed by another moving image of Ace riding, and then a final shot of Ace's mailbox being knocked down.

At the point at which we first see the moving image of Ace riding, Peckinpah blends in Ace's voice on the soundtrack saying, "Only costs five thousand dollars." One might almost think that Ace's voice, like his image, is emerging from the past via Junior's memory. However, after the final image of the mailbox falling down, the voice continues as Peckinpah cuts to a shot of the outside of the Prescott County hospital where, as we learn from the next shot, Ace is a patient. The image of the knocked-down mailbox and the view of Ace in bed with his head bandaged seem to confirm that the symbolism in the falling mailbox shot is valid, that Ace has in some sense been felled. Yet as we soon see, Ace is just as spirited and lively as ever; he still intends to act on his dreams, despite the fact that he has already spent all of the money that Curly paid him for his land.

The technique of abruptly cutting from the ranch scene to the hospital, along with the carried-over sound, implies that Junior may somehow be intuiting what Ace is saying to Curly. At the very least, as a result of the profundity of Junior's reactions at the site of Ace's house, Junior has entered into the spirit of the destructive condition in which his father now finds himself, with the visual and auditory result that he is apparently placed in contact with Ace. Moreover, it is certainly no coincidence that Curly is with Ace at this point, since the threat to Ace's integrity that Curly represents (and which Junior intuits while near his father's house) was graphically present at the house in the form of the bulldozers. The sum effect of the house and hospital sequences is that we first share Junior's anxiety about Ace through his internal visions and experience the reality of these anxieties coming true in the person of Curly Bonner.

During the hospital scene, Curly denies Ace's request for funding for his Australian trip. Later, Ace watches a televised commercial for one of Curly's ventures, the Curly Bonner trading post, and the scene ends when the disgruntled Ace throws a glass through the television screen.[8] (This derisive act anticipates Junior's knocking Curly through a plate-glass window.) The conflict between the past and the present then reemerges when Junior arrives at the site of the rodeo. Junior drives in from the right while Buck Roan, who owns Old Sunshine and who represents the present, drives in from the left. Junior goes through a brief confrontation with Old Sunshine, who, after being unloaded from a trailer, is eventually herded to a pen. As in the face-off between the car and the bulldozer, Junior is on the right side, with Old Sunshine on the left. Junior uses his hat to feint like a matador at the bull and is finally charged. (The sequence is peppered with more images of Junior's previous ride on Old Sunshine.) Junior then quickly jumps over the stockade fence to safety, pays his entry fees, and goes looking for Buck, whom he finds at the Palace Bar.

We know from the title sequence that Junior injured his ribs during his previous ride, and we note when we see him walking on the rodeo grounds that he is limping as well. Yet when he sits down at Buck's table and is told by Buck that he acts like he's "hurting," Junior says that he is "just fine." Buck's comment exemplifies the honest concern that rodeo men have for each other, while Junior's reply indicates a stoic approach to discomfort, which he views as a very personal matter. (In the same way, it should be obvious that Junior's memory images are not the result of his intentionally dwelling on the past but are merely reminders of it.) Buck's next question (like his offer of a job later in the film) indicates something of a misunderstanding of Junior's needs. Buck asks, "Money?"

Along with the inquiry about Junior's pain, the question makes it clear that Buck doesn't quite realize that there is a more profound, more intangible discomfort assailing Junior, one that manifests itself most significantly in the realm of the spiritual and ideal, not in the concrete realm of physical pain and finances. Junior replies, "Well, money's nobody's favorite, Buck, but I want to ride that Sunshine bull of yours again."

Buck then says, "The way your luck's been running, you're just liable to draw him again." Junior, though, is not the kind of person to let either fate or chance determine what is going to happen to him. "I just don't want to be counting on my luck," he says. Buck tries to make it clear that he is not in a position to act like one of the fates: "You know I don't set the draw, Junior" (something that is obviously not true, as we later see). Junior, instead of contradicting Buck with the truth, phrases his response diplomatically.

> JUNIOR: Now listen, most cowboys would pay you to stay off that bull.
> BUCK: I don't suppose you're thinking about paying me to draw him for you.[9]
> JUNIOR: Well, it's like I said, money's nobody's favorite.
> BUCK: I'll be damned if you're not serious.

In classic Old West style, Junior replies that the clash between him and Sunshine is a solitary and personal one, a situation that Junior obviously feels is just as it should be. "Um-hmm," he says, "just one of him and one of me." However, Buck has to make sure that Junior isn't acting on some petty principle here, not yet realizing that Junior wants another chance to ride the bull in order to prove his worth. "Look, Junior, neither me or my bull aim to make our living off another fellow's pride. Now you might as well face it: you're just not the rider you was a few years back."

Junior's reply gains subtle shadings from Steve McQueen's acting. McQueen looks down, hesitates, and half smiles, actions that convince us of his character's sincerity and slight embarrassment. "I need it, Buck," Junior says; "it's my home town."[10] Having revealed some of his inner need, Junior now reinforces the request by expressing his assertion in different terms that may totally convince Buck to let him once more ride the bull. "I'll ride that bull for half of the prize money," Junior says, to which Buck answers, "You sure are a man of confidence—and generous, too." Junior's reply overlooks the generosity aspect, since that refers to money, a topic that, as we shall see, Junior always approaches with great reluctance. "That's me, Buck, just full of confidence," he says. Junior offers the last statement ironically, in a mildly self-deprecating manner. Yet judging from his reply, it seems as though Buck meant his comment to be taken literally in order to underscore the fact that, despite Junior's recent failure, he still has faith in him. "I'll give you that [your confidence]," he says, and the interchange between the two men ends.

Up to this point we have seen Junior in two significant locations: at the site of his father's house and at the rodeo (the visit to the Palace Bar to discuss rodeo matters with Buck functions as an extension of the previous scene). In the opening scenes, then, Junior visits all of the locations and people who for him have the most significance: first Ace's house (thereby giving his father the primacy of place that his name connotes and paying homage as well to his father's idealism, which is bound up with attitudes concerning self-worth intrinsic to the rodeo way of life), then to the rodeo itself. Junior now moves on to his mother's house, where he comes in contact with the materialistic side of his family and where he figuratively confronts his brother, thereby completing for the time being his dealing with all of his family and showing us through the priority of his visits how, as always, he favors the ideal over the material.

What is most significant in the conversation between Junior and Ellie is what is left unsaid, the questions never asked, the comments never made. Indeed, as succeeding scenes with the Bonners indicate, it is rare for any of the Bonners to communicate their feelings or ideas directly to one another. Instead, these people usually either talk at cross-purposes or by implication. A representative example of the family's emotional indirectness is Junior's statement about arriving at Ace's home too late to see him. "Sorry I missed you, Ace," he says. The statement is the clearest assertion by Junior regarding his feelings about his father, yet it is made when no one is there to hear it. We suspect that with Junior, as with Ace, Curly, and Ellie, had anyone else been present, his feelings would never have been expressed as plainly and directly.

When Junior first arrives at Ellie's, he sees his mother emerging from around the side of the house carrying some tomatoes. Junior asks, "You farming now, are you?" Ellie replies, "Sure as hell am trying." Ellie later asserts that Curly is providing for her, but this comment, like Junior's later question about Ellie's boarders, suggests that she is in fact impoverished. Yet Ellie never once admits to her financial condition, maintaining a characteristic Bonner stoicism. In similarly restrained fashion, Ellie offers only simple replies to Junior's comment about how much money Curly paid Ace for his land.

> JUNIOR: That's all Curly paid him for that land is $15,000?
> ELLIE: That's all.
> JUNIOR: Four sections up there.
> ELLIE: I know.

The notion of money then naturally leads the conversation to the subject of the entrepreneurial activities of Curly and his wife, Ruth.

> JUNIOR: Curly and Ruth still running that place up the highway?
> ELLIE: Um-hm. They're the two busiest people in this county. Curly started a mobile home development on the ranch right in back of the trading post, and he isn't stopping there.

Ellie then modifies the meaning of the word "stop" by asking, "Junior, when are you gonna stop?" She wants to know, of course, whether Junior is ever going to forego his itinerant lifestyle and "settle down" and "be responsible" like Curly. Junior understands his mother's implication, although he doesn't acknowledge it directly. Instead, he addresses the only issue involving responsibility that he thinks is relevant here: not the way that he intends to live, but a debt that he owes Ellie.

> JUNIOR: Well, about that money I haven't been paying you— there's going to continue to be an interruption there.
> ELLIE: Is that what it's called, a continued interruption?

Junior looks down in embarrassment. Ellie sees that Junior is distressed not only about being unable to pay back the loan but also about the implied contrast between his poverty and Curly's prosperity. One might expect that at this point Ellie would shift the conversation to another topic, one less painful to her son. Instead, out of what appears to be a desire to ameliorate Junior's reaction and an unconscious need to accentuate the distinction between the two brothers, Ellie says, "Oh, well, don't worry about it; it doesn't matter. Your brother's taking care of things." The obvious implication is that neither Junior nor Ace is able (or willing) to "take care" of Ellie. Without meaning to, Ellie has let Junior know how disappointed she is in him and Ace, since their fiscal irresponsibility has placed her in Curly's power. "He [Curly] selling this place, is he?" Junior asks. Ellie tries to make it seem that the sale of her home is of little consequence to her and, further, that she approves of the constricted mobile homes that Curly is promoting: "Why not?" she demands. "Mobile homes are the thing of the future." This comment also implies that Junior is a creature of the past. Junior responds with a diplomatic "Yeah," an answer as measured as the assertions that his mother makes; he then learns that Curly is coming to supper that evening.

Ellie then remarks, "You and Ace, maybe you're the lucky ones, drifting the way you do." Although Junior seems to take his mother at her word here ("Maybe," he tactfully agrees), it's clear that Ellie's comment is only half serious. The underlying criticism of Junior and Ace's fiscal irresponsibility is still strongly in force. Yet Ellie is also envious of Junior and Ace's freedom, a quality that she undoubtedly resents because, as the film makes clear, this freedom is available only to men. Although *Junior Bonner* contains numerous men (Junior, Ace, Red, Buck Roan) who live a free, itinerant life, its most prominent female characters (Ellie, Ruth Bonner [Mary Murphy], Arlis [Sandra Deel], and Charmagne [Barbara Leigh]) are either firmly allied with a dominant male figure or are manipulated, abandoned, and in general acted on by the men whom they encounter. Ellie is destined to live under Curly's sway; Arlis, in her most prominent scene in the film, is for a very awkward moment left without a dance partner; and Charmagne, after a night with Junior, is left behind at the airport while Junior returns to the essentially womanless rodeo life that he prefers. From the "pretty little girls" (Ace's patronizing words) whom Ace sees on the rodeo grounds to the wives and lovers who line the sidelines at the parade that features their men, women in *Junior Bonner* are usually on the periphery of events, a sad comment on contemporary society by this traditional Western film.

After Junior leaves Ellie's, he stops at the Bonner trading post, which is located adjacent to one of Curly's Reata Ranchero mobile home sites. Here, he learns firsthand precisely what is being done with Ace's land. The scene is like something out of a carnival: Curly, speaking through a public address system, hucksters the sites while, in his own words, "ladies in hot pants" circulate through the crowd handing out maps and brochures. The rancheros themselves, each of which occupies a quarter of an acre (which means that on the 2,600 acres where Ace used to live, Curly is going to be able to accommodate more than ten thousand people), are touted as having sunken garbage cans and providing "total electric living."

The Reata Ranchero scene is both an example of Curly's manipulative fiscal adroitness and a striking contrast to the rodeo. Whereas the rodeo sells the dream of the past, Curly (unbeknownst to his patrons) is selling the nightmare of the future: for all of Curly's talk about the area's clean air, his development actually represents the beginning of the type of progress that is destined to bring pollution to the region. Moreover, the rancheros bastardize the myth of the West's wide-open spaces and, with their accent on retirement living, anticipate the notion of growing older and the fear that attends it; as we will see, the problem of ageing is one of the most significant issues at work within the Bonner family. Despite the hug between Curly and Junior (Junior touches Curly on his expansive girth, Curly touches Junior on the ribs, noting his pained response), what we are seeing here in Junior's stunned reaction to the entire scene is the beginning of the disagreement between the two brothers that will blossom into full conflict after the dinner at Ellie's. For now, though, all that Junior can do is stare in amazement as the Reata Ranchero tour bus departs to the strains of Curly's Ranchero theme song, whose lyrics emphasize the supposed attractions of this sterile place: "[After] the children have all grown up and gone their separate ways," the residents will here "spend their happy golden sweet retirement days." This is as depressing a prospect as one could imagine.

The first Bonner family gathering (Ace is not there) is the dinner at Ellie's, which is attended by Junior, Curly, Curly's wife Ruth, and Curly and Ruth's children. There is a pronounced awkwardness at the dinner, which is characterized by either silence or disquieting dialogue. Ruth in particular stares at Junior and the manner in which he is eating (taking healthy portions of food, mopping up his gravy with a biscuit) in a way that makes the viewer wonder just what there is about Junior that seems to offend Ruth so much.

Curly comments that Ellie's working for him (by selling the mobile homes) will give her the opportunity to "get rid of some of these antiques." Just as later in the film, when an ambiguous reference is made to a "curio shop," there is an unclear meaning here. Since Ellie doesn't react to Curly's statement, we never know whether or not she wishes to keep these objects; nevertheless, it seems likely that Curly is being insensitive to his mother's attitude toward her possessions. In a similarly manipulative way, Curly has taken control of Ellie in having her house sold, so that she can move into one of his mobile homes and act as a salesperson for him. In fact, both Curly and his wife are controlling Ellie: Ruth remarks to Ellie, "Do you have to smoke while you're feeding our baby?" Ellie complies by putting out her small cigar.

When Junior makes it clear that he is going to compete in the rodeo, Ruth again acts hostile toward him, belittling him by attacking his vocation. "Curly says you seen one rodeo, you seen 'em all," Ruth says. Curly tries to be a bit conciliatory by stating, "Well, I didn't mean our rodeo, darling," but he finishes by saying, "That's part of history." Thus, just as he has relegated his mother to the status of an antique by rendering her useless except in relation to his own business, so too does he confer this status on the rodeo and, by extension, his brother as well. By contrast, Curly apparently feels that he himself represents the desirable future. Unlike Junior, Curly does not seem to understand that one can learn from the past, as Junior will realize through his nondisparaging acknowledgment of tradition and a recognition of previous mistakes. For now, Ruth completes the verbal insults by saying, "There's never been a horse that couldn't be rode, never been a cowboy that couldn't be throwed." Junior gracefully parries the remark by commenting, "Famous old saying." Ironically, this statement evokes the benefits of the passage of time by acknowledging the wisdom in a remark that has endured. Junior is also telling Ruth that he's heard this saying many times before and that she doesn't have anything new to tell him. Nevertheless, there is no denying that what Ruth has said must have stung Junior.

By the time Curly and Junior retire after dinner to the front porch, we are ready for a more direct confrontation between these two characters, who represent the opposition between contemporary and traditional values. What is most remarkable about the brothers' conversation is how, while Curly and Junior seem to be discussing the same subject, each character is really pursuing only his own version of what is being talked about. Junior accentuates the ideal realm, Curly the material, so that the discussion functions as a kind of debate. As in the previous discussion between Ellie and Junior and the forthcoming discussion between Junior and his father, the two men talk at cross-purposes. First Curly refers to Ace. "You went to see 'im," he says. Junior's response is remarkably restrained: "Yeah." Junior then goes on to ask tactfully about his brother's purchase of Ace's land. Although Junior knows how much Curly paid for the property, while mentioning the price he phrases his reference to it in the form of a question in order to avoid having his brother construe the inquiry as a critical affront. "How much was it you paid for the old man's land, fifteen thousand wasn't it?" However, Curly does not want to address the criticism implicit in Junior's question (which harks back to Junior's discussion with Ellie), so he shifts the discussion away from what he paid Ace to what Ace did with the money. "Yeah," Curly says, "which he proceeded to gamble and whore away in Nevada." Curly then expands on his censure of Ace, making it quite clear that he considers Ace a failure because of his inability to pursue a particular project. "But he had to quit prospecting twenty feet from the mother lode," Curly says.

Plate 36. Junior and Curly Bonner.

Junior will not allow himself to be distracted by Curly's attempt to change the subject's focus, though. He returns to the topic of the paucity of payment for Ace's land. "Don't seem much, twenty-six hundred acres," he says. Curly, though, continues with his chosen topic: Ace's recklessness, now exemplified by his propensity to seize on what Curly considers ill-advised ideas. "Now he's got this scheme to go to Australia." Junior replies, "Well, why don't you send him?" Curly's response is sharp and vindictive. "Oh, come on, Junior. I'll put him on a weekly allowance and that's it. I told him so. Know what I mean?" Junior's reply is as curt as usual, although here he keeps his response restrained solely for the sake of promoting amity: "Yeah," he says.

Curly then attempts to involve Junior in the Reata Ranchero project by appealing to his brother's supposed desire to protect himself financially. Characteristically, Curly expresses himself in terms of the future, laying emphasis on what he obviously regards as the necessity for self-centered, entrepreneurial activity. He first says, "You oughta start thinking about your own self for a change." He then tries to tempt Junior by using an extremely worn cliché commonly employed in business ventures; its use reveals Curly's conventional mode of thinking and highlights the narrowness of what he considers to be his progressive vision. "You may not know it but you are in the right place at the right time," he says. "That's here. It's a regular land boom, Junior."

Having observed Curly's land project, Junior knows what a travesty of the traditional Western land boom it represents. Doubly offended at the affront to both his own views concerning the need for space (whether literal or personal), Junior now employs some uncustomary sarcasm. "Yeah, I saw your wide-open spaces," Junior says. Curly's reply is equally disagreeable. "You know less about those wide-open spaces than I do," he says. "I know it where it is." Curly then goes on to retaliate against Junior's implied criticism of him by using the same tactic that his wife had earlier used: attacking Junior's vocation. "You're just some kind of motel cowboy," Curly says. (The remark seems a bit uncharacteristic for Curly, though, since he is using the word *motel* in a pejorative way, something that you would not expect from someone promoting mobile housing.) Despite the intended insult, Junior is not to be deterred, still insisting that Curly confront what Junior feels is the disrespectfully small amount of money that Ace received for his land. "Fifteen thousand just seems a little bit short," Junior says in a remark that, although direct, signals the return of his essential good humor since the statement, which contains only the barest hint of irony, has its directness modified by the qualifying words *seems* and *little*.

Curly is still very offended, though. "Fifteen or thirty thousand, [Ace] would have blown it all," he says. However, as Junior undoubtedly recognizes, what Ace did with the money has nothing to do with the appropriateness of the amount that he received for what turns out to have been an extremely valuable piece of land. Curly may reason that he has merely carried out a sound capitalist transaction by buying cheap and selling dear, but such a contention would also be beside the point. The transaction with Ace makes it plain that Curly places finance before family. Curly then goes on to state, "Now he needed the money fast and I got it for him—me." Curly's repeated emphasis on his role in providing Ace with the money operates as a quite obvious criticism of Junior, just as Ellie's reference to Curly taking care of things had done.

Curly then changes the topic back to Junior again, invoking the supposed lure of the future, even though Curly has yet to define what, aside from making money at someone else's expense, is so tantalizing about it. "I just want you to get a grip on your future," Curly says.[11] "I want you to come work for me." However, Junior senses Curly's true motives and states his suspicions clearly. "You mean you want me to help you sell the old man's land," Junior says. Curly's subsequent reference to the property as "our land, Junior" is clearly a lie. The land is not a birthright; it is property that Curly has acquired solely in order to benefit himself. Curly refers to it as "our land" only in order to involve his brother in his capitalist scheme.

Curly then expands on how he conceives of Junior's role in his business, inadvertently alienating his brother even more by the way that he attempts to turn to commercial account Junior's involvement with the rodeo. "What a salesman you'd make for the rancheros. Big cowboy like you—sincere. Why you're as genuine as the sunrise."

The speech is interesting in a number of respects. Curly is obviously misrepresenting his beliefs here in order to convince Junior to work for him. Curly refers to Junior as a "big cowboy" as though he admired his brother's vocation; yet we know from his earlier "motel cowboy" reference that Curly believes that Junior only plays at being a cowboy. Of course, Curly may dimly perceive that Junior does truly possess some genuine cowboy traits. Curly's actual view on this topic doesn't really matter, though: regardless of whether he means to have his customers take the illusion of genuineness for the real thing, or whether he intends to corrupt actual genuineness for his own benefit, Curly is nonetheless promoting falsity for profit, a fact that makes his use of the word *sincere* rankly offensive. Curly's use of the word *sunrise* also reflects poorly on him. Throughout the film, the word *sun* is used for its connotations of genuineness, with regard not only to the literal sun as a revealer of the truth but also to the bull Old Sunshine, who helps reveal to Junior the truth about himself as a rider. Additionally, the word *sun* functions as a pun referring to Ace's two offspring, each of whom represents one of the poles in the spectrum from materialistic and insincere to idealistic and sincere. Again, this reference can work only to Curly's disadvantage. (An additional meaning emerges here: that Junior's fortunes may somehow be on the "rise," but only if they are allied with genuineness, a consideration that obviously excludes Curly.)

Eventually, Curly realizes that, unlike Ellie, Junior is not interested in slaving himself to him. "There's no fooling ourselves, is there," Curly finally says. "You got to ride." "That's right, Curly," Junior replies. "Salinas, California, day after tomorrow." These two sentences are another example of the brothers' cross-purpose conversation. Curly means to imply that Junior's compulsion to continue competing in rodeos is impractical. Junior, by contrast, refers to a specific time at which he is scheduled to ride, a concrete example of the compulsion to which his brother refers, which Junior regards as a way to bring the ideal realm into the real.

Finally, Curly makes the mistake of juxtaposing his insulting offer to Junior with a direct slur against Ace as well, a combination of offenses that even a good-natured man like Junior cannot tolerate. "I just don't want you to turn out like the old man," Curly says, at which point Junior knocks him through the porch's plate-glass window. Ellie shouts, "Junior!" Junior's reply, "Don't say it," seems to indicate that this kind of altercation has occurred before. "I'm going," Junior says, and the scene ends. The family get-together has concluded with everyone (except the matched pair of Curly and Ruth) being totally alienated from one another.

The following morning Junior and Buck Roan meet in a scene that contrasts strikingly with the Bonner family gathering, thereby underscoring the distinction between the way that rodeo and nonrodeo individuals interact. Junior first asks, "Do I get that draw or don't I?" Buck's reply—"A kick in the head, Junior, that's what it's about"—indicates that he believes that Junior will not be able to ride the bull successfully. Yet, as we see from subsequent events, Buck proves his friendship by giving Junior the chance to make another attempt; this is an especially admirable and nonmaterialistic gesture given the fact that it is in Buck's best interest for the bull to remain undefeated. Of course, Buck may believe that Junior poses no threat to the bull's championship. Yet knowing Junior's nature as he does, it's more likely that Buck thinks that Junior just may be able to ride the bull long enough to win.

However, to give Junior the option of an alternative to riding,

Buck offers Junior a job, which he may accept either before or after the rodeo. Buck's manner differs markedly from the way that Curly offered Junior a job. Buck couches his offer in the third-person conditional; by doing so, he causes the offer to seem less direct and real, thereby making it easier for Junior to decline without offending Buck. "You know, Junior, if a man was gonna expand his business, stop in more shows and more towns, he might be interested in an assistant, say a fellow who had been around some, a champion in his day."

The reference to Junior's past status as a champion, which might seem offensive if offered by a different speaker, does not cause animosity here. As before, when Buck had told Junior that he was no longer the rider that he had been, Buck is merely expressing his opinion, with no ulterior motive. If anything, Buck's statement is meant as a gracious and sincere testimonial to Junior's capabilities, with no emphasis placed on his championship being in the past. However, receiving no response, Buck retreats slightly from his offer. "Well, I just thought I'd mention it," he says. "Don't think so, Buck," Junior replies in his typically succinct manner, and the topic is closed. No animosity has been engendered between these two men, as there is between Junior and Curly. It thus seems quite appropriate that Buck and Junior now decide to participate in a bonding ritual: communal eating. Their decision to breakfast together puts a simple and touching end to the scene.

The first meeting between Ace and Junior occurs during the Frontier Days parade and is a fine representation of the way that father and son, while carrying on what appears to be a casual conversation, express their innermost feelings about issues that are vital to them. The conversation takes place in a symbolic setting that is arrived at symbolically. Ace and Junior, having ridden off from the parade in which they were both riding Junior's horse, are at the Prescott train station. Junior's horse is tethered near the bench where Ace and Junior are sitting. Throughout the conversation we hear the sounds of the horse's hooves moving back and forth on the concrete train station platform, thus yoking the two predominant strains in the film: the past, as represented by the horse, and the present, manifested not only in the train station but also in the actual train (an iron horse) that passes through the station at one point.

The conversation between Junior and Ace begins when Ace inquires about a couple of rodeo circuit men, thereby revealing a tendency toward nostalgia already noted during his earlier exchange with a rodeo veteran named Roy. In that conversation, though, Ace was talking to a contemporary of his and could admit his somewhat anachronistic status:

ACE: How many we rode in, Roy?
ROY: Not enough, Ace.
ACE: Not enough and maybe too many, huh?
ROY: Too many probably.

Ace would not make such a concession to members of his family, in front of whom (and other people as well) he is prone to braggadocio and bluster. In the scene with Junior, we first get the following exchange.

ACE: You ever hear from Johnny Mars?
JUNIOR: He's breaking horses out of Carlsbad—still makes the El Paso show.
ACE: And Buddy Cox—always hollered, "As long as women live, my name will never die."
JUNIOR: Well, he's dead, Dad—car crash between Abilene and Dallas.

The exchange makes it plain that Ace is out of touch with many of his contemporaries; indeed, he doesn't even know that one of them is no longer alive. Ace then goes on to make a remark that he intends to be taken as a friendly comment to Junior, part encouragement, part question to see how his son will react to what is, after all, a routine colloquialism. "Well, I hear you're doing very well," he says. As always, though, Junior prefers to deal with the unvarnished truth. "Where'd you hear that?" he asks.

Junior then follows with another truth that he wishes revealed: Ace's behavior toward Ellie, of which he is doubtless reminded by the similarity between his own impoverishment (his not "doing very well") and that of his mother. "Taking care of Mom, are you?" he asks. Ace is not only as much of an idealist as Junior; occasionally he is also, like Junior, ready to acknowledge the truth about certain situations. "Oh, not much," Ace replies. Yet unlike Junior, Ace will not admit that his actions are directly responsible for Ellie's current poverty. Of course, Junior exhibits some degree of fiscal recklessness toward Ellie as well (a quality we have already seen in his failure to repay Ellie). At the film's end, Junior compounds the situation. Instead of using part of his rodeo winnings to pay off some of this loan, Junior decides to finance Ace's trip to Australia, thereby not only revealing his greater affection for his father but also demonstrating his preference for the ideal life (which Ace represents) over the material attitudes represented by Ellie and Curly. Junior's action may also hint at the film's general slighting of women's roles. This attitude is much in evidence in the supposedly comic action during the fight in the Palace Bar when a man, after chasing a number of women through the bar, rushes into the women's bathroom, where he apparently engages in sex with a woman. Later, this same man is seen chasing a different woman, who is yelling and trying to get away from him. He justifies his behavior by explaining, "I love 'em," hardly a sufficient rationale for what amounts to assault.

Ace rationalizes his wife's present situation, attempting to represent it as though she is well off, since she is now under the protection of Curly. Ace contends that Ellie is doing precisely what she wants to do. "She's selling antiques out to the town house. She's happy. She's living right where she wanted to live all her life: right in the middle of things."

However, Junior points out to Ace a fact of which his father should be aware but isn't. "Curly's gonna sell that house," says Junior, "put her in a curio shop." The reference to the curio shop implies not only that Ellie will be working in the shop but also that she may very well be regarded as an anachronistic curio herself. All that Ace says to this assertion, though, is "Curly's doing right well." This meaningless colloquialism, which harks back to his similar statement to Junior, inadvertently implies that he somehow approves of the way that Curly is treating Ellie.

We have seen members of the Bonner family demonstrating emotional reticence before. In the present scene, though, Ace's refusal to react to what is happening to Ellie demonstrates not emotional restraint but selfishness. The circumstances obviously call for outrage or indignation—at the very least, some affective response. Instead, Ace doesn't even bother to empathize with Junior's concern about Ellie.

The conversation then turns to Ace's projected trip to Australia, the change in subject representing another example of Ace's being interested solely in his own activities. Ace tells Junior that he intends to go to Australia to prospect for gold and asks his son to "grub-stake" him. After Junior tells Ace that he cannot help him because he has no money, Ace—in despair and frustration—knocks Junior's hat off his head. Regretting this action, Ace stands up to retrieve the hat. However, to do so, Ace must cross a set of railroad tracks.

At this point, a train passes between Ace and Junior, blocking each man's sight of the other. The train separating Ace and Junior serves two functions. First, while it is passing, Junior turns his back on Ace and grasps his pained side, thus using the obstruction of vision to hide his discomfort from his father. Second, since the train, a machine, represents progress (as is customary in Peckinpah's work), its intercession also signifies the symbolic gulf in time between Ace and Junior, with the father allied with the rodeo's past and the son trying desperately to remain a part of its present. (However, this distinction between Ace and Junior is not quite as pronounced as it might seem. Junior's participation in the rodeo allies him with the past. Ace, too, is striving to be more than just a curio from the past, hoping to avoid that status and provide a new, economically secure future for himself by prospecting—ironically, a very traditional activity.)

After the train passes, Ace walks back to the platform and returns the hat to Junior, who accepts it graciously. A serious emotional rupture between the two men has been settled amicably. It remains for Junior to express his affection for Ace by telling him that he has entered them both, as a father-and-son team, in the wild cow–milking contest that is about to take place.[12] In both disbelief of, and silent appreciation for, Junior's touching gesture, Ace can only shake his head and mumble as the scene draws to a close.

During the steer-wrestling competition at the rodeo, Junior and his only real rival for the rodeo championship, Red Terwilliger, trade roles. First, Junior rides and then wrestles the steer and Red hazes (that is, Red, riding on a horse beside Junior, helps to guide the steer toward Junior's horse). As in the opening sequence, Junior is bested by Red. Junior's time for wrestling the steer to the ground is 8.2 seconds; Red's is 6.5. The way that Peckinpah depicts each man's performance is significant. Junior's steer wrestling is shown in slow motion, ostensibly to allow us to appreciate Junior's style. However, Red's actions are shown in real time. Although this approach might be explained by the need to use a different cinematic technique to avoid repetition, the style also works to exaggerate the fact that Junior's time is significantly longer than Red's.

At halftime, many of the spectators and participants retire to the Palace Bar, where the fight between Curly and Junior that began at Ellie's enters its second, and final, round. The fight represents more than just Curly's revenge on Junior for the blow that he received the night before; it also provides the occasion for some

Plate 37. The wild cow–milking contest: Ace and Junior don't exactly look like they're pulling together here.

important dialogue between the brothers as well as an exchange of gestures that might otherwise not have occurred. The action begins when Curly determinedly walks up to the bar, where Junior is having a drink. Sensing the strain between himself and Curly, Junior tries to establish good feelings by asking, "You want a beer, Curly?" At this point Curly knocks Junior down. (As Ellie had done the night before when Junior had hit Curly, Ace indicates that the brothers' fighting is a fairly regular occurrence. "Just like old times," he says.)

When Junior gets up, Curly seems to be anticipating some physical response from his brother, but Junior knows that Curly's blow is fair retaliation for the night before, so he simply says, "Would you like a beer?" Curly assents and goes on to express his affection for Junior, but in a highly qualified way: "You're my brother, Junior, and I guess I love you." He then qualifies the assertion even further, essentially withdrawing it by saying, "Well, we're family," as though this fact were something whose unalterable nature he regretted. Curly then expresses what he claims is the motivation behind his job offer to Junior: "I don't care if you sell one lot or one hundred lots; I'm just trying to keep us together." But when Junior replies, "I got to go down my own road," Curly, as he had the night before, once again feels offended and retaliates with hostility aimed at Junior's vocation. "What road?" he asks. "I'm working on my first million and you're still working on eight seconds." Junior looks somewhat hurt here, but then Ruth steps in, puts her arm around Curly, and leads him away to dance. Seeing them openly expressing affection, with the usually dour Ruth exhibiting an uncharacteristic tenderness and warmth, Junior cannot help but smile, a smile that seems to temporarily dispel the two brothers' alienation. As Curly walks away, Junior touches his brother and Curly touches Junior at the waist. This time, though, Junior does not wince in pain, as though the reconciliation with Curly has momentarily eased the discomfort and humiliation that had felt at being defeated by Old Sunshine.

At this point, Burt Huntsacker (Charles Gray) and Charmagne enter the bar. We have already met Charmagne and Burt in an earlier scene on the rodeo grounds, where Burt, Charmagne, and another couple approach Junior. In order to assert his superiority, Burt treats Junior like a sideshow attraction. "Well, if it isn't Junior Bonner. Hey, folks, this is Junior Bonner," Burt says while the man with him shoots pictures of Junior as though he is some form of oddity. When Junior fails to react, Burt says, "Burt Huntsacker. Oh, you remember me. Six years ago, a little place in Nogales, right after the Tucson show." Junior seems to remember Burt only vaguely, if at all, but he isn't about to be intentionally insulting if he can avoid it. "Six years is a long time, but you're sure looking good, Burt," Junior replies. The compliment is sincerely offered, which seems to disarm Burt, who looks quite disappointed.

In the present scene, Junior walks over to Burt's table and asks Charmagne to dance. As at the end of the other scene, when he had shepherded Charmagne away from Junior, Burt acts as though Charmagne is his possession and again tries to act superior to Junior. "You're a little out of line, Junior," Burt says, to which Junior simply replies, "Not really." When it looks as though Burt is going to respond physically, Charmagne forestalls a confrontation by saying that she will dance with Junior. However, Burt does not intend to acquiesce so easily. Speaking as though he is an old-style Western tough, Burt says, "One dance, Junior; I can't count much further."

Junior and Charmagne dance and talk a bit. When Red Terwilliger sees what an attractive woman Junior is dancing with, he tries to cut in on them. This interaction between Red and Junior provides a notable contrast with the way that Burt and Junior had behaved and parallels the scenes between Curly and Junior and Buck Roan and Junior. Whereas the rodeo men treat each other with respect and cordiality, the nonrodeo men react with defensiveness and hostility. What seems to account for these different attitudes is that the rodeo men are allied with a profession that mandates self-respect and mutual consideration, qualities that apparently derive from the fact that they are part of a group that shares a tradition of achievement and a concomitant sense of self-worth. Earlier in the film, when Junior had first arrived at the rodeo grounds, Red had asked him why he hadn't stayed at the Palace Bar the night before. Junior replied that he had slept outside, to which Red had simply responded, "Um-hm." Red's restraint was more than an example of characteristic cowboy terseness; it also indicated his respect for Junior. Realizing that Junior must have spent all of his money on registration fees, Red refrained from commenting on his friend's poverty.

When Red tries to dance with Charmagne, his intention is good-natured. Red asks Junior if he would mind his cutting in; Junior replies, "Well, I'll tell you the truth, Red, I kind of do—nothing personal." As Junior intends, Red doesn't take the rebuff personally, merely adding a comment to indicate that he wishes Junior all of the best in his relationship with the woman. "I hope she treats you better than Sunshine," Red says. Junior replies, "So do I." Red then goes back to his table.

When the next song begins and Junior and Charmagne start to dance again, Burt gets up to break them apart. Seeing this, and wanting to engage in a little fun at Burt's expense, Junior now allows Red to dance with Charmagne. When Burt comes up to Red he says, "You, git!" The incredulous Red replies, "What?" Burt says, "I mean it," and shoves Red. Red retaliates, and the fight in the bar has begun.

The fight is nothing more than a comic set piece, notable as an example of a successful wedding of chaos and good nature that is unique to Peckinpah's work. (The cafe altercation in *Convoy* tries for this tone but fails to achieve it.) Although the fight involves most of the people in the bar, Peckinpah makes certain that some of them do not participate, thereby providing a necessary counterpoint to the prevalent disorder. Throughout the fight, the country-and-western band plays its slow tune; Ellie and Ace, and Junior and Charmagne, continue to dance (although the latter couple eventually retire to a phone booth to finish their conversation); a group of men keep up their leisurely card game; and the bartender takes the opportunity presented by the melee to steal from the cash register.

With its cordiality and aggression, the Palace Bar scene acts as a microcosm of the film as a whole, providing the occasion for the resolution of Curly and Junior's disagreement and even allowing Ace and Ellie, who leave the bar, to become reconciled. Nonetheless, it is clear that the bar scene is chiefly intended as an interlude before the event toward which the entire film has been heading: Junior's second ride on Old Sunshine.

This time Junior is lodged in chute number one, the number referring to the champion status that Old Sunshine possesses and toward which Junior aspires. Peckinpah renders the majority of the ride at regular camera speed in order to give us a full appreciation of the bull's swiftness and power. However, by intercutting views of the timekeeper's stopwatch, inserting crowd reaction shots, and judiciously using slow-motion images of the ride, Peckinpah manages to stretch the ride's first eight seconds to at least forty seconds on screen, thus increasing the suspense about the outcome. After Junior has completed the ride, becoming the first man to have ridden the bull successfully, the crowd stands up in acclamation. The rodeo announcer comments, "I think you'll agree that after eighty-four years [the length of time that the Prescott rodeo has been held] they still make cowboys as tough as they ever did." This statement confirms that Junior has accomplished more than merely proving to himself that a significant part of his rodeo capabilities is still intact; he has also once again established himself as the legitimate heir to a great American rodeo tradition.

Like its characters, the film wastes no time on sentimentality, refusing to linger over Junior's triumph. The last part of *Junior Bonner* consists of leave-takings, each one ending with a freeze-frame of the character being left behind. The technique, which harks back to the titles sequence, suggests that these characters are already moving into the confines of memory. We first see Junior and Charmagne driving up to and entering the airport terminal. Here again, *Junior Bonner* demonstrates its restrained approach to emotional matters. It is the next morning; given that Junior and Charmagne had left the rodeo in each other's company and are obviously attracted to each other, we can assume that they have spent the night together. Yet the film does not directly acknowledge this personal situation. It is enough for *Junior Bonner* merely to suggest that Junior and

Charmagne have shared some intimacy in order for the present scene to be effective. When they enter the airport, neither character says anything. Charmagne looks at Junior; Junior looks back at her and then shakes his head, as if to indicate that words at this point would be both insufficient and superfluous. Affirming the fact that for him the rodeo is all-important, Junior appropriately expresses himself in Western terms by saying, "Rodeo time—gotta get it on down the road. So long." The image freezes as Charmagne watches Junior depart.

When Junior stops at Ellie's house, his mother says to him, "You had to win, didn't you?" The ambiguous phrase "had to" indicates the forces of ambition and fate that exert an influence on Junior. Junior didn't just need to win; in some sense, he was destined to do so. Unfortunately, in *Junior Bonner* the confluence of fate and ambition acts to distance the film's central characters from one another, either literally or figuratively. Junior's allegiance to the rodeo, and his continued success in it, separate him from his family and Charmagne; Ace's insistence on living out his dream, which he is able to do thanks to Junior's good fortune, compels him to absent himself from the rest of the Bonners. Ellie's need for security and Curly's desire for wealth—which, in a complementary fashion, cause Ellie to gravitate toward Curly for fiscal protectiveness, thereby making possible his influence over her—are purchased at the price of emotional contact. As Junior walks away from his mother's house, the camera freezes on Ellie's face. She is photographed through the screen door, which lends to her face a grainy quality similar to the rough-textured title sequence images from the past; like these images, Ellie seems to have entered the past already.

The leave-taking between Junior and Curly has previously taken place—at the Palace Bar. No direct good-bye occurs between Junior and Ace. Ace is last seen on a Prescott street shouting after Junior, who, driving by, apparently doesn't hear his father calling him. We last see Ace in a freeze-frame image, his head intersecting the four-sided window of a bar in front of which he is standing; this scene calls to mind Curly's comment about Ace drinking up the money he received for his land.

The film's penultimate scene (the credits, like the titles sequence, function as an integral part of the film) takes place in an airline ticket office. Junior spends virtually all of his prize money on a ticket to Australia for Ace and Ace's dog. (Ace's ticket is one-way, implying that Junior doesn't feel that Ace will be coming back; it is also for first class, as befits the way that Ace thinks of himself and the esteem in which Junior holds him.) When the sales agent asks, "Who shall we say paid for the ticket?" Junior, using typical Western rhetoric and restraint, says, "Tell 'em Junior sent you" and the scene ends.

The film cuts to a shot of Junior's car moving along the highway leading out of town. (The scene is photographed from a respectful distance except for one brief close-up of Junior, thus maintaining *Junior Bonner*'s objective approach to the sentimental realm.) It's a melancholy yet satisfying conclusion that finds Junior, having harnessed the sunshiny light of his dreams (as a son he has really shone) and successfully resolved for himself the conflict between the past (available to us through memory) and the future (where his desires lead him), driving away as the setting sun casts the ever-lengthening shadow of his car on the road that he has chosen to go down alone.[13]

Breaking Out for Love

          Like the beginnings of *The Wild Bunch* and *Junior Bonner*, the titles sequence of *The Getaway* conveys a great deal of information about the film and its characters. Even before the film's first image, we hear the sound of barking dogs, an effect that, along with the lack of image, communicates a feeling of unrest and anxiety that will prevail throughout most of the film. The first shot, which is accompanied by the sound of a neighing horse (which again implies a feeling of unease), is a close-up of a deer staring at the camera, an image that would usually communicate a sense of pastoral relaxation were it not that this feeling is quickly compromised by the sound of the neighing horse and the anxiety that lingers from the continuing dog sounds. Peckinpah cuts to a shot of other deer and then pans up from the deer to a guard tower, thereby letting us know that the deer are grazing outside a prison. The guard-tower shot is then complemented by the sound of sheep, an effect whose pastoral connotation is undercut by the realization that this juxtaposition of images and sound compares sheep and prison inmates, who, like sheep, are repressed by the prison rules. These rules are figuratively present in the barking of the dogs (presumably bloodhounds) and the neighing of the horses, which are ridden by many of the prison guards.

          Shots of the sheep, and then the deer again, are followed by a pull-back that eventually reveals the barbed wire that surrounds the prison, emphasizing the place's repressive aspect. This effect is then reinforced by a view of the prison's numerous and identical buildings; this architectural sameness reflects the way that the prison destroys individual identity. During the pull-back, the noise of a machine blends into the soundtrack, another effect suggesting not only impersonality but the fact that, like a constantly whirring machine, the repression here is endless.

However, the idea of never-ending repression conflicts somewhat with the next shot of Doc McCoy (Steve McQueen), which is accompanied by a voice-over from the parole board hearing toward which he is walking. The dialogue from the hearing continues throughout the next series of images. Yet the interminable machine sound continues here as well, suggesting that Doc stands little chance of being released until his full term is served. We then see prisoners working out with barbells; the men are trying to maintain their physical integrity in the midst of an institution that assaults the integrity of their personalities. This image is followed by a shot of the men at the parole board, which is then followed by a shot of Doc working at the machine that is the source of the sound we have heard: a loom at which wool—doubtless from the sheep that we earlier saw, the linkage reinforcing the comparison between Doc and the animals—is being woven. Doc's presence at the loom further suggests a linkage between him and the fates, who spin men's destiny, with the irony that Doc, as a prisoner, has no control over his fate. The parole board, which we would assume is far more in control of Doc's fate, is then seen again, followed by a shot of Doc on his way to the hearing.

Throughout *The Getaway*, Doc and his wife, Carol (Ali MacGraw), pass through many physical and figurative barriers on the way to their final escape. In the title sequence, we see Doc repeatedly walking through gates on the way to the parole board meeting. Yet even though he passes through these barriers, we know that Doc is trapped; indeed, each door releases Doc only into another part of the prison. The film's title appears just as Doc, on his way to the board room, passes another prisoner, who says, "Good luck, man"; the scene strongly suggests that Doc and Carol will need some kind of luck to achieve their final getaway.

Doc walks into the room where the parole hearing will be held; we are then given our first view of Benyon (Ben Johnson), who, we later learn, controls the parole board and who represents the bad luck that sets Doc free but also subjects him to many hazards before his luck changes. Doc looks at Benyon, who glances at Doc and then disdainfully looks away. However, Doc continues to stare at Benyon, who finally, in an unfriendly fashion, looks back at Doc;

all the while Benyon idly fingers a loose piece of skin on his thumb, an action that draws attention to the figurative member under which Doc is trapped.

Succeeding shots tell us that Benyon is the real power behind the board. While all of the board members sit forward at the table, the self-assured Benyon leans back from it, suggesting that he regards the meeting with indifference; this is an unusual attitude given the seriousness of the board's work. Additionally, although Benyon, like the board's other members, wears a tie in an acknowledgment of some degree of formality, he keeps his hat on during the meeting, emphasizing his disdain for the board's authority. All of these details combine to presage ill for Doc.

Doc's lawyer asks the committee to note Doc's good behavior while a prisoner; Benyon seems to ignore the lawyer's statement, just as he pointedly ignores the chairman of the parole board. The chairman, who is obviously a mere figurehead, states that Doc's request for parole is denied; Doc must now wait for an entire year before reapplying. Doc betrays his anxiety by beginning to bite his lip, all the while staring at Benyon, who stares back at him. During these shots, Peckinpah blends back in the sound of the oppressive and fateful loom, which grows progressively louder on the sound-track until we eventually see a shot of it.

The loom sound continues through the next long sequence of images. A shot of Doc being tenderly touched on the shoulder by someone whom we later realize is his wife communicates a sense of intimacy and freedom of action that are simply unavailable to Doc at the present. Yet the shot also suggests another possible source of freedom, since it emanates from the realm of memory, which ideally should be untouched by the physical constraints imposed by the prison. Unfortunately, as we soon see, Doc can take no comfort in this realm.

Doc walks back to his work area at the loom and turns on the machine. The ensuing close-up of his face intensifies our experience of his despair. There follows a view of the loom's on-off switch, an object that suggests that an insidious pecking order operates in *The Getaway*. We know that Benyon controls the parole board and that the parole board controls Doc. All that Doc has control over—and then only to a small extent, since he obviously cannot choose not to work—is the delivery of electrical power to the machine. Tragically, the man who controls the machine is controlled as if he himself were a machine.

The ideas of powerlessness and entrapment are reinforced by succeeding shots of the deer and of prisoners being counted off as they file back into prison. We next see Doc, who expresses his frustration over his imprisonment and asserts his limited power over the loom by jerking the machine's on-off handle back and forth. The pointlessness of Doc's gesture is emphasized by the next shot, photographed from the point of view of a dispassionate God, which shows prisoners filing into their individual cells. A guard says, "Lock 'em up," and all of the cell doors, also operated by an electrical mechanism whose actions are associated with confinement, close simultaneously. More close-ups of the loom mechanism and Doc working at it—accompanied, as always, by the oppressive sounds of the machine shop—are followed by a close-up of a prisoner in the work area looking at Doc's tortured face. A shot of Doc follows, then an extreme close-up of the loom gears jerking the machine's gear train back and forth in a repetition apparently as endless as the prisoners' routine movements from the inside of their cells to the outside and then back into their cells again. The back-and-forth movement also suggests the prisoners' depressing recidivism. This idea is stated explicitly by the guard who opens the gates for Doc after Benyon secures a parole for him. The guard says, "You'll be back, Doc." And were it not for the entrance into Doc and Carol's lives of a nearly divine figure, this prognostication would certainly prove true.

The gear-train image also functions as an analogue of the relationship between Benyon and Doc, with the master of mechanical fate, Benyon, as the gear, imparting movement to Doc—in this case, by having him paroled and then telling Doc that although he may think he is performing the bank job on his own volition, he is not. As Benyon says, "You run the job but I run the show." In an additional example of the film's pecking order, Doc does impart motion to some lesser characters, Rudy Butler (Al Lettieri) and Frank Jackson (Bo Hopkins) among them. Yet all of the characters, even Benyon, are ultimately part of a greater mechanism of fate. Only after Doc and Carol realize their devotion to each other and acknowledge that they are subject to forces beyond their control— an idea most strongly impressed on them when they become nothing more than trash being hauled in a garbage truck—are they ready to admit their inability to change their fate and thus come to accept it. In a paradigm that invites comparison with the acquisition of religious humility, Doc and Carol's recognition and acceptance of their need for each other changes their fate and makes possible a release from the ominous, mechanical series of events that have, ironically, led them to the place where their humility makes possible their new life.

The loom's gears are seen in more shots, some of which turn to freeze-frames while the soundtrack remains continuous, thereby setting up a tension between static images and sounds of movement. The suggestion of the possibility of release follows with the shot of two attractive pictures of Carol on Doc's cell wall. Yet as with all of the invocations of memory in the title sequence, these photos may offer both solace and pain: although the photos might afford a release into fantasy, they may also remind Doc that Carol is free while he is imprisoned.

Another extreme close-up of the loom mechanism follows; the shot then freezes. The stasis is broken first by another shot of Doc's face and then by a shot in which movement predominates: a view of prisoners running, their freedom belied by the fact that their actions are viewed through prison bars. We then see Doc through his cell's bars, lying corpselike on his bunk and idly scratching the back of his hand. In contrast to the confining connotations in this shot is the sound of a guard saying, "Open the gate," at which point the image once again freezes. The guard's statement derives from the scene with the running prisoners, who are headed to some outdoor location; once again (as in the loom–parole board juxtaposition) we realize that the editing technique has given us access to two different time sequences since, as it turns out, Doc is among the prisoners who are to pass through the gate. The prisoners, viewed this time through the grillwork of an iron fence topped with barbed wire (more restrictions), are then abruptly halted by another guard.

An important sequence now begins that represents the contradictory ideas under which Doc is operating. Again lying on his back, Doc turns toward the wall and looks at Carol's pictures. A series of memory images then starts that clashes with the activities of the prison work detail. The opposition suggested here is between the tenderness, familiarity, and freedom that Doc, at least at this juncture, associates with Carol and the impersonal, onerous situations that he associates with the prison. During this portion of the title sequence, Peckinpah renders four different times and places: Doc in the prison workshop, Doc in his cell, Doc on a work detail, and Doc with Carol. These realms, which are spatially striking in that they move from the exterior of the prison (the work detail) to its interior (the workshop and the cell) to the innermost reaches of Doc's consciousness (his memories of Carol), are nevertheless all oppressive. (As we will see, Doc's relationship with Carol initially seems as much of a trap as any of these other realms.) Regardless of where he is and whether he is concentrating on the interior or exterior world, Doc will always be a prisoner until he realizes that he is trapped by his negative attitude toward himself and the people around him.

In this sequence we first see a shot of the work detail as a guard begins to give the men orders. There follows a close-up of Carol looking down at Doc and tenderly touching his forehead. On the soundtrack we still hear the prison guard giving orders; guard dogs bark in the background. For Doc, the visual and aural realms here are in powerful conflict. What is most striking about this sequence is that no sounds accompany Doc's memory images of Carol; alternatively, all of the images related to the prison are supported by oppressive sounds. This characteristic not only points up the primacy of the prison for Doc but also radically compromises any positive effects that his memories of Carol might have.

Obviously pained by his recollection of Carol, which was doubtless prompted by the pictures above his bunk, Doc turns away from the wall. Images of the guard ordering the men on the work detail and views of Doc and Carol kissing are quickly followed by shots of Doc at the loom and another extreme close-up of the loom gears. During the last three shots, the conflict between these realms seems to be increasing in intensity since the loom sounds, which have been heard throughout this sequence, are now heard at full volume. The image then freezes on the gears.

More shots alternate between Doc and Carol's lovemaking and the loom gears, suggesting the antithesis between mechanical movements and human passion; this theme, which is one of the film's primary concerns, emerges most clearly in Doc's later criticism of Carol's use of her sexuality as a tool to influence Benyon. A shot of the peristaltic flow of work detail prisoners past a prison gate not only mirrors the jerking back and forth of the loom gears but also duplicates the way that Doc's thoughts move back and forth between the various times and places that he is remembering. More images of oppression and enforced labor ensue. We see part of the work detail, Doc among them, passing through the prison gates and jumping into trucks. This shot is followed by views of guards on horseback; more of the men being counted off into the detail; and a shot of an overweight guard carrying a shotgun and mounted on a horse.

Then, the idea of a fateful pecking order is once again offered. Now, though, Doc seems to be in control, manipulating a piece in a chess game that he is playing with another prisoner; however, the fact that it is merely a game considerably lessens the significance of Doc's influence. Another shot of the work detail features one of the guards telling another guard to "keep them dogs in close to them." This remark throws us back to the beginning of the title sequence, where we first heard the sound of the dog, and suggests that even when Doc tries to divert himself, he is unavoidably reminded of the most oppressive aspect of his confinement: his powerlessness.

That the chess game provides no release for Doc is made clear in the next series of shots. We see Doc staring at the chessboard; on the effects track, the sound of the loom mechanism returns, followed by a shot of work detail prisoners riding past a tower manned by armed guards. The tower resembles a rook, which has a greater range of movement than do the pawns, which the prisoners resemble. Shots of prisoners being frisked (another reminder of their powerlessness) is followed by a shot of Doc staring at the chessboard, during which sounds of the guards giving orders to the work detail intrude into Doc's consciousness. At this point, Doc angrily knocks over his chess pieces. His partner says, "Oh, man, it's just a game," but it's more than that to Doc: chess is a visible reminder of his status as a pawn controlled by Benyon.

We again see the work detail in action, rounding up some brush. We then see Doc trying once more to divert himself in his cell, this time by building a wooden bridge, a symbol of his desire to cross over from his present circumstances to something better. Yet the sounds of the work detail here remind us that Doc may never be free of the prison's presence. Another shot of the work detail is followed by a shot of Doc's cell door opening, which allows Doc entrance only to his place of confinement. Doc enters and lies down on his back, exemplifying dull sameness by assuming a moribund position identical to the one that he had taken in an earlier shot. Shots of the work detail and a view of Doc working on his bridge are followed by a series of images connoting some form of pleasurable release. We see prisoners taking showers; Doc is then seen working on his bridge. The sound of the showering, with its positive connotations, carries over to this last shot of Doc, suggesting that perhaps Doc may have found some form of release from pain through his model making. This notion is supported by scenes of Doc enjoying his shower and a memory shot of Doc and Carol kissing.

The speed of the editing then increases. In rapid sequence, we see Doc again with the bridge model; the pictures of Carol on Doc's wall; and Carol moving toward Doc to kiss him. At this point, Peckinpah very subtly cues us into the way that these rapid images are going to be resolved by blending in the sound of the loom mechanism, which he allows to surface through the sound of the water from the shower sequence, doing so in such a way as to show us how similar the two sounds are and thereby how fragile the barrier between pleasure and pain is for the prisoners. The fact that Peckinpah introduces the similarity between the sound of the water (a natural and positive sound) and the machine (a traditionally negative presence in Peckinpah's work) at the point at which we see an image of Carol tenderly moving toward Doc to kiss him presages the linkage between Carol's affection and Doc's anger toward her that *The Getaway* will later develop.

Again we see Doc showering. But the enjoyable nature of this activity is once more corrupted as images of pleasure and pain again begin to alternate. We see the "stop button" sign on the loom, a vicious reminder that the pain of these images cannot be stopped; Doc showering; the loom mechanism; a shot of a work detail guard; the loom mechanism again; Doc working on the bridge; two rapid shots of the loom mechanism; the feet of the men on the work detail; Doc showering. Finally, we see Doc with the bridge. In despair, Doc crushes the model, takes off his glasses, and hangs his face in his hands, at which point the action freezes. The prison's worst aspects have obviously predominated.

The film's action dissolves to the prison visitation room, where Doc meets Carol. Doc doesn't even look at Carol when he first sits down, and he only hesitantly touches her finger through the wire that separates them. "Hello, Doc," Carol says. Then, alluding to Doc's rejected request for parole, she says, "I'm sorry." Having accepted the fact that if he doesn't cooperate with Benyon he will never be paroled, Doc states his position plainly. "Get to Benyon, tell him I'm for sale, his price. Do it now," Doc says, apparently not realizing that by acceding to Benyon's "price" he will only be trading penal for personal servitude. Doc has set in motion a fatalistic mechanism that will point him and his wife toward destruction until they are released by a virtually divine intervention.

Carol goes to Benyon's office, telling Benyon that she is "ready

Plate 38. Carol, in the role of petitioner, talking to Benyon about Doc in *The Getaway*.

to talk about my husband." The statement obviously means that she is willing to accede to Benyon's terms for Doc's release. Benyon smiles smugly and offers her a drink. Carol, looking at Benyon, says, "Yeah, I could use one"; Benyon, speaking from his office bar, says, "Come on over." This statement suggests that, in a fateful action, Carol is actually coming over to Benyon's way of thinking, a notion reinforced by Peckinpah's fading in the sound of the loom at this point. Carol joins Benyon at his bar, at which point Peckinpah tells us that the deal is already finalized by cutting immediately to a shot of Doc walking through a prison gate, just as he had done on the way to his parole board meeting. This time, though, the circumstances are obviously different. Doc is in a suit and tie; he has been granted his parole. The apparent release from oppression is underscored by the loom sound's disappearing at the same time that the iron sound of the gate's opening is heard.

When Doc leaves the prison, though, Carol is not the first one there to meet him. Instead, a black Cadillac pulls up and its driver delivers a message to Doc. "Mr. Benyon will see you the day after tomorrow. Twelve-thirty, at the river walk." Through a production fluke, the driver's voice is heard although his lips never move. This disjuncture inadvertently lends an ominous tone to this pronouncement. The statement not only seems to emanate from an inhuman source but also foreshadows Benyon's unusual voice quality in the later meeting, during which Benyon's voice, echoing off the walls of a tunnel through which he and Doc are passing, also takes on a dark, unworldly, and ominous quality.

After Benyon's flunky leaves, Carol arrives and she and Doc drive away. *The Getaway* continues to represent different states of mind during the sequence in which, after being released from prison, Doc goes to a park with Carol. In this scene, though, unlike the situation in prison—in which the internal realities led only to discomfort—Doc's idealized desires are realized through what appears at first to be merely a fantasy.

In the park, where we hear barking dogs (but with a connotation obviously different from the one created in the prison sequences), Doc watches a young boy swing on a rope over a lake. Peckinpah immediately cuts to a shot of Doc, with only his jacket removed, swinging on the rope and dropping into the water; then Carol, also fully clothed, dives in. Given the fact that the only change from Doc's previous situation is that he is no longer in prison, this scene would seem to suggest that external circumstances are the major determining factor in one's ability to achieve happiness. Yet *The Getaway* will later contradict this implication, since the beginning of Doc and Carol's regeneration takes place in a garbage dump. Rather, the film grants Doc his pleasure here because he has not yet built up the animosity toward Carol that he will later evidence. Indeed, until he is able to view his wife as someone other than an enemy, Doc has extraordinarily bad luck. In *The Getaway*, then, psychological change is a prerequisite to a change in one's fortunes. The fact that it is Benyon who sets in motion the series of events that lead Doc and Carol to their phoenixlike rising from the ashes in the garbage dump testifies to the ironic quirks in what is nonetheless a cosmically balanced universe in which everyone gets what he or she deserves.

Nevertheless, at numerous points in the film the characters' fates seem to be hanging in the balance: during the bank robbery, when things go wrong; when Doc shoots Rudy and mistakenly believes that he is dead; the many times when it seems as though Doc and Carol's capture is imminent. At these and other points, for Doc and Carol the dividing line between success and failure, escape or

Plate 39. The fantasized swim that comes true.

capture, reconciliation or break-up, is painfully thin. Perhaps no other scene in the film dramatizes this situation so well as the one in which Doc and Carol go to Benyon's house to split up the stolen money. Benyon begins by hinting at his sexual involvement with Carol. This isn't the first time that the subject of Carol's fidelity has arisen. On the way to Benyon's, Doc had asked Carol if she had ever been to Benyon's ranch, to which Carol had replied no, although Doc seemed unsatisfied with her answer. Now, Benyon alludes most strongly to his dalliance with Carol. "Let's examine the situation. One—an extremely attractive woman. Then there's the woman's husband. Then there's a man with political influence."

At this point, Carol, unseen by Doc, slowly enters the room. Benyon continues by describing himself as "a man who can easily get a parole for a convict. Why should he? A simple reason, McCoy." We realize now how apt Carol's entrance at this point is, since what Benyon is referring to is the reason that he decided to get a parole for Doc: Carol's sleeping with him. Doc, though, is becoming increasingly annoyed with Benyon's nasty implications and stalling.

> Doc: Let's get down to it. The radio's rapping about 750,000.
> There's a half a million here.

206

BENYON: A little more was taken out before. You see, my brother's a director of that bank. We had a few problems we
had to iron out.
DOC: OK, we covered you.
BENYON: Yeah, you surely did, Doc.

This dialogue has a dual significance, since at this juncture Carol, whom Doc doesn't even know is in the room, raises her gun and points it at Doc's back, thereby "covering" him, although whose side she is on at this point is unclear. Referring to Carol's apparent betrayal of him (which to the audience must now seem even greater than Doc realizes), Doc says, "My old lady must have made you a lot of promises," to which Benyon replies, "Close. . . ." Doc says, "I wouldn't feel . . . ," but he never finishes his statement: at this point Carol shifts her gun and shoots Benyon five times.

Throughout the latter part of this sequence, just as in the park scene, the audience experiences anxiety deriving from the indeterminateness of the action. In the park, it was never clear whether Doc and Carol's swim was real or fantasized, a situation that created a pleasant anxiety. (The following scene, which shows us that Doc and Carol are wet, demonstrates that the swim was real.) In the present scene, though, our inability to divine Carol's intentions and allegiances makes us unpleasantly anxious. Indeed, until the ending, anxiety is the film's governing principle. *The Getaway* is a film of flight and pursuit, so we might expect such discomforts within it. As we shall see, what is surprising is the manner in which Peckinpah relieves us of our anxiety.

For now, though, the audience must deal with Carol's murder of Benyon. Has she killed him because of her loyalty to Doc? Or has she shot Benyon because he seemed too damned sure of her loyalty to him? To keep the scene's tension high, Peckinpah leaves the issue unresolved. What we see is Doc and Carol, photographed from the point at which Benyon's body landed (thereby implicitly including him in the action), leveling their guns at each other. Finally, in an equivocal gesture that may signal either allegiance to Doc or acquiescence to the impossibility of resolving their standoff, Carol slowly lowers her gun and the scene ends.

The scene in the train station is similarly replete with stress and anxiety, which is created not only by Doc and Carol's flight but also by Peckinpah's use of ambient details. Thus, while Carol sits in the station waiting for Doc, we hear the annoying sounds of a crying baby and a locker door being slammed shut. An ill-shaven man who sits down next to Carol looks at her askance. Doc's simultaneous situation is equally unsettling: he is recklessly driving through the station parking ramp. Tires squealing, Doc finally pulls to a halt at a spot on the top floor. Shooting from the driver's point of view, the camera shows the car rushing up to the ramp's barrier and stopping only inches away from it.

After Doc enters the station and realizes that Carol has lost the suitcase to a con man's ruse, there is an anxious sequence in which, after grabbing Carol by the arm, Doc says to her through clenched teeth, "Find him!" The handheld camera (its shakiness complementing the scene's anxiety) alternates between point-of-view shots and shots that track backwards in front of Doc and Carol as the characters weave their way through the crowded, noisy station, at one point finding a black bag that turns out to be the wrong one. As the tension mounts, the station announcer states that the train is about to leave. Finally, after Carol spots the thief, Doc rushes forward and boards the train that the man had entered. Doc does not immediately find the man on the still stationary train, so he disembarks. First showing Doc walking alongside the train, Peckinpah then underscores Doc's stealth and skill. The camera's view of Doc is for a second obscured by an intervening baggage truck. When the truck passes, we catch the barest glimpse of Doc's coattail (which is itself partially obscured by another intervening object, a concrete post) disappearing onto the train. It's almost as though Doc has dematerialized, only to reappear later on the train.

Just before Doc finds the con man (who also seems to have disappeared for a time), we see the man, photographed from the rear, seated on the train. A shadow passes across the back of the seat adjacent to him. It is Doc, again stealthily tracking the man like a dark presence. Doc sits down beside the man and, after apprising him of his ineptitude, knocks him out. When Peckinpah cuts back to the train station where Carol is waiting, he photographs her in a high overhead shot that emphasizes her helplessness. Then, in another collapsing of the film's physical realms, Peckinpah has some dialogue being spoken on the train accompany this shot of Carol. We hear Doc say to the train conductor, "Two—end of the line." In keeping with *The Getaway*'s intentional refusal to resolve its situations until its end, this statement is ambiguous and can be read as meaning either that Doc and Carol will stay together regardless of circumstances or that they have reached the end of their relationship. The following action does nothing to resolve this ambiguity.

When Doc returns to the train station with the suitcase, Carol demonstrates that she considers Doc more important than the money. She smiles, embraces Doc, and says, "You're all right." Only then does she refer to the money, asking, "How did you get it back?" Doc, though, responds neither to Carol's expression of concern nor her question about the money's retrieval. Implying that she is intentionally making mistakes in order that he be caught, Doc says, "If you're trying to get me back in Huntsville you're going about it the right way." Carol responds in kind, appropriately retreating from her emotional concern and demonstrating that she can be as callous as Doc if need be. The two trade insults.

> CAROL: Well I just wouldn't worry about it, Doc, because I can always get you out, you know. I mean I can screw every prison official in Texas if I want to.
> DOC: Texas is a big state.
> CAROL: I can handle it.
> DOC: Yeah, I'll bet you can.

There is an anxious pause between the couple. Then, in an attempt to defuse Doc's anger over an act that he sent her to perform, Carol finally bests Doc in the exchange by asking Doc a simple and forthright question that challenges all of the traditional assumptions about the manipulative uses of female sexuality. "You'd do the same for me, Doc, wouldn't you? I mean if I got caught, wouldn't you?" Carol asks. The question compels Doc to accept the fact that his wife's commitment to him is so complete that she can barter her most personal possession, her body, to help him.

Throughout this sequence, Peckinpah has been undermining our sense of visual stability by repeatedly shifting the camera's point of view, first shooting from Doc and Carol's right side, then their left; shooting over Doc's shoulder to photograph Carol; and shooting over Carol's shoulder to photograph Doc. (The last two techniques alone are standard and wouldn't call as much attention to themselves as do the four techniques together.) Doc observes, "You don't like the way things are, I don't like the way things are," and suggests that they split up; Carol responds, "I don't want to." As in the shoot-out scene in Benyon's office, Peckinpah again eschews a neatly resolved ending to a scene in favor of indeterminateness. Doc and Carol leave the station together, although on what terms is unclear. However, Peckinpah does emphasize how much the audience wants the couple to remain with each other. After Carol's statement, Peckinpah cuts back to a view of the spot in the train station where Doc and Carol had stood talking, showing us through the characters' absence how lonely the setting is without them. It is Doc and Carol's presence together that engages and holds our attention, a realization that reveals through purely visual terms that we care about them as a couple. This notion is highlighted by the fact that, although the train station had been filled with people throughout Doc and Carol's discussion, the crowd (especially on the film's first viewing) goes virtually unnoticed, as does the fact that we don't notice when all of these other people leave the scene, fixated as we are on Doc and Carol.

Coincidence, present in *The Getaway* in the form of Doc and Carol's extraordinarily bad luck before they meet Cowboy (Slim Pickens), is also evident in the subplot, which not only mirrors and comments on the changing relations between Doc and Carol but also extends the film's suspense. The action involving Fran and Harold Clinton (Sally Struthers and Jack Dodson) and Rudy contains a fair amount of grim humor. However, instead of providing a diversion from the anxiety that we feel about Doc and Carol, the subplot increases it, not only because Rudy is pursuing Doc and Carol but also because the dangerously mercurial Rudy is constantly alternating between harmony and fighting. He is accompanied by Fran and Harold, who is tremendously uneasy about his wife's affair with this gangster.

The film's repeated parallelism is striking. At one point, Rudy is listening to a radio in a motel room while Doc goes into a store to buy a radio; another coincidence occurs there, since just as Doc walks into the store, a television announcer reports about him while a picture of Doc flashes onto the screen. Rudy and Fran have a food fight in Harold's car at the same time that Doc and Carol pull into a drive-in, where another regrettable dovetailing occurs. The radio in Doc and Carol's car is broadcasting a news story about them. Doc turns off the radio and places his order; the carhop leaves, and Doc turns the radio back on to some music. At this point, Peckinpah cuts to Rudy's motel room, where Fran is listening to the same station.

Then, another unfortunate coincidence occurs to Doc and Carol as the workers at the drive-in, who at that moment are reading a newspaper, recognize Doc's picture, a coincidence gravely compounded by the arrival of a police car, which pulls in at that very moment.

A grim parallelism is present in a subsequent scene that takes place at dawn (a time that would normally suggest a possible new beginning). A garbage truck is seen on its way to the dump; Peckinpah then cuts to Rudy's motel room. In a brutal scene, Rudy enters the bathroom and discovers that Harold has hanged himself. Rudy blithely looks up at Harold and then tosses his cigarette butt into the trash can (thereby equating Harold with garbage). The radio is blaring a sermon by a revivalist preacher, who is screaming, "To all you sinners out there I simply say, receive the Lord, receive the Lord, open your hearts and let him in! Say Hallelujah! Let us pray." On the words "Let us pray," Rudy tosses away his cigarette, indicating his immense indifference to religion or morality. The combination of Rudy's action and the preacher's hypocritically pious words mock the solemnity and horror of Harold's suicide.

Plate 40. Doc and Carol's unhappy mirror images: Rudy and Fran on their way to the confrontation at the film's end.

In a final example of parallelism, which occurs before the penultimate confrontation between Rudy and Doc, we see Carol and Doc kissing in their hotel room while Rudy is yelling at Fran to hurry up and get ready to leave their room. These scenes emphasize the abusive nature of Rudy and Fran's actions and the manner in which, by contrast, Doc and Carol are attempting to remain faithful and compassionate toward one another.

To leaven such tragic timing, Peckinpah also injects a bit of comedy into the film. For instance, at one point Doc sits down at

Plate 41. Carol and Doc during the shoot-out.

a bus stop next to a woman who is reading a newspaper that prominently features his photo. The woman, though, ignores the news story, so intent is she in grabbing the bottle of soda that the departing Doc leaves behind.

With the exception of the incident involving the stolen money, which is brought back through Doc's skill, it is not skill but luck or fate that determines what happens to Doc and Carol. The two happen to be in the alley at the precise time that the garbage truck that eventually takes them out of the city comes by to make its routine pickup. (This garbage truck is a precursor of the scrap truck that will later take them out of the country.) Had the garbage truck not appeared at that point, it's likely that the fugitives would have been picked up by the police, who are seen cruising down the alley. By this point, we realize that *The Getaway* is a work of wish fulfillment in two senses, since in it things that you hope won't happen actually do, while things that you might never expect to happen manage to take place. The factor that determines what type of action will occur is the moral attitude of the people involved, a point emphasized in the garbage-dump scene.

> DOC: Listen, there's something I want to say.
> CAROL: I don't want to hear it.

212

DOC: Well listen, it's hard enough for me as it is. The things you said before, you might be right. It's not gonna mean anything if we don't make it together.

Carol then echoes Doc's earlier statement about their splitting up:

CAROL: I don't think we can make it. I think if we ever get out of this dump I'll just split.
DOC: We've made it together so far.
CAROL: We've come a lot of miles but we're not close to anything.

Carol's last statement suggests that the couple's flight is less a physical one than a spiritual journey toward greater compassion and understanding. Carol underscores her implicit point about Doc's essential callousness: "I always thought jails made people hard but not you, boy. I mean you're just not tough enough to forget about Benyon. I chose you, not him, you know that?"

To protect herself at this emotionally vulnerable moment, Carol then qualifies her assertion by saying, "Not that it makes any difference." "Pick it up and we leave and we leave it here. There's no other way," Doc says. Responding to Doc's offer of conciliation, Carol relegates Benyon to a subsidiary status, no longer referring to him by name but merely by pronoun. "No more about him," Carol says. Doc echoes the spirit of Carol's statement: "Whatever happens, no more about him."

For all of its chaotic action, *The Getaway* is mainly intent on displaying the happiness that can be derived from love and trust. The violence that surrounds Doc and Carol throughout most of the film should ideally be viewed as nothing more than the projection of the hostility between them. Once Doc and Carol resolve their differences in the dump, their fortunes change. The suggestion is that it was the unproductive nature of their relationship after Doc left prison that had determined the couple's fates.

Only the loving and amicable pair, Doc and Carol, survive the fighting at Laughlin's hotel. We know that Doc will emerge triumphant from the confrontations because he has finally repudiated his materialism, which was most tellingly present earlier in his comment, while holding some money, about what he believed in.

DOC (annoyed that the car radio doesn't work): You can't trust a thing nowadays.

CAROL: Tell you something, Doc, one of these days you're gonna have to trust somebody.

DOC (gesturing with a dollar bill): Wanna see what I trust? In God I trust; it's the words on the back of every bill.

CAROL: Just keep that up and it won't matter how far we get away because there won't be anything left between us. You understand that? Nothing.

At Laughlin's, the change in Doc's attitude is striking. Doc once again is seen handling some of the stolen money. However, this time, using the serial numbers to represent cards, he plays a friendly game of poker with his wife. (The fact that this game is usually called "liar's poker" yields a pleasant irony, since at this point Doc and Carol are at the height of their mutual honesty.)

Plate 42. With trust reestablished, money can be used for play.

Coming down the stairs during the shoot-out, Doc sees Benyon's men at the same time that they see him. The gang's surprise is communicated by the jump-cut shots of the men that Peckinpah employs at this point. After killing all of the men but one (whom Doc tells to "just run away"), and having shot Rudy in a fair way (Rudy fired first and missed), Doc is now almost completely free.

Yet at this point he needs something akin to a miracle if he and Carol are to escape the police. The couple's deliverance will appear in the quasi-angelic Cowboy, who is seen about to load some garbage (an action that links him to the transcendent action at the dump) from the back of the hotel. Once again, a garbage truck saves Doc and Carol, although this time they will escape not just from a single police car but from all police forever.

The slogan painted on Cowboy's truck, "Our business is picking up," refers literally to his activity (which includes picking up Doc and Carol) and also sounds a note of optimism in the face of what appears, from the truck and Cowboy's shabby condition, to be a rather destitute existence. Indeed, Cowboy tells Doc that the previous year he earned only "about five thousand dollars." Obviously, though, what is important to Cowboy is not money but respect and trust. Thus, he is pleased when he finds out that Doc and Carol are traditionally committed to each other: "Are you kids married? Hey, I'm glad. That's the trouble with this world: there's no dang morals. Kids figure if they ain't living together they ain't living." He doubtless sees in their relationship a reflection of his own long-standing commitment. In fact, the film emphasizes Cowboy's view of the importance of this type of commitment by having Cowboy refer to it in a statement that he makes to a Mexican border guard. Cowboy tells the guard that the truck in which Doc and Carol are riding contains "building material," a figurative reference to the new basis for Doc and Carol's relationship. Cowboy's statement of advice to Doc and Carol is worth quoting in full. "You know if I was you kids what I'd do? I'd quit this running around the country, you know, and get a little bit of money together and, hell, buy me a place, settle down, and raise a family. I been married to the same old gal for thirty-five years. She's a tough old hide. Everything I am I owe to her."

Although Doc and Carol decide to give Cowboy thirty thousand dollars for his truck and his silence, it's clear that he would have kept quiet about them whether he had received any money or not, since he has already told them that he sympathizes with their situation. "I been in trouble with the law myself," he says. Money, formerly used only for sordid purposes, becomes through Doc and Carol's gift to Cowboy a means of granting someone pleasure. The film's final image shows a row of telephone poles stretching into the distance; their crucifix shape suggests that Doc's selfishness and

215

oppression have been sacrificed on a cross of tribulations and that Doc and Carol have been reborn into a new and better world, one governed not by a malicious fate but by a loving and compassionate deity. In the end, as Doc and Carol disappear over the rise into this new land, they do indeed, to translate and appropriate Cowboy's final words to them, "Go with God."[1]

CHAPTER NINE

Star Packer

The 1989 Turner Entertainment video release of *Pat Garrett and Billy the Kid* initially presents us with a dilemma. The 122-minute videotape, which runs 16 minutes longer than the film version released by MGM, is being billed as "just the way director Sam Peckinpah wanted you to see it,"[1] but this wording is inaccurate. As a result of the post-production dissension between Peckinpah and producer Gordon Carroll on one side, and MGM president James Aubrey on the other, no one knows exactly what Peckinpah's final cut might have been.[2]

When we consider the other Peckinpah works that were truncated, *Major Dundee* and *The Wild Bunch*, we are at least on secure ground when referring to their texts. With regard to *Dundee*, information is available on the form that Peckinpah wanted the film to assume.[3] In the case of *The Wild Bunch*, the footage from the original release has been restored to the film; *The Wild Bunch* can now be seen virtually as the director intended it.[4] But with *Pat Garrett*, we can only speculate about what the film might have been if Peckinpah had been allowed to assemble it his way.[5] Critic Paul Seydor, who is extremely conversant with Peckinpah's editing style and sensitive to the way that Peckinpah's films "play," believes that the shorter *Pat Garrett* is closer to what Peckinpah would have wanted than is the longer film. Seydor, who is a now motion picture editor, feels that many of scenes in the 122-minute version go on far longer than Peckinpah would have allowed—that they do not, to appropriate a phrase from editorial parlance, end "on the moment" that Peckinpah would have chosen.[6] Peckinpah's other films

217

certainly suggest that Seydor's contention is correct, yet the problem is not merely aesthetic. Some of the longer version's additional footage does change for the worse the way that various scenes work (e.g., the scene between Garrett and the whores at Rupert's saloon, which degenerates into absurdity); however, this additional footage also contains thematic information that radically changes the manner in which we view various characters and events, making the 122-minute version at certain junctures a richer and more fascinating work.

Given the significant differences between *Pat Garrett*'s variant texts, we now have two aesthetically different works.[7] Fortunately, we need not become involved in disputes concerning authorial intention to resolve the problem of which version Peckinpah probably would have preferred: that is, once a simple issue is settled concerning the way that the video is being promoted. As Seydor pointed out to me, despite the fact that Turner Entertainment refers to the new video release of *Pat Garrett* as the "restored director's cut," the term "director's cut" itself is highly ambiguous. In the film industry, "director's cut" refers to the cut of a film that a director, free from any outside interference, prepares within ten weeks after completion of principal photography; this cut does not necessarily represent the director's final intentions (which is the way that Turner Entertainment wants consumers to understand the term). However, "director's cut" is also used casually to denote the version of a film that carries the director's final imprimatur. Keeping in mind the way that most of Peckinpah's films are edited, it seems likely that had the frame story, Garrett's visit to his house, and the entire meeting with Chisum[8] been restored to the theatrical-release version of *Pat Garrett*, the film would be far closer to a realization of Peckinpah's desires than is the film that Turner Entertainment, in a ploy to make money on what they undoubtedly realize is an early cut of the film, has released on video.

In *Peckinpah: The Western Films*, Seydor suggests that one of the most striking differences between *Pat Garrett*'s released version and the version that Peckinpah wanted is the presence of the frame story,[9] which Peckinpah always intended to have in the film. Yet the stylistically interesting frame device, which brackets the film with a scene showing the murder of the aged Garrett (James Coburn), does very little to change the meaning of the film's events. (In fact, the cut version begins and ends at Fort Sumner, doubling back on itself with results that are just as fateful as those in the longer film.)

However, the dialogue and action that have been restored to the film totally change the way that we view Billy (Kris Kristofferson). Garrett remains virtually the same in both versions, but the longer version's Billy is a more rounded character, at once both more sympathetic and more brutal.

Perhaps the most significant effect of the framing device is its creation of a major irony in that it shows us that all of Garrett's self-serving efforts result only in his being killed by men working for the propertied interests to whom he sold out. Moreover, the device reminds us of how far removed we are not only from the time of the frame but from the central story. Because we therefore feel more distant from the characters, we are prevented from totally identifying with them, an important effect in a film whose two central protagonists would be very difficult to like in any case.

It is certainly tempting, as Seydor does, to read the story within the long version's frame as Garrett's brink-of-death scanning of the events in his life, an approach that would make his death that much more ironic;[10] however, there is no justification in the film for adopting such a view. Indeed, since *Pat Garrett* narrates action of which Garrett could not possibly have had any knowledge (e.g., the dialogue between Billy and his two companions at Stinking Springs, the action between Billy and Bell after Garrett has left Lincoln), Seydor's approach is contradicted by the film. Instead, we should regard the frame merely as a device that adds a bit more shading to what is in any case a merciless retelling of a famous Western legend.

As a title indicates, *Pat Garrett and Billy the Kid* begins near Las Cruces, New Mexico, in 1909.[11] Garrett and John Poe (John Beck), one of the deputies with whom Garrett rode in pursuit of the Kid, are first seen in a long shot moving across a barren and uninviting landscape. Garrett, who is riding in a buggy, remarks bitterly on the sheep that are grazing on what he twice refers to as "my land." Poe reminds Garrett that it is no longer his land, since Garrett leased it to Poe. "I'm paying you off when I get back and breaking that goddamned lease," Garrett says. The exchange here is quite ironic. We know from history that Garrett can never "get back": he cannot return to his home, nor can he go back to the time before he had compromised his beliefs and entered the employ of the big landowners. The elitist ranchers were always in bitter conflict with the populist farmers, who felt that cattle and sheep were ruining their land and preventing them from growing crops.

(This conflict, traditional in Western literature and film, receives a lighthearted treatment in Rodgers and Hammerstein's *Oklahoma!*) Thus, in a further irony, Garrett's objection to the sheep places him in the position of opposing the kind of men with whom he was formerly allied. At the same time, Garrett states that he will not abide by a legal document, despite his having sworn as a lawman to uphold the law. In fact, Garrett repeatedly insists on ignoring the demands of legality and the rights of other people in favor of his own selfish interests; these are the precise qualities that have brought him to the sorry situation in which he now finds himself.

We can infer from the film's bleak tone that, given his destructive tendencies, Garrett was destined to betray himself and the Kid. Indeed, as soon as the film's first major event occurs—Garrett's announcement that he has become the sheriff of Lincoln County— we realize that his relationship with the Kid is doomed and that by becoming sheriff and placing himself in the employ of the region's moneyed interests he has mandated most of the film's subsequent events, including his own death.

Referring to the breaking of the lease between himself and Garrett, Poe says, "I don't allow the law'll agree to that," to which Garrett replies, "What law is that, Santa Fe Ring law? Shit. God-damned law is ruining the country." In retrospect, Garrett's assertion is quite ironic: of course, Garrett himself represented the Santa Fe Ring in the killing of the Kid, and while Garrett was working for the ring, Billy made virtually the identical assertion about the nation, stating that Chisum (Barry Sullivan) and the other landowners were "trying to put a fence around this country." Garrett's repetition of the statement's meaning is all the more telling since he never heard what the Kid said. At least part of Garrett is, and always will be, in sympathy with Billy's attitudes and politics. Unfortunately, for the sake of supposed self-comfort, Garrett does not act on these beliefs. Instead, by trying to provide for himself monetarily, Garrett succeeds only in impoverishing his future, disregarding the moral imperative that one consider the consequences of one's actions before acting. Yet even as an old man Garrett never realizes the true reprehensibility of the acts he committed when he was younger. He is not wise, merely bitter.

When Garrett says "Santa Fe Ring law is ruining the country," Peckinpah cuts to a distant view that shows us a man with a rifle crawling along the ground in order to get a clear shot at Garrett. Here, as later in the film, the word *law* is juxtaposed with lawless action. Throughout, the film shows Garrett to be a representative of the law who nonetheless kills men in a brutal and premeditated fashion; now, as Garrett is commenting on the law, we see a man about to commit a premeditated act of murder. Yet a further irony is also operating here: although the men who shoot Garrett are acting outside of conventional law, they are also inadvertently fulfilling the behests of a greater law by visiting justice on Garrett for his murder of the Kid.

Poe responds to Garrett's comment about the law, which seems to be the statement of an old man looking bitterly at the present and longing for a supposedly simpler past, by asking, "Ain't you still a part of that law? I believe they elected you and paid you good wages for killing the Kid." Despite Poe's use of the impersonal "they," it wasn't the people—"the electorate" later referred to by Garrett—who wanted Billy dead; it was the businessmen and bankers who desired it, the same men who controlled the elections and who bought Garrett like a hired assassin. However, Garrett doesn't want to hear this truth, even though he doubtless knows it himself. "You rotten son of a bitch," he says to Poe, at which point the man with the rifle is seen taking aim at Garrett.

Peckinpah then cuts away from this scene, leaving the action poised on the brink of Garrett's execution. We are thrown back in time to "Old Fort Sumner, New Mexico, 1881." (This is the date at which the short version begins.) The first shot we have is of a chicken buried in dirt up to its neck, a fitting symbol for an unrestrained, animal spirit trapped by circumstances. Moreover, the cutting back and forth between shots of the buried chickens and views of Billy and his friends draws an implicit comparison between the chickens, the Kid's present inertia, and his men, all of whom, like the chickens, will soon be slaughtered. Additionally, the presence of the chickens strongly suggests that a pecking order (no pun intended) operates in the film. The forces in power manipulate men like Garrett, who in turn manipulate men like Billy and his gang, who themselves are manipulating animals. The view of nature here is not that of a great chain of being aspiring upwards to perfection; it is of a chain of destruction that moves downward toward chaos and death. As we can infer from the film's prologue, what really descends along the pecking order is murder, a further indication that Garrett can be killed solely because he is no longer of use within this brutal chain of being.

The fact that in *Pat Garrett*'s long version the present and the past are virtually equivalent (a meaning communicated by the rapid cutting between shots depicting 1881 and 1909, which establishes not only an equivalence but a causality between these two realms) creates in the audience a sense of despair, since it indicates that there is really no possibility for moral progress or change, only the playing out of historical causality. This aspect is then reaffirmed. Billy shoots at a chicken; a rifleman in 1909 aims at Garrett. Sensing an impending danger, Garrett begins to move down off the buggy. We see Billy shoot at the chicken; in 1909, Garrett is shot. A temporal reversal has been asserted; reaching out from the past, Billy has avenged Garrett's shooting of him. However, the complementarity of the Kid and the rifleman who actually shoots Garrett is both affirmed and denied in the way that Peckinpah places the characters in the frame and then links succeeding shots. Billy is facing screen left; the rifleman is facing screen right, suggesting some sort of opposition between them; this opposition is confirmed in both versions of the film, which show us that despite the Kid's knowledge of Garrett's pursuit of him, he never wished Garrett dead. Indeed, by having both Garrett and Billy in the two matching shots facing screen left, Peckinpah indicates that despite what has happened between them, the two men are still linked in some sort of timeless affinity.

More temporal jumps then take place. The rifleman shoots at Garrett, and one of the chickens explodes, struck by a bullet. This editing again affirms the linkage between the two times and also equates Garrett with a chicken; for those in the audience who already know Garrett and Billy's history, the film suggests that Garrett's killing of the Kid was a cowardly act. A man with Garrett's 1909 party fires at Garrett; in 1881, another chicken explodes. (Like Garrett and the Kid, the man who shoots Garrett faces screen left, thus making it seem as though Garrett is executing himself; this is, of course, essentially true, although Garrett pulled the trigger more than twenty years before.) Now Poe shoots Garrett; like Billy, Poe is also facing screen left. Poe's shooting of Garrett seems to be the culmination of the antagonism toward Garrett that Poe seems to feel throughout the film, while the identity of placement with Billy links up with Poe's riding with Garrett (just as the Kid had done many years before). Garrett begins to fall and the image freezes, a technique that heralds the eventual death of the character in the frame by relegating him to a deathlike stillness. In the long version, Peckinpah complements this effect by shifting each of the frames of the 1881 sequence to black and white as it freezes, thus robbing the characters of chromatic vitality to foreshadow their later deaths.[12] (The 1909 sequence, with only the slightest hint of color, has been processed in black and white as a symbol of Garrett's lifelessness at that point.)[13]

Billy then shoots at one of the chickens; one of Billy's gang, in a statement that could apply as well to Garrett's being shot, says, "Got him goddamn near perfect." The statement suggests that Garrett's shooting is justified, a point of view that is consistent with the attitude of the members of Billy's gang, none of whom has any fondness for Garrett. Coincidet with the statement is a shot that ends with a freeze-frame as Garrett is seen falling off his buggy. Billy shoots again at the chicken, at which point Peckinpah cuts back to Garrett, now lying on the ground and reacting to the shot while on the sound track we hear the laughter of Billy's gang as though, returned from the dead, they are taking pleasure in Garrett's execution.

Eno (Luke Askew), another member of Billy's gang, then shoots at the chickens but misses. Garrett, lying on the ground, looks up, at which point we see Eno again. The shots from the two time periods are linked in such a way that it seems as though Garrett is looking at Eno. Eno shoots again, more laughter is heard, and in 1909 Garrett is hit. As Poe reacts to this shot, the image freezes and the film's title is superimposed.

Peckinpah then cuts to 1881. Garrett rides into Fort Sumner with his deputy, Bell (Matt Clark), and sees the game that Billy and his gang are playing. Garrett puts his hand out to stopBell from riding any further; his gesture is that of a father checking the actions of a wayward child, an example of Garrett's paternalistic presumptuousness.

Billy aims at a chicken; Garrett takes down his rifle and aims too. Peckinpah, now asserting through editing a causality that remains within the same time period, next gives us a shot from Garrett's point of view of the back of Billy's head, which makes it seem as though Garrett means to kill the Kid. And although there is an intervening shot of Billy once again aiming, we nonetheless conclude, as do Billy's gang after Garrett fires, that the shot may in some sense have been meant for Billy or them; they react by ducking down behind the wall they had been leaning against and spinning around. Billy says, "Goddamn, that's Garrett," and as Garrett shoots again, Peckinpah cuts back to Garrett, lying on the ground in 1909. The

223

meaning thus suggested is twofold. First, Garrett, by riding in behind Billy and his men and then firing his rifle, seems to be pursuing them with the intention of killing them, which of course he is. Second, Peckinpah suggests through the editing that Garrett is his own executioner; this notion is symbolically reaffirmed at the film's end when Garrett shoots his mirror image, but it is here communicated far more forcefully in that Garrett is not firing merely at his reflection but at his body.

A shot of an exploding chicken torso is now seen. The smoking torso rises up and settles back down in slow motion, precisely the movements that we had seen Garrett's corpse describe in one of the frame sequence shots, thus reaffirming the comparisons between the two times periods. After the views of Garrett's corpse in 1909 that are now shown, the film shifts to that time period, with the exception of the long version's brief reprise of Garrett's murder (including Billy's "shooting" of Garrett).

The scene with Billy, Garrett, Bell, and the members of Billy's gang that now takes place conveys most of its meanings through implication. This avoidance of direct statements derives primarily from Garrett, who sets the scene's tone. It is only when Billy in the next scene compels Garrett to speak directly that Garrett will tell Billy why he has come to visit him. Garrett greets Billy, who says, "That's pretty fair shooting for an old married man." Garrett replies, "Just lucky I guess; how are you, Kid?" Although Garrett and Billy demonstrate a certain amiability, we already feel somewhat unsettled by the implications of the cross-shootings created by the editing. This feeling is compounded by the different implications arising from Garrett and Billy's statements. Garrett is referred to as "married" and "old"; Billy is obviously single and is referred to as "Kid," a nickname that aptly reflects the character's liveliness in contrast to Garrett's deathlike aspect. Referring to Billy and his gang's activities, Garrett asks, "You having some kind of fiesta?" Billy replies, "No, we always live like this; you ought to visit us more often." Billy's sincere smile and demeanor suggest that he misses Garrett's company. In response, though, Garrett only grunts.

Luke (Harry Dean Stanton) then says, "Well, I reckon the whole damn territory is gonna be one big open jug for us now, is that right, Pat?" The question gives us three bits of information simultaneously: Garrett is apparently in some position of authority; the gang obviously holds that position in disdain; and the men feel constrained to tease Garrett about the situation. Beaver (Donnie Fritts) echoes

Luke's taunt by saying, "Ain't that right, Pat?" and Beaver's image freezes in a foreshadowing of the character's impending doom. In another sarcastic taunt, Black Harris (L. Q. Jones) says to Garrett, "Take a two-day ride from Lincoln just to pay me back the two dollars you owe me, Pat?" Black's image freezes in a linkage between money and death; in fact, Garrett eventually pays Black back by killing him.

The action continues in this grim vein as Holly (Richard Bright) says, "Better collect it now, Black. I understand we ain't gonna be seeing much of Pat these days," thereby hinting at further alienation between Garrett and the gang. Garrett takes up the taunting tone of these remarks, suggesting that Billy and his gang leave the country: "Say, I understand those Mexican señoritas are as pretty as ever down there." In the long version of the film, Garrett and Holly exchange assent restricted to the literal meaning of Garrett's statement, and Holly's image freezes. Billy then recalls Garrett's giving a prostitute a dime when she asked him to pay her whatever he thought she was worth. (This callous action prefigures Garrett's treatment of the whores at Rupert's bar later in the film.) Billy goes on to recount that the woman had said, "If that's all it's worth, I might as well sew it up."

The short version cuts the dialogue at this point, thus robbing us of further interplay. According to Billy, Garrett had told the prostitute, "You could use a few stitches"; Garrett's reaction shot shows that he is not at all pleased by Billy's relating this example of his cruelty. In the long version, Billy then says, "Now I didn't feel she did," implying that his penis is larger than Garrett's. (Later, Garrett seems to respond to this taunt; when he beds down with four whores at Rupert's, he seems to be overcompensating for some anxiety about his prowess.) The longer film thereby reveals that the Kid can often match Garrett in his taunting, albeit with the difference that Billy is not cruel to women or people who are defenseless, as Garrett is. Billy's remark is merely a somewhat crude but humorous aside to his friend.

At this point, Garrett and Billy begin to veer off from the gang and move toward the cantina. Although the long version cuts the following dialogue, it is a worthy complement to the interaction we have witnessed among these men. "You don't figure he's [Garrett] too good to drink with us, do you?" one of the gang asks, to which another gang member replies, "Maybe it's the other way around."

Garrett then says, "Jesus, don't you get stale around here, Bill?

Maybe a year or so down in Mexico will do you some good." At
least here, Garrett seems to be truly concerned for his friend's well-
being; if Billy leaves the country, Garrett won't have to kill him.
Garrett may be partly correct when he says that he has taken over
as sheriff of Lincoln merely to provide for himself in his old age,
but the situation is obviously more complicated than that, especially
considering that in order to retain the job he must betray a man
whom many of the film's characters contend has been his closest
friend. Having made what is in many ways a very bad decision,
Garrett goes on to punish himself for it by destroying all of his
feeling for life and pleasure. This view would explain the deathly
demeanor that Garrett assumes throughout the film.

A further implication is that since Garrett seems to represent a
stage in the country's development, his turning away from his life-
affirming impulses (oriented toward love and friendship) and toward
materialism signals the fulfillment of a similar death wish on the
part of the nation. What we witness in *Pat Garrett*, then, is more
than just the end of a friendship; we see the death knell of the loving
spirit of America as well. *Pat Garrett* presents us with the Western's
traditional opposition between money and love, the material and
the spiritual, death and life. And though I certainly want to stop
short of asserting that there is an absolute correspondence between
Billy and the idealized sensibility of the American pioneer, it is
nonetheless certain that the Kid's affability and sympathy for the
lower classes are attractive traits, especially when contrasted with
Garrett's materialism.

Despite Garrett's negativity, Billy tries to reinvoke the bond of
friendship between them. Instead of directly reacting to Garrett's
remark about Mexico, Billy uses it as a departure point for narrating
a story about a man they both knew who attempted to reach Mexico.
"You heard about old Eben; he drowned in the Rio Grande trying
to get back to that old Mexico you're talking about. He took two
of the posse with him." Despite Billy's attempt to move the discussion away from the adversarial tone that Garrett is adopting, this
statement nonetheless reflects it, since the story about Eben concerns
the man's demise and also contains within it a possible warning to
Garrett concerning the fate of any men whom Garrett might recruit
for a posse. Billy thus invokes death and separation at the same
time that he is trying to affirm his friendship with Garrett, thereby
revealing the contradictory tendencies that his character embodies.
This story also shows us that the only significant difference between

Garrett and Billy is a matter of degree with respect to their being oriented toward either life or death, with the Kid leaning more to the former and Garrett to the latter.

Garrett replies, "I'm sorry to hear that. I always liked old Eben." Then, having briefly indulged his sentimentality, Garrett turns the conversation back to his desire to have Billy leave the territory. "Least he knew when it was the right time to leave," Garrett says, although given the fact that Eben was being pursued by a posse, it is hardly likely that he *chose* the time to depart. Nevertheless, Garrett seems to be inadvertently suggesting that death may be the only escape from a country that seems rapidly headed toward corruption. Garrett's remark turns the Kid back toward reminiscence, as though all that he and Garrett will now ever have is the past, since Garrett, through his assumption of the "responsible job" to which he will soon refer, has precluded the possibility of any amicable future between them. Billy first reinvokes the bond he still feels with Garrett by saying, "We did have some times, didn't we?" Yet as the remark makes clear, these times are over. Unlike *The Wild Bunch*, *Pat Garrett* does not celebrate the past, nor does it give its characters the benefit of great deeds and honorable deaths. At Garrett's hands, the Kid dies rather ignominiously, while Garrett is left to live out the rest of his sad life. *Pat Garrett* is a grim film that expresses its director's despair regarding the possibilities for spiritual renewal. *The Wild Bunch* is Peckinpah's celebration of possibilities; *Pat Garrett* is his meditation on limits.

Billy observes, "It's gotta be pretty hard to turn your back on all of that, ain't it?" Garrett's reply, which looks forward to the upcoming "changing times" remark, is in the form of a sentence fragment, reflecting the distracted mood that now takes hold of him. "Times changing, Billy," he says. Then, having realized that his suggestions about Billy's leaving the country have been ignored, Garrett must now state his case directly, a situation that obviously disturbs him. "You want it straight?" Garrett asks, to which Billy candidly replies, "If that's what you're here for." "The electorate wants you gone, out of the country," Garrett says. As throughout the film, the term *electorate* refers not to the general populace of the territory but to its moneyed ruling class, which Garrett hypocritically refers to with a populist term. "Well, are they asking me or telling me?" Billy says. To a degree still invoking a friendship that is for the most part ended, Garrett replies, "I'm asking you, but in five days I'm making you."[14] Peckinpah then freezes on a shot of Billy,

227

thereby telling us that the only way that Garrett will be able to make Billy leave the territory for good is to kill him.

In *Pat Garrett*, Peckinpah brings the Kid back to life for an extremely didactic reason: to show us that the intriguing stories that grew up around Billy are only part of the story.[15] Although *Pat Garrett* features Billy's friendship with poor characters such as Paco (Emilio Fernandez) and the Horrells (Claudia Bryar and Gene Evans), it also shows Billy demonstrating amiability with, but very little convincing compassion for, those who fight with him. Most of Billy's gang are shot and killed while the Kid isn't there to react to the murders; as for Paco's death and the Kid's outraged reaction to it, the incident seems to me less an example of Billy's capacity for sympathy than a plot device to maneuver Billy away from his trip to Mexico and (ultimately) back to Fort Sumner for his final confrontation with Garrett. As for Garrett and Billy's friendship, even if it did at one time achieve some halcyon state, Peckinpah ignores this period in favor of the time during which their friendship deteriorated and died. In this respect, the film is the most revisionist, and pessimistic, of all of Peckinpah's films set in the Old West; as the last of Peckinpah's literal Westerns, it stands as his grim goodbye to the period.

Peckinpah himself appears in the film as Will, a coffin maker, an especially apt role given the fact that the film itself is not only ruled over by death but is also a coffinlike repository for the body of legends and myths about Billy, Garrett, and their friendship. It is thus fitting that Will is working on a child's coffin, since *Pat Garrett* takes the childish attitude about Billy's unalloyed purity and decency and buries it once and for all.

Garrett declares that in five days he will "take over as sheriff of Lincoln County." Billy proposes a toast to this fateful situation. Again invoking the disparity between his age and Garrett's, with all of the associations regarding idealism and integrity versus materialism and compromise that such a reference entails, Billy refers to Garrett as "Old Pat." Billy then goes on to emphasize what he regards as the contrast between himself and Garrett by using Garrett's new title, drawing attention to the clearly marked opposite sides of the law that the two men now occupy. "Sheriff Pat Garrett, sold out to the Santa Fe Ring. How does it feel?" "It, uh, feels like times have changed," Garrett says, as though the nature of the times molds men's behavior and not vice versa. Garrett thus makes it clear that he wishes to avoid personal responsibility for his actions.

Billy, though, assumes full responsibility for what he does. "Times, maybe, not me," he replies. Garrett rejects Billy's request that he "stick around; we got a few days left ain't we?" "No, I gotta get back," Garrett says, at which point he picks up his rifle, which now represents the vengeance that will be a prime part of his new office.

When Garrett rises to leave, Billy, in another reference to the gambling metaphor that will be developed in the next scene, says, "Don't press your luck." Garrett replies, "I'm not worried about my luck." Garrett's slight emphasis on "my" indicates that he considers Billy to be in danger, a measure of Garrett's high opinion of his own prowess. In the longer version, Holly laughs grimly at this point, indicating that the gang members foolishly feel that the forces behind Garrett will not be sufficient to destroy them. Garrett then leaves the room, turning his back on the gang and thereby demonstrating that he doesn't fear that Billy or one of his men will shoot him in the back. (The film never again allows Garrett to display much dignity.)

The longer version continues with a reinvocation of the gambling metaphor. Bell says, "You boys are playing a losing game. I figure on staying alive." This assertion gains further significance since it looks forward both to Garrett's statement after the Stinking Springs massacre ("I'm alive, though") and a remark Norris (John Chandler) makes to Garrett at the meeting with Governor Wallace (Jason Robards, Jr.) about how the pursuit of the Kid and the accretion of power and influence in the territory are all part of a game. Then, in striking contrast to Garrett's audacious exit, Bell backs out of the room.

In both film versions, Holly then asks Billy, "Why don't you kill him [Garrett]?" "Why?" Billy responds. "He's my friend." The short version ends the scene at this point, and the titles begin; this cut affirms Billy's affection for Garrett despite the acrimonious nature of their exchange. However, the film's longer version makes it clear that at least intellectually, if not emotionally, Billy has accepted the fact that his friendship with Garrett is over. As Black walks out, he says to Billy, "He ain't no more [your friend]," a statement to which Billy assents. "I reckon," he says. Thus, whereas the cut version at least holds out the hope for the survival of Billy and Garrett's friendship, the longer film makes it plain from its opening minutes that only death lies ahead for this relationship.

Contrasts between the film's two versions are also evident in the next scene, the shoot-out at Stinking Springs, which takes place

229

the day after Garrett assumes his new office. Billy and two compatriots, Tom (Rudolph Wurlitzer) and Bowdre (Charlie Martin Smith), are in a cabin. As a bit of dialogue makes clear, they plan to steal some of Chisum's cattle, a blatant affront to Garrett, who became sheriff with Chisum's help. Bowdre goes out to water the horses and is shot by some of Garrett's men, among them Bob Ollinger (R. G. Armstrong), who will appear in subsequent scenes. At one point during the assault on the cabin, there is a virtual repetition of the type of editing juxtaposition used in the Las Cruces scene. First we see Billy fire his gun; this image is followed by a shot of Garrett, suggesting that Billy is aiming specifically at him. (In fact, Billy's shot comes so close to Garrett that we can see the shadow from the explosion that is caused by the bullet's impact.) Yet we must keep in mind that this "shooting" is implied by the editing only; it is clearly unjustified by what we know about the Kid's attitude to Garrett.

The gunfire at Stinking Springs eventually becomes more violent. Billy, Bowdre, and Tom are surrounded without any apparent mode of escape. Eventually, Bowdre and Tom are killed and Billy surrenders. The film's cut version eliminates an important part of this scene, though: the early part of the card game that the three men play in the cabin while they are being fired at. (All that is left of the game in the film's short version is a brief shot of Tom tossing a card onto the cabin floor.) The fact that these men are playing poker and betting on the game not only invokes the game's use in Westerns as a metaphor for life (taking chances, bluffing, demonstrating skill) but also signals their camaraderie and highlights their attempt to ignore their desperate circumstances. It also subtly reflects the continual raising of the stakes caused by the progressive destruction of the cabin by Garrett's men's bullets. After Tom and Bowdre bet, actions indicating that they intend to play out this last game right to the end, Billy uses a phrase that duplicates *The Wild Bunch*'s "Why not?" and that indicates not a bitter resignation but an acceptance of the positive aspects of the "game" being played. Indeed, the Kid symbolically makes it plain that he is not only ready to participate in resisting Garrett's assault but is also willing to try to best Garrett in this deadly game. "Raise you five," Billy says.

As the shooting continues, though, Bowdre, who was shot when he stepped outside the cabin, begins to die. "I can't see the cards no more," he says. At this point, the longer version gives us reaction shots from Billy and Tom that show their sympathy for their young companion. The cut version shortens Billy's reaction to Bowdre's dying and totally eliminates Tom's response, denying us these men's compassionate reactions and changing our view of them. The shorter film shows us only Billy's saying to Bowdre at this point, "Maybe it's time you took a walk." Bowdre, joining in the spirit of Billy's challenge to Garrett's aggression, responds, "Hell, yes; why not." The short version makes it seem that Billy wants Bowdre to divert the posse's gunfire so that he and Tom can try to escape. However, the longer version allows Billy to say, "We're framing you up, Charlie; it's the only chance we got"; thus, the Kid openly acknowledges the use to which he intends to put his friend, with the additional meaning that both he and Tom (the men are still acting as a group) are grateful for Bowdre's gesture. By once again eliminating dialogue, the cut version radically alters the way that we view the Kid's behavior.

After pushing Bowdre out of the cabin, Billy and Tom try to escape. However, Tom is killed. After retreating back into the cabin and accepting the impossibility of eluding capture, the Kid gives himself up. Holding his gun above his head, Billy emerges from the cabin, at which point Ollinger tries to shoot him, an action that Bell prevents. This attempt at brutal murder, in clear contradiction to Garrett's intention to bring the Kid in alive, not only characterizes Ollinger as the kind of fanatic who would shoot an unarmed man but also tempers our reaction to Billy's shooting of Ollinger a bit later in the film.

The Stinking Springs scene concludes with Garrett approaching Billy. Remarking on the ragtag group that Garrett has assembled, Billy comments, "You're in poor company, Pat." "Yeah, I'm alive, though," Garrett responds, a weak rejoinder, as Billy realizes. "So am I," says the Kid, and all that Garrett can do is smile at the Kid's bravado.

The dialogue in the next scene, which takes place in the Lincoln County jail, is notable for the manner in which the characters distort and build on one another's remarks. (This technique is also used in *Junior Bonner*.) The scene opens on a shot of Bob Ollinger, who is seated in a corner with his shotgun slung across his lap. When we first see Ollinger, Peckinpah blends in the sound of money clanking, thereby providing an aural bridge between the gambling activity from the previous scene and that in the present one, a linkage reinforced when we see that Garrett, Billy, and Bell are playing poker. At Stinking Springs, Billy and his friends, involved in a deadly situation, were gambling in order to lighten their oppressive circumstances. Here, three men are also playing cards in a room associated with entrapment and death, and each of them is also equivalently trapped by circumstances. Billy is literally enchained; Garrett, Bell, and Ollinger are bound by the poor choice they have made to serve the law because it profits them to do so. (Ollinger's choice seems especially problematical; he seems too fanatical to have well-founded opinions.)

The irony, of course, is that the man in chains, who serves no law but his own, is freer than the men guarding him precisely because their enchainment is self-willed and therefore that much more difficult to break. The sound of the coins clanking during the card game also resembles the sound of chains, which we hear later when Billy gets up to move around. This aural linkage conveys its own meaning: that there is a connection between money and entrapment, which we know to be so in the cases of Garrett, Bell, Ollinger, and the other members of Garrett's posse, all of whom have compromised themselves in return for the money they receive from the area's big landowners.

Plate 43. The tense card game in *Pat Garrett and Billy the Kid.*

The card scene reinvokes Billy's disappointment in Garrett's compromising, which he eventually extends to Bell; the scene also develops the idea that various people use Billy to justify their own decidedly tenuous beliefs, a characteristic that we will see in operation through the dialogue given to Ollinger. Billy says to Garrett, "I never figured on hearing you brag on being a working man. I never figured you for the law, either"; the statement implies that the law is neither an honest nor a working man's occupation, a direct insult to his former friend, whom he thereby challenges to justify his assumption of the post of sheriff. Garrett replies, "It's just a way of staying alive: no matter what side you're on you're always right." Garrett's first assertion is a patent falsehood; there are many other ways of earning a living other than working as a shill for a group of big-money ranchers. Additionally, the "staying alive" remark also relates back to the interchange between Garrett and Billy after Billy's surrender at Stinking Springs. Despite Garrett's previous and present comments, though, it's clear that he is not alive in the way that the Kid is; he lacks Billy's spontaneity and capacity for pleasure.

Garrett's second assertion also makes it plain that he realizes how corrupt the law he serves really is by suggesting that, regardless of the morality of your acts, you're always safe if you have the power of legal authority on your side. Garrett thus either intentionally misuses the term *right*, equating it with the coercion that money buys, or indicates through his misuse that he doesn't understand that he is wrong to act as the puppet of the moneyed forces. Garrett's further comment that he "aim[s] to live to be rich, old, and gray" is not only ironic in light of the knowledge we have of Garrett's bitter old age and murder but is based on the assumption that the mere attainment of old age or wealth is itself desirable, regardless of the quality of your life or the source of your money.

Billy replies, "That's a fine ambition, Pat. You keep thinking like that and I'll keep thinking on how I'm gonna spend your money." The verbal interplay now expands to include Bob Ollinger, who rises from his chair in the corner and approaches the table at which the other men are seated. Reacting to Billy's use of the phrase "thinking on," Ollinger attempts to impose his point of view on Billy: "Only thing you got to think about, Mr. Bonney, is when you stand before the highest court there is, may it sit in judgment on your rotten soul." Ollinger's statement translates the references to money in Billy's statement to a coinage of another kind. Perhaps more important, Ollinger also indicates that it is not God who will pass judgment on Billy but Ollinger himself; indeed, he has already done so, and his use of the term *rotten* places him in the role of a judgmental deity.[16] Like the other "law-abiding" characters in the film, Ollinger uses the Kid for his own purposes. Garrett uses Billy to advance himself politically; Bell, to advance himself financially.

Chisum and the other moneyed men use Billy to divert attention away from their corruption. Ollinger uses Billy as a scapegoat in an attempt to confirm what appears to us to be suspect religious obsessions. Ollinger concludes his statement by saying, "You listen, listen to me good. Just before that rope snaps it's gonna hit you like a bolt of lightning that what I've been telling you is the truth. Now you'll learn to believe before I'm finished with you."

Billy chooses to ignore Ollinger's remark, merely extracting the word *believe* to turn the conversation away from Ollinger's fanaticism and back to Bell and Garrett, who, unlike Ollinger, may still be capable of acknowledging their own excesses. "What do you believe in, Bell?" Billy asks. In the film's cut version, the first sentence of Bell's reply is cut, thus limiting his statement solely to a reference to the card game and suggesting that he does not wish to comment on matters of conviction. However, in the longer version Bell acknowledges the moral issues that are being brought up in the jailhouse conversation and touches on the implications in Billy's question. Bell's statement in full (with the long version's dialogue in italics) is, *"Only belief I have, Billy, is knowing I'm a little man with a job to do. But* I do believe I'm gonna have to see that bet and raise you five."

Ollinger persists in his assertions about God, quoting inaccurately from Ecclesiastes by saying, "Billy, somewhere in the good book it says, there's a time for everything, a time to hate, a time to kill." The quote's source highlights Ollinger's sanctimonious personality, while its inaccuracy reveals either how poorly versed he is in the Bible or how little regard he has for its integrity. Then, unlike the other characters, who react to each other's statements, Ollinger reacts to one of his own in a further affirmation of his insular psychology. "But now it's time you got close to God, boy," he says in a continuation of the scene's time references. Billy, who does not attempt to turn this statement to his own purposes but merely tries to deflect Ollinger's annoying presence, characterizes the deity in his own terms by relating his idea of God to two activities at which he excels, gunfighting and gambling: "I heard God's fast, but I'll have to go up in front of him myself before I bet on it."

Garrett cannot help contributing his little reminder of the Kid's impending execution. "You will [go up before God]," he says in a hypocritical invocation of a belief system in which he does not believe. Garrett appropriates Ollinger's terminology merely to taunt the Kid with his impending death.

In the cut film, Garrett remains silent after this remark. The long version has Garrett question Ollinger about his convictions, thus indicating that even before he admonishes him (as he soon will do), Garrett doesn't think very highly of Ollinger. "Say, Bob, what else do you believe in besides God?" Garrett asks, to which Ollinger replies, "Me." Garrett's next statement indicates the low esteem in which he holds Bob. "Just like old Ollinger; always got to have a minority opinion on everything." But since Ollinger is one of Garrett's deputies, his character ultimately comments on Garrett himself, who is here revealed as someone willing to employ men whom he doesn't respect. These men—the "poor company" referred to before—are very likely the only ones willing to help trap the Kid, an indication of both the fear that the Kid engenders and the high regard in which he is held.

Garrett prepares to leave to collect taxes (an additional invocation of the scene's concern with money as a locus for ideas about power and control and a reminder of Garrett's status as a lawman for hire). Garrett tells Billy that he will be back in two days, a none-too-subtle reminder of the passage of time, which for Billy is running out. (The statement can also be read as Garrett's subtle way of informing Billy of how much time he has to make his escape.) Ollinger again seizes on the notion of passing time in a further attempt to frighten Billy into repentance. "I count eight days 'til dawn, Billy; best be on your knees and making the acquaintance of your lord and master." Referring to Ollinger, Billy tells Garrett to "keep that mule's asshole away from me before I have to break him." To this affront, much of whose significance doubtless eludes him, Ollinger replies, "I truly wished you'd try, son. I got my shotgun full of sixteen thin dimes, enough to spread you out like a crazy woman's quilt," a statement that reinvokes the film's yoking of money and death. Ollinger tells Billy to "sing a song of Jesus while there's still a way," at which point Garrett, recognizing that Ollinger has gone too far, restrains him. "Now you mess around with him one more time, I'll have to send your ass back to Texas," Garrett says. But Billy doesn't want this. "Don't," he says; "think I'd like to keep him here a while," doubtless to remind him of what self-righteous people are really like and, perhaps, to give him the chance to kill Ollinger. At this point, Ollinger goes back to the corner and sits down, virtually duplicating the position he was in at the scene's beginning and rounding out this elegantly self-contained action.

Garrett then leaves. The next scene, between Billy, Bell, and

Ollinger, begins with a dissolve to Billy at the poker table looking over in Ollinger's direction, thus linking the scene with the previous one. When, in a facile attempt to placate Billy, Bell pretends that he does not have a good hand of cards, Billy admonishes him. "You must be afraid I'll go out a loser, Bell. As long as I'm still breathing let's just play it straight up," Billy says, using his phrase for forthrightness. Billy goes on to remind Bell of his opinion of the moral stance of Bell and the posse (and, by extension, Garrett). "I ain't sold myself like you and the rest of the town boys, Bell." Then, making sure he includes a comment on everyone in the room, Billy says, "That's just Bob that smells like street shit over there." Billy thus subtly turns Ollinger's former comment about breaking Billy, which equated the Kid with a horse, against Ollinger by referring to him as that animal's waste product.

At this point, Ollinger rises and tells Billy to get on his knees; this order recalls Ollinger's previous admonishment to Billy ("Best be on your knees and making the acquaintance of your lord and master"), thereby again placing Ollinger in the role of God. Billy replies, "Kiss my ass." Ollinger knocks Billy out of his chair and onto the floor. "Repent, you son of a bitch," Ollinger says, to which Billy replies, "Sweet Jesus I repent." A Mexican standoff ensues between Ollinger, who shoves his shotgun into Billy's chest, and Bell, who points his gun at Ollinger and tells him, "Leave off, Bob, you've gone loco." Ollinger releases Billy and prepares to go to the saloon, saying he's "thirsty as hell" in a reference whose colloquialism invokes once again the idea of damnation.

The cut version edits the dialogue at this point, denying us Ollinger's wonderfully stylized comments to Billy. "Not until you taste the fear of the Lord [will you repent]," Ollinger says in a comment that makes it clear that he wants to deliver this "taste" to Billy. "I'll show you. I'll take you for a walk across Hell on a spider web. Your trouble, boy, is you don't know about God." Ollinger then prepares to leave, taunting Billy with a statement that appears in both the film versions. "Wanna tell you one last thing personal, Kid. It's gonna be a loose rope and a long drop." The cut version ends the speech here, but the long version lets the speech continue to its logical conclusion, allowing Ollinger to indulge further his hatred of the Kid. "Why, good people are coming just to see your poor sinner spirit meet the devil, and I'm aiming to please them by making sure you say the Lord's prayer before you do a proper cakewalk and soil your drawers." Ollinger attempts to turn the "street shit" remark back against Billy by linking it with the dying man's loss of sphincter control and, quite possibly, inadvertently comparing him to a diapered baby through an unflattering reference to the Kid's nickname. Further, Ollinger's acting as the hangman places him in the role of the sacrificial priest. Ollinger has gone Bell and Garrett's use of the law one better, since he acts in the name not only of man but of God as well.

After Ollinger leaves for his drink, more conceptual linkages appear. His physical abuse has loosened Billy's bowels, to which Ollinger referred in his parting remarks. On the way to the outhouse with Billy, Bell comments on how his horse "locoed on [him] once." The "loco" reference harks back to the statement Bell had made to Bob when he was abusing the Kid. The sound of unruly horses neighing at this point not only links up with Ollinger's previous wild actions and the references to breaking horses and "street shit" but also provides a commentary on the Kid's unruly spirit, which seems impossible to tame. Additionally, the wild horse evocation looks forward to two other sequences: the one in which, after breaking out of jail, Billy is thrown by an unruly horse, and the scene in which anxious, shuffling horses are in the background when Billy and his gang dispatch some men who have come to kill them. In each scene, death accompanies the appearance of the animals, suggesting that violence, like an animal spirit, is a perennial force.

Bell goes on to talk about a bunch of Mescaleros. "They was just off the reservation and I suspicioned of them. But I had some biscuit on me; I give it to them and they just rode off." The story, which is about a group of men who seem untamed and alien to the culture of which Bell is a part, also invokes ideas about wildness, thus rounding out this section of the scene.

In the outhouse, Billy discovers a gun buried among the newspapers used for toilet tissue.[17] He retrieves it and rejoins Bell. Billy then succinctly expresses his feelings about Garrett. By taking Bell into his confidence, Billy reveals that he still considers Bell a close friend, despite his feelings about Bell's hypocrisy. "You know, I think old Pat's lost his sand; he won't come on a man," Billy says. "You hadn't ought to talk about him that way, Billy; you and him used to be pretty close," Bell replies. "He ain't the same man," Billy says. Then, looking at some corraled horses and doubtless thinking about the carefree times that he and Garrett once had, Billy says, "He's signed hisself over to Chisum and every other goddamned landowner that's trying to put a fence around this country." At the statement's end, a horse neighs. The editing juxtaposition suggests a conceptual connection: the horses represent not just Garrett and Billy's true spirits but also that of the country in its youth, which has now been corralled by the dubious benefits of civilization.

Billy finishes his statement by saying to Bell, "Hell, that's what you been doing, ain't it Bell, selling us out and getting fat." Billy accompanies his assertion by quickly flicking his eyes up and down Bell's body. "Ain't that easy, Billy," Bell says, indicating that what divides these two men isn't just a different attitude toward the law but something more primal: a different attitude toward reality. A romantic in thought (albeit not always in deed), Billy sees everything in absolute terms; Bell sees many sides of the same issue. The film drops the conversation here, yet the point has been made; each man has chosen to live a certain way. Yet given the manner in which *Pat Garrett* portrays these characters (and others like them), it's simple to see that despite this veneer of jaded resignation, Peckinpah at this point in his career believes in romanticism even though he apparently despairs of the attitude's ever being put into practice.

After a shot of children swinging on the hangman's rope (an action watched by Ollinger, who smiles at the children after he emerges from the saloon), we see Billy and Bell mounting the steps back to the jail's upper room. The two men talk about a friend of theirs, Carlyle. "I don't mean to be contrary," says the Kid, "but I ever tell you how he died? I shot him three times in the back; blew his goddamned head off." Although these seem to be two rather harsh statements, their brutality is tempered somewhat by the dialogue that the longer version places between them. Bell says, "I heard [about how Carlyle died] from Sam Dedrick," to which Billy says, "Yeah; now I'd like you to hear it from me." The implication in the longer film is that the story Bell had previously heard was not true. The Kid's insistence that he be the one to tell Bell the truth about Carlyle is remarkable when you consider that the portrait Billy paints of himself is extremely unfavorable. Nor can we assume that Billy tells Bell the truth merely because he wants Bell to know that he's a ruthless killer, since Bell surely already knows this. The fact remains that this is merely another instance in which Billy plays things "straight up" with someone.

After pointing his gun at Bell, Billy says, "I don't wanna kill you, Bell," a sentiment with which Bell concurs. "Well, now, I sure hope you don't, Billy." Billy's cautionary story hasn't had the desired effect on Bell, though. Bell begins to back down the stairs, to which

Billy says, "Don't, please." "You wouldn't shoot me in the back, Billy," Bell says, although this is precisely what happens.

Following Bell's death, the Kid runs upstairs and, quite possibly wanting to visit an appropriate justice on Ollinger, grabs Ollinger's shotgun out of the gun rack. When he emerges onto the jailhouse upper porch, he sees Ollinger coming toward the jail. "How's Jesus look to you now, Bob?" Billy asks. The reference is not intended merely to encourage an equation of Billy and Jesus; the film's repeated comparisons between Billy and Jesus are also reflections of Billy's view of himself as sacrificial victim. Here, Billy offers his remark as a taunt in response to Ollinger's previous self-serving sermonizing about standing at judgment. An off-screen townsperson says, "Bonney's killed Bell." Ollinger, so close to being killed that he expresses his death as a foregone fact, says, "Yeah, he's killed me, too." In slow motion, we see Ollinger's shotgun discharge the dimes and watch them pass through his body; this shot is followed by another reminder of Billy's unbridled spirit, the neighing of a horse and, in the longer version, a flash-cut shot of two children on the planks of the gallows who quickly duck for cover. Given Ollinger's employment by Garrett, his death by dimes is metaphorically apt and looks forward to Garrett's death at the hands of the moneyed interests for whom he previously worked.

After shooting Ollinger, Billy says, "Keep the change, Bob."[18] Then, in consonance with its unsparingly honest portrayal of the Kid's brutality, the long version shows Billy shooting Ollinger again. Billy sings an extemporaneous song to the gathering townspeople about the "lowdown town" of Lincoln, breaks his leg chains, and mounts a horse to ride out of town. Billy says to a man whose horse he commandeers, "I'll throw in about $1.60 worth of change if you can dig it out of old Bob there."

Days later, when Garrett rides back into town, he does not take immediate action to recapture the Kid, possibly because he knows where Billy will be and possibly because he wants to give the Kid enough time to leave the country. Instead, Garrett proceeds to the barber shop, whence he issues orders to form a posse. The first member, Alamosa Bill (Jack Elam), acknowledges to Garrett that he shot a fellow card player in the back after the man had accused Bill of cheating at cards. This piece of information actually appears to please Garrett, who downs his drink and says with a smirk, "Well, Bill, I'm gonna make you my deputy."

However, like the other men whom Garrett subsequently enlists in his campaign, Alamosa doesn't seem particularly enthusiastic about riding in pursuit of the Kid. Seen in extreme close-up after Garrett tells him he'll be a deputy, Alamosa looks virtually terror stricken; other people whom Garrett enlists, among them Sheriffs Baker (Slim Pickens) and McKinney (Richard Jaeckel), help Garrett with extreme reluctance. The crusade to capture the Kid is very unpopular, a fact that sets up a rather unusual situation for the audience. On the one hand, we have a popular outlaw who is clearly a remorseless and brutal killer. On the other hand, we have the traditional law-abiding characters, virtually all of whom seem extremely unsympathetic. We are thus placed in a moral dilemma: we can neither sympathize with the Kid nor trust the characters who represent the law. Essentially, the view that *Pat Garrett* takes is an unusual one for Peckinpah, who tends to favor the outlaw with morals: he presents us with a film in which no character, with the exception of Sheriff Baker, is likable.

After Garrett leaves the barber shop, he walks over to his house, which is at the edge of town. Despite Seydor's assertion about the long film, the "director's cut" doesn't show Garrett entering his house and playing out a scene with his wife.[19] Instead, the long version merely shows Garrett opening the gate in the picket fence, which lets out a squeak that foreshadows the deadly sound of the porch swing in which Garrett sits after murdering the Kid; this scene also looks forward to Garrett's opening the picket fence gate at Fort Sumner toward the film's end. The aural linkage is appropriate given not only the love/hate relationship between Garrett and Billy and (as asserted by Seydor) Garrett and his wife but also the complementarity between Garrett's hesitancy to confront his wife, who according to Seydor's account of the film powerfully disapproves of his actions, and to confront the Kid, whose objections mirror those of Mrs. Garrett.

In the longer film, there follows a series of scenes without dialogue whose gentle dissolves and lyrical photography communicate the unhurried nature of Garrett's pursuit of the Kid. We see Billy riding during the day, followed by a shot of Billy removing his leg irons, which dissolves to Billy riding past a body of water at twilight. His reflection in the water reminds us of his being shadowed by Garrett and emphasizes the Kid's imminent status as a legend, a status that will be based more on reflections on his acts than on the acts themselves. (Indeed, the scene is so dark that the Kid, who is scarcely discernible, seems to have already passed into history.) The idea of Billy's being shadowed leads us to the next shot: Garrett, during the late afternoon, riding in the same direction as the Kid. This shot dissolves to Billy riding at dusk past some barbed wire, which reminds us of the Kid's remark to Bell about Chisum and other men trying to throw a fence around the country.

The time of day at which these shots take place is significant. In the opening shots, Billy and Garrett are seen riding during the day. The other shots of Billy take place at sunset or near dusk, whereas Garrett's other shots take place in the late afternoon, implying through the light imagery that the Kid is far closer to death than is Garrett. The sequence's final shot is also noteworthy. Whereas in the previous shots Garrett and Billy had both been riding screen right, in the series' last shot Garrett is facing screen left, casually leaning against a tree and examining his watch. It's almost as though Garrett, like the grim reaper, is counting out the Kid's remaining hours. Moreover, instead of pursuing Billy, Garrett now seems either to be waiting for him or to be stalling in order to give the Kid enough time to leave the country. (This image also foreshadows the film's climax, when Garrett waits until Billy is finished making love to Maria before he shoots him.) The ambiguity here testifies to *Pat Garrett*'s brilliance, in that it shows how varied Garrett's motivations may be.

The next scene, which takes place at Governor Wallace's (Jason Robards) mansion, introduces us to two of the men financially backing the Kid's capture. Garrett enters extremely deferentially. After removing his hat and walking toward the governor, he even goes so far as to pat his hair down like a schoolboy approaching a teacher. Wallace introduces the two men at his table. He first identifies Luellen Howland (Jack Dodson) and then goes on to say, with a grimace of distaste emphasized by his using only the character's last name, "and, uh, this . . . man is Norris." The two pauses here function as a clear criticism of Norris; Wallace further denigrates him by offering only his last name. The hesitation also establishes a linkage between Wallace and Garrett, who had used a similar rhetorical pause during an earlier scene: when Garrett returned to Lincoln and found Ollinger's body still on the street, he said, "Would some of you . . . people get this man off the ground and into it?"

Sarcastically referring to his guests as "these, uh, gentlemen," Wallace says that Howland and Norris are "very concerned about the escape of William Bonney, a concern I'm sure you also share." Garrett assents, saying, "He escaped from my jail"; Wallace responds, "Exactly," emphasizing his feeling that Garrett blundered in allowing the Kid to get away. The governor's statement so upsets Garrett that he first stares across the table at Wallace as though he has just been slapped or ridiculed and then peevishly expresses his displeasure by leaning back in his chair in order to increase the distance between himself and Wallace.

Wallace then delivers a speech about the necessity of Billy's capture. He justifies his attitude by appealing to the concern of the moneyed interests with the maintenance of the status quo.

> This territory is vast and primitive. There is money here [the governor looks at Howland and Norris], growing investments and, uh, political interests. [He again looks at Howland and Norris.] We must protect these investments so that the area can continue to prosper and grow.

Howland and Norris's insulting of Garrett begins with Howland's response to Garrett's statement that the Kid's movements are unpredictable. "Oh come now, sheriff," Howland says. "For a man who's half outlaw himself and still smart enough to be elected sheriff by Chisum and the other ranchers, I expect better than that. Now can you bring him in or shall we look elsewhere?" Garrett replies, "Oh, I can bring him in." He then goes on to reveal his view of the stupidity behind the politics with which he has allied himself: "If the big peckerheads don't mess things up by starting another cattle war." Howland answers, "I can assure you, Mr. Garrett, that Chisum and the others have been advised to recognize their position"; this answer reveals quite plainly that even Chisum occupies a subsidiary status with regard to the territory's political jockeying.

Howland goes on to say, "In this particular game there are only a few plays left. I'd advise you to grab onto a winning hand while you have a chance." The statement not only reinvokes one of the film's primary conceits, card playing as a metaphor for risky machinations, but also implies that the speaker, as dealer, knows to whom he is dealing winning hands, thereby indicating that the entire political game is rigged against the poor and disadvantaged, an idea with which we are already familiar.

Norris patronizes Garrett by offering him in advance half of the $1,000 reward for Billy's capture. Garrett replies, "Well, I aim to bring the Kid in, but 'til I do, better take your 500 dollars and shove it up your ass and set fire to it." The show of bravado, approved by Wallace after he and Garrett excuse themselves from the table

("A commendable notion," Wallace says), can't hide the fact that despite their air of superiority they are both working in the employ of men like Leland and Norris.

In parallel scenes, as Billy is seen rejoining his men, Garrett is shown gathering more men for his posse. Garrett enlists the aid of Sheriff Baker to roust out members of Billy's gang. However, Sheriff Baker joins Garrett's cause extremely reluctantly.

BAKER: Understand you been riding for Chisum. [At this point, Garrett turns his back on Baker, in all likelihood to hide his embarrassment, and takes a drink.] I'd rather be on the outside of the law than packing a badge for that town of Lincoln and them that's a running it.

GARRETT: It's a job. There comes an age in a man's life when he don't wanna spend time figuring what comes next.

BAKER: Well it's gonna cost you some change. I got to the point where I don't do nothing for nobody less there's a piece of gold attached to it. [At this point, Garrett tosses Baker a gold coin.] One of these days when I get my boat built I'm gonna drift out of this damn territory. This town's got no hat size nohow.

Baker's reply makes it clear that Garrett is not respected by those men of conscience who are sworn to uphold the law. Yet when Baker does finally decide to help Garrett, he throws Garrett's money back to him to indicate that he will help Garrett out of friendship but will not be paid (as Garrett is) for enforcing a law in which he does not believe. When Baker's wife (Katy Jurado) says, "I don't like it [the situation in which Garrett has involved them]," Baker says, "Tell you the truth, mama, I don't take a shine to it myself."[20] It is thus all the more tragic that Baker, the only admirable character in the entire film, is mortally wounded in the shoot-out with Billy's men.[21] He dies facing a body of water on which he conceivably could have sailed out of the territory, away from compromise and deceit and hypocrisy (an end that looks forward to the conclusion of *The Killer Elite*). Yet in this scene, as in the upcoming raft episode, there is no escape from reprehensible qualities. *Pat Garrett*'s water imagery only points up the contrast between the film's predominantly morbid tone and the alternative milieus of which it admits no possibility.

Pat Garrett's most extraordinary meditation on fertility and futility occurs during an evening scene.[22] Garrett is sitting by a river. While he is looking at the water, Garrett hears shots that immediately—given our preconditioning by the previous shootings we've already witnessed in the film—key us to expect trouble and death. Instead, we see a barge silently floating by, from which a man is contentedly practicing his aim by shooting at a floating bottle. What we might take to be a honing of aggressive skills is portrayed as simply a casual entertainment, as is plain from the peaceful details with which Peckinpah has populated the barge: a young woman, two children, an idly smoking stove. At first, though, Garrett violates this serenity by using his pistol to shoot at the bottle from a concealed vantage point, just as he had earlier come up on the Kid unaware and fired his gun, demonstrating his shooting prowess while simultaneously frightening the Kid and his friends. For a second, the man on the barge doesn't know where the shot is coming from. We can certainly forgive him for assuming that the shot may signal danger. In fact, the man reacts as though he might personally be under fire and aims a shot in Garrett's direction. Garrett picks up his rifle (at which point the woman and the children duck down for cover) and gets the man in his sights; the man carefully aims at Garrett as well. Only at this point does Garrett realize that he might very well have erred in shooting and thus have provoked a hostile response. A stalemate is therefore reached, with each man aiming his rifle at the other and neither willing to take any further action. The barge man's river idyll has been destroyed, while Garrett, always a symbol of sterility and death, has for once been brought to some form of humility. All that can now ensue is for the barge to continue drifting silently downstream, with both Garrett and the man reduced to staring. What might have been a friendly contest has instead resulted in the creation of ill feelings on both sides. Through Garrett's morbid self-obsession, a potentially fruitful and peace-connoting waterside scene has been transformed into a powerfully ominous, death-connoting moment.

The film's striking parallelism resurfaces when Garrett visits Lemuel's "bar" while Billy is at the Horrells. The entire scene at Lemuel's points up Garrett's essential cruelty, which is in telling contrast to Billy, who kills only for retribution (as when he shoots the men who have killed Sylva [Jorge Russek] and tortured Paco). Garrett, though, draws out his abuse of Holly, Beaver, Lemuel (Chill Wills), and Alias (Bob Dylan). He tells Alias to knock out Beaver with a gun butt, doing so in such a way as to ensure that Beaver is aware of the terrible thing that is going to happen to him. Garrett then has Alias push Lemuel's hat down over his eyes so that the man can hear but not see what is going on, as though Garrett knows how terrible it must be to listen to horrors in the dark. He then orders Alias to read out loud the labels of the "air tights" (canned food) on Lemuel's shelves and finally makes Holly play cards with him, all the while compelling Holly to get powerfully drunk on the liquor both men are drinking. Holly draws a knife on Garrett, who then shoots him; after Holly falls, Alias keeps on reading: "Plums, beans, tomatoes. . . ." Alias's continued reading adds a grimly humorous counterpoint to a terribly morbid scene.

By contrast, in a parallel scene Billy rides up to the Horrels, where he expects no trouble; he is merely stopping by to pay his respects and get something to eat. Unfortunately, Alamosa Bill, already deputized by Garrett, is there, and the two men must return to the front of the house for a shoot-out. Seydor contends that because Billy turns around to face Alamosa before the requisite count of ten, the Kid cheats.[23] However, Alamosa is a well-known rascal, as revealed in the discussion he has with Garrett before being deputized; moreover, in the present pace-off Alamosa cheats by turning around at the count of eight. (As he dies, he explains to Billy, "I never could count.") Thus, it seems fairer to assert that Billy was only protecting himself. The contrast between Billy and Garrett's scenes should be obvious: Garrett takes pleasure in killing; Billy kills for protection.

During the meal at the Horrels, Billy makes a significant observation about the law. After Billy notes how ironic it is that Alamosa should be a deputy, Alamosa says that he never intended to volunteer and that he had, in fact, ridden in to Lincoln merely to see Billy hang. (Alamosa's attempt to avoid responsibility for being deputized mirrors Garrett's repeated disclaimer of personal responsibility for his own actions.) Billy then observes, "Wasn't long ago I was the law riding for Chisum and Pat was an outlaw. The law's a funny thing, ain't it?" The point here is important: Billy recognizes that the meaning of "the law" depends on the person for whom you work. If, like Garrett, you are in the employ of powerful men, then you have the law on your side. The law, then, equals money, which equals power. It's as succinct and pessimistic a statement on the status of justice in the United States as Peckinpah has ever made.

Aside from the frame story, the only other major difference between *Pat Garrett*'s shorter and longer versions is the presence in the longer film of the scene involving Garrett, Chisum, and Poe, which is notable chiefly for further characterizing the forces behind

Garrett's pursuit of the Kid. (Ironically, the shorter film seems superior with regard to Chisum, whose absence makes him appear to be more mysterious and powerful.) When Garrett and Poe ride up, some of Chisum's men are breaking wild horses. When one of Chisum's men is unable to tame one of the horses, Chisum says, "All right, somebody else try him." Given the film's equation of wild horses with an indomitable spirit, Chisum's statement makes it plain that, just as Norris had told Garrett, if Garrett isn't successful in "breaking" the Kid, the men with money and power will find someone else to do their work for them.

Chisum then says, "Bonney tried to steal a few head a couple of weeks ago." Garrett is not about to let the statement go unchallenged, though. "Well, he says you owe him 500 dollars back salary," Garrett says, being careful to ascribe the remark solely to Billy so as to protect himself from any involvement in the assertion. "He rode for me; I treated him just like any other man," Chisum replies. The remark sidesteps the point about the truth or falsity of Billy's contention; it is therefore met with a scornful look from Garrett. Chisum then asks why Garrett has ridden out to see him, a question that Poe, somewhat presumptuously, answers. "Thought maybe you'd heard somethin'," Poe says. Chisum's reply reveals how disdainful he is of the capabilities of the men with whom he's talking. "Yeah, I'll tell you what I heard. Billy the Kid is in Tuscosa; Billy the Kid is in Tombstone. Billy the Kid is in Mexico, Tularosa, Socorro, White Oaks. And, Billy the Kid is at my table right at this moment eating tacos and green chili peppers with my niece, just like old times."

The last assertion reveals not only that at one time Billy had been fond of Chisum's niece (doubtless in a romantic way) but, further, that Chisum apparently had been fond of Billy, too, or else he would not have allowed Billy to keep time with his niece and eat at his table. This last quality establishes a link between Chisum and Garrett, both of whom feel that Billy has disappointed them in their affections. Chisum then asks Garrett, "You staying for supper?" Garrett refuses the invitation with a tired sigh and then, looking over his flask with an evaluating eye at Chisum, takes a drink. Chisum is not through yet, though; he confirms his elitist attitudes, shared as well in varying degrees by Wallace, Howland, Norris, and Garrett himself, by asking Poe to supper. When Poe, somewhat taken aback by the unexpected invitation, accepts, Chisum replies, "Fine, bunkhouse is right behind the large barn." Chisum then underscores the class-based pecking order that, in his obsessive and neurotic fixation on status, he finds it necessary to confirm through the degradation of others: "Men usually eat when the cook lets them." He therefore insults Poe by denying him his table and relegating him to the status of a hired man; worse, he makes him the underling of the ranch cook. "Interesting meeting you, Mr. Poe; perhaps I'll see you again sometime," Chisum says, thereby dismissing Poe in a superficially polite yet clearly hostile way.

Then Chisum once more finds it necessary to degrade Garrett: "Glad to be of service, Garrett; but don't overuse it." Garrett knows that he, too, is being casually dismissed. He caps his flask but does not leave without paying important deference to Chisum. "I appreciate the loan," Garrett says, making it clear how literally indebted to Chisum he really is. Chisum first looks away without reacting, making Garrett's statement merely hang in the air, its speaker twisting emptily along with it. Then, acknowledging the statement with only the barest nod of his head, Chisum reminds Garrett of how he expects this "loan," which is really betrayal money, to be repaid. "You gonna get him?" Chisum asks and Garrett, unable to answer without sounding either childishly overconfident or downright stupid, merely rides away. Seeing Garrett leave, Poe follows like a kowtowing acolyte, but not before putting his finger to his hat to pay one final gesture of obeisance to Chisum.

From this point onward, *Pat Garrett* settles down to an almost languid pace, and the audience falls into a strange dreaminess. Time appears to move very slowly; Garrett seems less to be pursuing the Kid (whom he has all along been giving plenty of time to leave the country) than to be merely drifting toward him. During this period, which occupies the film's middle third and prepares us for its languorously paced finale at the compound managed by Pete Maxwell (Paul Fix), we are lulled by the repeated shootings and the almost uniform sterility of the landscape. In essence, we become like Garrett and Billy—tired, almost indifferent to violence, anxious for some change that will herald an end to this sameness.

The change comes when Garrett, Poe, and Sheriff Kip McKinney—who walk toward the fort very slowly, looking like grim figures emerging out of the darkness—converge at dusk on Pete Maxwell's, where Billy is in bed with Maria (Rita Coolidge).[24] Garrett stops for a few moments to talk to Will, the coffin maker. Will begins by making a rather curious statement about Garrett's having "figured it out," which we may take to refer not to Garrett's finding Billy (surely this was easy enough) but rather to Garrett's rather poorly considered decision about what to do with the rest of his life. In Will's (and the audience's) view this choice is wrong, as Will's next statement makes evident. Will insults Garrett, comparing him to chickens (thus calling the sheriff a coward and also reinvoking the longer version's opening titles) and accusing him of being not only a foraging animal but one that feeds on waste products: "I thought you'd be out picking shit with the chickens, cutting yourself a tin bill." "Tin bill" refers to Garrett's sheriff's star, which Will feels has devolved to Garrett thanks to his association with Chisum and the men above him, whom he also implicitly compares to shit-eating cowards.[25]

Urging Garrett to "go on, get it over with," Will then proceeds to reject the manner in which the territory is moving toward materialism and mercenary attitudes. Much as Sheriff Baker had done, Will intends to use a wooden vessel (not surprisingly, the coffin is shaped like a boat) to free himself from the region: "You know what I'm gonna do? Put everything I own right here and I'm gonna bury it in the ground. Then I'm gonna leave the territory." Despite his bitterness, though, Will—like other characters in the film who bear Garrett ill will but nonetheless give him good advice (Baker and Holly, for example)—warns Garrett that the reasoning he has been using to justify capturing and killing the Kid is faulty and self-serving, since it will result only in frustrating Garrett's desire for self-protection. "When are you gonna learn you can't trust anybody, not even yourself, Garrett?" Will says. When Garrett moves off, Will finishes his insult in a parting shot at the sheriff, calling him a "chicken shit badge-wearing son of a bitch." He thus remarks directly on Garrett's essential cowardice and links it with the sheriff's star. (Interestingly, Garrett does not wear his star when he shoots Billy, perhaps to indicate that he is acting on his own and not as a lawman in the employ of the Santa Fe Ring).

By this point in the film, the weary and grim Garrett seems like death incarnate, a role confirmed in the way in which he is repeatedly seen as a shadow skulking around the fort and in the manner in which he insinuates himself into Pete Maxwell's kitchen, sitting down next to Maxwell like some dark presence. Garrett's otherworldly aspect is further reinforced by his almost magical disappearance from Maria's room when she tries to discover who is there; this same quality is also present in the deathly creak of the porch swing when Garrett sits down in it before the murder.

Plate 44. Garrett standing over Billy, whom he's just killed.

The actual shooting of the Kid is over rather quickly. Coming back into Maxwell's, Billy sees Garrett and seems glad of the fact, but he has virtually no time to react before Garrett shoots him once in the chest. When Billy dies, Garrett realizes just how dead he himself is. Having killed his better self, Garrett turns and murders his mirror image, affirming his living death and repudiating the ugly picture that the mirror gives back to him. (Significantly, Garrett's shot blows a hole in the mirror just where his heart would be.)

The endings of *Pat Garrett*'s two versions differ only slightly, but significantly. After Garrett rides away from Maxwell's, the long version reprises the 1909 shooting of Garrett seen at the film's beginning, but with a number of important differences. For one thing, the opening title's views of Garrett reacting to being shot are all, save one, eliminated; thus, the three men firing at Garrett seem to hit him from the same vantage point. This foreshortening of the original shooting suggests a far more impressive unanimity of purpose among these men than was communicated in the sequence's initial appearance. Additionally, there is a shot of Poe firing at Garrett, which is followed by a flash cut of Billy shooting. The juxtaposition, which crowds the two images together so swiftly as to make Poe and the Kid seem equivalent, achieves two effects: it repeats the suggestion in the prologue about Poe succeeding to Billy's place as Garrett's traveling companion, and it also allows the dead Billy an opportunity to have his revenge on Garrett. (However, this action would be highly uncharacteristic of the Kid; its depiction represents a misguided or self-contradictory notion of the filmmakers more than anything else.)

Plate 45. The final freeze-frame of the shortened *Pat Garrett*.

Ironically, the long film's ending is no more satisfying than the one that MGM appended to the end of *Pat Garrett*'s cut version. In the shorter film, after Garrett rides away from the scene of Billy's death, we see as a final image a reprise of a shot from the film's opening sequence near Fort Sumner, when Garrett and Billy, for the only time in the film, had for a very brief moment seemed happy together. This image, which appears in a still frame (an appropriate stylistic representation given the ultimately deadly nature of Garrett and Billy's relationship), shows Garrett and the Kid smiling. As a reminder of their friendship and the way that it tragically turns out, that final, frozen two-shot couldn't be improved on.

CHAPTER   TEN

Head Games

We may take Peckinpah at his word when he states that *Bring Me The Head of Alfredo Garcia* is the one film in which he fully realized his intentions.[1] Indeed, the film is an exhilaratingly effective mélange of all of Peckinpah's thematic and stylistic concerns.

Alfredo Garcia starts out with a scene that at first appears most atypical for Peckinpah, since it begins placidly, in Mexico, whereas in most of the director's films a Mexican idyll is reached only after a great deal of chaos. From its very beginning, then, *Alfredo Garcia* inverts the normal order of things. This scene of pastoral beauty and repose finds a young, pregnant woman (Janine Maldonado) sitting by a calm body of water, gazing peacefully into its depths while on the water's sun-dazzled surface pairs of ducks and geese slowly glide. However, since Mexico in Peckinpah's films is a land of contradictions, we shouldn't be too surprised by the violent turn that the film's action now takes. A woman bearing a message for the scene's central figure enters, telling the young woman that she is wanted back at the ranch; this summons not only disrupts the wordless repose but also presages danger. The pregnant woman returns to the ranch and is brought before her father, El Jefé (Emilio Fernandez), who is in his private chapel; he demands that she name the father of her unborn child, which she does only after one of El Jefé's minions breaks her arm. By now, we have already been plunged into what we later realize is a microcosm of *Alfredo Garcia*'s entire universe, within which exaggeration, violence, and fierce contradictions prevail.

Up to this point, *Alfredo Garcia* has refrained from communicating to us any sense of time period. In fact, given the settings of the film's two opening scenes—first the unblemished countryside and then the lavishly and traditionally adorned house, which is filled with women in black shawls and men in the perennial costumes of the landed gentry—we may conclude, despite the presence of two men in modern dress, that what we are watching is taking place in some timeless fairyland. Consequently, when agents are sent out at El Jefé's behest to bring him proof of the death of the bastard child's father (in the form of Alfredo Garcia's head), and these agents are suddenly seen leaving the palace not only by horseback but also by motorcycle, automobile, and jet plane, we experience a shock at the violent leap into the present. Yet the remainder of the film makes clear that similar juxtapositions of tone—temporal, moral, and aesthetic—are the very basis of *Alfredo Garcia*'s structure.

In other Peckinpah films we have seen characters embody traits such as love, compassion, cruelty, morbidity, alienation, anachronism, and nihilism. However, only *Alfredo Garcia* gives us these humors and states of mind in such undiluted forms. Two of El Jefé's henchmen, Sappensly and Quill (Robert Weber and Gig Young), go to a sleazy Mexico City piano bar where Bennie (Warren Oates) is the instrumentalist.[2] Eventually, Bennie takes on the quest for Garcia's head so that he may earn the money with which Sappensly and Quill tempt him. As the film progresses, we find that Garcia is already dead; the action necessary to secure his head is therefore much more unsettling than originally anticipated, since it's no longer merely a question of killing a man but the decapitation of a corpse. Of course, previous Peckinpah films have accustomed us to undiluted representations of murder and mayhem, and surely even a beheading would not significantly raise the stakes of terror. However, the proposal to do violence to someone already dead, who must be disinterred and then violated, calls down on this proposed act all of the social prohibitions concerning the sanctity of the dead. In *Alfredo Garcia*, though, this sanctity is just one more taboo that is approached, confronted, and transcended.

As Bennie continues on his mission, the potential for revulsion and horror becomes greater at the same time that the amount of reward money promised him increases. The offers grow from the small bribe for information about Garcia offered in the piano bar, to the 1,000 dollars that Quill first offers, to the 5,000 and then 10,000 dollars that El Jefé's agent, Max (Helmut Dantine), promises, and, finally, to the million dollars in cash contained in the case that El Jefé offers Bennie toward the film's end. As the reward grows, so too does Alfredo's severed head become progressively more corrupt. The rotting head—which Bennie finally acquires—requires increasingly more efficacious methods of preservation: first a cloth wrap, then regular ice, then dry ice. And just as the money grows and the head rots, Bennie moves simultaneously toward a truly psychotic state of mind. Indeed, the longer Bennie is with the head, the crazier (or more sane, if sanity is a state of mind consistent with one's milieu, which in this case is decidedly pathological) Bennie becomes. As time passes, more and more corpses pile up as Bennie works his way toward the two primary figures from the film's beginning: El Jefé and his daughter.

Plate 46. Chopping ice to keep the "dead cat" cool in *Bring Me the Head of Alfredo Garcia*.

Unlike the film's other murderers, Bennie never kills any innocents; for example, he doesn't kill any of the members of the moral Garcia family, and he is responsible only for the deaths of the motorcycle marauders and the henchmen of El Jefé who are out to acquire the head. Nonetheless, we can have very little sympathy for Bennie, who is often cruel to his lover, Elita (Isela Vega). After

Elita's death, which takes place toward the end of *Alfredo Garcia*'s graveyard sequence, Bennie goes truly mad. Yet there seems to be a purpose behind his erratic behavior: to locate the source of the film's horrors. At the same time, though, we are also given an equivalent amount of evidence to suggest that the only force driving Bennie forward is the anarchic need for action of any sort.

Alfredo Garcia easily qualifies as the most stylistically excessive of Peckinpah's films. The film giddily juxtaposes horror and humor, as when Bennie pours some tequila over the clothbound head and says, "Have a drink, Al." On another occasion, Max, fully dressed except for his trousers, is discovered in his hotel room being given a pedicure by two women while he simultaneously scans a copy of *Time* whose cover is adorned by the bloated face of Richard Nixon. (Nixon's distorted cover picture has already been anticipated by a phony Nixon dollar bill that hangs on the nightclub wall behind Bennie's piano.) Such exaggerated comic pairings are fashioned in the classic surrealist mode, in which improbable actions or events are melded within a stylistically antithetical context: in Lautreamont's phrase, "The fortuitous encounter on a dissecting table of a sewing machine and an umbrella."[3] The yoking together of objects and ideas that are individually sane and integral but that become effectively insane when juxtaposed (e.g., Alfredo's head and Bennie) creates in us a state of mind that moves us beyond conventional notions of good and evil, right and wrong, into a realm in which we merely perceive—precisely the result that Lautreamont wished to achieve.

With our vision so cleansed, what we see in *Alfredo Garcia* is the nihilistic energy of a man seeking an end whose nature he could never possibly imagine. We accept what would normally qualify as absurd impossibilities—for example, Bennie's being able to pass Alfredo's head through the usual airport baggage checks on one of his journeys. We refrain from speculating on what Bennie hopes to accomplish at El Jefé's place, nor do we wonder where Bennie thinks he is going when, having killed El Jefé, he drives off down the road toward what turns out to be his end in a hail of machine-gun bullets—à la *Bonnie and Clyde*. The film contains wild slayings (the massacre of the Garcias; the shoot-out in Max's hotel room), incredible events (the massive number of shootings), and giddy dialogue. For example, when a young Mexican boy asks what is in the fly-covered cloth wrapped around Alfredo's head, Benny says that it's a "cat—dead cat—used to belong to a friend of mine." At another point, commenting on the horrible hotel he and Elita stay in one night, Bennie says, "You oughta be drunk in Fresno, California. This place is a palace."

The film is also characterized by humorously inappropriate ambiance (the continuous Muzak that Peckinpah has filtering into Max's suite during the slaughter there) and comic characterizations (e.g., Bennie sleeps with his sunglasses on). All of these elements help to create a milieu in which action is its own justification. By the film's end, before the close-up of the eye of the phallic machine gun that has been wagging its stupid visage at us, we have had our conventionally defined sanity blown away. *Alfredo Garcia* is a machine gun of a film that explodes in our heads while we sit there and laugh in the face of the chaotic universe that the director has portrayed. Ultimately, the insanity of such a response is the sanest reaction of all.

Although *Alfredo Garcia* embodies many of Peckinpah's concerns in intentionally excessive forms, it also contains a great deal of linear dialogue, traditional symbology, foreshadowings of events, and figurative movements. It is almost as though Peckinpah is trying to confound critics of his films who have accused him of indulging in meaningless violence by overloading this violent film with meaning wherever one looks, thereby parodying through excess this type of criticism. The result is that *Alfredo Garcia* is the most elusive (because of its contradictory actions and dialogue) and accessible (because of its multitudinous references) of any Peckinpah film.

Peckinpah demonstrates the connection between religion and violence (which he has previously dramatized through *Ride the High Country*'s Joshua Knudsen, *Major Dundee*'s Reverend Dahlstrom, and *Pat Garrett*'s Bob Ollinger, all played by R. G. Armstrong) by showing us clergy who are directly involved with corruption and death. Thus, a priest and two nuns blithely stand by while El Jefé has his daughter's arm broken. Associated as it is with violent action and symbols of violence (El Jefé's thugs wield weapons during the chapel sequence), the church is depicted as being an actual harbinger and, indirectly, purveyor of pain and death by virtue of its failure to protest them. When Elita objects to Bennie's plan to remove Alfredo's head, Bennie points out how the church has been known to cut off the fingers, feet, and even heads of saints for relics. Bennie's comment implies, first, that Alfredo is in some perverse sense a saint, a Grail-like object of veneration (an attitude that links up with Bennie's earlier sarcastic reference to Alfredo as "the golden fleece" that he and Elita are "gonna find"). Bennie also argues implicitly that what he plans to do is no different from what the church does with its celebrated dead (although the church's actions could be viewed as more objectionable since they regard the bodies that they dismember as holy).

In *Alfredo Garcia*, Peckinpah at once denies us many of the visual results of violence and, using an aural and verbal approach, makes violence's results more accessible than ever before. Peckinpah cuts away from the chapel scene at the precise point when we hear El Jefé's daughter's arm break. He also persists throughout the film in failing to grant us a full view of its central symbol: Alfredo's severed head. Compensating for this lack of visual heads is the film's saturation with verbal references to heads. Bennie makes a nasty comment to Elita, asking her if during her time with Alfredo he gave her "good head." A little while later, when Bennie tells Elita to get dressed because they're going on a picnic, Elita says, "Don't play with my head," a statement that has both a colloquial meaning (don't tease me) and a prescient and literal one, the latter realized when Bennie toys with Alfredo's severed head. (The line also looks forward to Bennie's claim that the contents of the sack "used to belong to a friend of mine.")

Posing as lost tourists, Sappensly and Quill stop at the site of the showdown between Bennie and the Garcia family. In a blatant pun on decapitation, Sappensly asks Bennie, "Where's the cutoff?" When Bennie replies, "It's right here, but you're gonna have to take it," the statement so obviously refers to the head that we can't help but laugh and groan at the same time.

Of course, at the center of the film there is a basic visual pun: one of the "heads" that Bennie brings back with him to El Jefé is the cameo headshot photograph of Alfredo (which El Jefé has already seen). Other puns in the film take visual form as well. To prefigure Bennie's going mad (that is, he "loses his head"), Bennie is shown after the graveyard assault against him and Elita waking up, half-buried. After a shot from Bennie's point of view of his reaching out through the dirt with which he is covered, we get a pulled-back objective shot of Bennie. The camera is situated in such a way that a plant obscures Bennie's upper body, making it seem that his head is gone.[4]

There is even more to the film's playfulness, though. When Sappensly and Quill enter the piano bar where Bennie is leading a chorus of patrons in singing "Guantanamera," the singing suddenly dies down and stops. This action is obviously a parody of the old B Western

Plate 47. Quill, just one of *Alfredo Garcia*'s well-adjusted characters, immediately before he murders the Garcia family.

routine in which a raucous barroom is reduced to awkward silence by the entrance of a stranger. Also parodied is the overplayed and heavyhanded symbolism in the sequence in which Bennie kisses Elita while driving, at which point they nearly crash. (The fact that Alfredo died in a car crash, and that the sound of squealing tires is heard when Sappensly first shows Alfredo's picture to Bennie, makes this connection between the pursuit of the head and death by automobile that much more obvious.) At the time, Bennie and Elita are driving by a series of white road markers that look like cemetery headstones. They also pass by a bus on the road, recalling the bus that drives by just before the Garcia family is massacred by Quill and Sappensly.

Irony surfaces at numerous points in the film. After Quill stuffs some money into Bennie's tips glass in the cafe, Bennie says, "Take me to your leader," which is exactly the point of his eventual mission. Bennie's allegiance to his cause and the head is reflected in his later telling Sappensly and Quill, "You've got me" while we hear in the background a car crash that not only foreshadows the film's literal automobile collisions but also symbolizes the many collisions of purpose among the film's various characters.

In keeping with the steadily progressing sense of morbidity, the

257

film's water symbols start out connoting life but eventually symbolize only death. We have already seen that the placidity of the film's opening is associated with water. The shower that Bennie mentions Elita's having taken at his apartment during an amicable period in their relationship recurs twice with morbid overtones: during the hotel scene, a distraught Elita collapses like a corpse on the shower's floor; and during the scene in which Bennie gives Alfredo's head a shower, he tells the head, "A friend of ours used to take a shower in there." Given this morbidity, we can appreciate the foulness of the pool of slimy green water at the graveyard, water whose taint is mocked by the clean water that drips into it.

Corruption and liquids surface again when Bennie, in bed with Elita, wakes up in the middle of the night and discovers that he has crab lice. He crushes some of the bugs (in keeping with the film's exaggerations, the sounds of their cracking carapaces is very loud) and then douses his crotch with tequila.[5] Tequila is the film's only substitute for all of its corrupt water, which includes even the supposedly holy water used at the child's baptism, a ceremony polluted not only by El Jefé's hypocrisy but also by the sycophantic ministrations of the morally compromised presiding priest. However, the film's antitheses (violence and peace, corruption and reverence) are no more absurdly contradictory than some of the outfits that Bennie sports, in particular the one he wears to Max's suite, which includes an orange-and-white plaid tie worn along with a raucously contrasting print shirt; the tie, a supremely cheap clip-on, slips off while Bennie is stuffing some of Max's money into his pocket.

One of the film's prime qualities, which might be overlooked given its periodic outbursts of violence, is that above all else *Alfredo Garcia* is a love story. There are moments of tenderness between Bennie and Elita that are as touching as anything that Peckinpah has ever directed. In one scene, for instance, Bennie and Elita are reclining under a tree, and she asks him why he's never proposed to her; in the following scene, though, Bennie and Elita are accosted by two bikers (Kris Kristofferson and Donny Fritts), one of whom attempts to rape her. Such striking juxtapositions of sentimentality and violence occur throughout the film. Given these juxtapositions, Peckinpah seems to be saying that love and murder, tenderness and brutality, are virtually inseparable.

Underscoring this linkage are some of the subtle sexual juxtapositions that Peckinpah achieves. When Sappensly is first seen, he is emerging from a carriage in which sits a pretty blonde girl of nine

Plate 48. The antipodes of *Alfredo Garcia*'s universe: Bennie and Elita in one of the film's rare quiet moments.

Plate 49. Bennie about to shoot one of El Jefé's minions. "Why? Because it feels so goddamn good."

or ten who is holding a flower, a strange linkage considering what we subsequently learn about Sappensly's brutality. In the barroom scene, two prostitutes approach Sappensly and Quill, and Bennie asks, "Something for the ladies?" Quill responds, "Burro piss?" Then one of the women starts to run her hand over Sappensly's crotch. He quickly knocks her out with an elbow punch; Quill looks on bemusedly while the woman is dragged off. Indeed, one of *Alfredo Garcia*'s most fascinating qualities is the way that the relationship between Sappensly and Quill suggests, if not homosexuality, at least a powerful homophilia, one that obviously excludes women. The details of the men's relationship are never made clear, which is as it should be, since Peckinpah intends to keep us off balance.

Regardless of *Alfredo Garcia*'s excesses, the audience must nonetheless ask a rather reasonable question: what is the ultimate purpose behind Bennie's mission? Bennie certainly appears to be acting without any discernible design, yet there may be some pattern to his actions after all. Despite his statements about wanting only the reward for the head, Bennie also wants to divine some reason for the film's senseless killings and assaults, many of which he either causes or is involved in. As we might expect given the escalating violence and morbidity, Bennie's inquiries about purpose become more and more incisive as the film progresses, moving from straightforward questions to Sappensly and Quill such as "What do you want him [Alfredo] for?" to his similar question to Max, to inquiries not only about other people's motives but also his own. For instance, when Bennie is faced with the Garcia family, who ask him if he wants the head only for money, he answers, "No—sí," thereby revealing the contradictions underlying all of his acts.

Yet Bennie does want to know the meaning behind the film's fantastic plot. He says to Alfredo's head at one point, "We're gonna find out, you and me." By using the head as his passport into the company of increasingly more corrupt characters, Bennie proves the truth of the adage that two heads are indeed better than one, especially when trying to unriddle the film's series of essentially chaotic events.

Alfredo Garcia's last two references to purpose occur as Bennie makes the final two moves toward the film's source of meaning (or, as it turns out, meaninglessness): El Jefé. The first occurs in Max's hotel room, where Bennie says, "This [the picnic basket containing the head] belonged to a very special lady. Once upon a time she filled it up with food and we went on a picnic. We turned off a dirt road and we ate the food she prepared with her hands, very special hands. And that's why I'd like to know why you don't take it [the head] and tell me what the hell the head of Alfredo Garcia is worth, and to who. Comprendo?" As this speech indicates, Bennie realizes that the whole journey with Elita began auspiciously (thus the fairy-tale "once upon a time" beginning) but turned morbid when they turned off the road for a picnic, during which the first of the film's many murders occurs. More important, for the first time Bennie not only verbalizes his curiosity about the head's value but also states that he needs to know who offers the reward.

The second reference to purpose occurs in El Jefé's chapel, where Bennie finally begins to realize that his entire quest has been an attempt to find meaning where none exists. "Sixteen people are dead because of him [Alfredo] and you and me," Bennie says to El Jefé, thereby protesting the film's violence while apparently recognizing that all of the deaths have served only to deliver an object that is essentially meaningless: it was intended to satisfy El Jefé's blind demand for vengeance, which, as El Jefé himself reveals, is now of no consequence to him. When El Jefé says, "I have everything that I want: I have my grandson," Bennie realizes that the head is without significance to El Jefé. El Jefé underscores the point by telling Bennie to throw the head "to the pigs." El Jefé's remark explains why he is the only important figure in the film whom Bennie does not ask to explain his motives for wanting the head. As Bennie realizes when he is in El Jefé's presence, El Jefé's desire for the head is as inherently absurd as the force that propels Bennie throughout the majority of the film.

The way that Bennie completes the statement about sixteen people being dead indicates that he has finally realized the objection-able lack of purpose in his quest. "One of them [the sixteen dead] was a damned good friend of mine," he says, obviously alluding to Elita, who for Bennie apparently represents the major innocent among the dead. When Bennie refuses to accede to El Jefé's order to take the money and leave, he signals his repudiation of pointless violence, a repudiation ironically underscored by his taking out his gun and, in self-defense, killing a number of El Jefé's guards. At this point, what else can Bennie do but effect justice by acceding to the daughter's request to kill El Jefé? Finally, a fusillade of bullets joins Bennie in death with Alfredo.

In *Alfredo Garcia*, Peckinpah intentionally links children's curi-osity and delight with horror: for example, the Mexican boy fasci-

Plate 50. The face-off between Bennie and El Jefé. One head (in the sack) and one million dollars (in the attaché case) lie between them.

nated by the head; the children enjoying El Jefé's fireworks, which Peckinpah aurally connects with the simultaneous gunshots in El Jefé's chapel; the little boy who, after the shoot-out, walks among the bodies scattered along the chapel's floor. However, these intentionally crude juxtapositions do not celebrate the grace inherent in death, despite the satisfying end to which Bennie comes. Rather, the film affirms its director's good-natured love affair with violence and reconciles two apparently irreconcilable realms: beauty and horror. These two realms, in the form of natural loveliness and unnatural cruelty, are present in the pair of freeze-frame images that close the film: the daughter by the lake, and Sappensly gazing into the bag that contains the head. Given our visual and aural re-education at *Alfredo Garcia*'s hands, it is not too much to imagine that the placid woman looking out on the calm face of the water and the nervous Sappensly finally looking on the face of terror see exactly the same thing: beauty becoming horror, and horror becoming beauty, with the ultimate realization that the two concepts are, in the end, identical.[6]

CHAPTER ELEVEN

Cold Killers

Although all of Peckinpah's films dramatize the dehumanizing aspects of progress, no film is more concerned with cold, calculating, duplicitous behavior than is *The Killer Elite*. The film's main characters are undercover agents in the employ of shadowy organizations such as the ComTeg Corporation, which in turn serve other shadowy organizations—in this case, the CIA. The actual reasons behind the missions assigned to the characters Mike Locken (James Caan) and George Hansen (Robert Duvall) are never clearly revealed. Compounding this motivational vagueness is the fact that the two men are sent out on the film's initial "job" by their superior, Cap Collis (Arthur Hill), who is simultaneously serving the interests of at least two opposing sides in the conflict. In his insistence on working to benefit only himself, Collis emerges as a twisted reflection of Mike, who until the film's end seems exclusively interested in revenging himself on George, his former friend and fellow agent.

One of the hallmarks of *The Killer Elite* is its economy of plot, action, and characterization; the film is as lean and direct as its main characters. Peckinpah characterizes his central players in an astoundingly small amount of screen time. The titles sequence shows the planting of a dynamite charge, an action that Peckinpah contrasts with two forms of innocence. The first, natural innocence, is suggested by a shot of a robin feeding its young. Tainted, human innocence is manifested through the background sounds of a children's jump-rope rhyme whose lyrics tell the story of "Cinderella . . . [who] went upstairs to kiss her fella, made a mistake and kissed the snake"; these lyrics suggest the kind of corruption of romance we'll encounter in the film. After the titles, a brief dialogue occurs between Mike, George, and Vorodny (Helmut Dantine); Mike and George's verbal horseplay and relaxed physical attitudes (which contrast with Vorodny's harried seriousness) reveal how casually the two seem to take their jobs. However, in a later scene the kidding between Mike and George starts to take on overtones of taunting and sadism (especially in the cruel joke that George plays on Mike about Mike's possibly having been exposed to venereal disease); apparently, the two agents' buddy-buddy affability is only a thin veneer over the inevitable hostilities and jealousies that arise from the competitive nature of their business, which demands that their allegiance be only to the organization for which they work, not to each other.

Plate 51. George Hansen, Mike Locken, and Vorodny in *The Killer Elite*.

In what seems to be a horrible visual pun on a previous bit of dialogue, the emotionless shooting of Vorodny by George occurs right after Vorodny says, "You can't know what it's like to live in a closed society"; George then opens up the back of Vorodny's head with a gunshot. The act's suddenness startles us. In a way, though, we have been prepared for this brutality by the nastiness of George's character. As a consequence, when Mike, emerging from the shower, looks over at George (who is seated on the cover of the closed toilet holding a gun between his legs) and asks his unresponsive partner, "What are you, nuts?" we can see how incorrect the question's literal meaning is. At this point in the film, Hansen is totally in control of what he is doing. If anything, it is the emotionally open (and therefore vulnerable) Mike whose psychological attitude is inappropriate; and it is only at the film's end, when he indulges himself by realizing an emotional fantasy, that Mike begins to jettison the calculated behavior that he has considered necessary to settle his score with George.

Plate 52. The shooting of Mike by George.

For now, though, it is George who has the advantage. He very carefully shoots Mike at two crucial body joints, the elbow and the knee, wounding him so that Mike will be permanently removed from agency field work. (There may be a hint of compassion in George's choosing to cripple rather than kill his partner. However, given George's inherently dispassionate nature, it seems more likely that he doesn't want to kill Mike but wants to leave him worse off than dead, tortured by his own uselessness.)

Mike is hospitalized and eventually returns to total effectiveness, a recovery that strains our suspension of disbelief. Mike's shattered knee had left his leg in a state accurately described by Cap as a "limp noodle," but he is later seen jogging along the hilly streets of San Francisco. Nevertheless, we accept his regeneration, not only for the sake of the plot but, more important, because the film's matter-of-fact tone makes want to believe in what we see.

In *Killer Elite*, Peckinpah for the first time reveals himself as a master of an intentionally clinical approach to human suffering. The film's surgery scene, which gives us the doctors examining and treating Mike's body as though it were a damaged machine, is as detached in style as the manner of the scene's doctors, who calmly ask for a blood pressure reading here, a piece of gauze or tape there. Then, in comparably even vocal tones, a doctor comments on Mike's condition: "The patella is completely shattered and the knee seems completely unstable." It is only at the sequence's end, when Peckinpah allows a shot of a harried doctor wiping his sweaty forehead, that we get a direct communication of how trying an event this must have been for the doctors and nurses. Yet by the time Mike is wheeled out of the operating room, we recognize as well that the surgical team's abstraction is a function of their professionalism, which is necessary if Mike is to survive. The fact that Mike himself must adopt a similar stance only underscores the vital function that the medical sequences play.

Peckinpah takes a productive and successful cue from the operation sequence's depiction of human duress and uses it in *Killer Elite*'s most discomforting scene. When Mike's casts and underlying surgical wrappings and stitches are removed, Peckinpah—partially through Caan's acting but largely by virtue of the scene's exaggerated sound effects—makes us wince every time that a piece of plaster, gauze, or stitching is peeled off or extracted. The inevitable tearing of tissues beneath the surgical wrapping comes through the soundtrack at full force, especially when Mike's arm cast, while being taken off, painfully pulls at some unseen body part.

If Mike didn't already have our sympathy, he doubtless would after these scenes, which distinguish him from the cold-blooded individuals who surround him: the dour Hansen and the wonderfully dissipated and compromised pair of ComTeg directors, Lawrence Weyburn (Gig Young) and Cap Collis. Cap's alienating coolness is aptly summed up in a question put to him by a CIA man: "Did you ever consider, my dear Cap, how much energy you've wasted over your forty-seven years mustering up that 'good fellow' smile and that insincere handshake?" These men and others like them quickly earn our disdain. For contrast, Peckinpah gives us other characters,

266

no less dispassionate in their killing and no less obsessive, who are immediately sympathetic. Miller (Bo Hopkins) and Mac (Burt Young) are attractive because they're on Mike's side, but we also respond to them because of the playfulness of their demeanors, their essentially softer facial features, and the comic vocal inflections that they use to deliver their wry comments and asides. At one point, Mike asks Miller why he chooses to skeet-shoot on a bluff overlooking the San Francisco Bay Bridge. In a soft Southern dialect, Miller replies, "I like it up here," and you really can't help but smile. In another scene, the skewed-looking Mac says to Mike apropos of his own mercenary activities, "I used to think what I did was nice and necessary"; he ends the speech by saying, "What the hell do I know." This humility indicates that Mac is a suitable ally for the somewhat humbled Mike and contrasts effectively with the attitudes of the other characters with whom Mike comes into conflict, characters who are predominantly hypocritical braggarts.

However, *The Killer Elite* is far too complex a film to let us classify its characters as easily as that. Although Mac and Miller always meet with approval (albeit to varying degrees), the same cannot be said for

Plate 53. Jerome Miller, whom Mike calls "the patron poet of the manic depressives," with Mike.

Mike, who has some reprehensible characteristics that make him quite similar to George, Cap, and, ultimately, Weyburn. Most notable in this respect is the fact that Mike is taking advantage of his assignment to protect Chung and his daughter in order to draw out Hansen. As Mac puts it, "Hey, this is a mousetrap, Mike. You're using them as bait." Yet if Mike *is* using the two Asians, he is also simultaneously being manipulated by Hansen, Weyburn, and Collis.

Appropriately, Mac makes all of these observations on the nature of the business in which the agents are engaged; he exhibits the kind of direct emotional expression that the film's other agent characters either deny or repress. After commenting on the Asian pair's powerlessness, Mac moves to an observation about this same quality in Mike. "He [Hansen] really blew you apart, didn't he? Whatever he does dictates the way you go. You're getting to be his prisoner, Mike, up here [points to his head]."

Mac goes on to deliver the film's most analytical speech, which continues the train of thought by extending the notion of powerlessness to all individuals, private citizens or supposedly elitist killers, who are trapped in servitude to corrupt organizations, governmental or otherwise. "I know the rationale: self-defense, God and country, another assignment in the national interest. . . . Damn it, Mike. You're so busy doing their dirty work, you can't tell who the bad guys really are."

Mike counters that he can recognize friends from enemies: "I know who the bad guys are; anybody who tries to hurt me" (a statement revealing the kind of solipsism that makes possible all of the film's excesses). However, Mac effectively meets his friend's objection: "They're *all* trying to hurt you, Mike, all the goddamned power systems, all the wheelers and dealers at the top with their gin and fizzes. They need guys like you to do their bloodletting while they're making speeches about freedom and progress. They're all full of bullshit. There's not one power system that really cares about its civilians." At this point, though, Mike (like Cable Hogue) is still shackled by his obsession with revenge. It is only after the film's final battles that he responds to the suggestions for action implicit in Mac's speech.

The Killer Elite gives us the clichéd Occidental observation that Orientals hold life cheap.

> MIKE: You know, it must be true about you people. I mean, you
> don't care if you live or die, right?

CHUNG: Of course we do. It's in the manner of living and dying that one finds relevance.

The exchange is quite ironic, since it is the film's Occidental characters who apparently believe that all people are easily replaceable and therefore of little worth. It's not only the repeated killings that tell us this but a statement delivered by Hansen when he and Mike are once again face-to-face. "If it hadn't been me [who shot you], it would've been somebody else," George says. At least up to this point, we have suspected that Mike and George are roughly equivalent (as Vorodny told George, "You all look alike, you young mercenaries—no matter what country"). Yet we also suspect that this similarity is merely illusory and that the distinctions between these two characters will not only emerge but will extend to their counterparts in ComTeg's higher echelons. It is therefore gratifying to find that, like George, Cap (for whom George is covertly working) is morally and emotionally stilted hereas Weyburn, like Mike, is a somewhat ruthless individual who is nevertheless sufficiently emotional (and possibly moral, although this aspect is unclear) to render him attractive to us.

When visiting Mike in the hospital, for example, Cap is all phony compassion; Weyburn, though, allows himself a bit of self-revelatory emotional indulgence. "My father was a minister; that's what he wanted me to be," he says. Regardless of the remark's apparent irrelevance, it is still poignant, a quality that neither Mike nor Cap can deal with or acknowledge.

The apparent distinction between Cap and Weyburn is reiterated in a later, remarkable sequence in which Weyburn prevents Cap from contacting George (or vice versa). Weyburn again appears sympathetic because he foils Cap's scheming. (It is never clear, though, whether Weyburn acts intentionally or inadvertently.) The harried Cap keeps wanting to answer his phone but is prevented from doing so by Weyburn, whose dialogue Gig Young delivers with a priceless collection of comic grimaces.

WEYBURN: [IBM stock is] going down; that's bad management. Well, it's not my problem; they're in the hotel business anyway. What about plastics, condoms; anything in there about condoms?[1] This I don't believe: the stock's up! They didn't even have a company. [Pause] A.D.P. is down. [Weyburn looks up, smiles, then lets the smile slowly fade away.]

The wild contrast between Weyburn's mundane talk about Com-Teg's investments and the truly hazardous situation in which George and Mike are soon to be plunged (a situation developing simultaneously with the present scene) creates dramatic tension and nervous comedy. "Work, work," says Weyburn, and all that the harried Cap can do is mumble his unwilling assent.

However, the distinction we may infer between Collis and Weyburn is just as false as the one we might draw between their conceptual doubles, George and Mike. George is to Mike as Cap is to Weyburn: the cold as opposed to the supposedly emotional partner. Yet at the film's end, we see that Mike and Weyburn can be as ruthless as anyone else. In *Killer Elite*'s universe, everyone, apart from the misfits Mac and Miller, is a louse.

At this point, it seems that Weyburn frustrates Cap's plans only by accident. Weyburn is here perceived as a more powerful yet less sinister version of Cap, exhibiting none of Cap's duplicity. However, we eventually realize that Weyburn is even more depraved than Cap: Weyburn wields more power and thus has far more opportunities to put his malign influence into practice. Again, it is the insightful Mac who later delivers the summary judgment on the subject: "Mike, when are you going to listen to me? He used you; Weyburn used you to clean up some office politics. Walk away; come with me and be a civilian. You're not gonna stay with this son of a bitch, this Weyburn, after he set you up too."

When Weyburn replies, "That's all he knows," Mike responds, "Ah, you could be *half* right" (my emphasis). Mike is being far more accurate in this remark than he realizes. Mike is a divided person, something made evident by the conflict in his character between cruelty and humanity and by his choice of his two better halves, Mac and Miller. Cap says of Miller and Mac, "One's retired and the other's crazy." Nevertheless, they do a great deal to assure that despite Mike's brutality, the audience will remain on Mike's side. The two characters' interaction is very amusing in the exchange concerning Mac's weapon.

> MAC (explaining why he is carrying a gun): Josephine [Mac's
>   wife] was robbed a couple of times last month.
> MILLER (looking around at Mac's garage): Nice place like this.
>   May I see it [your gun]?
> (Miller weighs and appraises the gun by rapidly twirling it
> around on his trigger finger.)
> MIKE: What are you, Wyatt Earp?

MILLER (to Mac): I got something better if you want it.
MAC: No, that's fine.
MILLER: Old weapon—slow rate of fire—heavy—hard to aim.
 [Gingerly hands the gun back to Mac.] Nice chrome.
MAC: What's your first name, Miller?
MILLER (turns away in embarrassment and mumbles): Jerome.
MAC: What?
MIKE: Jerome.
MAC: Jerome?
MILLER: Jerome.
MIKE: Come on, let's go.

Although both Mac and Miller (who, along with Mike, form a kind of Three Musketeers with similar-sounding names) have our approbation, there is an important distinction between them, one that, unlike the apparent difference between Weyburn and Cap, is quite valid. This difference is brought out during the only sequence in which Mac and Miller are alone together.

MAC: Jerome, I know a lot about you, you know that? Don't
 hurt anybody just for fun, OK? That's not nice.
MILLER: How would you like me to take that .45 and shove it
 where it belongs, cabbie?
(Mac pulls out his gun and aims it point blank at Miller's face.)
MILLER (slowly puts his hands behind his head, assumes a re-
 laxed posture, and smiles): You like stewardesses?
MAC (smiling): Sometimes.

The comic ending doesn't change the fact that, as Mac realizes, Miller is an emotionless, amoral killer. We suspect that, having worked for ComTeg before, doubtless on many kinds of assignments, Miller takes his jobs without considering the moralities of the various parties involved. By contrast, Mac is also a former ComTeg employee but has voluntarily retired, presumably for moral reasons: thus his repeated statements and questions about morality. Mac is on Mike's side not only because he likes Mike (as does Miller, who repeatedly calls Mike "partner") but also because he believes in his friend. As a result, Mac works to steer Mike away from revenge and compromise toward a moral stance.

Killer Elite also includes some outright comic scenes, such as the one involving the motorcycle policeman who runs down the street with the bomb that was planted under Mac's cab. Yet in keeping with the film's underlying serious tone, the comedy here is ruthlessly undercut: at the beginning of the next scene, we hear a bomb go off and wonder if perhaps the policeman was unable to toss the device into the bay and was killed. Indeed, the entire film continually moves between serious and comic elements, an alternation that compels the audience to experience the dual states of the characters. Thus, the film's serious beginning, which shows the laying of explosives, is followed by the seriocomic interplay between Mike and George in the escape car; the light tone of the party at Mike and George's apartment is followed by the seriousness of George waking Mike to go to the hideout where Vorodny is being held; and so on. Additionally, such alternation keeps us in a state of constant irresolution, a condition that mirrors the difficulty of our realizing any definitive truths about allegiances in the film.

The shift in *Killer Elite*'s emotional thrust, which changes Mike from a predominantly affectless to an emotional character, is occasioned by George's death. After George's murder, Mike is delivered from the revenge scheme. Miller shoots George, an action to which Mike at first objects. Mike punches Miller for doing so, either because he wanted to kill his former partner himself or because he somehow regrets its being done. (The motivation is unclear, perhaps being compounded of both impulses.) After this point, the triumph of Chung (whom Mike is helping) over his own adversary, Negato Toku, seems like a foregone conclusion. (Although Mike wants to shoot Toku, Chung insists on using a sword, an insistence on traditional weaponry that looks forward to the equation of basic weapons with morality that we see in *The Osterman Weekend*.) However, two further acts of justice are yet to occur. First, there is the dispatching of Cap, whom Mike wounds in the same places where he himself was wounded, appropriate in that it seems likely that Cap, acting through George, was directly responsible for Mike's shooting. (Mike further affirms the similarity of situations by saying to Cap, "You just retired," precisely what George had said when he shot Mike.) Next, Chung triumphs over Toku.

In a finale that yokes together the film's two primary emotional strains, ruthlessness (evident in Mike's telling Mac to leave Josephine behind) and sentimentality (Mike's desire to take Mac on his romantic journey), the perfect couple, Mike and Mac, prepare to sail away from compromise and the tangled web of ComTeg's deceptions toward an eastern sea that represents an invitation to a new day (the rising sun) and hints at the East's emphasis on honor (present in *Killer Elite* in the persons of the T'ai Chi instructor and Chung).

Although they literally sail away, Mike and Mac are figuratively heading for that special Peckinpah realm of wish fulfillment, where, as in traditional American myth (e.g., "Rip Van Winkle"), they will supposedly become innocent. Yet when Mac and Mike do finally withdraw, their exit is far more deplorable than it might at first seem. True, they leave Cap behind and turn their backs on Weyburn. At the same time, though, the two men also abandon an important aspect of themselves: the part devoted to their relationships with women. It's clear from Amy's roles as a nurse and a devoted lover to Mike during his recovery, and from Josephine's futile insistence that Mac stay out of undercover agent work, that they represent for both men a combination of physical and moral health, qualities that until the film's penultimate scene Mac urges Mike to emulate as well. Nonetheless, Mike encourages Mac to abandon Josephine in as unfeeling a manner as he had himself exhibited when he walked out on Amy. When Mac asks, "What about Josephine?" Mike answers, "Leave her for Mr. Davis." (When Mike is around, Josephine calls everyone "Mr. Davis," an emblem of the hydra-headed moral taint embodied in the agents of companies like ComTeg.) Mike evidently believes that Josephine in particular, and women in general, belong to the morally compromised world of agents, which is clearly not the case. Although corruption and disease are attributed to women (e.g., the woman at George and Mike's party who supposedly has a sexually transmitted disease), it is the film's men who are pathological. Nevertheless, Mac obliges, jettisoning his feelings and effectively insulting Josephine in a repudiation of sentimentality that invites comparison with the coarse way that Mike had scorned Mac's sentimentality when Mac had visited the hospital bearing flowers and good wishes.

Mike and Mac's last act makes it plain how death-oriented and pointless their escape really is; more important, it points up the weakness of the film's conclusion, which fails to confront the moral problems inherent in the lives of secret agents. Still, as is characteristic of many Peckinpah films, our reaction to *Killer Elite*'s end is compounded of contradictory feelings. If we condemn Mike and Mac for their selfishness (and Peckinpah for resorting to a facile resolution), we also feel that some sense of closure has been reached and that Mike and Mac have earned their place in the sun and are sailing off to a justified reward.

The Graveyard Where the Iron Crosses Grow

Cross of Iron, Peckinpah's self-characterized attempt to "do World War II,"[1] is a very idiosyncratic war film. The film is characteristic of Peckinpah in that it is primarily concerned with opposition, in this case the conflict within the film's central character, the German soldier Steiner (James Coburn), between his commitment to serve his country and his abhorrence not only for the war but for all forms of authority, an attitude that opposes him to the cowardly and supercilious Captain Stransky (Maximilian Schell).

Quite early in the production the conceptual split that characterizes the film is manifested in Stransky, an emotionally atrophied Prussian aristocrat for whom the war's major significance is that it will provide him with the opportunity to garner an Iron Cross. The symbol of achievement is obviously more important to Stransky than is achievement itself, as we see later when he earns the decoration through the false accounts of men who testify to his leading an attack when in fact he had been nowhere in the vicinity of the encounter. Thus, when Colonel Brandt (James Mason), responding to Stransky's statement that he wants the Iron Cross says, "Here, have mine," and later when Steiner, in a similar gesture, tosses his Iron Cross at Stransky, the captain on both occasions refuses it. Stransky is determined to have the medal awarded to him, even if it means he will have to lie in order to "deserve" it.

Cross of Iron is situated at the turning point of the war, during 1943, and takes place during the retreat from Russia. What we witness, then, is a Germany on the brink of defeat. As a result, we readily empathize with the film's German soldiers, who seem to be under constant bombardment and attack and who are fighting from a pitifully weak defensive position. Moreover, the film places its major focus not on the officers, sympathetic or not, but on the war's dog soldiers, who were culled from the German working class. These men did not start the war, do not stand to benefit from it, and certainly don't want to continue fighting. They merely want to go home.

In the characteristic Peckinpah mold, Steiner, the film's major figure of integrity, is self-made, self-knowledge able, and resigned to the occasional nasty vagaries of fate. Although he serves in body, Steiner reserves his spiritual allegiance for those aspects of existence that he considers of greatest importance: friendship and peace. Steiner is the film's moral center. What is essential to him is not which side is winning or losing but the safety of his men. Early on it is clear that the film's concerns transcend mere politics. As with Lewis Milestone's *All Quiet on the Western Front, Cross of Iron* distinguishes itself by invoking a humanism that, in compelling us to acknowledge it, transforms the audience from an undifferentiated mass into individuals who, like the film's German soldiers, are less men of a particular country than simply human beings. By concentrating on war's human (as opposed to military or political) elements, *Cross of Iron* demonstrates that what is most important in life are interpersonal relationships; everything else qualifies as some form of politics and is therefore absurd. In keeping with this focus on humanism, we find that the film's most significant kinds of destructions of men are not the actual killings in battle but the petty assassinations of the spirit that occur between one human being and another. A prime example of such cruelty is the insidious assault against two soldiers, Triebig and Kessler, that Stransky undertakes when he asks them about their sexual preferences.

The soldier's embattled circumstances also help earn our sympathy. As Colonel Brandt says in response to Stransky's pontificating about ideals, "The German soldier no longer has any ideals. He's not fighting for the culture of the West, for one form of government that he wants, not for the stinking party. He's fighting for his life, God bless him." Although the entire unit's pathetic situation unites the soldiers, it does not integrate any of the officers aside from Steiner, regardless of whether they are elitists, like Stransky, or liberals, like Brandt and his aide, Kiesel (David Warner). Steiner makes this distinction quite plain when he says to Kiesel, "Do you think that just because you and Colonel Brandt are more enlightened than other officers that I hate you any less? I hate all officers, all the Stranskys, all the Triebigs, all the Iron Cross scavengers and the whole German army." However, since Steiner obviously does not include the men in his platoon, his use of "German army" applies only to men who are so regimented in thought and behavior as to have jettisoned their identities in exchange for power. Perhaps the supreme example of this type of person is the hospital sequence's visiting general, whose actions epitomize the insulting high-handedness of the officer class.

As with most war films, most of the action in *Cross of Iron* takes place in a world without women. This universe is first directly alluded to in Stransky's taunting discussion with Triebig and Kessler about their homosexuality, which Stransky views as an absolute aberration. (Toward the end of his talk with these men, Stransky pats Triebig's cheek in as vile a way as Hitler, in the film's title montage, patted the cheek of a young boy.) Given all of the exclusively male war scenes that show us destruction, one might expect a contrast between scenes involving only men and those that include women, who usually humanize a scene. Yet the potential for violence arising out of heterosexuality is also accentuated in *Cross of Iron*, not only during the extraordinary interlude at the military hospital— where the tender but eventually repudiated sexual relationship between Steiner and his nurse, Eva (Senta Berger), coincides with Steiner's horribly insightful visions concerning the war—but also later, when Steiner's batallion encounters a group of Russian soldiers who are all women.

The meeting between the men and women unleashes a series of forces previously only suggested in the film, forces that prove to be the undoing of the platoon's weaker members. Thus, the platoon's resident innocent, a young recruit, is stabbed by a Russian woman who cries after she performs the deed. The young soldier's stabbing results from his first trusting and then attempting to become sexually involved with this woman, whom he is supposed to be guarding. In a parallel, virtually simultaneous scene in which the roles of victim and victimizer are reversed, the platoon's most despicable member, an SS man planted there by Stransky, compels a Russian woman to fellate him; she severs his penis with her teeth.

Regardless of the women's sex, what is essential to remember is that Steiner's men are here dealing with the enemy, something that the young recruit and, to a certain extent, the audience tend to forget. Our condemnation of the Russian women's factionalism is especially interesting given the emphasis on humanism already present in the film. Indeed, our reaction to the women's actions is twofold. We deplore the murder of the young soldier (the SS man clearly deserves his treatment) at the same time that we must admit that these women are merely acting as they should: killing men with whom they are at war. In the encounter between the Russian women and Steiner's men, then, we watch the action from both personal and political vantage points, the latter a perspective that until this juncture *Cross of Iron* has worked hard to dispel.

Plate 54. Steiner with Eva in *Cross of Iron*.

Even more striking in their power, though, are sequences that take place in a locale where we would expect relative calm: the military hospital to which Steiner is sent to recuperate from a concussion. In these scenes, Peckinpah most effectively communicates insights into Steiner's psychology. Throughout the film, we have known Steiner as an impressive fighter and a man of fierce independence. Yet now we see that for all of his supposed individuality, he does not feel that he really exists outside of the war. When Eva asks, "Do you love the war so much; is that what's wrong with you? Why are you afraid of what you will be without it?" Steiner cannot answer. Apparently, it is conflict, and the male camaraderie that the war engenders, that Steiner misses and needs. "I thought you were going back home," Eva says. Steiner replies, "I have no home," to which Eva answers, "My home, our home." Steiner's response is clearly a falsification, though. Steiner leaves the hospital grounds in a troop truck with one of his men, Schnurrbart (Fred Stillkraut), and establishes an immediate affinity. This easy acceptance demonstrates that the war is where Steiner lives; horror is his home. (In this sense, Steiner, like all of Peckinpah's paired characters, needs his double—Stransky—to affirm the validity of his existence.)

During his hospital stay, Steiner undergoes a remarkable series of hallucinations induced by his concussion. After Peckinpah shows us Steiner receiving his wound (during which Steiner intuits images of Kiesel and Brandt, as though he is wondering what they are doing while he is being injured), and soon after Steiner's admission to the hospital, we are granted a number of visions that shuttle back and forth between images of life and death, hope and despair, qualities inherent in war. First, in a shot that signals the opening of the hospital image series, we see Eva (who is rendered objectively until the series' end) entering Steiner's room. This is followed by a shot of a dead man's eyes being closed by a fellow soldier, a sign of the end of image perception. We then see Steiner, while in his bunker, hoisting a celebratory cup, an indication of happiness; this is followed by an extremely grainy image of a soldier, who has obviously been shot, moving downwards. The raising of the cup is opposed by the fall of the injured soldier, suggesting a powerful opposition between human bonding and armed combat. Then Eva once more enters the room (the repetition of action creates a sense of failed progression); this is followed by a shot of Steiner running alongside a wooded area. In his unconscious mind, Steiner is obviously attempting to break free of the hospital's confines. Once again we see the soldier falling as a reminder of war's deadliness.

Eva is seen shutting the door of Steiner's room, an affirmation of closure. Then, in a curiously bifurcated image, we see Steiner catching the Russian boy's harmonica, even though the boy himself is not seen; the boy's absence from the sequence here creates an annoying sense of incompleteness and strongly suggests the boy's uncompleted life. (The scene in which Steiner sustains his injuries is immediately preceded by one in which he bids the Russian boy good-bye and the boy tosses him his harmonica; soon after, the boy is shot to death. Thus, the moment of open emotion between Steiner and the boy ironically results in closure and death.) Steiner's catching the harmonica is followed by a complementary shot that connotes finiteness: a mortally wounded soldier is seen. A shot of the light that Eva is using to determine just how abstracted and withdrawn Steiner has become as a result of his concussion signals both openness (the desire to divine the extent of Steiner's injuries) and closure (Steiner's shell-shocked state). The following series of images alternates shots of the examination light, which is associated with the hospital, and Steiner running. Interestingly, part of this latter shot seems virtually clairvoyant (like Doc McCoy's vision of swimming in *The Getaway*) in that Steiner sees himself dressed in the very clothes he wears later in the hospital, right down to the sling that supports his injured left arm.

Plate 55. The ritualistic passing of the Russian boy's harmonica to Steiner.

The sense of limitation is then opposed again, this time by a shot of Steiner, once more free, standing by a body of water that might connote redemption and renewal were it not that Steiner, whom we know prefers the war, seems to take pleasure in immersing himself in it. (Indeed, Steiner's running away from the hospital and escaping into the water suggests that his immersion represents a wish-fulfillment return to the paradoxical, death-oriented feeling of oneness that war, and the exclusively male camaraderie that goes along with it, occasion in him.) After removing his arm from his sling and spreading out his arms like Christ, Steiner allows himself to fall into the water (another echo of *The Getaway*).

There are more shots of the light being directed into Steiner's eyes (Eva says, "Look at me," a statement that has both a negative connotation, since Steiner is ill, and a positive one, since she is trying to help him); these images are followed by a shot of Steiner in the water and a shot of Eva saying, "Follow the light with your eyes." This is succeeded by the dreamlike resurrection of the Russian boy, who, once more in his army uniform (which has a negative connotation; appropriately, Steiner had removed the boy's uniform before freeing him), is seen running to the water's edge. (The image's connotation is not wholly positive, though; the shot of the boy running is broken in two, creating a strong sense of fragmentation.) Subsequent shots of Eva looking into Steiner's eyes and the Russian boy looking at Steiner suggest a strong affinity between the two characters, who come to represent emotional openness and affection, qualities that Steiner unfortunately repudiates in the film. Steiner sees the Russian boy and looks at him in amazement, as though thnking, "Can he be alive?" Eva then says, "Look at me again," a statement suggesting that Steiner should remain open to sensory impressions.

Another close-up of the examining light is followed by a shot of the boy throwing his harmonica to Steiner. The latter action is abstracted, though, because at this point we never see Steiner catching the instrument. Steiner looks at the boy, and we then see Eva, who is now part of Steiner's image series, at the water's edge. When she sees Steiner in the water, she throws up her hands in exasperation and calls out "Sergeant!" However, the similarity between her hand gestures and those of the boy tossing the harmonica reaffirm that both characters represent positive emotions for Steiner. After another light/eye image alternation, we see Eva at the water's edge taking off her shoes and getting into the water to retrieve Steiner; unlike the boy's harmonica gesture, Eva's removal of her shoes is a completed action (we subsequently see her in the water with Steiner, beginning to lead him out), a fact that suggests that she might have a more beneficial effect on Steiner than the boy did. (Unfortunately, this does not turn out to be true; as I've noted, Eva is unsuccessful in leading Steiner away from the war.) Finally, Eva turns on the overhead light in Steiner's room, and the image series ends.

Later, when Steiner is brought out onto the hospital veranda, another series of startling images begins. We first see Steiner's point-of-view shot of a one-legged man in a wheelchair, who is seen from the waist down; this sight is momentarily obscured by another one-legged man's hobbling by on crutches. The sense of death and displacement that emanates from these objectively rendered, alienating images of the war's effect on men gives rise to Steiner's desire to see someone whom he knows, someone who connotes life affirmation and bonding. Steiner therefore imagines that one of the patients on the veranda, who is dancing with a nurse, is Kruger, a member of his platoon. Steiner gets out of his wheelchair and approaches the couple; but when Steiner turns the man around to look at him, we see that it is not Kruger but a horribly scarred young soldier, another incarnation of the war's brutalities. Apparently, Steiner's wish-fulfillment hallucinations are not sustained long enough to deliver him from horror. (Yet, in an amazing brief shot, glimpsed over Steiner's shoulder, we see that it is indeed Kruger dancing with the nurse. It is almost as though, after looking at so many casualties, the camera itself has become disoriented.)

More oppositions follow. When walking up to the man he imagined was Kruger, whose face during the approach was never seen, Steiner anticipated a brief image of Kruger turning toward him (the image is culled from the past, thus sustaining the oppositions in this and the previous sequence's visions). Now, as Steiner realizes that the dancing man is not Kruger, he intuits another memory image of Kruger, who appropriately, given Steiner's disappointment in not finding him, is turning away. Steiner then looks back to where he had been sitting. In a striking representation of alienation, Steiner sees himself in the wheelchair and Eva at his side. Where previously the veranda was crowded, it is now deserted, a further abstraction from context that complements the abstracted state of Steiner's mind. Steiner looks again and, once more trying to establish contact with one of his men, sees Schnurrbart sitting in his wheelchair. Yet when Steiner looks once more, there is nobody there at all.

After an objective shot of the approach of a high-ranking German officer, we see Steiner walking back to Eva, who is standing by the wheelchair; the veranda is once again occupied. But the hallucinations are not over. Peckinpah inserts a jump cut (a perfect corollary for the disruption of perceptual continuity in Steiner's consciousness) that shows us Steiner sitting down in his chair, alone on a completely unoccupied veranda.

Plate 56. The officer's visit to
the military hospital.

The gloominess continues into the next sequence, in which the
German officer visits the hospital's inmates. After pausing in front
of Steiner, asking him how he is, and receiving no answer, the
general stops to shake the hands of a seated soldier. The general
waits for the man to extend his right hand, which turns out to be
a stump. Taken aback, he tries to grab the man's left hand, which
is also a stump; at this point very few people in the audience could
fail to react with revulsion and pity. But Peckinpah is not done with
this bit of business. The soldier, quite aware of the moment's awful
terror and awkwardness, does not intend to let this officer off easily.
He turns the general's phony conviviality against him, revealing its
insincerity by extending his foot in a gesture like a goose step. The
officer is invited to grasp the foot, an action that would necessitate
his publicly admitting the artificiality of his good will; instead, he
turns away. The final statement is communicated in the soldier's
mocking expression.

The officer then instructs that the smorgasbord meat be carried
away, leaving behind only the vegetables. (Is there an intentionally
nasty pun here, asserted from the general's point of view, about the
status of many of the patients?) Steiner gets up, again in a shocked
state. With intercut images from a comparable celebration (Lieutenant Meyer's birthday party) occurring in his consciousness, Steiner

walks past the food table, smashing dishes but having the presence of mind to take with him two bottles of wine.

Steiner and Eva are next seen on the hospital grounds.

STEINER: Did I have a bad spell?
EVA: Yes. You were very violent.
STEINER: Violent?
EVA: Violence should stop. It must stop.
STEINER: You say violence must stop. [Steiner laughs.]

At this point, Peckinpah cuts back to the veranda, where the men are ripping up and tossing the vegetables in protest. Obviously, violence will not stop, a realization confirmed by the image with which Peckinpah ends this sequence: the scarred soldier looking straight into the camera, confronting us with his injury.

The magical reappearance toward the film's end of the platoon's dead Russian youth, who served as their mascot, reinvokes the spirit of humor that Steiner seemed to lose after his hospital stay. Indeed, humor, which mocks fools like Stransky, not only stands as the inherent morality behind the film but also indicates the wry, devilish sensibility of the director. Although in *Cross of Iron* peace may be imminent, war is ever-present, always looming on the periphery of events—thus the film's closing epigraph from Brecht about the "bitch of war" already in heat with another deadly brood.

Don't rejoice in his defeat, you men.
For though the world stood up and stopped the bastard
The bitch that bore him is in heat again.[2]

Armed conflict must always qualify as the ultimate expression of human stupidity, in response to which the only sane reaction is laughter, derision, and the kind of black humor that offer the sole way to live with such utter madness. To quote Brecht from another context, "He who laughs has not yet heard the bad news."[3] In *Cross of Iron*, though, the man who laughs (as Steiner does at the film's end) is not foolish but admirable; having heard the bad news, such a man is nonetheless able to stay human, something achieved by virtue of laughter.

Cross of Iron's penultimate situation, the slaughter of the majority of Steiner's platoon, takes place as a result of Stransky's orders. (Stransky is repaying Steiner for not testifying that Stransky bravely led a counterattack, when in fact Stransky had been hiding in his bunker.) The act is the perfect expression of Stransky's cowardice

Plate 57. Steiner and Kern coming back to base.

and perfidy and is carried out by Triebig, who has weakly succumbed to Stransky's blackmailing him over his homosexuality. (Triebig justifies his actions by saying, "It's all Stransky's orders," a defense that recalls the Nuremberg trials.) That Steiner should then want to machine-gun Stransky is perfectly understandable; when Steiner reaches Stransky's bunk and aims the weapon at him, we want him to fire. Yet for Steiner to kill Stransky at this point would spare Stransky the far more satisfying humiliation that *Cross of Iron* has planned for him.

Stransky asks, "Where is the rest of your platoon?" Steiner, now determined not to kill Stransky but to make him prove himself in the field (thus indicating that despite its humanism, *Cross* believes that valor in battle is somehow meritorious), replies, "You are, Captain Stransky; you are the rest of my platoon." Stransky accepts the challenge. "I will show you how a Prussian officer can fight," he says, to which Steiner replies, "Then I will show you where the Iron Crosses grow."

However, *Cross of Iron* is far more complex than this scene would indicate. Outside, Stransky trips, falls down, and reveals that he doesn't know how to reload his machine gun. Then, as the

Plate 58. Stransky with Steiner at the film's end.

children's song from the film's opening title sequence briefly reappears, so too does the dead Russian boy. (Unlike the vision of him in the hospital sequence, though, the boy is now rendered objectively.) Through a juxtaposition of images (the art of film conquering death), the boy seems to shoot off Stransky's hat; the boy is then seen shaking his head, as though in disgusted resignation, while Steiner begins to laugh.

The final image series (which runs between the credits) clarifies the film's attitude toward youth and war. During the film's opening titles, we saw movies of adults fighting and suffering and images of healthy youths either meeting Hitler or gazing reverently upon him. At the film's conclusion, we see the awful results of war on youths, manifested through views of suffering children and, in the identical first and last images, a hanging involving two adolescents, one of whom is already dead. These final images, unlike the fluid shots of the film's opening (which were only periodically frozen) are all stills, dead images. (Indeed, the last glimpses we have of Brandt, Steiner,

Stransky, and the Russian boy are in freeze-frames, as though they too have been relegated to the war's gallery of the dead.) This somber mood has derived from the film's depiction of war and its terrors.

After the last of the freeze-frames, the children's song from the opening title sequence is reprised, only to end when the distinctly unfunny shot of the hanging is first shown. Steiner's laughter briefly reappears behind the next-to-last still, that of a group of children behind barbed wire (perhaps at a concentration camp?), but quickly trails off when the hanging photo is once more shown. At this point, the sound of a slide projector (a mechanism that delivers frozen images, an appropriate quality at this late juncture), which has been heard behind all of these stills and whose sound throughout the sequence has been made to resemble that of a gun magazine being loaded, is subtly altered. Now, the projector–gun magazine sound seems more like that of a heavy steel door being shut, suggesting that we are trapped with the depressing ambiance that is here being created.

At the appearance of the Brecht quote, a little bit of the children's song is again heard, although the only part of it that appears here is one line: "Hanchen klein ging allein" (The little cockerel went forth alone). Given the film's depiction of war, we may take this line to refer to a child's introduction to the world's horrors. The line is repeated three times; at the fourth repetition it is broken off after the words "hanchen klein." Like the fantasy image of Steiner's tossing the harmonica to the Russian youth, the movement of the cockerel is incomplete; the amputation of the line's last half connotes a terrible finality, like a life ended too soon. Since the linkage suggests the Russian youth, as does the allusion to the "little cockerel," the effect is doubly depressing. The song's termination leaves us with a sense of irresolution, an appropriate response to a film that cautions us against war while simultaneously acknowledging its inevitability.

The repetition of the hanging in the credits' opening and closing images creates a sense of blind, unavoidable repetition and fatality (affirmed as well in the Brecht quote; war is constantly being reborn). Yet the repetition and awfulness is also present in the connotations of the sound of the slide projector. The machine's cold, mechanical sound itself connotes finality, thereby implying that knowledge of war (communicated through sights and sounds) must nonetheless eventually give way to ignorance, thus making war inevitable. In this sense, *Cross of Iron*'s conclusion communicates its director's belief that art cannot enlighten or warn us; instead, it can do little except entertain. This view throws us back to an only apparently routine remark of Brandt's to Kiesel, whom Brandt considers more intelligent and sensitive than most men and thus representative of Germany's future. "In the new Germany, if such a thing is allowed to exist, there will be a need for builders, for thinkers, for poets," says Brandt. Between "builders" and "for poets," Peckinpah inserts a slow-motion cutaway of a man being shot. The slow-motion effect lends a graphic poetry to the image, suggesting that it is something like the director's carefully built, thoughtful poetry that is being referred to in Brandt's remark, a poetry that nonetheless shows how destructive of poetry war can be.

Regardless of its presence in the film, poetry at *Cross of Iron*'s despairing end has its efficacy debunked. The film's final, repeated images suggest that art ultimately means nothing, that it has no instructive effect, and that despite Brandt's optimism, not only will there will be no new Germany, but there will also be no new world either, just the same old tired, morally depleted universe whose characteristics will derive not from thinkers, poets, and builders but from people who are unreflective, materialistic destroyers. Through its art, *Cross of Iron* shows us how useless in the face of war even the greatest art really is.

CHAPTER THIRTEEN

Dead Truck Stop

Peckinpah's comment that in *Convoy* he was trying to produce *The Wild Bunch* with trucks involves an unfortunate comparison, since *Convoy* is far from satisfactory.[1] Muh of the truckers' rhetoric seems unconvincing and forced; the characters are poorly realized; and the profusion of car and truck stunts seems intended to gloss over glaring deficiencies in the acting. *Convoy* does have some qualities to recommend it, which I will discuss, but overall it is Peckinpah's weakest film.

Convoy almost loses its audience at the outset. The film's first thirty minutes will probably fail to engage the attention of any viewer who is not already enthralled with citizens' band radio and the terminology that CBers use. Indeed, the beginning sequences seem rather pointless and not at all amusing, and although they do serve to introduce the major characters—among them Kris Kristofferson's Rubber Duck (also referred to as "R. D."), Ernest Borgnine's Dirty Lyle, and Burt Young's Pigpen—one can't say that they are pleasant. You can almost hear the groaning of the film's plot machinery as it wearily begins to get up to speed. Even when Peckinpah tries to lighten up the proceedings a bit by staging a no-holds-barred fight in a truck stop, the sequence is barely diverting; in fact, it feels like an etiolated replay of the barroom brawl in *Junior Bonner*, but without that film's good humor. The fight in *Convoy* has too many slow-motion shots of men falling down, so that even this usually successful technique fails to keep us from being bored.

The problem with *Convoy*'s opening reels is that we really don't care about the opposition between the truckers and Dirty Lyle because it seems so clichéd. The redneck lawman is hostile to the truckers for no apparent reason other than that such harassment nets him some money every time he pulls one of them over on a trumped-up charge. After his initial tentative feints at a black trucker, Spider Mike, Lyle delivers a remark whose nastiness is underscored by the sneering smile that Borgnine assumes. Mike's wife is nine months pregnant; Mike protests that Lyle can't arrest him for vagrancy (Mike has no money left after paying Lyle's bribe) because he needs to get home. When Lyle asks, "Anybody know who the father is?" we know that undiluted evil is about to start making the conflict between Lyle and the truckers interesting.

Plate 59. Dirty Lyle racially insulting Spider Mike in *Convoy*; Rubber Duck intervenes while Pig Pen looks on.

After the full extent of the racism in Lyle's remark is experienced, the truckers determine to pass out of the shit-kicking state of Arizona and the state (New Mexico) where compromise nearly destroys them and into what they perceive to be the land of freedom: Mexico. In Arizona and New Mexico more trucks join the convoy in order to protest against all sorts of oppressive conditions in the United States. The truckers rally behind the reluctant Rubber Duck, who, when asked if he's the leader, responds in true democratic fashion, "No, I'm just out in front." Stretching along the road for miles and ignoring the attempts of local and state police to stop it, the convoy becomes a visible symbol of the free spirit once again let loose in America.

It's certainly true that in an America that is boxed in with speed traps, populated by racist sheriffs, and circumscribed by all sorts of repressive behavior, the highway suggests itself as a symbol of freedom. Indeed, films such as *Thunderbolt and Lightfoot*, *Scarecrow*, and *The Rain People* have used it for precisely that purpose. *Convoy* appropriates this idea as well. Peckinpah emphasizes the fact that truckers command a monstrously powerful machine that frees them from the restraints of their bodies. The trucks in *Convoy* run on gas while the truckers are fueled primarily by the energy emanating from rapid movement and two kinds of primal gratification: sex and edibles. As a wizened old trucker says, "All we need is three things: fast trucks, fast women, and fast food."

Having created possibilities for conflict by revealing Lyle's racism and the truckers' revolutionary liberalism, *Convoy* takes oppression one step further by introducing the political element into the struggle. Of course, politics has already been present in the film in the form of the opposition between Lyle and the truckers. The conflict between the truckers and the police is complicated by New Mexico politicians who try to make it seem that they are allied with the well-publicized convoy by soliciting the truckers' opinions. At one point, the governor's aide rides alongside the convoy in the back of a van (within which is perched a Panavision camera and a soundman, who is played by Peckinpah) and shouts questions to the truckers about their concerns.

Some of the truckers respond with comments on well-known subjects: Watergate, the fifty-five mile-per-hour speed limit, and so on. As might be expected, the more knowledgeable truckers refuse to answer questions about their beliefs. A trucker called the Old Iguana responds to the question about where he was born with an intentional absurdity: "Originally?" Rubber Duck states that the convoy is not interested in issues: "The purpose of the convoy is to keep moving." A gravel-voiced trucker says, "I'm just along to kick ass and for the ride." When the governor's aide objects, "Certainly you must have some kind of personal grievance against the laws of this state," the trucker responds, "No, I just like kicking ass." Then the trucker goes on to taunt and humiliate his inquisitor: "You sure are a pretty, red-headed little boy; wanna ride in my truck? We oughta have supper."

The political ramifications of the truckers' movement are allied with a hope for the future symbolized by children (e.g., Spider Mike's baby and the high school marching band that welcomes the convoy in one town). The truckers also take on a counterculture status. Lyle obviously represents stultified law and order: at one point he says, "I am the law; don't you understand, I represent the law," to which Rubber Duck replies, "Well, piss on you and piss on your law." Lyle also personifies a narrow-minded point of view. The Merle Haggard song "Okie from Muskogee," which is playing in the jail where Spider Mike is being held, blares forth a lyric that clearly applies to the police in the film: "We don't smoke marijuana in Muskogee; / We don't take our trips on LSD." Clearly, the truckers' passions and pleasures threaten the instincts and behaviors of the country's traditionalists, who are represented in the film by short-haired policemen. (The subversive in the midst of the police is the Texas jail janitor, who, with his beard and long hair, looks like a trucker; it is he who sends the CB signal asking the truckers to tell R. D. that Spider Mike is in jail.)

The major problem with *Convoy* is that no real focus is given to the truckers' status as outlaws. We know, for example, that *Pat Garrett*'s Billy prefers freedom to compromise and that he wants to return to the "good old days" in which a man could fulfill his destiny. Despite *Convoy*'s attempt to portray its truckers as rebels, they seem to be nothing other than working-class men with no significant political ethic—at least, none that we can divine through *Convoy*'s awkward script. In this respect, *Convoy* invites comparison with Richard Serafian's *Vanishing Point*, which features a relentless cross-country driver who is intent on speed.[2] However, Serafian's film gives us background information on its protagonist, showing how his hostile attitude toward the law had been formed. *Convoy* never provides its characters with personality shadings; the film just assumes that we will accept the truckers as they are. Imagine *The Wild Bunch*'s Thornton and Pike updated but without the information on their past and minus any convincing action and characterizing touches, and what you have is *Convoy*.

Peckinpah tries to rescue the film by raising the stakes in *Convoy*'s last third. Getting off the highway and thus temporarily halting their convoy, which in protest to Spider Mike's imprisonment has been running roadblocks, the truckers take the New Mexico governor's suggestion to spend the night at what he guarantees is a safe area. At this point, Rubber Duck's essentially volatile freedom seems most in danger of being co-opted. (His freedom is volatile both

Plates 60–61. *Convoy*'s stunts are the only truly interesting sequences in the film.

morally and literally: he is transporting highly explosive chemicals, a symbol for the destructive potential of his opposition to the smug liberalism of contemporary America.) Fortunately, Rubber Duck is delivered from the possibility of compromise by the intercession of Pig Pen and by the necessity of leaving to save Spider Mike. After using his truck to demolish the jail in which Mike is being held captive, Rubber Duck goes on to crash through a roadblock manned by the National Guard, who are equipped with tanks and machine guns. In a scene reminiscent of the bridge explosion in *The Wild Bunch*, Rubber Duck apparently demolishes his truck and himself; the bridge collapses and the truck plunges into the river.

The politicians and media try to turn the Duck's death to their own account. They stage a memorial service on the highway, replete with empty coffin and attended, somewhat unwillingly, by the truckers, making it virtually inevitable that the Duck be reborn from the ashes of destruction if only to save the film from total despair. The ceremony is barely half over when Rubber Duck reappears like a resurrected water god. (Explaining his return, he says, "You ever see a duck that couldn't swim?" The comment hardly accounts for his escaping alive from the shattered, bullet-ridden truck; not even the usual Peckinpah romanticism can make this plot device seem plausible.) With all of the rejoicing truckers in tow, Rubber Duck and a news reporter, Melissa (Ali MacGraw), head out for the characteristic Peckinpah region of possibilities, Mexico, leaving in their wake the politicians, the gaping media idiots, and Dirty Lyle, who is seen laughing at the whole situation.

During and after the filming of *Convoy*, Peckinpah reportedly felt that the film's various aspects didn't cohere.[3] He had good cause to feel anxious. *Convoy* is a film of tired appropriations of dialogue and action from Peckinpah's other productions. We sense throughout that the director is merely going through the motions. In spite of this depressing situation, Peckinpah is occasionally able to convince us that America's last frontiers, the open roads, are still there beckoning to us if only we are strongly enough motivated—and therein is our own liberating, propelling force—to walk away from compromise and pretense and take advantage of the highway's invitation.

His Last Bow

That Peckinpah's final film, *The Osterman Weekend*, is radically different from all of the director's previous work is evident from the film's opening moments. We are watching an extremely grainy shot of a man and a woman in bed. The man eventually gets up and leaves the room, after which the woman—in an action whose alienating, graphic terror exceeds anything else in Peckinpah's other films—is assaulted by two strangers, one of whom thrusts a hypodermic needle into her left cheek, injecting a drug that quickly kills her.

The camera then pulls back to reveal that we have been watching a film within the film. As we subsequently learn, what has been depicted is the murder of the wife of CIA agent Lawrence Fassett (John Hurt), an act supposedly carried out by members of the KGB. Of the two men watching the film, the most important is Maxwell Danforth (Burt Lancaster), the head of the CIA, who subsequently calls in Fassett to help to expose and bring back to the American side three Americans working as Russian agents: Bernie Osterman (Craig T. Nelson), Richard Tremayne (Dennis Hopper), and Joseph Cardone (Chris Sarandon), who are friends of television talk show host John Tanner (Rutger Hauer).

Before Fassett enters the room, Danforth remarks of the footage, "A nasty piece of film." Precisely how nasty this piece of film really is will be revealed as *The Osterman Weekend* continues. However, Danforth's remark has a further applicability. The comment may also be taken to refer to *The Osterman Weekend* itself, which mercilessly depicts high-level governmental intrigue, a subject that has already been dealt with in *The Killer Elite*. Since the emphasis here is on both the deceptive actions of the CIA and similar organizations (as it was in the earlier film) and the electronic means by which deception is achieved, *Osterman* has more than just moral resonance. The film also functions as a comment on media manipulation of all kinds (even the kinds that *Osterman* itself employs), regardless of whether such manipulation is used for political, social, or economic purposes.

Plate 62. CIA head Maxwell Danforth in *The Osterman Weekend*.

The Western-style lone avenger, the cowboy figure, is recognizable in two of the film's characters: the maverick interviewer John Tanner, who is supposedly interested only in facts (although, as we subsequently realize, at the film's beginning Tanner is more of a poseur than anything else); and Fassett, who initially is viewed as an alienated renegade with a strong sense of morals. Even after we see how maniacal Fassett is, we can still appreciate the justness of his outrage over his wife's death, although we never know for certain that she was murdered at Danforth's instructions, as Fassett claims. (According to Danforth's aide, the murder was only "sanctioned" by the CIA chief.)

Fassett's presumed morality is obvious from Danforth's comment to his aide about Fassett. The aide protests against Fassett's status; Danforth replies, "He's something you're not and never will be: he's a field operative." At this point, Danforth's aide tellingly states, "I don't think nostalgia is the right instinct at this time, sir." The word *nostalgia* directly pinpoints the bygone past peopled by lone vigilantes for justice, a past for which the conservative Danforth obviously yearns. Ironically, Danforth's nostalgia, more than any other factor, seems responsible for his accepting Fassett's proposal to use Tanner against his friends and thus makes possible Fassett's exposure of Danforth's dangerous qualities toward the film's end.

As the plot begins to unfold, we can quickly tell that something unusual is transpiring. For one thing, the blatant self-reflexivity of *Osterman*'s repeated references to media (e.g., the film within a film at the beginning) is a new concern for Peckinpah. The only previous examples of this concern were exaggerated graphic effects (as in *The Wild Bunch*'s titles and precredits sequences, whose style drew attention to their cinematic status). In this respect it is somewhat unfortunate that *The Osterman Weekend* is verbally and visually so diverting that we frequently forget that we are watching a fictive representation of reality. As a result, we often fail to pause and consider precisely what the significance of the film's events really is.

Although *Osterman* begins in the bright lights of a television studio and then moves on to a daylight scene, the film's most important action takes place either in the dark or at night. These are significant settings, for it is only in the utmost darkness that Tanner and Osterman can hope to respond successfully to Fassett and his men, who intend to kill them. Early on in the film we are implicitly told that the most decisive confrontations will take place in the dark when Bernie Osterman faces off with his karate instructor, who turns out the gym's lights, stating that such darkness imposes "conditions of maximum equality." Osterman emerges from this encounter victorious, just as Osterman, Tanner, and Tanner's wife, Ali (Meg Foster), will finally triumph over Fassett and his men. (However, darkness is ultimately overturned, since the final victory over Fassett and Danforth is achieved through electronic means, with the electronics still on instead of switched off into blackness as Tanner suggests we do toward the film's end.) However, the most dramatic face-off, which occurs between the men working for Fassett and the Tanners and Osterman, consists of a series of encounters that have all the traditional aspects of the hunt.

Osterman's extended hunting references surface toward the

film's beginning. Ali talks about an expeditionary trek that she and her son had taken. Describing the animals they were after, she says, "They were down in this little ravine; then they caught wind of us and we needed your [Tanner's] help," a statement made immediately after Tanner's son had mentioned that he and his mother "couldn't get a clear shot." The hunting terms used in the quote come to fruition when Osterman and Tanner are under siege from Fassett's men; Ali, armed with a crossbow, kills one man and seriously disables another. Ironically, at this later point Tanner and Osterman are the quarry and are indeed situated down in a little depression: a flat, low-lying area at the base of a surrounding wood where the Tanner house is located. And although Ali quite capably deals with two of Fassett's men, she and her son are nevertheless eventually captured, leaving it up to Tanner and Osterman to rescue them toward the film's end.

In metaphoric form, hunting permeates the film, first resurfacing in Ali's remark after she learns that Maxwell Danforth is on the phone to Tanner, ostensibly to agree to appear on Tanner's television show. "Your trophy buck just broke cover," she says. (The pun on *cover*, a term used in both venery and espionage, is doubtless intentional, as is the ambiguity in Tanner's son's earlier question to his father, "Mom says you're a big trophy hunter; what does she mean?") Ali's statement equates Danforth with prey, but it also has a far greater significance. We have already seen Tanner successfully "run to ground" and "bag" a man (General Keever) on his show, but this military man was decidedly small game, awkward and unintelligent, in apparent contrast to the sleek, cool efficiency of Danforth, who is watching the show.

Tanner fancies himself a media hunter of great prowess, yet he is initially out of his element with Fassett and Danforth (that is, until the CIA chief appears on Tanner's media turf at the end). Tanner also needs the assistance of other people and traditional weaponry (he and Ali with crossbows, Bernie Osterman with a poker and his bare hands) to deal with Fassett's men, who are hunting him. Moreover, Tanner's electronic hunting implements (video cameras, recorders, and so on) are at first of no help in defending himself from Fassett. In fact, why should he expect them to be? If only from the contrast between the title of Tanner's show, "Face to Face" (Fassett mocks the show when, appearing on televisions at Tanner's house, he says, "Time for a face to face"), and the fact that the show never brings people together physically but only on television monitors, we should know that the program and, by extension, Tanner's role in it are a sham. The implication is clear: electronic confrontations are an inappropriate substitute for direct encounters; the technologies of the mass media offer a massive potential for deception through manipulation not only of sound and images but of personality as well.

Undoubtedly, Tanner's slick, relaxed presence on television is the major factor accounting for the general's being bested by Tanner. (Tanner's slickness vividly contrasts with physical assurance, a quality exhibited in the film only by Osterman and Danforth; note the awkward way that Tremayne, Cardone, and, especially, Tanner—when he walks away from his meeting with Danforth—physically handle themselves.) Danforth says of the general while watching the program, "Why in hell did they send such a fool?" Fassett replies, "He must have been the fool on duty." What is most significant on television, then, is not truth but the audience's perception of the personalities involved. From the very beginning, *Osterman Weekend* asserts that the main emphasis of television (and, by extension, of all the mass media) is not on truth but on illusion. This fact is made evident in the most telling part of the discussion between Danforth and Tanner.

> DANFORTH: Suppose I were to tell you that our enemies are capable of impairing rational thought, of dismantling our willingness to defend ourselves, of disassociating whole societies from their value systems.
> TANNER: You mean they've got TV as well?

Primarily, *The Osterman Weekend* is a treatise on media. Danforth employs film and tape to view events involving his agency. Fassett is a joyfully masterful user of various electronic devices ranging from VCRs, video cameras, and monitors to sonic devices and the rifles with laser scopes with which his agents are equipped. As for Tanner, his career depends on vast banks of broadcast equipment, which he uses during his show with the intention of revealing the truth behind his guests' various assertions. Like Harry Caul in *The Conversation* and Jack Terri in *Blow Out*, Tanner feels that electronics can help him penetrate to the truth.

For a variety of reasons, such an attitude is dangerously deceptive. Initially, it reveals that Tanner believes that there is such a thing as truth, something separable from the range of opinions and ideas that make up the spectrum of perceptible reality. Compounding Tanner's belief in the ability of electronics to reveal the truth is his trust that the truths delivered electronically are objectively presented. Thus, when Fassett shows Tanner a tape of the latter's friends talking about betraying their country, Tanner at first objects that the tape might have been falsified. Having broached this possibility, Tanner uses the very same electronics in Fassett's studio to monitor the tape for tampering. (Tanner also fails to note that the dialogue on the tapes could easily have been taken out of context.) Thus, despite his protests Tanner succumbs to the seeming reality of electronics and begins mistaking the image of the truth for the truth itself. A media manipulator on his show, Tanner unwittingly becomes nothing more than a manipulated audience in the electronic scenario of deception being projected, maintained, and played out by Fassett.

Repeatedly in *Osterman Weekend*, characters and the viewer are warned that perceptions are largely illusory. The film's central characters all have professions involving deceptions of one sort or another. As head of the CIA, Danforth is doubtless involved in covert and duplicitous operations. Tanner uses television's inherent deceptions in order to aggrandize himself. Joseph Cardone is a stockbroker specializing in investment tax shelters, which offer ways of "cloaking" one's money to avoid taxes. As a plastic surgeon, Richard Tremayne changes the appearance of others; Bernie Osterman writes television scripts, thus feeding the media beast that traffics in diversion. However, all of these manipulators eventually become the victims of manipulation and deception. Danforth is tricked, first by Fassett with his contrived story about treason and then by Osterman and Tanner at the film's end. Like Danforth, Tanner is initially duped by Fassett's manufactured evidence and then is further deceived during what we subsequently realize is the staged abduction of his wife and son. At this point, though, the audience may still believe in Fassett's veracity. Yet by the time of the trick with the fake severed dog's head that is found in the refrigerator, it's clear that not only all of Tanner's guests but Tanner too (in spite of his pact with Fassett) is being deceived by someone outside their group. Possibly suspecting something, Tanner tries to delve behind Fassett to divine the source of his motivations, asking, "Who's pulling your strings?" The only answer he gets is Fassett's mocking movements, as though the agent were a marionette.

Although it is true that it was Danforth's (supposed) murder of Fassett's wife that compelled Fassett to seek revenge, until the film's conclusion Fassett, a master puppeteer, is the only character who

Plate 63. The puppeteer who pulls everyone's strings: Fassett on the prowl after his manipulative scheme starts to break down.

seems beyond manipulation. At the end, though, Fassett doubts what he sees: Tanner in his trailer, ready to kill him. This is an ironic, albeit apt, reversal, since at this late point Fassett, the great manipulator of electronic images, cannot seem to place credence in a physical manifestation: Tanner, with gun poised to shoot.

The most significant unraveling of personalities, though, occurs during the three-way television hookup during which Tanner brings Danforth into electronic confrontation with Fassett, causing Danforth to reveal himself as a dangerous reactionary. Here, it is Tanner (in the studio) and Osterman (in the director's booth) who manipulate Danforth and Fassett, not vice versa. Danforth and Fassett's appearances are live; however, by this point, Osterman and Tanner have passed beyond television's unrealities and turned the medium's inherent unreliability to their own account. Bernie Osterman disappears from the control room while the show is still going on. (Indeed, toward the film's end the control room and studio are completely deserted.) Tanner's part of the show is on tape, a fact that allows Tanner to appear in Fassett's trailer, dressed like a commando, while the agent is still watching the show. The appearance seems almost magical from our point of view: although we witness a portion of the tape's initial run-through before the program begins, we nevertheless assign immediacy to Tanner's appearance on the show, thus casting ourselves in media-duped roles–à la Danforth and Fassett. Fassett's belief in the present-tense reality of Tanner's portion of the program indicates that he has fallen prey to illusion. The fault becomes Fassett's undoing; not only does he not expect Tanner to be there, but he also doesn't believe that Tanner will have the nerve to shoot him. Apparently, Fassett hasn't realized that the intervening action between Tanner's recruitment and the present moment has toughened up Tanner and that this former media junkie is now fully capable of acting, a capability that Fassett has virtually compelled Tanner to acquire. (Despite its pacifist veneer, the film affirms the value of military-style preparedness.)

The various examples of evidence to which Fassett subjects Tanner's friends—the initial film shown to Tanner, the parking ticket given to Osterman (which is really a Swiss bank draft), the Omega marks that appear on Tremayne's mail and on a television broadcast that Cardone is watching—are all instances of information that lead to faulty conclusions on the part of the perceivers. By the time that *Osterman Weekend* has shifted gears slightly, parting one curtain of lies by revealing in its last third that the three friends are not, after all, traitors but merely pawns in the insidious game that Fassett is playing with Danforth, we seem at last to be approaching something resembling the truth. We are encouraged to accept this conclusion although we are no closer to the truth than we ever were. It is only when Tanner, his wife, his son, and Osterman pass beyond electronics, by being reduced to using conventional weapons against the heavily technological devices with which Fassett's men are supplied, that the film's air of obfuscation begins to clear.

Yet *Osterman Weekend* would be far less of a film, and appreciably less true to its main premise concerning the unreliability of all technologically communicated information, were its story simply one of an agent such as Fassett gone mad and seeking revenge. (Fassett's name implies the glimpse of only a small part, or facet, of reality.) The three-way confrontation among Tanner, Danforth, and Fassett; Danforth's raging response; the commando-garbed Tanner's shooting of Fassett; and then, after Fassett's death, the reappearance in the studio of the clean-cut, conventionally dressed Tanner philosophizing on television's ultimate unreality and the inability of its illusion-addicted audience to switch off the set—all of these scenes represent stunning pullbacks from the film's present-tense action that impose context after context on an already convoluted plot. Following Tanner's offer of advice, we get a long shot of the studio control room and "Face to Face" set, which are totally empty, as though the television audience remains fixated on the television set (as we are on the cinema screen) long after the actors have walked off; this emptiness implies that the content (or lack thereof) of film or television is unimportant in the engaging of our attention and that it is the very medium itself that mesmerizes us. Indeed, Fassett made this point most convincingly a bit earlier in the film. Fassett first reveals that his entire campaign against Tanner and his friends was his way of avenging himself on Danforth (although what Fassett hopes to gain from all of this maneuvering is unclear). He then informs Tanner that the supposed KGB agent with whom Tanner saw Osterman talking was really a film producer.

> FASSETT: Now don't you feel better knowing that all your old friends are just tax evaders after all? Or are you just a little disappointed?
> TANNER: You were setting us up. Why?
> FASSETT: We're in prime killing time. All it took was to have my wife murdered while my employers watched on closed-circuit TV. It's just another episode in this whole snuff soap opera we're all in.

Osterman tells Tanner to "switch off" the television, but Fassett replies, "You know better than that, Bernie. It's your business, both of you. Addicting people so they can't switch off." And when Osterman advises Tanner to "smash it" (the television through which Fassett is speaking to them), the crazed Fassett shows them the Cardones and Tremaynes trying to escape in a motor home, daring them to "switch this off."

The point of the film's numerous media images is clear: *nothing* is plain; the media deceptions feed off of one another and reproduce themselves spontaneously. The only way out of the contemporary world's illusion factory is through complete avoidance of the mass media, an impossibility given their pervasiveness. Yet though *The Osterman Weekend* is itself part of the mass media, a well-oiled, technologically realized fiction casually gliding between tenderness and terror, verisimilitude and exaggeration, it nonetheless manages to warn us against technology. Obviously, then, technology itself is not inherently evil; its moral status is a function of the humans behind the machines.

Ironically, the film's message is first delivered by a madman,

Plate 64. John Tanner and Bernie Osterman use one of Fassett's television hookups in an attempt to warn their friends of danger.

thus linking Fassett with *Network*'s crazed newsman, Howard Beale, who says, "Turn off your television sets, turn them off . . . and leave them off." Simplistic though this message might seem, it is worth considering. When the moment of truth in *Osterman Weekend* has passed, the only proper response is to abandon the studio, to leave television behind, to switch off, thereby plunging the hypnotically luminescent television eye into the darkness from which the truth may emerge. However, through this film Peckinpah implies that we may be unable to do so. After Tanner advises us to "switch off"— even though he believes that viewers "can't do it"—Peckinpah cuts to a shot of Tanner's whimpering dog, chained to a wall with its mouth taped shut. The comparison between the dog and what the film regards as the typical viewer of television does not seem complimentary to the latter.⁴

Osterman Weekend's most startling aspect is its abstract, inhuman tone. Its precision, which is its dominant characteristic, is almost totally untempered by humor and wit. There is virtually no comic relief in *Osterman* except for some scattered ironic asides offered by Bernie Osterman. (In this respect, the film invites comparison with *Pat Garrett*, which is even more humorless.) *Osterman* seems almost soulless, bearing only the slightest signs of its director's

303

Plate 65. The Cardones and Tremaynes in flight.

sensibility behind its sounds and images (e.g., the trademark slow-motion sequences). This quality may be the result of Peckinpah's conforming his technique to the material (an inversion of his usual response) by playing it cool, but such an explanation can be offered only as a hypothesis. Nevertheless, the absence of a pronounced directorial presence in the film grimly ties in with the fact that this was to be Peckinpah's last work; this point is underscored by the message about the need to desist from creating deceptive images. At the same time, the film's plot thread concerning an organization named Omega inadvertently acts as a morbid foreshadowing of the end of Peckinpah's career. Yet since Peckinpah achieves in *The Osterman Weekend* notable heights of self-assurance, it may very well be fitting that his final creation should be this subtle whisper of a film, which for us does indeed leave the film studio empty and says good-bye to the work of one of American cinema's most diverse and amazing practitioners.

A F T E R W O R D

Sam Peckinpah left behind a body of work as unique as it is inconsistent. His films range from the brilliant achievement of *The Wild Bunch* to the appalling disorder of *Convoy*, a film that would be an embarrassment for any director, but especially so for Peckinpah, whose trademark was the intelligence of dialogue and characterization that he usually brought to his work. Yet even his last film, *The Osterman Weekend*, made after Peckinpah had not directed a film for five years, shows the director demonstrating new interests, in this case the manner in which media can be deceptive and manipulative.

Peckinpah was a master of dialogue and atmosphere. When these qualities are wedded to action, whether exaggerated (as in *The Wild Bunch*) or restrained (as in *Ride the High Country*), the results can have extraordinary effect. This is not to say that Peckinpah didn't evidence an occasional weakness. His propensity for roughneck male horseplay and jokes about virility were sometimes in poor taste, nowhere more than in *The Killer Elite*. Yet even in that film the director managed to turn bad taste to good account, since the jokes tend to reflect back on their perpetrators, Locken and Hansen, whom we're not meant to like very much anyway.

Much has been made of the (supposed) biographical details of Peckinpah's life: the womanizing, the booze, the reports of drug use.[1] For me, these "facts" have nothing to do with our assessment of the man's films, with which they are often linked. What should matter to us is only what Peckinpah did when he was working. Concerning ourselves with the films themselves, we discover a generous, loving, vulnerable director whose innovative editing and uncompromising devotion to the need for a personal code of behavior are unique in American filmmaking.

It's difficult to account for the present diminishment of Peckinpah's reputation in the United States. Currently, he is usually referred to, if at all, for his direction of *The Wild Bunch*, and then primarily with regard only to that film's violence. *The Wild Bunch*'s brutally honest depiction of violence was undoubtedly striking for its time. Yet even today, after more than two decades of increasingly graphic filmic bloodletting, *The Wild Bunch*'s excessive actions still strike us with emotional force because they're intricately bound up with, and play off of, our feelings about the film's characters, a lesson in effective scriptwriting lost on most of the filmmakers who have appropriated violence as a motif.

Complementing the achievement of *The Wild Bunch*'s action sequences is Peckinpah's ability to work out those intricate pieces of characterization that make his films so endearing, bits of business like the point in *Ride the High Country* when Steve Judd, in order to read the bankers' contract, must hold it ever further away than he is already holding it, thereby revealing that Steve is too poor to buy a new pair of glasses; likewise, both Coffer in *The Wild Bunch* and Mac in *The Killer Elite* fumble with objects, thereby revealing their nervousness. (Peckinpah built up a coterie of character actors— among them R. G. Armstrong, L. Q. Jones, Warren Oates, and Dub Taylor—who perfected this kind of playing.)

Peckinpah is undoubtedly the last of the great American directors in the tradition of Stroheim and Ford, larger-than-life figures who left an indelible stamp on their films and who were ready to do battle with studios and producers who dared to compromise the integrity of their productions. It is in films such as *The Wild Bunch* and *The Ballad of Cable Hogue* that Peckinpah is most alive, looming large as a creator whose personal and artistic vision of the world can encompass the most humane gestures and the most inhuman villainies. Through his films, Peckinpah becomes himself, becomes a creature characterized by braggadocio and doubt, expansive humanity and deplorable pettiness. Known by reputation as a cynic, Peckinpah revealed through his films that he was actually a closet romantic. Peckinpah was reluctant to show his vulnerable side, perhaps for fear of being called weak (although he unabashedly reveals his romanticism at the conclusion of *The Wild Bunch*, when he brings the Bunch back from death to the serenading tune of "La Golondrina"); instead, he cloaks his romanticism, permitting it to speak only through his characters' aspirations. Peckinpah's indulgent love of Mexico, and his touching acceptance of the Mexican people's emotional forthrightness, shows how much he yearned for an honest expression of affection among all people.

It was Peckinpah who gave us a privileged look at the West's great vistas in stunning panoramic shots in films such as *The Wild Bunch* and *Pat Garrett and Billy the Kid*; who dared to sing the swan song of the cowboy in that paean to the West, *Junior Bonner* (only Clint Eastwood's *Bronco Billy* has been as unabashedly nostalgic about the cowboy's virtues); who condemned the money men and sell-out artists in films such as *The Getaway* and *The Killer Elite*; and who exploded the notion of violence as manly in *Straw Dogs*. If today we have become overaccustomed to the kind of slow-motion deaths that were perfected in *The Wild Bunch*, that's primarily a fault of the filmmakers after Peckinpah who handled the technique so awkwardly and repeated it so blindly. Coming as it did after Arthur Penn's *Bonnie and Clyde*, *The Wild Bunch* nonetheless outshone the drama of Penn's film by protracting the balletic aspect of violent death without glorifying it, as Penn's film tended to do. Peckinpah successfully trod the fine line between realism and romanticism, showing us violence without approving of it.

Unlike John Ford and Howard Hawks, his immediate predecessors in the Western genre, Peckinpah had to fight for recognition. Unfortunately, he lost the battle because he came to be known for the wrong things, violence and bloodletting, when he would have preferred to be remembered for the manner in which he presented melancholy stories about lost love, as he did in *Cable Hogue* (the director's personal favorite) and the exaggeratedly romantic *Bring Me the Head of Alfredo Garcia*. If other filmgoers find, as I do, moments of unparalleled greatness in Peckinpah's work, the least that we can do is to accord him that rare combination of respect and affection that he has long deserved but far too seldom received.

NOTES

FILMOGRAPHY

BIBLIOGRAPHY

INDEX

NOTES

Introduction

1. Turner, "Significance of the Frontier," 2–3.
2. Frye, *Secular Scripture*, 6–7.
3. Ibid., 170.
4. See, for example, Frye, *Myth and Metaphor*, 252.
5. Ibid., 50.
6. See Smith, *Virgin Land*, 95, 96, 99, 100–102, 109, 111, 116–19.
7. Turner, "Significance of the Frontier," 3.
8. Ibid., 15.
9. Ibid., 19–20.
10. Ibid., 20.
11. Ibid.
12. Ibid.
13. Ibid.
14. Smith, *Virgin Land*, 4
15. Frye, *Myth and Metaphor*, 5.
16. Evans, *Dialogue with C. G. Jung*, 78. See also Jung, *Man and His Symbols*, 23–25.
17. Smith, *Virgin Land*, 92.
18. Ibid., 95.
19. Ibid., 109.
20. Ibid., 119–20.
21. Ibid., 123.
22. Ibid., 71.
23. Freud, *Civilization and Its Discontents*, 42.
24. Ibid., 44.
25. Kitses, *Horizons West*, 168.
26. Simmons, *Peckinpah*, 232.
27. French, *Westerns*, 17.
28. See, for example, Wood, "Introduction to the American Horror Film."
29. Cawelti, *Six-Gun Mystique*, 39.

30. Kitses, *Horizons West,* 11.

31. Ibid., 25.

32. Seydor, *Peckinpah,* 32.

33. That Peckinpah was intimately involved in the scripting of his films, even those on which he did not receive screenwriting credit, is attested to by Seydor (*Peckinpah,* 106, 145n, 190–91), Simmons (*Peckinpah,* 37, 44, 180), and Fine (*Bloody Sam,* 61, 70).

1. Couples

1. Seydor, *Peckinpah,* 16–17.

2. The comic juxtaposition of temperance and religion occurs again at the beginnings of *The Wild Bunch* and in *The Ballad of Cable Hogue.*

3. The phrase strongly parallels the resolution of another moral innocent. Mark Twain's Huckleberry Finn, after lying about Jim's color in order to protect him, also rejects conventional values and resigns himself to the fact that he will go to Hell. Moreover, the cave in which Kit Tilden shoots the Apache seems derivative of Twain's *Tom Sawyer,* in which Tom and the malicious Injun Joe clash in a cave.

4. Soon after entering the room, Billy fires at his mirror image, treating the reflection as an adversary, which suggests that all of Billy's gun duel rivals are extensions of himself. The thematic touch will reappear in *Pat Garrett and Billy the Kid.*

5. The sequence in which the doctor reserves most of his anesthetic whiskey for himself instead of his patient is a precursor of the scene in John Ford's *The Man Who Shot Liberty Valance* in which, after Liberty Valance (Lee Marvin) is shot, the doctor (Ken Murray) calls for whiskey and then drinks it himself before pronouncing Valance dead. In another Ford film, *The Searchers,* we see Indians restaging a raid, just as they do in *The Deadly Companions.*

6. The scene in which Billy forces himself on Kit, after which the two struggle on the ground until they bump up against Yellowleg, (who is again only initially revealed by our seeing his feet) precisely duplicates the scene in *Ride the High Country* in which Heck and Elsa's fight is ended by Steve Judd's intercession. Indeed, in the way that *The Deadly Companions* involves sending a group of characters into a wilderness where they confront a member of essential passions within themselves, the film's basic plot can be seen repeated in Peckinpah's next work.

7. After Kit and Yellowleg have arrived at Siringo, Yellowleg says in response to Kit's statement about affection between them, "Love? You don't even know me. I'm just a face under a hat." Here we can for the last time see Yellowleg invoking Kit's supposed lack of knowledge about him as a rationalization for his fear of being known.

8. The scriptwriter apparently didn't realize what a slight against Kit's husband this remark represents.

9. A character's desire for aggression against someone who has taken advantage of him in a defenseless moment resurfaces in *The Killer Elite*, in which Mike Locken is attacked by his friend George Hansen after Mike emerges from the shower. See chapter 11.

10. The use of buckshot to compensate for poor aim reemerges in *Ride the High Country*, in which Gil Westrum uses buckshot in his shooting booth.

11. Seydor, *Peckinpah*, 17.

12. Seydor, *Peckinpah*, 20–21; McKinney, *Sam Peckinpah*, 45–46; Butler, *Crucified Heroes*, 37; Simmons, *Peckinpah*, 38.

13. McKinney reasons that the film would have been richer had Yellowleg shot both Turkey and Billy, stating that then the "resolution between Kit and Yellowleg [would have been] more ambiguous" (*Sam Peckinpah*, 45). However, given Kit's statement, if Yellowleg had shot both men, such a resolution would have been impossible.

14. McKinney, *Sam Peckinpah*, 45; Seydor, *Peckinpah*, 16–18.

15. Although it's not awkward, the film's use of black leader slugs between scenes is quite unusual. The practice is used in television to mark where commercials are to appear; thus, this technique may be a curious carryover from Peckinpah's television work.

16. Peckinpah and Brian Keith managed to rewrite most of Yellowleg's dialogue but could not alter Kit's—which isn't surprising considering that Maureen O'Hara is the sister of producer Charles FitzSimons, with whom Peckinpah fought throughout the production.

2. Riding High on Morality

1. It is ironic that in his films, Peckinpah decries technological progress at the same time that, through film's magical technology, the glorious past (which the director claims is killed off by the progress that technology represents) is resurrected. Peckinpah apparently does not see the contradiction in his attitude. Consider, for example, this extremely interesting comment that Peckinpah once made: "I detest machines. The problem started when they discovered the wheel. You're not going to tell me the camera is a machine; it's the most marvelous piece of divinity ever created" (quoted in Seydor, *Peckinpah*, 250). Despite the rhetorical flourish, the statement hardly sidesteps the fact that although it may seem divine, the camera is nonetheless a piece of technology.

2. Seydor renders the name of the town as Coarsegold (see, e.g., *Peckinpah*, 29), as does McKinney (*Sam Peckinpah*, 53). Kitses (*Horizons West*, 156) and Butler (*Crucified Heroes*, 39) represent the name as two words. The film, as in the sign outside of Kate's saloon, uses the latter version, which is therefore the one I have chosen.

As Seydor notes, the actual town of Coarse Gold, California, was familiar to Peckinpah since it was situated "just below his grandmother's ranch." According to Seydor, Peckinpah visited the town "when he was five years old and it was still being mined" (*Peckinpah*, 27).

3. This assertion also links up with Knudsen's statement to Elsa (after he discovers her with Heck) that he has to keep "the dirt" (unsuitable young men) away from her.

4. There are other examples of wordplay in the film. Steve's last name, Judd, echoes the words *just* and *judge*; the first syllable of his partner's last name, Westrum, clearly evokes the region in which the film takes place, and the second syllable ties in with the liquor that Gil drinks to put himself to sleep each night. One could playfully continue in such a vein, deriving "piglike men" from the name Hammond (ham-men), with obvious reference to their behavior. One might also distill from Heck's last name, "Longtree," a sense of emotional yearning (longing) for what is natural (e.g., a tree; cf. the shots of the forest at the film's opening).

Steve, Gil, and Heck's first names are also significant. Steve's name means "crown," a word that can be read as an allusion to Steve's desire for the heavenly crown of life as a reward for virtue. Gil's name means "illustrious through hostages," which could apply to Gil's distinguishing himself when Steve, Heck, and Elsa are, effectively, being held hostage at the Knudsen farm by the Hammonds' gunfire. Heck's name (a shortened form of "Hector") means "holding fast," a state that seems applicable to Heck's resolve to remain faithful to Steve once he has given him his word to act virtuously.

5. Biblical references, which occur frequently in the film, surface in the name "Elsa" (derived from Elizabeth), which means "God has sworn" (an allusion to the vengeful attitude that Mr. Knudsen has taken toward Elsa's mother) and Knudsen's first name, "Joshua," which not only calls to mind the Old Testament book of Joshua, whose latter part includes an exhortation to keep the law (an attitude that would please a strict disciplinarian like Knudsen) but also suggests judgment and salvation in its Hebrew meaning, "Yahweh saves." ("Heck" itself is a euphemism for "hell," a meaning that reinforces the film's religious motif.)

6. Knudsen further alters the passage. In Isaiah, it is not "the young and old lion" who are "carry[ing] their riches upon the shoulders of young asses"; instead, it is "a rebellious people, lying children, children that will not hear the law of the Lord" who do so (Isa. 30:9).

7. Indeed, one of Knudsen's later quotes seems to be based on a verse in Steve's favorite book, Proverbs. When Knudsen tells Elsa, "Receive my instructions, not silver; knowledge rather than choice gold. For wisdom is better than rubies," he echoes the sentiment and phraseology of Proverbs 2:15: "There is gold and a multitude of riches: but the lips of knowledge are a special jewel." The complementarity between Steve and Knudsen is greater than might at first appear.

8. Psalms 22:14 actually reads, "The mouth of strange women is a deep pit."

9. Not surprisingly, Isaiah asserts many similar equivalences of terms denoting material wealth and corruption with terms connoting moral poverty and moral lapses. See, for example, Isaiah 1:22, 25.

10. Of course, in other respects the two films' paired characters are extraordinarily different; Garrett lacks Gil's sense of humor, while the Kid hardly qualifies as Steve's moral equivalent.

11. Seydor proposes (*Peckinpah,* 37) that there is a difference between "making a deal" and "keeping your word" and that this distinction makes Gil and Heck's deal invalid. However, Seydor never deals with the fact that the type of person with whom one makes an agreement may affect that agreement's validity.

12. Steve's piety is reinforced by the film's theme music, which bears a striking resemblance to the Shaker hymn "Simple Gifts."

13. Although *Ride the High Country* doubtless elicits in us a sense of nostalgia for a morality that seems to be progressively receding, it is just as certain that Peckinpah's subsequent films contradict this reaction. Witness the reappearance of morality with equal fervor in the central protagonists of Peckinpah's contemporary films: Junior (*Junior Bonner*), Doc McCoy (*The Getaway*), Mike Locken (*The Killer Elite*), Steiner (*Cross of Iron*), Rubber Duck (*Convoy*), and John Tanner (*The Osterman Weekend*), all of whom are (sooner or later) just as resolutely upright in their own ways as are their counterparts in the period films. (*Alfredo Garcia*'s Benny is a moralist, but a unique one; the morality of *Straw Dogs'* David is so perverse as to be totally objectionable).

3. Dandy Tyrant

1. Kitses (*Horizons West,* 139–40) details the cuts that Columbia made in *Major Dundee,* although he never cites his source for this information. Seydor (*Peckinpah,* 52–53) repeats this information and points out an error in Kitses's citations (namely, that the discovery of Riago's mutilated corpse does appear in the film's released version, contrary to Kitses's assertion). Seydor goes on to quote part of John Cutts's interview with Peckinpah, in which the director draws attention to some specifics of the film's cut footage. (See Seydor, *Peckinpah,* 62–63; Cutts, "Shoot! Sam Peckinpah Talks to John Cutts.")

According to Simmons, Peckinpah was asked (Simmons never says by whom) to restore *Major Dundee* to its original length. However, Peckinpah refused to do so, saying that he didn't have the time that the undertaking would require: "If they can't live with it now, they shouldn't have fucked with it then," he remarked (Simmons, *Peckinpah,* 72).

2. The awkward sexual imagery and action in the film doesn't involve

only Ryan, though. Although it assumes a humorous form, there is also the use of phallic cannon by the naive Lieutenant Graham and, in an awkward representation of maturation that invites comparison with Ryan's post-intercourse shaving, Graham's choking on the cannonlike, phallic cigar that Dundee offers him in their first meeting, and Dundee's later reward of a cigar to Graham after the lieutenant successfully contradicts Dundee about his right to give orders in Dundee's absence.

> DUNDEE: When I left I gave you a specific order. You failed to carry it out.
>
> GRAHAM: No, sir. You gave me a command. After that, I gave the orders.
>
> DUNDEE: You surely did. Have a cigar.

Presumably, Graham will not choke on his cigar this time.

3. Many aspects of the scenes involving Teresa's village look forward to the scenes in *The Wild Bunch* that depict Angel's village, in particular the skinny dogs grazing outside of town (an image that recurs at the end of *Cable Hogue* in the form of the emaciated coyote), the atmosphere of frolicsome abandon allied with a feasting that takes place after famine, and the manner in which the benefactors, as they are serenaded out of town, pass by a character who represents humanistic values (Teresa in *Dundee*, Don José in *The Wild Bunch*).

4. The water symbolism in the film intensifies the significance of the hymn "Shall We Gather at the River," which draws attention to water's connotations of life and death in that it is often sung at funerals to comfort the living (as it is in *Dundee* during the burial of the troop members killed in the Apache ambush). The song achieves additional significance in *Dundee* since this same song is sung in the *The Searchers* at the funeral of people also killed by Indians; and, as in *Dundee*, the singing occurs just before the film's central, racist character begins his mission of vengeance against a single Indian character conceived of as manifestly evil.

5. Seydor, *Peckinpah*, 69.

6. The shot after Hadley is killed is quite interesting. With the musical themes playing in the background, Peckinpah has the camera very slowly pan up Hadley's body, cutting the shot at the point when the camera discovers the Confederate insignia on Hadley's coat. Notable as well are the flash cuts of Hadley's brother Arthur (L. Q. Jones), Lieutenant Graham, Ryan, and Ryan's girlfriend (Begonia Palacios) that Peckinpah gives us as split-second reactions to the extremely precipitous shooting.

7. A further reading of the line "You're getting leave" is also possible. "Getting leave" may be taken not only as a reference to the major's removal from command but also as an indication that having been relieved of command, Dundee—outside of the trappings, prestige, and power of authority—will now be allowed to be himself, which in view of the Durango

episode means to be a shiftless, purposeless, drunken wanderer. Apparently, the only things standing between Dundee and utter degradation are his position and title, which nonetheless don't totally prevent him even when he in uniform from reckless and potentially self-destructive behavior (e.g., his actions at Gettysburg and his pursuit of Charriba, the latter against the dictates of self-preservation and common sense).

8. Fittingly, as Tyreen taunts the major to get up by kicking the prostrate Dundee and challenging him, the "Dundee" and "Battle Hymn" themes, which invoke a call to battle, chime in on the soundtrack.

9. Kitses, *Horizons West*, 145.

10. Seydor, *Peckinpah*, 57.

11. Teresa's statement is intriguing in that it presages a line delivered by *Cross of Iron*'s Eva, who, like Teresa, is played by Senta Berger. In *Cross*, Eva tells James Coburn's Steiner that he, too, cannot live without war.

12. Cf. the similar mythologizing of *The Searchers*' Ethan Edwards and Martin Pawley by the Apache, who respectively refer to them as "Big Shoulders" and "He Who Follows."

13. Kitses, *Horizons West*, 139–40. However, Kitses never reveals the source of his information about the film's original form.

4. Like It Used to Be

1. Although the screenplay refers to the town as San Rafael, and there is a sign in the town with the same name, it is nonetheless referred to as Starbuck in the film.

2. Interestingly, before Huerta's seizure of the presidency, he and Villa had been friends, a situation that bears comparison with the relationship between Pike and Thornton. See Clendenen, *United States and Pancho Villa*, 23–24, 28–30.

3. Although it doesn't immediately follow an act of violence, there is still an effectively anxious moment when Pike tells Mapache that he needs Angel for the train heist, at which point Mapache strongly objects until he is dissuaded by Zamorra.

4. Indeed, Angel involves the Bunch in two redemptions: once when they rescue him from Mapache after Teresa's shooting, and once at the film's end, when, after his death, the Bunch figuratively redeems him through violent retribution.

5. In the screenplay, the Gorches' desire—minus the seductive aspect—actually comes true, since the woman with whom the Gorches play cat's cradle is identified as Angel's sister and the woman who calls her away to help with the food is Angel's mother. The script also indicates that Don José is Angel's grandfather, an aspect that makes Don José's later remark about the relative unimportance of who killed Angel's father that much more significant, given the fact that he is referring to the death of his own son.

6. As might be expected, the temporary unity deriving from consumption is also present among Thornton's gang, but in a reduced form that is consistent with the group's status as a poor reflection of the Bunch. In one scene, Peckinpah cuts from the Bunch drinking to a shot of Thornton's men indulging in a comparable, albeit less intense, communal activity: eating. These and other parallel scenes constitute additional linkages in the film.

7. One aspect of the fiesta sequence that is never explained is how, despite the village's obvious poverty, the villagers are able to provide an abundance of food during the fiesta.

8. This animal imagery recalls the skinny dogs outside of the sacked village in *Major Dundee* and looks forward to the image of the mangy coyote roaming around the water station at the end of *Cable Hogue*.

9. There are many comic moments in the film. My favorite is when Herrera, realizing that Pike has rigged the munitions wagon with dynamite, says, "Very smart, that's very smart for you damn gringos," a statement whose delivery (the exaggerated Mexican accent) and form (the repeated word, here an adjective) hark back to the famous "badges" speech in *The Treasure of the Sierra Madre*, delivered by Goldhat (Alfonso Bedoya).

> GOLDHAT: We are the federales—you know, the mounted police.
> DOBBS: If you're the police, where are your badges?
> GOLDHAT: Badges? We ain't got no badges. We don't need no
> badges. I don't have to show you any stinking badges.

10. Via a dissolve, the image of the ants and scorpions also carries over onto this scene, further affirming the linkage.

11. Laughter that functions as a tension reliever also occurs when the Bunch is waylaid by the mountain Indians, who threaten them with machetes. The anxiety level here is quite high, since the Indians are very suddenly discovered by the Bunch to be in their midst. Once the situation is understood (for once, it is not Angel but the Bunch's Caucasian members who are made to feel like outsiders), the Bunch relaxes, an effect hastened by the comedy deriving from the characteristic mutual accusatory statements between the Gorches.

> LYLE: It's getting so a feller can't sleep with both eyes shut for
> fear of getting his throat cut. Where in the hell were you?
> TECTOR: Now you listen to me, Lyle. You get up off your ass
> and help once in a while, I wouldn't have got caught
> near so easy.

12. Actually, not all of the shots of the Bunch come from this scene. Although Angel was seen during this sequence laughing along with the others, Peckinpah instead reprises the shot of Angel laughing after the

train heist and bridge explosion, when the Bunch was amused over denying liquor to Lyle. The choice of image was obviously dictated by Peckinpah's not having appropriate footage of Angel laughing during the original sequence. Nevertheless, the choice of shot has the effect of suggesting that even after the film's assertion of the Bunch's unity, Angel is still somewhat removed from the group's other members.

13. Salinger, *Catcher in the Rye*, 277.

14. As viewings of *The Wild Bunch* and other Peckinpah films should indicate, the meaning that Peckinpah intends by his use of still frames is not consistent from film to film, although the still images always have the same meaning within individual films. I am intrigued, though, by Seydor's suggestion that "the alternation of desaturated and color images at the beginning of *The Wild Bunch* is . . . Peckinpah's way of suggesting that the story is emerging from old newspaper accounts, and by the time the film has ended the last escapade of [the Bunch] has become the subject of the peasants' folksong, festival, and mythmaking" (*Peckinpah*, 273). This reading not only brings an added dimension to *The Wild Bunch*'s title sequence but also implicitly posits an alternate reading of the desaturated stills at the beginning of the long version of *Pat Garrett*, especially since the character Alias (who is first seen working as a printer's devil) might well have been involved in chronicling Billy and Pat's exploits in newspaper articles.

15. Although it doesn't involve the Bunch as a whole, there is actually a fourth example of this type of image: in Agua Verde, Angel, while being dragged on the ground behind Mapache's car, is tormented by young children who point at him sticks whose ends have been fitted with lit sparklers. Note that in all of these instances (with the exception of the Bunch's entrance into Agua Verde), fire comes down on the Bunch from above, a duplication of a major aspect of the ants/scorpions/children image. However, it is clear that the image's meaning is not immutable. Thus, although the film approves of the Bunch (who are at one point apparently equated with ants), it also criticizes the insectlike occupants of Agua Verde and Starbuck, the latter of whom certainly don't deserve to be slaughtered. The ants and scorpions image works primarily as a characterization of turmoil, with the children operating as power figures manipulating them.

16. This rather jaded view of Starbuck's citizens is given voice by Harrigan, who in response to Thornton's suggestion that the people in Starbuck should have been told of the planned ambush of the Bunch asks, "Do you think anybody in this shit pile could keep a secret?"

17. Seydor, *Peckinpah*, 80–82. However, Feldman's role in the film's cutting is not as clear as it first seemed to be. With new information available, Seydor has rewritten his chapter on *The Wild Bunch*, making it clear that although Feldman initially went along with the cuts, feeling that they improved the film, he later attempted (unsuccessfully) to have

prints of the film's full-length, European version struck so that they could be exhibited in New York and Los Angeles.

18. One other excised, present-tense flashback involves the interaction among members of the Bunch during the fiesta in Angel's village. Dutch asks Pike if he can dance with his woman; later, Sykes cuts in on the couple. The deleted footage is very short, which leaves me at a loss to explain why Warner Brothers wanted it removed.

19. Pike's statement is implicitly echoed in the mistaken certainty of his former lover that her assignation with Pike is safe because her husband will not soon be returning.

20. Seydor, *Peckinpah*, 87.

21. During the Agua Verde scene, overtones of this scene will recur when Pike enters a room in which a woman is located; sensing danger, Pike shoots through a bureau mirror, killing a man who had been hiding there.

22. Seydor, *Peckinpah*, 89.

23. Ibid., 88.

24. This dialogue appears only in the full-length film.

25. Peckinpah is counting on the viewer's realizing that the machine gun's appearance here suggests World War I, which began only a year after the period of *The Wild Bunch* (1913). The weapon figured prominently for the first time during this war, when it accounted for more than ninety out of every one hundred casualties and changed the face of war. The gun also links up with the characters of Mohr and his second-in-command, Germans who are in Mexico presumably because they are trying on behalf of their government to establish an alliance with Mexico against the United States in anticipation of the imminent global conflict. Thus, when Pike, after killing Mapache, chooses to shoot Mohr next, he is not only inadvertently striking a blow against this political subterfuge but also demonstrating his unconscious alliance with his own country; this act recalls Dutch's earlier statement, "That's hitting pretty close to home," and Pike's equivocal reply to Mohr's question about whether the Bunch is sympathetic to the aims of the United States government.

I should also note that the machine gun ties in with Pike's reply to Sykes's comment about Mapache's car. When, in reference to the car, Sykes says that he has seen one that can fly, Pike mentions airplanes. It was, of course, in World War I that machine guns were first mounted on airplanes, thus opening a deadly new realm of warfare.

26. Just as the film raises the stakes of destructiveness (measured in terms of numbers of dead) between the Starbuck and Agua Verde massacres, so too does the weaponry keep pace with this increase in destructive potential, progressing from the pistols and rifles in Starbuck to the dynamite used to blow up the bridge and finally to the combination of dynamite, grenades, and machine-gun fire used to devastate Agua Verde. Because

this progression in intensity is in keeping with the Bunch's groping progress toward an acceptance of their mutual responsibilities (as they move from speeches about sticking together to a higher realm in which such sentiments are acted on), we must conclude that the increasingly powerful ordnance signals an attendant raising of the moral stakes, which eventually makes it possible for Pike's predominantly untested assertions about mutual responsibility to be put to the ultimate test: one by fire.

27. Seydor offers two complementary explanations for Pike's defense of Thornton. At one point, he states that Pike is "obstinately disinclined to judge Thornton for teaming up with the railroad . . . because [it was as a result of] Pike's carelessness that Thornton wound up facing the alternative of remaining in prison to be whipped day after day or joining the posse" (88). (Of course, this latter assertion is based on the assumption that Pike knows why Thornton is working for Harrigan, something that Seydor never establishes.) Later, Seydor states that Pike respects Thornton's remaining true to his word regardless of the person to whom he gives it (97). It is this latter consideration that makes the exchange between Dutch and Pike so fascinating, especially when we consider that other Peckinpah films (e.g., *Major Dundee, The Getaway*) show us characters making deals with individuals whom they do not respect and yet remaining true to their word. The most telling example of this dilemma occurs in *Ride the High Country*, where Gil attempts to sway Steve away from his compact with the bankers. (Indeed, to appropriate the meaning behind Dutch's words to Pike, one can imagine Gil saying to Steve, "You gave your word to a bank; the deal doesn't count.") Yet for Steve as for Pike, it's a man's word that is the most important, not "who you give it to." (And since we admire Steve, perhaps even more so than we do Pike, we are reluctant to contradict him.) Obviously, there is no simple answer to this issue; what can be said with certainty is that Peckinpah obviously felt that the moral question raised here is one of great importance.

28. Interestingly, Tector's bird is tied with a piece of string so that it cannot fly away. The image of the tied bird recalls Angel, who is tethered at the end of Mapache's rope and, like the bird, is being used as a toy; in another example of the film's textural richness, this notion in turn reinvokes the ideas associated with the image of the ants and scorpions.

29. At one point, contact is made between the Bunch and the Mexicans when Tector angrily shoulders a Mexican out of his way.

30. The continuation of the Bunch's tradition is symbolized after the massacre through Thornton's appropriation of Pike's gun; similarly, Mapache, through the child's rifle, briefly exerts influence after hi death. Interestingly, both pieces of armament were stolen from the U.S. government, a fact that goes to prove that regardless of their source, the end to which weapons are put is determined by the person wielding them. Thus, another piece of American issue, the machine gun, first passes to the Bunch,

then to Mapache—who, fortunately, never has the chance to use it in battle—then back to the Bunch, who turn it against Mapache, and finally to Sykes, Thornton, and Don José, who will use it in furtherance of the cause that the Bunch, through the Agua Verde massacre, have unwittingly assisted.

31. The gestures are also similar to those exchanged among Pike and the Gorches in the Agua Verde adobe.

32. This ending, which reinvokes the feelings of reverence associated with the Bunch's departure from Angels village, was not in the original script; indeed, the Bunch's touching departure from the village was not in the script either. Both scenes were added later by Peckinpah, which shows what a romantic sentimentalist he really is.

33. Through a device whose self-reflexivity recalls the black-and-white still frames used intermittently at the film's opening (which have deadly connotations almost identical to those resulting from the freeze frames at the beginning of the uncut *Pat Garrett and Billy the Kid*), Peckinpah reminds us at the film's end (when our sentimentality concerning the Bunch is at its height) that *The Wild Bunch* is a crafted, storytelling vehicle that creates, and fosters the continuation of, the Bunch's myth. The director accomplishes this effect by having the final anamorphic Panavision image (a freeze frame of the Bunch riding out of Angel's village) recede within the original frame after the final credits and just before "The End" appears on the screen. Like the song that is used to serenade the Bunch out of Angel's village, the film is a mnemonic device that in the future will be used to evoke feelings and ideas, in the same manner that the stories about Major Dundee (to which Sam Potts refers in the earlier film) will be used.

5. This Cactus Eden

1. Peckinpah is able to carry off this scene (despite the strong antijingo-istic sentiments of the early 1970s, in particular those associated with protests against the Vietnam War) primarily because the flag raising affirms a patriotism that transcends the individual foreign policy mistakes for which the country's politicians were responsible.

2. The verbal interplay between stage driver Ben and the man in the stagecoach recalls the catechistic duel between Steve Judd and Joshua Knudsen in *Ride the High Country*. Angry at the delay occasioned by the coach's stopping for Cable, the man tells the drivers that he'll have them fired. " 'The wrath of God cometh on the children of disobedience.' Ephesians, chapter 5, verse 6," he says. In response, Ben unties the man's belongings, which are on the stagecoach's top. As the stagecoach pulls away and the man's goods fall off, Ben shouts out, " 'The Lord giveth and the Lord taketh away,' Matthew, chapter 2."

3. Actual children appear in the film as well, most significantly in the scene in which Cable is physically thrown out of the stage company office.

Cable falls down in the street at the same time as a group of children are singing "Ashes, ashes, all fall down." The children's song mocks Cable, as does their subsequently following him for a while. By treating Cable as a curiosity, something the townspeople also do, the children show us how typically adult in their values they are, as are virtually all of the children who appear in Peckinpah's films.

6. Dogs of War

1. A horrible anticipation of terrible acts is also present in an interchange on the moor between the two sexual assailants, Venner and Scutt. Scutt says, "You drive them [the ducks] to me, Charlie," to which Venner says, "I will," a reference that contains within it an accurate description of the rape sequence, in which first Venner and then Scutt rapes Amy, who is thereby equated with an animal of prey. Moreover, the description also serves as an apt summary of the way that David, the apparent prime mover behind the assault on the farmhouse, drives the rowdies toward him by performing various acts that provoke the attack. In these and many other dialogue exchanges, as well as in its sexually suggestive imagery, *Straw Dogs* sets up anticipations that come true, thereby giving its action a quality of horrible inevitability.

2. Assault on the eyes is often a symbol of castration; it is probably especially so here, since the workers had been involved in a visual rape of Amy.

3. Many of the characters in *Straw Dogs* have tag names that reflect the character's function in the film. Charlie Venner's last name recalls "venery," a word that refers to both hunting and sexual activity. Norman Scutt's last name hints at his supposed sabotage ("scuttle") of David's marriage and also refers not only to his objectionable status (a "scut" is defined as "a contemptible fellow") and lowly duties (the colloquial usage for odious duties is "scut work") but also to his sexuality ("scut" also means "a short, erect tail," with obvious phallic overtones, and the slang phrase "back-scuttle" means to commit sodomy, the act Scutt performs on the unwilling Amy after Venner has raped her). As for the Sumners (both of whose actions *summon* a great deal of violence), their first names link up with the ways that they are related to the violence. Amy, whose name means "love," is connected with it emotionally through her former relationship with Venner; David's biblical name suggests that he is the small man who will slay his larger, Goliath-like opponent (size in this case takes the form of David's opponents outnumbering him).

On "scut," see *Webster's Seventh New Collegiate Dictionary*; on "back-scuttle," see Partridge, *Dictionary of Slang*, 986.

4. However, Amy does shoot Riddaway, who reappears after having been subdued.

5. A case could be made for the interdependency of the forces of law

and disorder by drawing attention to the virtual identity of the names Scott (the character who most strongly represents the law) and Scutt (the rapist).

6. For a fine discussion of this traditional aspect of the horror film, see Wood, "Introduction to the American Horror Film," esp. 12–22. Indeed, Wood's article comprehensively elucidates the horror film's social and sexual subtexts. In particular, Wood identifies horror films' concern with sexuality (repressed in the family and released through the monster) and elucidates their Marxist concerns (in Western culture, conventional marriage emerges as a corollary for capitalist repression, with the female typically viewed as property by the imperialist male). These aspects also find expression in *Straw Dogs*.

7. Edgar Allen Poe's "The Fall of the House of Usher" is the most famous example of a work that makes the continuity between a house and its major occupant graphically evident.

8. This sequence's technique of anticipatory tension followed by release followed by renewed terror (e.g., the unexpected reappearance of Riddaway) is also present in the attack sequences at the beginning and end of *The Wild Bunch*.

9. Chan Wing-Tsit, *The Way of Lao Tzu*, 107.

10. Ibid.

11. Although I believe one should always trust the tale, not the teller, it's still interesting to note that Dustin Hoffman seems to share this view of David's character. "I saw [David] as fleeing the violent campus situation in America for the peaceful English countryside on a conscious level, while on an unconscious level he would begin to set up the situation of conflict in the small town he went to. In other words, I saw the town as being completely indifferent towards him at the outset of the film, and then in snide little ways he would turn them against him because he carried his violence with him" (quoted in Simmons, *Peckinpah*, 126). Although Hoffman felt that the script version of David "differed somewhat" from the one in the film, I believe that the personality traits to which Hoffman is drawing attention still emerge in the film.

7. Memory and Desire

1. This dissolve acts as a gentle transition between images, in contrast to the abrupt, unannounced, and therefore unconscious shifts between past and present that occur through most of the film.

2. Actually, Junior does have money in his pocket, at least $135, but he's saving it for his rodeo entrance fees. However, we only learn this later, so that our feeling at this point that Junior has no money remains unchanged. Later, our reaction is only slightly different; looking back on Junior's sleeping outside, we see that it is more important to Junior to spend the money on the rodeo, and thereby attempt to regain his status

324

as a champion, than it is to sleep comfortably indoors. This emphasis on the satisfaction to be derived from personal achievement, as opposed to the comforts to be gained from wealth and concrete possessions, will re-emerge as the basis of the essential differences between Junior and his mother and Junior and his brother.

3. A bulldozer had also passed in front of the gas station at which Junior stopped, suggesting how virtually omnipresent these vehicles, and the progress that they represent, seem to be.

4. The sun also functions as a stand-in for Curly, who is the agent behind the construction. Later in the film, more puns on *sun* will appear.

5. Interestingly, since we are not at this point given shots of Junior looking back at the other bulldozers, these shots could be objective representations of the continuing demolition. However, given the powerful effect that the destruction of Ace's house is having on Junior and the fact that—as we saw in the title sequence—Junior has a tendency to review scenes with which he is obsessed, these images are probably only repeating in Junior's mind, a reading supported by later repeated images in this same sequence.

6. However, my observation about Junior's sensibility not only assumes that he has consciously chosen his psychology but also ignores the possible causes for why Curly and Ellie have adapted in the way that they have. We might speculate that Curly places a great emphasis on money for two reasons: first, Ace's philandering and recklessness have always kept the family poor, a situation that Curly despises; and second, his profound desire for wealth is a compensatory response to his alienation from his father's affections, which may have always been directed primarily toward Junior. We can view Ellie a bit more kindly. Instead of acting in order to gain wealth, Ellie has withdrawn into inaction and passively accepted relative poverty. She protects her desires and feelings, probably because of Ace's unfaithfulness and profligacy. Curly acts; Ellie is acted on: thus Ellie's allowing Curly to put her on an allowance and give her a job, actions that confirm our suspicion that Curly has appropriated the role of parent that Ace has abandoned, and that he has turned this role, with the possibilities that it offers for manipulation, against his mother.

7. Junior's loneliness is alluded to in the exchange between him and one of Red Terwiliger's women friends when Red, also traveling to Prescott, has his car pull up next to Junior's on the highway. The woman asks, "How's the cowboy?" Junior answers, "Lonesome." The woman then replies, "Not for long; wait 'til you try our brand of sunshine." What we seem to have here, though, is the one line of dialogue in the film that fails to make any real sense. If the reference is to literal sunshine, Prescott's is certainly not going to differ from the kind that Junior encountered in the previous rodeo town; if the reference is to the bull Old Sunshine, it is also meaningless, since Junior has already experienced him as well. And if the

reference is to the can of beer that she tosses to Junior, then the line is at best trivial.

8. *Junior Bonner*'s stress on realism in its objective sequences is complemented by the aural ambiance that Peckinpah creates. Thus, there is an impressive verisimilitude to the hollow sound quality in Ace's hospital room; this hollowness complements the awkward pause in Curly's television commercial. (Curly says, "Come out and visit me at the . . . Bonner trading post.") Although Curly aspires to a well-polished presentation, the pause emphasizes his feeling of awkwardness.

9. The serious juncture that is reached at this point is underscored by the background music (the jukebox is playing the theme "Rodeo Man") stopping at this point, so that all that we hear are Junior and Buck's words and a few of the bar's ambient sounds.

10. Junior's decision to ride the bull again also involves his spending a fair amount of money on the entry fee, a point subtly underscored by the ringing of the bar's cash register as this line is delivered.

11. Curly's use of the phrase "get a grip on" inadvertently refers to the manner in which bull riders must securely grip the rope attached to the bull, which they hold with one hand. Of course, the contrast between the materialist future that Curly wants Junior to grasp, as opposed to the idealistic promise held out by the ride that Junior intends to take on the bull (which, if successful, bodes well for his immediate future), is quite obvious, since it derives from the distinction between the material and the ideal that has been prominent throughout Curly and Junior's discussion.

12. The event is very entertaining. Junior defers to his father in it by doing the mugging for Ace, who had bragged about his prowess as a roper. ("I'm accurate number one," Ace says, the word *one* indicating Ace's view of his status.) For Ace and Junior, the contest is a series of comic misadventures, with father and son eventually losing the race to the finish line (to be the first pair to hand in their bottle of milk) because of the interference of Ace's dog (who has somehow gotten into the arena); Junior's difficulty in holding on to the cow; and the arguing between father and son about who is going to run back to the finish line with the bottle. At the end of the contest, Ace says, "We coulda won"; Junior replies, "We did, Ace," and we realize what Junior means. He and Ace have triumphed by demonstrating their affection for each other. Through Ace and Junior's antagonistic but nonetheless loving interaction, this affection has been made plain to the rodeo audience as well.

13. The sun is now behind Junior, indicating his new position of power and authority.

8. Breaking Out for Love

1. Jim Thompson's book *The Getaway*, on which Walter Hill's screenplay is based, ends far more grimly than does the film. In the book, Doc

and Carol are reduced to plotting against each other, with murder as the ultimate goal. Like the sentimental touches that Peckinpah added to the script of *The Wild Bunch*, the change here suggests that Peckinpah is less brutal than his reputation would suggest.

9. Star Packer

1. Quote from the box of the Turner Entertainment video release.

2. For information on the difficulties that occurred during the film's shooting, see Seydor, *Peckinpah*, 186–96; Simmons, *Cinema of Sam Peckinpah*, 304–310; and Fine, *Bloody Sam*, 247–53. For the best details available on what happened to the film in post-production, see Seydor, *Peckinpah*, 196–204; Simmons, *Cinema of Sam Peckinpah*, 314–20; and Fine, *Bloody Sam*, 254–60.

3. For cuts to *Major Dundee*, see Kitses, *Horizons West*, 139–40; Seydor, *Peckinpah*, 52–53, 62–63; Cutts, "Shoot! Sam Peckinpah Talks to John Cutts"; Simmons, *Peckinpah*, 72.

4. The only parts of *The Wild Bunch* that are still missing (at least as far as the restored videotape version—which, unfortunately, is not in the letterboxed, wide-screen format—is concerned) are the intermission title and the intermission music. When this book was in its final editing stage, I learned from Paul Seydor that in Europe *The Wild Bunch* was originally released in 70 millimeter with a six-track stereophonic soundtrack. The 70 millimeter version of the film still exists, and there is now a movement to encourage Warner Brothers to make this version available for viewing, if not theatrically then at least on laserdisk.

5. Just what Peckinpah's "way" actually would have been is not entirely clear, since Peckinpah wasn't always involved in discussions about the film's final form. In fact, there seems to have been a great deal of negotiating among Carroll, Roger Spottiswoode (one of the film's main editors), and Aubrey about what form the film's release version should have assumed. To take just one example: as Seydor points out, Carroll and Spottiswoode wanted the raft episode retained; Aubrey agreed to the scene's retention as long as the frame story was removed (Seydor, *Peckinpah*, 198).

6. Letter from Paul Seydor to Michael Bliss, 12 Feb. 1992. In a conversation I had with Seydor during November 1992, he pointed out to me that it was Peckinpah's usual working method to shoot scenes long and then edit them down later. This method—which Seydor noted was familiar to editors such as Roger Spottiswoode, who worked with Peckinpah on *Pat Garrett* and two other films—makes it abundantly clear that many of the scenes from the "director's cut" are not in the form that Peckinpah intended them finally to assume.

7. For a discussion of the problems inherent in choosing between alternate versions of the same work, see Thorpe, "Aesthetics of Textual Criticism," 107. Obviously, I cannot detail all of the differences between

NOTES TO PAGES 218–237

the film's two versions. I suggest that interested readers rent both tapes to enjoy them for themselves—and, if possible, try to watch the film when it plays on commercial television, since according to Seydor (*Peckinpah*, 202n), the television release contains footage not included in either version of the film. Some additional variant footage from *Pat Garrett* appears in the theatrical trailer that is appended to Turner's videodisc release of the "director's cut," which—except for the fact that the disk is "letterboxed"—is otherwise identical to the 122-minute videotape version.

8. Even the Turner Entertainment *Pat Garrett* is missing footage from this scene, primarily the part during which Garrett and Chisum discuss the money that Chisum has lent Garrett.

9. Seydor, *Peckinpah*, 189, 202–204.

10. Seydor, 204.

11. As Seydor points out (*Peckinpah*, 189), the correct year for these events is actually 1908.

12. The short version uses stills behind the opening titles, but the effect is hardly the same as that achieved in the longer film. The stills, which for some indiscernible reason are intentionally out of focus, are in color; in addition to shots of the film's principals, they feature characters who do not die in the film, among them Garrett and some townspeople from Lincoln.

13. The color, which is muted (in keeping with the sequence's morbidity) and is restricted to characters' flesh, was apparently added by hand after the footage was initially developed.

14. In Peckinpah's script for *One-Eyed Jacks*, the following exchange takes place between the sheriff, Dad Longworth (who, like Garrett, was once an outlaw), and his former friend, the outlaw Rio.

> RIO: Sounds like you're telling me to get outta town, Dad.
> DAD: No. (*Pauses; then quietly:*) I'm asking you.

The conflict between friendship and what a person conceives of as "duty" is only one of the similarities between this script, which was completed in February 1959, and Peckinpah's later films. Indeed, most of Peckinpah's work—most prominently *The Wild Bunch* and *Pat Garrett and Billy the Kid*—incorporates the themes of revenge and betrayal dramatized in *One-Eyed Jacks*.

15. A comparison between Billy the Kid and the Australian bandit Ned Kelly provides a fascinating commentary on the manner in which many outlaws regard themselves as free-spirited opponents of capitalism and highlights the way in which myths about outlaws are created. See Clark, *Earth Abideth Forever*, esp. 327, 329.

16. In this sense, Ollinger is quite like *Ride the High Country*'s Joshua Knudsen, who is also played by R. G. Armstrong.

17. Seydor believes that the film suggests it was Garrett who planted

the gun in the outhouse in order to give the Kid an additional chance to break out of jail and leave the country (*Peckinpah*, 222). I agree with Seydor, although Garrett could not have been assured that it would be the Kid who would find the gun.

18. Not only is this statement callous, but it also serves as another example of the Kid's disdain for people who are willing to compromise themselves for money.

19. Seydor, *Peckinpah*, 202n, 212. Seydor pointed out to me that when MGM was assembling the "director's cut," he told them that they could find the scene with Garrett's wife in the negative of *Pat Garrett*'s television version, which MGM has in storage. For some inexplicable reason, MGM never included the scene in the supposedly "full-length" videotape and videodisc versions of the film.

20. Interestingly, Baker's wife tosses his badge to him just as Garrett had tossed the gold piece to Baker. It's as though she is reminding Baker that the entire mission in which Garrett is involving her husband is pointless, a meaning underscored by her telling Baker that the town "isn't worth it [that is, his dying in defense of it]."

21. This scene differs between the long and short versions of the film most significantly in that in the longer film Peckinpah blends in Bob Dylan's music for the song "Knocking On Heaven's Door" before Baker begins walking to the water's edge. Mercifully, given the song's awkward lyrics, the longer film uses only the instrumental version of the song. The music over the credits also differs between the two films. Although both films use the same score, the version in the longer film is more stately. Indeed, throughout the MGM version of *Pat Garrett*, Dylan's music is injudiciously used.

22. The fact that this scene is preceded in the long version by a bunkhouse scene in which Poe knocks out Cody (Elisha Cook, Jr.) to convince Josh (Dub Taylor) to reveal the Kid's whereabouts not only prepares the way for the raft scene's bleakness but also asserts a parallel between Garrett and Poe's deadly ruthlessness, a comparison impossible to draw in MGM's version.

23. Seydor, *Peckinpah*, 219. The issue raised here parallels the one in *The Wild Bunch* in which Pike and Dutch argue about whether Thornton's agreement with the railroad is binding. In my view, one doesn't cheat if one cheats a cheater, which is another way of saying that an agreement with someone whose word is not reliable is not binding.

24. I especially like the way that McKinney moves as though he is in a trance, one no doubt induced by a powerful reluctance to be on such a mission.

25. The reference to chickens recalls the negative connotations associated with the buried chickens from the film's first scene at Fort Sumner. The phrase "tin bill" elegantly combines the image of the chickens with

that of Garrett's tin sheriff's star, yoking cowardice with cheapness; thus, Will means for Garrett to understand that his sheriff's badge, like his mission and his self, is of little value.

10. Head Games

1. Simmons, *Peckinpah*, 208.
2. Sappensly and Quill are never identified by name in the film.
3. Quoted in Nadeau, *The History of Surrealism*, 25.
4. The effect is repeated shortly afterward when Bennie, grieving over Elita's death by suffocation, hangs his head so low down that it is obscured by a mound of dirt.
5. Bennie has caught the crab lice from Elita, who works as a "hostess" in a club. Bennie comments, "Change the sheets, darling, or get another job."
6. The film's ending and beginning sequences are finely balanced. Most of the opening titles appear over a still shot of the water; the moving action begins simultaneously with the introduction of the film's music. At the film's end, the close-up of the machine gun's firing eye involves a fade-out of the sound followed by a freeze-frame of the shot. The resulting balance is especially striking considering that it appears in a film devoted to disorder.

11. Cold Killers

1. It's hard to believe that there aren't two word doublings operating here. One doubling occurs on the word *plastics*, which could just as easily refer to plastic explosives (used in the opening titles sequence) as to other, harmless forms of plastic. The other pun is on the word *condoms*, probably short for "condominiums" but equally applicable to prophylactics, which have already implicitly appeared in the film in the repartee between George and Mike about venereal disease.

12. The Graveyard Where the Iron Crosses Grow

1. Simmons, *Peckinpah*, 255.
2. Although not credited in the film, the quote is from the epilogue to Brecht, *The Resistible Rise of Arturo Ui*, 128.
3. A statement of Brecht's recorded in Green, *Morrow's International Dictionary of Contemporary Quotations*, 94.

13. Dead Truck Stop

1. Peckinpah is quoted in Simmons, *Peckinpah*, 232.
2. "Speed" has dual meanings here: the driver in Serafian's film likes both fast cars and amphetamines.
3. Simmons, *Peckinpah*, 233–35.

Afterword

1. Marshall Fine's *Bloody Sam* is the most obvious offender in this respect. After reading Fine's stories of Peckinpah's extended debauches, one begins to wonder how Peckinpah found the time to direct films.

FILMOGRAPHY

The Deadly Companions (1961)

DIRECTION: Sam Peckinpah
SCREENPLAY: A. S. Fleischman, based on his novel
CINEMATOGRAPHY: William H. Clothier
EDITING: Stanley E. Rabjohn
MUSIC: Marlin Skiles; song "A Dream of Love" by Marlin Skiles and Charles FitzSimons, sung by Maureen O'Hara
SOUND: Gordon Sawyer and Robert J. Callen
SPECIAL EFFECTS: Dave Kohler
MAKE-UP: James Barker
HAIRSTYLES: Fae Smyth
WARDROBE: Frank Beetson, Sr., Sheila O'Brien
PRODUCTION MANAGER: Lee Lukather
PRODUCER: Charles FitzSimons
RELEASED BY: Pathé-American
RUNNING TIME: 90 minutes
CAST: Maureen O'Hara (Kit Tilden), Brian Keith (Yellowleg), Steve Cochran (Billy), Chill Wills (Turkey), Strother Martin (Parson), Will Wright (Doctor), Jim O'Hara (Cal), Peter O'Crotty (mayor), Billy Vaughn (Mead), Robert Sheldon (gambler), John Hamilton (gambler), Hank Gobble (bartender), Buck Sharpe (Indian)

Ride the High Country (1962)

DIRECTION: Sam Peckinpah
SCREENPLAY: N. B. Stone, Jr.
CINEMATOGRAPHY: Lucien Ballard
EDITING: Frank Santillo
MUSIC: George Bassman
RECORDING SUPERVISOR: Franklin Milton
ART DIRECTION: George W. Davis, Leroy Coleman
SET DECORATION: Henry Grace, Otto Siegel
COLOR CONSULTANT: Charles K. Hagedorn

MAKE-UP: William Tuttle
HAIRSTYLES: Mary Keats
ASSISTANT DIRECTOR: Hal Polaire
PRODUCER: Richard E. Lyons
RELEASED BY: Metro-Goldwyn-Mayer
RUNNING TIME: 94 minutes
CAST: Randolph Scott (Gil Westrum), Joel McCrea (Steve Judd), Mariette Hartley (Elsa Knudsen), Ron Starr (Heck Longtree), Edgar Buchanan (Judge Tolliver), R. G. Armstrong (Joshua Knudsen), Jenie Jackson (Kate), James Drury (Billy Hammond), L. Q. Jones (Sylvus Hammond), John Anderson (Elder Hammond), John Davis Chandler (Jimmy Hammond), Warren Oates (Henry Hammond), Carmen Phillips (saloon girl)

Major Dundee (1965)

DIRECTION: Sam Peckinpah
SCREENPLAY: Harry Julian Fink, Oscar Saul, Sam Peckinpah
STORY: Harry Julian Fink
CINEMATOGRAPHY: Sam Leavitt
EDITING: William A. Lyon, Don Starling, Howard Kunin
MUSIC: Daniele Amfitheatrof; title song ("Major Dundee March") by Daniele Amfitheatrof and Ned Washington, sung by Mitch Miller's Sing-Along Gang; song "Laura Lee" by Liam Sullivan and Forrest Wood
SOUND SUPERVISOR: Charles J.Rice
SOUND: James Z. Flaster
ART DIRECTION: Al Ybarra
PROPERTY MASTER: Joe La Bella
SPECIAL EFFECTS: August Lohman
COSTUMES: Tom Dawson
MAKE-UP: Ben Lane, Larry Butterworth
SECOND UNIT DIRECTION: Cliff Lyons
PRODUCTION MANAGER: Francisco Day
ASSISTANT DIRECTORS: Floyd Joyer, John Veitch
ASSISTANT PRODUCER: Rick Rosenberg
PRODUCER: Jerry Bresler
RELEASED BY: Columbia Pictures
RUNNING TIME: 134 minutes
CAST: Charlton Heston (Major Amos Dundee), Richard Harris (Capt. Benjamin Tyreen), Jim Hutton (Lt. Graham), James Coburn (Samuel Potts), Michael Anderson, Jr. (Tim Ryan), Senta Berger (Teresa Santiago), Mario Adorf (Sgt. Gomez), Brock Peters (Aesop), Warren Oates (O. W. Hadley), Ben Johnson (Sgt. Chillum), R. G. Armstrong (Reverend Dahlstrom), L. Q. Jones (Arthur Hadley),

Slim Pickens (Wiley), Karl Swenson (Capt. Waller), Michael Pate (Sierra Charriba), John Davis Chandler (Jimmy Lee Benteen), Dub Taylor (Priam), Albert Carrier (Capt. Jacques Tremaine), Jose Carlos Ruiz (Riago), Aurora Clavel (Melinche), Begonia Palacios (Linda), Enrique Lucero (Dr. Aguilar), Francisco Reyguera (old Apache)

The Wild Bunch (1969)

DIRECTION: Sam Peckinpah
SCREENPLAY: Walon Green, Sam Peckinpah
STORY: Walon Green, Roy N. Sickner
CINEMATOGRAPHY: Lucien Ballard
EDITING: Louis Lombardo
ASSOCIATE EDITOR: Robert L. Wolfe
MUSIC: Jerry Fielding
MUSIC SUPERVISION: Sonny Burke
SOUND: Robert J. Miller
ART DIRECTION: Edward Carrere
SPECIAL EFFECTS: Bud Hulburd
MAKE-UP: Al Greenway
WARDROBE: Gordon Dawson
SCRIPT SUPERVISION: Crayton Smith
SECOND UNIT DIRECTION: Buzz Henry
ASSISTANT DIRECTORS: Cliff Coleman, Fred Gammon
PRODUCTION MANAGER: William Faralla
ASSOCIATE PRODUCER: Roy N. Sickner
PRODUCER: Phil Feldman
RELEASED BY: Warner Brothers/Seven Arts
RUNNING TIME: 145 minutes (European version), 143 minutes (original domestic version), 139 minutes (final domestic release version)[1]
CAST: William Holden (Pike Bishop), Ernest Borgnine (Dutch Engstrom), Robert Ryan (Deke Thornton), Edmond O 'Brien (Freddie Sykes), Warren Oates (Lyle Gorch), Jaime Sanchez (Angel), Ben Johnson (Tector Gorch), Emilio Fernandez (Mapache), Strother Martin (Coffer), L. Q. Jones (T. C.), Albert Dekker (Harrigan), Bo Hopkins (Crazy Lee), Bud Taylor (Wainscoat), Jorge Russek (Zamorra), Alfonso Arau (Herrera), Chano Urueta (Don Jose), Sonia Amelio (Teresa), Aurora Clavel (Aurora), Elsa Cardenas (Elsa), Fernando Wagner (German army officer), Paul Harper (Ross), Bill Hart (Jess), Rayford Barnes (Buck), Steve Ferry (Sergeant McHale), Enrique Lucero (Ignacio), Elizabeth Dupeyron (Rocio), Yolande Ponce (Yolo), Jose Chavez (Juan Jose), Rene Dupeyron (Juan), Pedro Galvan (Benson), Graciela Doring

(Emma), Major Perez (Perez), Fernando Wagner (Mohr), Jorge
Rado (Ernst), Ivan Scott (paymaster), Sra. Madero (Margaret),
Margarito Luna (Luna), Chalo Gonzalez (Gonzalez), Lilia Castillo (Lilia), Elizabeth Unda (Carmen), Julio Corona (Julio), Matthew Peckinpah (child in Starbuck)

The Ballad of Cable Hogue (1970)

DIRECTION: Sam Peckinpah
SCREENPLAY: John Crawford, Edmund Penney
CINEMATOGRAPHY: Lucien Ballard
EDITING: Frank Santillo, Lou Lombardo
MUSIC: Jerry Goldsmith
SONGS: "Tomorrow Is the Song I Sing" by Jerry Goldsmith, Richard
    Gillis, sung by Richard Gillis; "Wait for Me, Sunrise" by Richard Gillis, sung by Richard Gillis; "Butterfly Mornings" by Richard Gillis, sung by Stella Stevens and Jason Robards
ORCHESTRATION: Arthur Morton
MUSIC SUPERVISION: Sonny Burke
SOUND: Don Rush
ART DIRECTION: Leroy Coleman
SET DECORATION: Jack Mills
PROPERTY MASTER: Robert Visciglia
SPECIAL EFFECTS: Bud Hulburd
DIALOGUE SUPERVISION: Frank Kowalski
COSTUMES FOR STELLA STEVENS: Robert Fletcher
MAKE-UP: Gary Liddiard, Al Fleming
HAIR STYLIST: Kathy Blondell
WARDROBE: Robert Fletcher
TITLE DESIGN: Latigo Productions
UNIT PRODUCTION MANAGER: Dink Templeton
ANIMAL HANDLER: John Walrath
ASSISTANT DIRECTOR: John Gaudioso
EXECUTIVE PRODUCER: Phil Feldman
PRODUCER: Sam Peckinpah
ASSOCIATE PRODUCER: Gordon Dawson
CO-PRODUCER: William Faralla
RELEASED BY: Warner Brothers
RUNNING TIME: 121 minutes (original version); 119 minutes (final release version)
CAST: Jason Robards (Cable Hogue), Stella Stevens (Hildy), David Warner (Joshua Sloane), Strother Martin (Bowen), Slim Pickens (Ben Fairchild), L. Q. Jones (Taggart), Peter Whitney (Cushing), R. G. Armstrong (Quittner), Gene Evans (Clete), William Mims (Jensen), Kathleen Freeman (Mrs. Jensen), Susan O'Connell (Clau-

dia), Vaughn Taylor (Powell), Felix Nelson (William), Max Evans (Webb Seely), Darwin W. Lamb (first customer), James Anderson (preacher), Mary Munday (Dot), William D. Faralla (Lucius), Matthew Peckinpah (Matthew), Victor Izay (stage office clerk), Easy Pickens (Easy)

Straw Dogs (1971)

DIRECTION: Sam Peckinpah
SCREENPLAY: David Zelag Goodman, Sam Peckinpah, based on the novel *The Siege of Trencher's Farm*, by Gordon M. Williams
CINEMATOGRAPHY: John Coquillon
EDITING: Roger Spottiswoode, Paul Davies, Tony Lawson
EDITORIAL CONSULTANT: Robert Wolfe
MUSIC: Jerry Fielding
SOUND: John Bramall
SOUND EDITING: Garth Craven
ART DIRECTION: Ken Bridgeman
SET DECORATION: Peter James
PRODUCTION DESIGN: Ray Simm
DESIGN CONSULTANT: Julia Trevelyan Oman
PROPERTY MASTER: Alf Pegley
SPECIAL EFFECTS: John Richardson
WARDROBE: Tiny Nicholls
MAKE-UP: Harry Frampton
HAIRSTYLES: Bobbie Smith
ASSISTANT DIRECTOR: Terry Marcel
PRODUCER: Daniel Melnick
RELEASED BY: ABC Pictures
RUNNING TIME: 118 minutes; cut to 113 minutes for U.S. release[2]
CAST: Dustin Hoffman (David Sumner), Susan George (Amy Sumner), David Warner (Henry Niles), Peter Vaughan (Tom Hedden), T. P. McKenna (Major Scott), Del Henney (Charlie Venner), Ken Hutchison (Norman Scutt), Colin Welland (Reverend Hood), Jim Norton (Chris Cawsey), Sally Thomsett (Janice), Donald Webster (Phil Riddaway), Len Jones (Cobby Hedden), Michael Mundell (Bertie Hedden), Peter Arne (John Niles), Robert Keegan (Harry Ware), June Brown (Mrs. Hedden), Chloe Franks (Emma Hedden), Cherina Mann (Mrs. Hood)

Junior Bonner (1972)

DIRECTION: Sam Peckinpah
SCREENPLAY: Jeb Rosebrook
CINEMATOGRAPHY: Lucien Ballard

EDITING: Robert Wolfe, Frank Santillo
MUSIC: Jerry Fielding
SONGS: "Arizona Morning," "Rodeo Man" written and sung by Rod Hart; "Bound to Be Back Again" by Dennis Lambert and Brian Potter, sung by Alex Taylor
SOUND MIX: Charles M. Wilborn
ART DIRECTION: Edward G. Haworth
SET DECORATION: Jerry Wunderlick
SET DESIGN: Angelo Graham
SPECIAL EFFECTS: Bud Hulburd
STUNT COORDINATOR: R. Michael Gilbert
RODEO STUNT COORDINATOR: Casey Tibbs
PROPERTY MASTER: Robert Visciglia
COSTUMES: Eddie Armand
WARDROBE: James M. George, Pat L. Barto
MAKE-UP: Donald W. Roberson, William P. Turner
HAIRSTYLES: Lynn Del Kail
TITLE DESIGN: Latigo Productions
ADDITIONAL DIALOGUE: Sharon Peckinpah
SECOND UNIT DIRECTION: Frank Kowalski
ASSISTANT DIRECTORS: Frank Baur, Malcolm R. Harding, Newt Arnold
PRODUCER: Joe Wizan
RELEASED BY: ABC Pictures
RUNNING TIME: 103 minutes
CAST: Steve McQueen (Junior Bonner), Robert Preston (Ace Bonner), Ida Lupino (Elvira [Ellie] Bonner), Joe Don Baker (Curly Bonner), Barbara Leigh (Charmagne), Mary Murphy (Ruth Bonner), Ben Johnson (Buck Roan), Bill McKinney (Red Terwiliger), Sandra Deel (Nurse Arlis), Donald "Red" Barry (Homer Rutledge), Dub Taylor (Del, the barman), Charles Gray (Burt), Matthew Peckinpah (Tim Bonner), Sundown Spencer (Nick Bonner), Rita Garrison (Flashie), Roxanne Knight (Merla Twine), Sandra Pew (Janene Twine), Francesca Jarvis (rodeo secretary), William Pierce (rodeo official)

The Getaway (1972)

DIRECTION: Sam Peckinpah
SCREENPLAY: Walter Hill, based on the novel by Jim Thompson
CINEMATOGRAPHY: Lucien Ballard
EDITING: Robert Wolfe
EDITORIAL CONSULTANT: Roger Spottiswoode
MUSIC: Quincy Jones
SOUND: Charles M. Wilborn

SOUND CONSULTANT: Garth Craven
SOUND EDITING: Joe von Stroheim, Mike Colgan
ART DIRECTION: Ted Haworth, Angelo Graham
SET DECORATION: George R. Nelson
PROPERTY MASTER: Robert Visciglia
SPECIAL EFFECTS: Bud Hulburd
MAKE-UP: Al Fleming, Jack Petty
HAIRSTYLES: Kathy Blondell
TITLE DESIGN: Latigo Productions
SECOND UNIT DIRECTION, ASSOCIATE PRODUCER: Gordon T. Dawson
ASSISTANT DIRECTOR: Newt Arnold
PRODUCERS: David Foster, Mitchell Brower
RELEASED BY: First Artists
RUNNING TIME: 122 minutes
CAST: Steve McQueen (Doc McCoy), Ali MacGraw (Carol McCoy), Ben Johnson (Jack Benyon), Sally Struthers (Fran Clinton), Al Lettieri (Rudy Butler), Slim Pickens (Cowboy), Richard Bright (thief), Jack Dodson (Harold Clinton), Dub Taylor (Laughlin), Bo Hopkins (Frank Jackson), Roy Jensen (Cully), John Bryson (the accountant), Tom Runyon (Hayhoe), Whitney Jones (soldier), Raymond King, Ivan Thomas (boys on train), Brenda W. King, C. W. Shite (boys' mothers), W. Dee Kutach (parole board chairman), Brick Lowry (parole board commissioner), Martin Colley (McCoy's lawyer), O. S. Savage (field captain), A. L. Camp (hardware store owner), Bob Veal (television shop proprietor), Bruce Bissonnette (sporting goods salesman), Dick Crockett (bank guard), Maggie Gonzalez (carhop), Jim Kannon (Cannon), Doug Dudley (Max), Stacy Newton (Stacy), Tom Bush (Cowboy's helper)

Pat Garrett and Billy the Kid (1973)

DIRECTION: Sam Peckinpah
SCREENPLAY: Rudolph Wurlitzer
CINEMATOGRAPHY: John Coquillon
EDITING: Roger Spottiswoode, Garth Craven, Robert L. Wolfe, Richard Halsey, David Berlatsky, Tony De Zarraga
MUSIC: Bob Dylan
SOUND: Charles M. Wilborn, Harry W. Tetrick
ART DIRECTION: Ted Haworth
SET DECORATION: Ray Moyer
SPECIAL VISUAL EFFECTS: A. J. Lohman
PROPERTY MASTER: Robert Visciglia
SECOND UNIT DIRECTION: Gordon Dawson

SECOND UNIT PHOTOGRAPHY: Gabriel Torres G.

WARDROBE: Michael Butler

MAKE-UP: Jack P. Wilson

PRODUCTION MANAGERS: Jim Henderling, Alfonsa Sanchez

ASSISTANT DIRECTORS: Newton Arnold, Lawrence J. Powell, Jesus Marin Bello

PRODUCER: Gordon Carroll

RELEASED BY: Metro-Goldwyn-Mayer

RUNNING TIME: 122 minutes (preliminary director's cut), 106 minutes (release version)

CAST: James Coburn (Pat Garrett), Kris Kristofferson (Billy the Kid), Bob Dylan (Alias), Jason Robards, Jr. (Governor Lew Wallace), Barry Sullivan (Chisum), Richard Jaeckel (Sheriff Kip McKinney), Katy Jurado (Mrs. Baker), Slim Pickens (Sheriff Baker), Chill Wills (Lemuel), John Beck (Poe), Rita Coolidge (Maria), R. G. Armstrong (Deputy Ollinger), Luke Askew (Eno), Richard Bright (Holly), Matt Clark (J. W. Bell), Jack Dodson (Howland), Jack Elam (Alamosa Bill), Emilio Fernandez (Paco), Paul Fix (Pete Maxwell), L. Q. Jones (Black Harris), Jorge Russek (Silva), Charlie Martin Smith (Bowdre), Harry Dean Stanton (Luke), Claudia Bryar (Mrs. Horrell), John Chandler (Norris), Mike Mikler (Denver), Aurora Clavel (Ida Garrett), Rutanya Alda (Ruthie Lee), Walter Kelley (Rupert), Rudolph Wurlitzer (Tom O'Folliard), Gene Evans (Mr. Horrell), Donnie Fritts (Beaver), Don Levy (Sackett), Elisha Cook, Jr. (Cody), Dub Taylor (Josh), Sam Peckinpah (Will)

Bring Me the Head of Alfredo Garcia (1974)

DIRECTION: Sam Peckinpah

SCREENPLAY: Gordon Dawson, Sam Peckinpah, from a story by Frank Kowalski and Sam Peckinpah

CINEMATOGRAPHY: Alex Phillips, Jr.

SUPERVISING EDITOR: Garth Craven

EDITORS: Robbe Roberts, Sergio Ortega, Dennis E. Dolan

MUSIC: Jerry Fielding

SONGS: "Bennie's Song" written and sung by Isela Vega; "Bad Blood Baby" by Sam Peckinpah; "A Donde Ir" by Javier Vega; "J. R." by Arturo Castro

SOUND: Manuel Topete

SOUND EDITING: Mike Colgan

ART DIRECTION: Augustin Ituarte

SET DECORATION: Enrique Estevez

SPECIAL EFFECTS: Leon Ortega, Raul Falomir, Frederico Farfan

PROPERTY MASTER: Alf Pegley

WARDROBE: Adolfo Ramirez
MAKE-UP: Rosa Guerrero
TITLE DESIGN: Latigo Productions/Pacific Title
ASSISTANT DIRECTORS: William C. Davidson, Jesus Marin Bello
EXECUTIVE PRODUCER: Helmut Dantine
PRODUCER: Martin Baum
ASSOCIATE PRODUCER: Gordon Dawson
RELEASED BY: United Artists
RUNNING TIME: 112 minutes
CAST: Warren Oates (Bennie), Isela Vega (Elita), Gig Young (Quill), Robert Webber (Sappensly), Helmut Dantine (Max), Emilio Fernandez (El Jefe), Kris Kristofferson (Paco), Donny Fritts (John), Chano Urueta (bartender),[3] Jorge Russek (Cueto), Don Levy (Frank), Chalo Gonzalez (Chalo), Enrique Lucero (Esteban), Janine Maldonado (Theresa), Tamara Garina (Grandmother Moreno), Farnesio De Bernal (Bernardo), Ahui Camacho (El Chavito), Monica Miguel (Dolores de Escomiglia), Paco Pharres (El Carpintero), Juan Manuel Diaz (Paulo), Rene Dupeyron (Angel), Yolanda Ponce (Yolo), Juan Jose Palacios (Juan), Manolo (tourist guide), Neri Ruiz (Maria), Roberto Dumont (Chavo)

The Killer Elite (1975)

DIRECTION: Sam Peckinpah
SCREENPLAY: Marc Norman, Sterling Silliphant, from the novel by Robert Rostand
CINEMATOGRAPHY: Phil Lathrop
EDITING: Garth Craven, Tony De Zarraga, Monte Hellman
MUSIC: Jerry Fielding
SOUND: Richard Portman, Charles M. Wilborn
SET DECORATION: Rick Gentz
SPECIAL EFFECTS: Sass Bedig
PROPERTY MASTER: Robert Visciglia
PRODUCTION DESIGN: Ted Haworth
STUNT SUPERVISION: Whitey Hughes
WARDROBE: Ray Summers
MAKE-UP: Jack Wilson, Jack Petty
HAIRSTYLES: Kathy Blondell
SECOND UNIT DIRECTION: Frank Kowalski
TITLES: Burke Mattson
ASSISTANT DIRECTOR: Newton Arnold
PRODUCERS: Martin Baum, Arthur Lewis
EXECUTIVE PRODUCER: Helmut Dantine
RELEASED BY: United Artists
RUNNING TIME: 122 minutes

CAST: James Caan (Mike Locken), Robert Duvall (George Hansen), Arthur Hill (Cap Collis), Bo Hopkins (Jerome Miller), Mako (Chung), Burt Young (Mac), Gig Young (Weyburn), Tom Clancy (O'Leary), Tiana (Tommie Chung), Katy Heflin (Amy), Sondra Blake (Josephine), Helmut Dantine (Vorodny), James Wing Woo (Tao Yi), George Kee Cheung (Bruce), Simon Tam (Jimmy Fung), Rick Alemany (Ben Otake), Hank Hamilton (Hank), Walter Kelly (Walter), Billy J. Scott (Eddie), Johnnie Burrell (Donnie), Matthew Peckinpah (young boy), Carole Mallory (Rita), Tommy Bush (Sam the Mechanic), Eddie Donno (fake policeman), Victor Sen Young (Wei Chi), Wilfred Tsang (Wilfie), Milton Shoong (Miltie), Kim Kahana (guard), Eddie White (security cop), Alan Keller (cop), Mel Cenizal (waiter), Gary Combs (security cop), James De Closs (soldier), Joseph D. Glenn (man at ComTeg), Eloise Shoong (Eloise), Charles A. Titone (soldier at party), Kuo Lien Ying (Tai Chi master), Christy Weston (Weyburn's secretary)

Cross of Iron (1977)

DIRECTION: Sam Peckinpah
SCREENPLAY: Julius J. Epstein, Herbert Asmodi, from the novel *Das Geduldiqe Fleisch* (*The Willing Flesh*) by Willi Heinrich
CINEMATOGRAPHY: John Coquillon
EDITING: Tony Lawson, Mike Ellis
MUSIC: Ernest Gold
SOUND: David Hildyard
SOUND EDITING: Rodney Holland
PRODUCTION DESIGN: Ted Haworth, Brian Ackland Snow
ACTION ARRANGEMENT: Peter Braham
SPECIAL EFFECTS: Richard Richtsfeld, Helmut Klee
MILITARY CONSULTANTS: Major A. D. Schrodek, Claus Von Trotha
WARDROBE: Joseph Satzinger
MAKE-UP: Colin Arthur
HAIRSTYLES: Evelyn Dohring
SECOND UNIT DIRECTION: Walter Kelley
ASSISTANT DIRECTOR: Bert Batt
PRODUCER: Wolf Hartwig
RELEASED BY: E.M.I.
RUNNING TIME: 133 minutes
CAST: James Coburn (Sgt. Steiner), Maximilian Schell (Capt. Stransky), James Mason (Col. Brandt), David Warner (Capt. Kiesel), Klaus Lowitsch (Kruger), Roger Fritz (Lt. Triebig), Vadim Glowna (Kern), Fred Stillkraut (Schnurrbart), Burkhardt Driest (Maag), Dieter Schidor (Anselm), Michael Nowka (Dietz), Senta Berger

(Sister Eva), Veronique Vendell (Marga), Arthur Brauss (Zoll), Mikael Slavco Stimac (Russian boy soldier)

Convoy (1978)

DIRECTION: Sam Peckinpah
SCREENPLAY: B. W. L. Norton, based on the song by C. W. McCall
CINEMATOGRAPHY: Harry Stradling, Jr.
SUPERVISING EDITOR: Graeme Clifford
EDITORS: John Wright, Garth Craven
MUSIC: Chip Davis
SONGS: "Convoy" by Chip Davis, Bill Fries, sung by C. W. McCall; "Don't It Make My Brown Eyes Blue" by Richard Leigh, sung by Crystal Gayle; "Blanket on the Ground" by Roger Bowling, sung by Billie Jo Spears; "Keep on the Sunny Side" by A. P. Carter, Gary Garett, sung by Doc Watson; "Okie from Muskogee" by Merle Haggard, Eddie Burris, sung by Merle Haggard; "Lucille" by Roger Bowling, Hal Bynum, sung by Kenny Rogers; "Southern Nights" by Allen Toussant, sung by Glen Campbell; "Walk Right Back" by Sonny Curtis, sung by Anne Murray; "Cowboys Don't Get Lucky All the Time" by Dallas Harms, sung by Gene Watson; "I Cheated on a Good Woman's Love" by Del Bryant, sung by Billy "Crash" Craddock
SOUND: Bill Randall
SOUND EFFECTS: Fred Brown, Ross Taylor, Michele Sharp Brown, Robert Henderson
ART DIRECTION: J. Dennis Washington
PRODUCTION DESIGN: Fernando Carrere
SPECIAL EFFECTS: Sass Bedig, Marcel Vercoutere, Candy Flanagin
PROPERTY MASTER: Robert Viscigilia, Sr.
STUNT COORDINATOR: Gary Combs
COSTUMES: Kent James, Carol James
MAKE-UP: Steve Abrums, Gene McCoy
HAIRSTYLES: Marina Pedraza
PRODUCTION MANAGERS: Tony Wade, Tom Shaw
SECOND UNIT DIRECTION: Walter Kelley, James Coburn
ASSISTANT DIRECTORS: Tom Shaw, Richard Wells, Pepi Lenzi, John Poer, Cliff Coleman, Newton Arnold
EXECUTIVE PRODUCERS: Michael Deeley, Barry Spikings
PRODUCER: Robert E. Sherman
RELEASED BY: United Artists/E.M.I.
RUNNING TIME: 110 minutes
CAST: Kris Kristofferson (Martin Penwald, a.k.a. "Rubber Duck"), Ali MacGraw (Melissa), Ernest Borgnine ("Dirty" Lyle Wallace), Burt Young (Bobby, a.k.a. "Pig Pen"), Madge Sinclair ("Widow

Woman"), Franklyn Ajaye ("Spider Mike"), Brian Davies (Chuck Arnoldi), Seymour Cassel (Governor Gerry Haskins), Cassie Yates (Violet), Walter Kelley (Federal Agent Hamilton), J. D. Kane ("Big Nasty"), Billy E. Hughes ("Pack Rat"), Whitey Hughes ("White Rat"), Bill Foster ("Old Iguana"), Thomas Huff ("Lizard Tongue"), Larry Spaulding ("Bald Eagle"), Randy Brady ("Sneaky Snake"), Allen R. Keller (Rosewell), James H. Burk (Frick), Robert Orrison (Bob Bookman), Tom Bush (Chief Stacy Love), William C. Jones, Jr. (Fish), Jorge Russek (Tiny Alvarez), Tom Runyon (Runyon), Vera Zenovich (Thelma), Patricia Martinez (Maria), Donald R. Fritts (Reverend Sloane), Bobbie Barnes, Turner S. Bruton, Sammy Lee Creason, Cleveland Dupin, Gerald McGee, Terry Paul, Michael Utley, and Wayne D. Wilkinson (Jesus freaks), Charles Benton (Deke Thornton), George Coleman ("Septic Sam"), Greg Van Dyke ("Silver Streak"), Ed Blatchford (Roger), Paula Baldwin (Samantha), Herb Robins (Mechanic Bob), Robert J. Visciglia, Sr. (ice-cream seller), James R. Moore (motorcycle cop), Spec O'Donnell ("Eighteen-Wheel Eddie"), Don Levy (Senator Myers), Jim Edgecomb (Doug, press man), John R. Gill (Jack, garage attendant), Daniel D. Halleck (Bart), Stacy Newton (Bubba), Sabra Wilson (Madge), Pepi Lenzi (news crewman), John Bryson (Texas governor), Sam Peckinpah (news crewman)

The Osterman Weekend (1983)

DIRECTION: Sam Peckinpah
SCREENPLAY: Alan Sharp, based on the novel by Robert Ludlum
SCREENPLAY ADAPTATION: Ian Masters
CINEMATOGRAPHY: John Coquillon
EDITING: Edward Abroms, David Rawlins
ASSISTANT EDITOR: Randy D. Thornton
MUSIC: Lalo Schifrin
SOUND: Jim Troutman
VISUAL CONSULTANT: Cloudia
SET DECORATION: Keith Hein
SPECIAL EFFECTS: Image Engineering
SPECIAL EFFECTS COORDINATOR: Peter Chesney
WARDROBE: George Little, Bernadene C. Mann
MAKE-UP: Robert Sidell
HAIRSTYLES: Shirley Padgett, Paul Abascal
SECOND UNIT DIRECTION: Rod Amateau
ASSISTANT DIRECTORS: Win Phelps, Robert Rooy, Laura Andrews
EXECUTIVE PRODUCERS: Michael Timothy Murphy, Larry Jones, Marc W. Zavat

PRODUCERS: Peter S. David, William N. Panzer
RELEASED BY: Twentieth Century–Fox
RUNNING TIME: 105 minutes
CAST: Rutger Hauer (John Tanner), John Hurt (Lawrence Fassett), Meg Foster (Ali Tanner), Dennis Hopper (Richard Tremayne), Craig T. Nelson (Bernard Osterman), Helen Shaver (Virginia Tremayne), Cassie Yates (Betty Cardone), Burt Lancaster (Maxwell Danforth), Chris Sarandon (Joseph Cardone), Sandy McPeak (Stennings), Christopher Starr (Steve Tanner), Cheryl Carter (Marcia Heller), John Bryson (honeymoon groom), Anne Haney (honeymoon bride), Kristen Peckinpah (Tremayne's secretary), Marshall Ho'o (martial arts instructor), Jan Triska (Mikalovich), Hansford Rowe (General Keever), Merete Van Kamp (Zuna Brickman), Bruce Block (floor manager), Buddy Joe Hooker (kidnapper), Tim Thomerson (motorcycle cop), Deborah Chiaramonte (nurse), Walter Kelly (first agent), Brick Tilley (second agent), Eddy Donno (third agent), Den Surles (assailant), Janeen Davis (first stage manager), Robert Kensigner (second stage manager), Buckley F. Norris (technician), Gregory Joe Parr (helicopter pilot), Don Shafer (helicopter agent), Irene Gorman Wright (executive assistant)

Notes

1. For details on the disputes between Peckinpah and Warner Brothers that led to these variant versions of the film, see Seydor, *Peckinpah,* 80–84.

2. *Straw Dogs* was trimmed before U.S. release in order to avoid an X rating from the Motion Picture Association of America. Although most of the deleted footage is from the farmhouse assault sequence, I think that for the MPAA, the film's most objectionable aspect was the anal penetration of Amy by Scutt. Part of this latter sequence was also excised to make it seem less graphic.

3. In all other Peckinpah filmographies, Urueta's character is described as the "one-armed bartender"; however, the character in the film clearly has two arms.

BIBLIOGRAPHY

Many of the screenplays for Peckinpah's films may be purchased from either Script City, 8033 Sunset Blvd., Suite 1500, Hollywood, CA 90046 (213-871-0707), or Hollywood Scripts, 5514 Satsuma Ave., North Hollywood, CA 91601 (818-980-3545).

Brecht, Bertolt. *The Resistible Rise of Arturo Ui.* New York: Samuel French, 1972.

Butler, Terence. *Crucified Heroes: The Films of Sam Peckinpah.* London: Gordon Fraser, 1979.

Cawelti, John. *The Six-Gun Mystique.* Bowling Green: Bowling Green University Popular Press, 1975.

Chan Wing-Tsit. *The Way of Lao Tzu.* Indianapolis: Bobbs-Merrill, 1963.

Clark, C. M. H. *The Earth Abideth Forever, 1851–1888.* Vol. 4 of *A History of Australia.* Carlton, Victoria: Melbourne University Press, 1978.

Clendenen, Clarence. *The United States and Pancho Villa.* Ithaca: Cornell University Press, 1961.

Cutts, John. "Shoot! Sam Peckinpah Talks to John Cutts." *Films and Filmmaking* 16, no. 1 (Oct. 1969): 4–8.

Evans, Richard I. *Dialogue with C. G. Jung* New York: Praeger, 1981.

Fiedler, Leslie. *Love and Death in the American Novel.* London: Jonathan Cape, 1966.

Fine, Marshall. *Bloody Sam.* New York: Donald I. Fine, 1991.

French, Philip. *Westerns: Aspects of a Movie Genre.* New York: Viking, 1973.

Freud, Sigmund. *Civilization and Its Discontents.* New York: Norton, 1961.

Frye, Northrop. *Myth and Metaphor.* Charlottesville: University Press of Virginia, 1990.

———. *The Secular Scripture.* Cambridge: Harvard University Press, 1976.

Green, Jonathon, comp. *Morrow's International Dictionary of Contemporary Quotations*. New York: William Morrow, 1982.

Hill, Walter. *The Getaway* (screenplay). Hollywood: Script City, 1971.

Jung, Carl G. *Man and His Symbols*. New York: Doubleday, 1964.

Kitses, Jim. *Horizons West: Anthony Mann, Budd Boetticher, Sam Peckinpah: Studies of Authorship Within the Western*. Bloomington: Indiana University Press, 1970.

McKinney, Doug. *Sam Peckinpah*. Boston: Twayne, 1969.

Nadeau, Maurice. *The History of Surrealism*. New York: Macmillan, 1966.

Partridge, Eric. *A Dictionary of Slang and Unconventional English*. New York: Macmillan, 1961.

Peckinpah, Sam. *One-Eyed Jacks* (screenplay). Hollywood: Script City, 1959.

Peckinpah, Sam, and David Z. Goodman. *The Siege of Trencher's Farm* (screenplay). Hollywood: Script City, 1970.

Peckinpah, Sam, and Walon Green. *The Wild Bunch* (screenplay). Hollywood: Script City, 1968.

Salinger, J. D. *The Catcher in the Rye*. New York: Grossett and Dunlap, 1945.

Seydor, Paul. *Peckinpah: The Western Films*. Urbana: University of Illinois Press, 1980.

Simmons, Garner. *The Cinema of Sam Peckinpah and the American Western: A Study of the Interrelationship Between An Auteur/Director and the Genre in Which He Works*. Ann Arbor: University Microfilms, 1975.

———. *Peckinpah: A Portrait in Montage*. Austin: University of Texas Press, 1976.

Smith, Henry Nash. *Virgin Land: The American West as Symbol and Myth*. Cambridge: Harvard University Press, 1950.

Thompson, Jim. *The Getaway*. New York: Random House, 1991.

Thorpe, James. "The Aesthetics of Textual Criticism." In *Bibliography and Textual Criticism*, edited by O. M. Brack, Jr., and Warner Barnes, 102–38. Chicago: University of Chicago Press, 1969.

Turner, Frederick Jackson. *The Frontier in American History*. New York: Holt, Rinehart, and Winston, 1962.

Tuska, Jon. "The American Western Cinema: 1903–Present." In *Focus on the Western*, edited by Jack Nachbar, 25–43. Englewood Cliffs, N.J.: Prentice Hall, 1974.

Wood, Robin. "An Introduction to the American Horror Film." In *The American Nightmare*, 7–28. Toronto: Festival of Festivals, 1979.

INDEX

Michael Bliss, a Ph.D. in English, teaches writing, literature, and film criticism at Virginia Polytechnic Institute and State University. His books include *Brian De Palma* and *Martin Scorsese and Michael Cimino.* His new book on the films of Martin Scorsese, *The Word Made Flesh,* will be published in 1994. Forthcoming through SIU Press is *Doing It Right,* Bliss's casebook on *The Wild Bunch.* Having just coauthored (with Christina Banks) *What Goes Around Comes Around,* a study of the films of Jonathan Demme, Bliss is currently researching the work of director Terry Gilliam for a book on his films.

DATE DUE

DEC 0 9 99			
MAR 1 1			
GAYLORD			PRINTED IN U.S.A.